ÆTHELSTAN

SARAH FOOT is Regius Professor of Ecclesiastical History at Christ Church, Oxford, and a foremost scholar of early medieval history.

Also in the Yale English Monarchs Series

EDWARD THE CONFESSOR by Frank Barlow

WILLIAM THE CONQUEROR by David Douglas*

WILLIAM RUFUS by Frank Barlow

HENRY I by Warren Hollister

KING STEPHEN by Edmund King

HENRY II by W. L. Warren*

RICHARD I by John Gillingham

KING JOHN by W. L. Warren*

EDWARD I by Michael Prestwich

EDWARD II by Seymour Phillips

RICHARD II by Nigel Saul

HENRY V by Christopher Allmand

HENRY VI by Bertram Wolffe

EDWARD IV by Charles Ross

RICHARD III by Charles Ross

HENRY VII by S. B. Chrimes

HENRY VIII by J. J. Scarisbrick

EDWARD VI by Jennifer Loach

JAMES II by John Miller

QUEEN ANNE by Edward Gregg

GEORGE I by Ragnhild Hatton

GEORGE II by Andrew C. Thompson

GEORGE III by Jeremy Black

GEORGE IV by E. A. Smith

* Available in the U.S. from University of California Press

ÆTHELSTAN

THE FIRST KING OF ENGLAND

Sarah Foot

YALE UNIVERSITY PRESS
NEW HAVEN AND LONDON

For information about this and other Yale University Press publications, please contact:
U.S. Office: sales.press@yale.edu   www.yalebooks.com
Europe Office: sales@yaleup.co.uk   www.yalebooks.co.uk

Set in Baskerville MT by IDSUK (DataConnection) Ltd
Printed in Great Britain by The MPG Books Group

Library of Congress Cataloging-in-Publication Data

Foot, Sarah.
  Æthelstan : the first king of England/Sarah Foot.
    p. cm.
  Includes bibliographical references.
  ISBN 978-0-300-12535-1 (cl:alk. paper)
  1. Athelstan, King of England, 895–939. 2. Great Britain—Kings and
rulers—Biography. 3. Great Britain—History—Athelstan, 925–940. 4. Great
Britain—History—Anglo-Saxon period, 449–1066. I. Title.
  DA154.1.F66 2011
  942.01'71092—dc22
  [B]

                                                                2010051046

A catalogue record for this book is available from the British Library.

ISBN 978-0-300-18771-7 (pbk)

10 9 8 7 6 5 4 3 2 1

For Michael

CONTENTS

ILLUSTRATIONS

PLATES

FIGURES

MAPS

ACKNOWLEDGEMENTS

It has proved an odd experience to find myself writing a biography at the same time as my husband, the modern British historian and historiographer Michael Bentley. While I have explored a shadowy tenth-century king, he has worked on the life of a leading twentieth-century historian, Regius Professor, head of a Cambridge college and Vice-Chancellor of his university. Outwardly, our tasks could not be more different: his subject, Sir Herbert Butterfield, left not only a large body of historical writing but also a huge personal archive, complemented by a wider public record. Mine left no personal records at all and, despite his claim to fame as England's first monarch, is ill-attested in the contemporary record and subsequent historiography. Yet in many ways we have grappled with similar difficulties and have benefited substantially from sharing our methodological perspectives. This life reflects that mutual journey towards making our subjects biographable. Without Michael's historical perceptions, his unsentimental criticism and unstinting support, this book would have been greatly impoverished; it is dedicated to him with loving gratitude. He bears no responsibility, however, for my decision to make the attempt, which is one I owe to my former research students, particularly Morn Capper and Martha Riddiford. It was they who first persuaded me that I should resurrect a project first begun as an undergraduate and revitalized by the invitation to write a short biography of Æthelstan for the *Oxford Dictionary of National Biography*. They went on asking, 'How's Æthelstan?' at regular intervals not only until I started to write, but whenever I seemed to be flagging as the project progressed. I hope they – and also Geoff Little, who took with typical equanimity this invasion onto what he might have seen as his own territory – feel that the resulting book was worth the wait.

Simon Keynes has been a constant source of information and advice throughout the gestation of the project; he supervised the original BA dissertation from which all followed and has continued to offer help and stimulating advice throughout. That I have not always followed his lead is not for want of his trying to persuade me to see things differently. I could not have completed this without his guidance. At a critical moment – when the project seemed to have flagged to the point of morbidity – Nicholas Brooks provided a badly needed appraisal of what ought to happen, the more valuable for his robust refusal to soften critical recommendations. Susan Kelly has consistently provided much support and substantial assistance with the charter material. I am extremely grateful to George Molyneaux for sharing a chapter of his Oxford DPhil thesis with me and for reading and commenting in detail on two of my chapters, thereby saving me from numerous errors and infelicities. Jinty Nelson and Edmund King have also struggled with writing lives of medieval kings, albeit ones whom history has served a good deal better than Æthelstan, and I am grateful for a number of discussions over the years and their advice on specific problems.

The completion of the project would have been impossible without a research leave award from the Arts and Humanities Research Council, for which I acknowledge my gratitude, and also to the History Department at Sheffield for matching that leave and releasing me from teaching and especially administrative burdens. In the final stages my new colleagues in Oxford have offered continuing support. Among them I should thank particularly Judith Maltby, whose sense of what a seventeenth-century king might do and think have often provided helpful comparisons, and also John Watts, who once approached a medieval English monarch's life from an entirely different perspective. Latterly, Laura Ashe has provided a useful foil on whom to bounce some of my wilder ideas and an invaluable source of advice on points of detail, especially in the translation of Old and Middle English. For letting me have advanced sight of unpublished material I am especially grateful to Simon MacClean, David Pratt, Gareth Williams and Alex Woolf. Michael Wood has generously discussed his ideas about Æthelstan with me over many years, and shown me some of his as yet unpublished work towards his own biography of King Æthelstan. I am extremely grateful to Richard Sowerby for assistance with the maps and also to my publishers, Yale University Press, for their patience over the gestation of this project; to Robert Baldock for first commissioning it, Heather MacCallum for seeing it to completion and to all the production staff, especially my eagle-eyed copy-editor, Beth Humphries, and Tami Halliday. All errors and infelicities that remain are my own.

Sarah Foot
Christ Church
27 October 2010

ABBREVIATIONS

Abbo, *Passio*	Abbo, *Passio S Eadmundi*, ed. M. Winterbottom, *Three Lives of English Saints* (Toronto, 1972), 67–87
ANS	*Anglo-Norman Studies*
ASC	Anglo-Saxon Chronicle. If no other manuscript is specified, citations of the Old English text are taken from K. O'Brien O'Keeffe, *The Anglo-Saxon Chronicle: A Collaborative Edition, 5 MS C* (Cambridge, 2001). Translations follow that made by D. Whitelock in *English Historical Documents I: c.550–1042* (2nd edn, London and New York, 1979), no. 1
ASE	*Anglo-Saxon England*
Asser	*Life of King Alfred: together with the Annals of Saint Neots erroneously ascribed to Asser*, ed. W.H. Stevenson (Oxford, 1904; reprinted with an introductory essay by D. Whitelock, 1959); trans. S. Keynes and M. Lapidge, *Alfred the Great: Asser's Life of Alfred and Other Contemporary Sources* (Harmondsworth, 1983)
AU	*The Annals of Ulster (to AD 1131), Part I, Text and Translation*, ed. S. Mac Airt and G. Mac Niocaill (Dublin, 1983)
Æthelweard	*The Chronicle of Æthelweard*, ed. A. Campbell (London, 1962)
BAR	British Archaeological Reports
Blunt, 'The Coinage'	C. Blunt, 'The Coinage of Athelstan, 924–939: a Survey', *British Numismatic Journal*, xliv (1974), 36–160
BL	British Library
C&S	*Councils & Synods, with Other Documents relating to the English Church. I, AD 871–1204*, ed. D. Whitelock, M. Brett and C.N.L. Brooke (Oxford, 1981)
Dumville, *Wessex*	D.N. Dumville, *Wessex and England from Alfred to Edgar: Six Essays on Political, Cultural and Ecclesiastical Renewal* (Woodbridge, 1992)
EETS	Early English Text Society
EHD	*English Historical Documents I, c.500–1042*, ed. D. Whitelock (2nd edn, London and New York, 1979)

EHR	*English Historical Review*
EME	*Early Medieval Europe*
EPNS	English Place-Name Society
Flodoard	*The Annals of Flodoard of Reims 919–966*, ed. and trans. S. Fanning and B.S. Bachrach (Peterborough, Ontario, 2004) [cited by AD date and then, in parenthesis, by numbered paragraph]
GP	William of Malmesbury, *Gesta Pontificum*, ed. and trans. M. Winterbottom with the assistance of R.M. Thomson (Oxford, 2007)
GR	William of Malmesbury, *De gestis regum Anglorum I*, ed. and trans. R.A.B. Mynors, R.M. Thomson and M. Winterbottom (Oxford, 1998)
HBC 3	*Handbook of British Chronology*, ed. E.B. Fryde *et al.* (3rd edn, London, 1986)
HE	*Bede's Ecclesiastical History of the English People*, ed. B. Colgrave and R.A.B. Mynors (Oxford, 1969)
HH	Henry of Huntingdon, *Historia Anglorum*, ed. D. Greenway (Oxford, 1996)
H&H	N.J. Higham and D.H. Hill, *Edward the Elder, 899–924* (London and New York, 2001)
HR	Simeon of Durham, *Historia regum*, ed. T. Arnold, *Symeonis monachi opera omnia*, Rolls Series lxxv, 2 vols (London, 1882–5), II, 2–283
HSC	*Historia de sancto Cuthberto*, ed. and trans. T. Johnson South (Cambridge, 2002)
I As.–VI As.	Æthelstan's law codes according to conventional numbering
JW	*The Chronicle of John of Worcester* II, ed. and trans. R.R. Darlingon *et al.* (Oxford, 1995)
Keynes, *Atlas*	S. Keynes, *An Atlas of Attestations in Anglo-Saxon Charters, c.670–1066* (Cambridge, 1995)
Keynes, 'Books'	S. Keynes, 'King Æthelstan's Books', in *Learning and Literature in Anglo-Saxon England*, ed. M. Lapidge and H. Gneuss (Cambridge, 1985), 143–201
Keynes, *Diplomas*	S. Keynes, *The Diplomas of King Æthelred 'the Unready'* (Cambridge, 1980)
Keynes, *Liber Vitae*	*The Liber Vitae of the New Minster and Hyde Abbey, Winchester: British Library Stowe 944: Together with Leaves from British Library Cotton Vespasian A. VIII and British Library Cotton Titus D. XXVII*, ed. S. Keynes (Copenhagen, 1996)
Lapidge, 'Poems'	M. Lapidge, 'Some Latin Poems as Evidence for the Reign of Athelstan', *Anglo-Saxon England*, ix (1981), 61–98

MGH	*Monumenta Germaniae Historica*
MR	Mercian Register
NCMH	*New Cambridge Medieval History* (7 vols, Cambridge)
S	P.H. Sawyer, *Anglo-Saxon Charters: an Annotated List and Bibliography* (London, 1968); charters are cited from the Electronic Sawyer: http://www.esawyer.org.uk
SEHD	F.E. Harmer, *Select English Historical Documents of the Ninth and Tenth Centuries* (Cambridge, 1914)
Stenton, *ASE*	F.M. Stenton, *Anglo-Saxon England* (3rd edn, Oxford, 1971)
Thomson, *Commentary*	*William of Malmesbury, Gesta Regum Anglorum, The History of the English Kings II, General Introduction and Commentary*, ed. R.M. Thomson (Oxford, 1999)
TRHS	*Transactions of the Royal Historical Society*
TSD	J.A. Robinson, *The Times of St Dunstan* (Oxford, 1923)
VW	S. Foot, *Veiled Women: the Disappearance of Nuns from Anglo-Saxon England*, 2 vols (Aldershot, 2000)
WM	William of Malmesbury
Wormald, *MEL*	P. Wormald, *The Making of English Law* (Oxford, 1999)

Figure 1

The West Saxon royal family

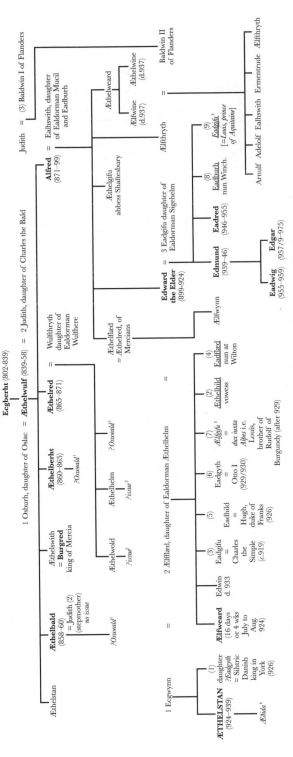

Kings named in bold; *italics indicate doubt*; underlined names: sisters of Æthelstan reported only by William of Malmesbury; (1) numbers indicate the birth order of Edward the Elder's daughters, according to William of Malmesbury: *Gesta Regum Anglorum*, II, §156 (ed. and trans. Mynors et al., pp. 198–201).

1. Osweald, *filius regis* attests charters S 340 (AD 868), 1201 (AD 868), 1203 (AD 875).
2. Ealdorman Æthelweard claimed descent from King Æthelred (*Chronicle of Æthelweard*, ed. Campbell, p. 2); presumably via one of his sons.
3. William of Malmesbury identified one daughter too many for Edward: Ælfgifu, daughter of Ælfflæd (whom William married to a duke near the Alps), and the second Eadgifu (married to a Louis of Aquitaine) were probably one girl, for whom we need find only one husband. Which should be deleted from the genealogy is less clear. Hrotsvitha of Gandersheim, the spare sister who accompanied Edith to Germany, gave the name *Adiva* to: *Gesta Ottonis*, lines 112–20, ed. Berschin, pp. 279–80; Æthelweard did not know her name.
4. *Liber Eliensis*, III.50, ed. Blake, p. 292: 'Æðida, filia regis Æðelstani'; probably error for 'sister'.

Figure 2

The West Saxon royal family in Europe

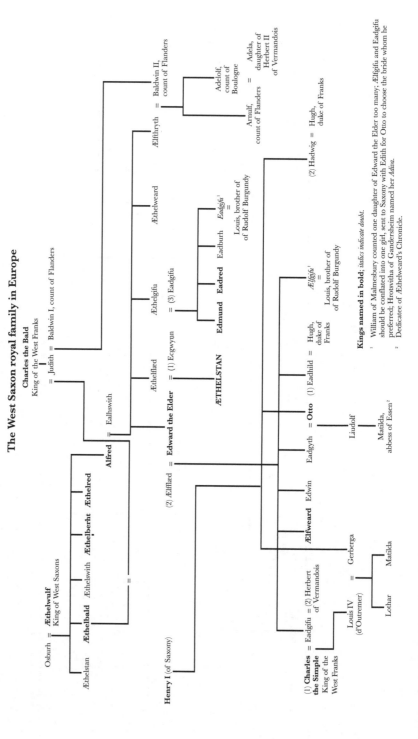

Kings named in bold; *italics indicate doubt.*

[1] William of Malmesbury counted one daughter of Edward the Elder too many; Ælfgifu and Eadgifu should be conflated into one girl, sent to Saxony with Edith for Otto to choose the bride whom he preferred; Hrotsvitha of Gandersheim named her *Adiva.*

[2] Dedicatee of Æthelweard's Chronicle.

Map 1. Britain in the tenth century.

Map 2. Tenth-century Britain and Europe.

Map 3. English Mints, 924–939.

Prologue:

WRITING A MEDIEVAL LIFE

On leaving Westminster Abbey on 5 November 1923 following the funeral of Andrew Bonar Law (who had held the office of prime minister for just 209 days), his political rival Asquith reportedly said, 'It is fitting that we should have buried the Unknown Prime Minister by the side of the Unknown Warrior.' Robert Blake chose that phrase as the title for his biography of Bonar Law, not because he thought it just or fair, but to dispel the erroneous impression it created of the significance of his premiership and wider career. On similar grounds 'The Unknown King' would make a good title for a life of King Æthelstan, who equally does not deserve his position as one of the least recognized English monarchs.[1]

Æthelstan's fifteen-year reign (924–939) constitutes one of the most significant periods in the history of England before the Norman Conquest. He was the first monarch to create and rule over a unified kingdom of the English, and proved himself adept at defending that kingdom against rival powers in northern Britain and Ireland as well as from Scandinavian incursion. In life, Æthelstan's contemporaries regarded him as 'the most excellent and illustrious among the earthly kings of our own day'.[2] Tributes on his death show him far from unknown, but held in high regard not just in England but in the Celtic world and on the continent. Still viewed approvingly around the year 1000, Æthelstan maintained his high reputation after the Norman Conquest. A twelfth-century chronicler recalled that he had 'first ruled alone the kingdom of the English over all England' and many post-Conquest historians referred favourably to his deeds.[3] He featured in later medieval romances, if not always in complimentary tones; ironically, his portrayal reached its lowest point in a fourteenth-century poem named after him: *Athelston*. Just as Æthelstan's star waned, so that of his grandfather, King Alfred, rose. Matthew Paris writing in St Albans in the thirteenth century first called Alfred 'Great'; that label stuck and still rests secure. At the millennial celebrations of Alfred's death (wrongly thought to have occurred in 901) thousands thronged the streets of Winchester to commemorate a king to whom the British empire owed much. In stark contrast, a single notice in *The Times* of London for 25 October 1940 (buried under 'Ecclesiastical

---

[1] Robert Blake, *The Unknown Prime Minister: the Life and Times of Andrew Bonar Law* (London, 1955), 531

[2] Radbod, abbot of Dol, letter to Æthelstan, *c.*927, *EHD*, no. 228.

[3] Oxford, Corpus Christi College, MS 157, 52.

News'), noted the supposed millennium of 'Æthelstan the Great' (dating his death to 940, in error for 939). Lamenting that there might in happier times have been some celebration of this event, the correspondent remembered the king as the greatest and most munificent benefactor of St Paul's Cathedral in London, his donations making that cathedral the richest in England.

In part Æthelstan's failure to prove, in Sellar and Yeatman terms, a memorable king, arises from the difficulties presented by the sources for his reign, which compare badly with the quantity of personal and biographical information relating to King Alfred. This must in part explain Æthelstan's lack of standing in the English historical consciousness, where his rightful claim to be seen as the first English monarch is supplanted by his grandfather. His name scarcely helps to fix him in the modern popular imagination, and may seem particularly rebarbative to a North American audience; should we call him Æthelstan, or Athelstan, or even Ethelstan?[4]

Outwardly Æthelstan thus represents a distinctly unpromising subject for a life. Mentioned in just six annals in the Anglo-Saxon Chronicle, his deeds found lengthy narrative treatment only at the hands of a twelfth-century historian, William of Malmesbury, who supposedly drew on a now lost tenth-century account.[5] Without contemporary narratives, one can only begin to build a picture of an individual (rather than an archetypical prince or king performing the various duties his role demanded) by reading a range of disparate sources creatively to find the man behind the stereotype. We can trace the key events of Æthelstan's life and explore his actions as king through Anglo-Saxon sources ranging from charters (documents recording grants of land and privilege), coins, law codes, poems written in his honour or dedicated to his memory, individual manuscript books associated with the king, and accounts of the relics he bought, received as gifts and gave to religious houses, as well as via texts written in other parts of Britain and in tenth-century Europe. Æthelstan emerges from such material as a ruler active in military, diplomatic and religious spheres; he appears as a more rounded individual when we concentrate our attention on references to him in the context of his own family, among his courtiers, with law-makers and royal counsellors, with bishops and monks, in the company of rulers of other parts of the British Isles and in entertaining foreign embassies. Anxieties about the future security of the large realm he had conquered dictated many of the king's policies, yet we shall observe an equal preoccupation with family affairs, the needs of his siblings, and of those foreigners whom he sheltered at his court, concern for his wider subjects' spiritual and intellectual heritage, and a care for his own eternal soul.

---

[4] W.C. Sellar and R.J. Yeatman, *1066 and All That: A Memorable History of England* (London, 1930).

[5] See Appendix I for a detailed discussion of the interpretative problems presented by William's account in his *Gesta regum Anglorum*.

One of the more substantial previous surveys of the reign comes in Sir Frank Stenton's magisterial study, *Anglo-Saxon England*. Reading the book on its first publication in 1943 not long after the millennium of Æthelstan's death, Kenneth Sisam of Oxford University Press wrote to Stenton: 'I think we want now a book in essay form on Æthelstan who is at the beginning of so many developments'.[6] As the first king to rule over all the English people together in a united kingdom, Æthelstan completed the work begun by his grandfather Alfred and father Edward the Elder to restore Christian rule over those parts of eastern and northern England that had fallen under pagan Scandinavian lordship in the late ninth century. Further, Æthelstan's unification of all the Anglo-Saxon kingdoms under a single monarch achieved a political English unity that, in the eighth century, Bede had only imagined. His reign laid the foundations for the governmental advances of the later tenth century that would make late Anglo-Saxon England the most sophisticated 'state' in contemporary Europe.[7]

Choosing a biographical treatment (rather than an examination of Æthelstan's life in the context of his times) has enabled me to put Æthelstan the individual at the heart of a narrative of the making of the kingdom of England. In every chapter Æthelstan the king takes centre stage – whether in his role as brother, diplomat, warrior, legislator, administrator, Christian or generous host; even so, Æthelstan the man remains elusive. In one sense biographers have the essentials of their plot presented to them, the narrative shaped by the life cycle of the person about whom they have chosen to write. Birth, youth, marriage (or celibacy, whether enforced or elective), old age, death: these constitute the key biological moments in any life, the co-ordinates around which the biographer crafts a more sophisticated narrative of the individual, refined by the social rhythm of the environment in which they lived and operated. A conventional biography need not stick rigidly to this temporal framework, perhaps running parallel and overlapping strands in the story where the subject played significant roles on more than one stage, or where private and public spheres conflict. But chronology usually remains an essential organizing principle. Biographers of medieval people can, however, struggle to apply that biological model consistently, since portions of a medieval life, particularly those relating to birth and childhood, often find scant mention in written sources. Mature years, even in the lives of prominent figures, can also pass unreported. Structuring a coherent biography of a medieval subject thus involves from the outset a greater degree of self-conscious construction and manipulation of material to fit artificial categories than might prove necessary for a better-attested person from a modern age. This is not to argue, of course, that biographies relating to whatever period are not as artificial and 'constructed' as are all other exercises in historical writing, or that any

---

[6] Sisam to Stenton, 5 Jan., 1944; Reading University Library, Stenton MSS, 8/27/1.
[7] James Campbell, *The Anglo-Saxon State* (London and New York, 2000), 1–30.

subject's life comes already pre-plotted for the biographer; merely that medieval biography can require particular artifice. Given the scanty, often formulaic and depersonalized material upon which most biographers working in the early medieval largely depend, anyone attempting this task needs to adopt inventive strategies for organizing the available evidence into useful categories and in structuring the final text of the life they ultimately write.[8]

Writing lives of kings presents specific difficulties. While on the one hand kings may seem more accessible than commoners – after all, historians have complained for generations that leaders and statesmen dominate the historical record and thus the writing of historians, to the detriment of other sorts of people – on the other hand, monarchs are distanced from us by the fact that they are so often conveyed as 'kings' rather than as men. The institution of kingship frequently appears more transparent than the mind of the kings who exercised kingly power, but this does not apply to all medieval kings. Medievalists may become embarrassed when they find themselves mining particularly rich seams, whether because their training makes them uncomfortable about or suspicious of plural accounts (let alone conflicting narratives) or simply because it seems ungrateful to complain when evidence is usually so hard to come by. The contrast between this reign and that of Æthelstan's grandfather Alfred could, in this respect, hardly be greater. Reflecting on the three different lives written of Alfred the Great by Charles Plummer, Alfred Smyth and himself, Richard Abels marvelled that

> the narratives told by these very different historians are, when all is said and done, remarkably similar. This, I believe, is because the narrative is common to the sources that underlie all three historical accounts, sources that ultimately derive from Alfred's court. These are the stories that Alfred himself wanted told to 'preserve his memory in good works'. In other words, the underlying narrative which had seduced so many historians, including me, is Alfred's own narrative – the story and image that he and his courtiers shaped to make sense of his life. This, of course, is not to say that this story and image are historical truth, only that it is the closest to historical truth that the surviving sources will permit us to get.[9]

Abels's caveat does not wholly convince, for that narrative is surely far from any abstract historical 'truth'. This court monopolization of the

[8] Pauline Stafford, *Queen Emma and Queen Edith: Queenship and Women's Power in Eleventh-Century England* (Oxford, 1997); Stafford, 'Writing the Biography of Eleventh-Century Queens', in *Writing Early Medieval Biography: Essays in Honour of Frank Barlow*, ed. David Bates *et al.* (Woodbridge, 2006), 100–1. Michael Clanchy, *Abelard: a Medieval Life* (Oxford, 1997), 19–21.

[9] Richard Abels, 'Alfred and his Biographers: Image and Imagination', in *Writing Early Medieval Biography*, ed. D. Bates *et al.*, 75.

information and its careful crafting into a usable past, a past which ensured that Alfred himself could control how he would be remembered, is precisely what makes it so dangerous. Biography points up rather starkly the problems of source-led historiography; the evidence from which the biographer confects her account does not reside in a distant past but in the concepts and formulations she crafts in the present while she investigates her subject. Her questions determine what evidence she will bring to bear, and equally where she can point only to silence.[10]

These are important considerations for the biographer of King Æthelstan. We know when he acceded to the throne (in 924), and that his accession was disputed, delaying his coronation until 925, but we do not know when he was born. Æthelstan's mother's identity and status are uncertain and his childhood remains largely blank; he seems never to have married and probably left no offspring. After his death in 939, Æthelstan was buried not in one of the monasteries in Wessex where one or more of his forebears lay, but in an abbey in Wiltshire. Malmesbury had few previous royal associations, although it had received donations from the king in life. That Æthelstan conquered Northumbria, brought the rulers of other parts of Britain to swear oaths of loyalty to him, and twice defeated those who dared rebel against those oaths we can assert with confidence. His greatest military victory found celebration in a lengthy poem in the Anglo-Saxon Chronicle and in a Norse saga, and Æthelstan's reputation extended in his own day far beyond British shores. The historian's, if not the biographer's, task is made easier by the survival of substantial documentary and administrative records from this reign; if one's questions about the king relate to his holding of royal councils, granting of lands, promulgation of law, administration of the regions, or minting of coins, one has plentiful material to explore. Æthelstan's ideas about the nature of royal power (or at least the ideas of those who crafted documents on his behalf) emerge from the same sources. Diplomatic exchanges with foreign kings and princes shed light on a family strategy and show a willingness to engage in contemporary continental politics. The king's book-collecting and the lists of relics associated with his name reveal another side of his personality; his contemporaries saw him as a notably pious king, even by the religious standards of his own day. Some even made direct comparison with the great ninth-century Frankish king and emperor, Charlemagne.

Yet Æthelstan the man still remains largely invisible. If 'what did he do?' can only sometimes be answered, 'what did he think?', 'how did he feel?', 'why did he do that (and not take a different course of action)?', 'how did he spend his free time?' and 'what was he like as a person?' are far harder questions, although all lie at the heart of any biography. This life seeks to

---

[10] A point made forcibly, and with much greater elegance, by Michael Bentley, *Modernizing England's Past: English Historiography in the Age of Modernism, 1870–1970* (Cambridge, 2005), 12–14.

determine whether answers can be offered for some of these questions, but in order to get behind the public persona of the king and nearer to the private individual it has necessarily adopted a thematic approach that will seem unconventional to readers expecting a life more akin to the studies of English monarchs of later eras already published in this series. For a straightforward chronological narrative of Æthelstan's life, tracing his thoughts and actions from youth to maturity, cannot be written. Given that uncomfortable truth, is any sort of biography of him possible?

One argument used to support the value of biographical study is that the form offers a means of putting the question of agency back into analysis of the past, something that has tended to fall out of favour in a postmodern climate. Adopting Anthony Giddens's useful model of structuration, a dialectical argument that sees individuals and deep structures working reciprocally, biography can demonstrate how underlying social, economic and political structures may have formed and taught the agent (the individual subject), who then helped to shape the structure of the world around him.[11] This was the model Ian Kershaw used for his biography of Adolf Hitler, showing how Hitler emerged from German society of the 1920s: he was formed by underlying social trends in Germany after the First World War, but also himself shaped those structures; his actions helped German society as a whole move in a particular direction and towards the creation of National Socialism.[12] Gerd Althoff employed an essentially similar technique in his study of Otto III. Adopting this method for studying Æthelstan would involve depicting the king in relationship to his own society, not simply by creating a picture of the times in which he lived and ruled, but by attempting to show that the wider context of his own age was in some measure one that Æthelstan himself had created through his own agency. The essential weakness of this model for my purposes lies in the nature of the evidence. Do we in fact know enough about what the king did (let alone why he did it) to be able to ask questions about what Æthelstan created and generated through his performance of his role as king such that we can show how his actions helped to move Wessex and England into new places? Can we answer the question, what changes were effected through his agency? Or enquire, equally, how Æthelstan himself was shaped by, influenced and changed by those new contexts? Æthelstan had a visible and demonstrable impact on a newly created realm encompassing all the English peoples and he (or at least his court) played some role in shaping a newly imagined political community from those Anglo-Saxon (and Anglo-Danish) subjects, and other British dependants. Yet, one may question whether we have sufficient material to

---

[11] Anthony Giddens's key statement is *The Constitution of Society* (Berkeley, 1984); see also his 'Structuration Theory: Past, Present and Future,' in *Giddens' Theory of Structuration: A Critical Appreciation*, ed. Christopher G. A. Bryant and David Jary (London, 1991), 201–21.

[12] Ian Kershaw, *Hitler, 1889–1936: Hubris* (London, 1998) and *Hitler, 1936–1945: Nemesis* (London, 2000).

be able to say anything about how the creation of that realm and invention of those fresh identities coloured Æthelstan's own sense of his role in that process, or his vision of himself as a king of a different sort from his grandfather, Alfred.

In the preface to the English translation of his life of Otto III, Gerd Althoff admitted that he had been criticized on the book's first publication for having purposely written a biography without a subject; he felt that he had avoided constructing a subject where the sources did not seem to provide enough grounds for doing so.[13] The principal danger of adopting a model of medieval life-writing that dwells as much on the wider times of a king as on his own life is that the times will come to take over the plot. Instead of engaging with the king as a person, one risks producing a series of intersecting studies of the nature of tenth-century government, of the state of religion and the Church, of the various peoples living within the king's realm. Given the difficulties of the evidence for this particular reign, a case could of course be made for not even attempting a biographical treatment (and indeed no one has previously tried to write one).[14] Predominantly the evidence offers images of Æthelstan as a type, a figurehead, a man in a performative role. One might argue that it offers little more than a *mise-en-scène*: a stage set furnished with a well drawn, quite detailed backcloth, some furniture and props but only a series of unconnected fragments of a script. Lacking a flesh-and-blood actor, we have only a cardboard figure propped up on a throne: a character in search of an author able to breathe some life into him, who could only animate him effectively with recourse to fiction.

Inevitably (and whatever the age in which one's subject lived), the man created and constructed by the biographer is no more a 'real' person who once existed than were the various versions of him invented by his family, his close associates, or his wardrobe-keeper. The Æthelstan who lived through the first four decades of the tenth century had experiences, thoughts, spontaneous connections with people and places that can never now be revived. But the fact that the man whom my book will create is not a 'true' person does not render the project of writing his life invalid. Biography becomes most powerful where the author can locate her subject both temporally and spatially in ways they could not themselves have known; my created subject is a compound of images and reflections only some of which were produced by Æthelstan personally, on his behalf, or at his command. Much of our access to his actions and the consequences that flowed from them arises from observations of others unknown to the king. So we can locate Æthelstan's actions and sometimes elements of his thought-world in the world of others both in his own generation and in generations where his reign was still a

[13] Gerd Althoff, *Otto III*, trans. Phyllis G. Jestice (University Park, PA, 2003), xii.

[14] Michael Wood argued that although some biographical artefacts survive, bringing us close to his life, it would be fruitless to try to write a biography in modern terms: *In Search of the Dark Ages* (London, 1981; 1991 edn), 127.

living memory. And most powerfully, we know what neither he nor any of his direct contemporaries knew: we know what happened next; we know when and where he died and can reflect on the legacies of his achievements.

Since I began this study more interested in questions about Æthelstan the man than in the royal office he held, I chose a structure for this biography that would enable me to push to the limits questions about intention and personality, one that focuses less on time than on the different spaces in which the king and the man performed together. In part, of course, that decision reflects the nature of the surviving evidence, yet it also has positive benefits.[15] To view the king not via a narrative of his deeds in chronological sequence but rather through the various lenses of the different environments and spheres in which he lived and worked helps us to construct a more rounded picture of his character. Before we can analyse the separate environments in which we can observe Æthelstan's actions and behaviour, readers will need to be located within the chronological framework of his life which underpins the book as a whole. A first chapter therefore supplies an overarching narrative of the king's life and his achievements, dwelling on his claims to kingship over the whole English people. Thereafter, the book has a spatial design, taking our enquiry outwards in a series of ever-widening circles beginning with the most intimate (familial) contexts in which we might hope to observe the child and then the man, and progressing ultimately on to the widest national and international stages.

Biological inheritance and the dynamics of the immediate family play key roles in the early development of any child's psyche, serving to form his character and personality before wider social and environmental factors come into play to shape and mould those in new directions. In placing Æthelstan within his family in Chapter 2, we can come closest to tracing his individual life cycle, exploring him as child, nephew, brother, foster-father, and head of his own household. That household had both private and public dimensions and so we move outwards in the next chapter from the family circle to the royal court. There we will still want to know what we can see of the king's domestic life, but will find greater light cast on his public entourage. Gaining a sense of which people stayed close to the king, who his immediate associates were (court officials and others), and which nobles (secular and ecclesiastical) and foreign leaders attended on him occasionally will all help to place Æthelstan in a specific social context. The Church represents another critical sphere in which the king was active but which equally influenced his character and shaped his mind. Beginning with the churchmen who were close to Æthelstan personally, the fourth chapter explores the place of religion in his reign. One of the distinctive features of the surviving evidence for Æthelstan is that although short of prose narratives, his deeds and reputation found

---

[15] In devising this structure I was much influenced by the thematic approach adopted by Clanchy's *Abelard*.

commemoration in verse. The religious and cultural environment that fostered and promoted poetry, the books that the king collected and those he gave away all offer us a fresh perspective on his person.

Moving away from the king's immediate court circle and looking out beyond cloistered doors we consider the whole kingdom in Chapter 5. Asking how Æthelstan performed his kingly role in governing the realm entrusted to his charge will inevitably take us away from the man and towards the public figure. Although the texts often portray the results of the deliberations of his councils in stereotypical language, couching the king's words or drawing his image conventionally, we can still use this material to answer some questions about Æthelstan's conceptions of rulership, the areas of responsibility he felt most keenly, the sorts of problems he chose to solve. Formulaic language only masks character and individuality; it need not conceal them completely. In Chapter 6 we come eventually to the place in which one might (given his modern reputation) have thought Æthelstan most at home: the battlefield. This chapter explores the king at war, concentrating on the three major military engagements of the reign: the conquest of Northumbria in 927; the Scottish expedition of 934; and the battle at *Brunanburh* in 937. Chapter 7, called 'Death', moves us towards the end of the king's life. There we consider Æthelstan's celebrated interest in the acquisition of relics and in the cults of the dead, exploring what this reveals of his continental connections and his patronage of English churches; we may also hope to learn something about his attitudes towards death and the afterlife, as well as about his own choice of site for burial.

This thematic treatment of the places and environments in which the king lived and worked builds an image of the king as a person by accretion. Each chapter addresses its chosen theme across the whole chronology of his reign (924–39); only in the first two does the narrative stray back into Æthelstan's childhood. Paralleling the first, the final chapter reconsiders the entirety of the reign in the light of what we have learned about Æthelstan's personality; it considers his hegemony not just over the Anglo-Saxon peoples of Britain but over the whole island and discusses the quasi-imperial language adopted at his court to mark his new status. An epilogue considers Æthelstan's legacy and explores how he has been remembered in the public consciousness over the millennium since his death.

The twelfth-century historian William of Malmesbury ended the lengthy account of King Æthelstan's life and reign in his History of the Deeds of the Kings of England (*Gesta regum Anglorum*) with the statement: 'his years, though few, were full of glory'.[16] Æthelstan has long merited biographical treatment; this life reveals the glory of those few years, coaxing this major figure into the light he deserves.

---

[16] *GR*, ii, 140, 228–9.

Chapter 1

ENGLISH KING?

King Æthelstan, when he had succeeded to kingship after his father
Edward . . . through God's grace ruled all of England alone which
before him many kings held among themselves.[1]

King Æthelstan has a substantial claim to the epithet 'the first English
monarch', for no ruler before him governed all the Anglo-Saxon kingdoms
as a single realm. He succeeded in 924 to an expanded kingdom of Wessex
that encompassed all of England south of the River Humber, and
assumed responsibility for a dominion created by the military achievements of his grandfather, Alfred the Great, and father, Edward the Elder.[2]
Yet, by the time of his death in 939, Æthelstan ruled as king over all the
English peoples of Britain. In the creation of this wide hegemony, he built
on foundations laid by his predecessors both militarily and administra-
tively. Needing swiftly to devise effective mechanisms for the retention and
control of an extended realm, Æthelstan created a more centralized
governmental machine than England had previously seen. Those administrative and legal systems he matched with novel expressions in word and
image of his own conceptions of royal power and authority fit for his
changed status. Scribes and artists in Æthelstan's court circle not only had
to invent discourses suitable for his assumption of kingship over the
English and the unification of England, but also increasingly had to assert
his claims to quasi-imperial rule over other parts of Britain. His leading
men, meeting with their king in council at different places across his realm,
worked strategically to ensure the acceptance and maintenance of the
West Saxon king's authority and of obedience to his law. Their efforts laid
the foundations on which Æthelstan's brothers and nephews would build
later in the tenth century, their collective endeavours creating one of the
wealthiest and most sophisticated governments in contemporary Western
Europe.

[1] Eleventh-century list of relics belonging to the church at Exeter preserved in Oxford,
Bodleian MS Auct D. 2. 16; fo. 8r, ed. and trans. Patrick Conner, *Anglo-Saxon Exeter*
(Woodbridge, 1993), 176; discussed in detail in ch. 7.
[2] The epithet for Æthelstan's father was coined by Wulfstan of Winchester in his *Life of
St Æthelwold*, presumably to distinguish Alfred's son from the later tenth-century king,
Edward the Martyr.

ÆTHELSTAN'S EARLY LIFE, *c.*894–*c.*909

The early years of Æthelstan's life remain unfortunately the most opaque to the historian, for we know neither the date nor place of the future king's birth and can only guess at where he spent his infancy and childhood. His father Edward, the eldest son of King Alfred, was by the last decade of the ninth century the acknowledged heir to the West Saxon throne. He probably married around 893 and his first child Æthelstan may have been born in *c.*894. Following Alfred's decisive victory over an invading Danish army in 878, Wessex the southernmost English kingdom – then stretching from Kent in the east to Cornwall in the west and as far north as the River Thames – had experienced a prolonged period of peace. In the years after 878, King Alfred had extended his realm north of the traditional boundary of Wessex, acquiring control of London and also of the western part of the midland kingdom of England, Mercia. At the time of Æthelstan's birth, Mercia was governed as a dependency of Wessex by Ealdorman Æthelred, who had married Alfred's daughter Æthelflæd and ruled the midland kingdom under his father-in-law's overlordship. The formerly independent kingdoms of East Anglia and Northumbria lay in Scandinavian hands, their native royal lines supplanted.

We have no information about where the young prince Æthelstan spent his early life, and can only assume that it was in one or more of the royal palaces in Wessex. Danish forces attacked England again between 892 and 896. Although King Alfred's defensive strategies implemented in the more peaceful 880s proved sufficient to prevent the Viking armies from inflicting undue damage on Wessex or western Mercia, the necessity to participate in the realm's military defence must have taken the prince's father away from home during much of his eldest son's infancy, leaving Æthelstan with his mother. Later sources give her name as Ecgwynn, but otherwise we know little about her; she had one other child (a daughter) with whom Æthelstan was brought up. Combined military (and naval) responses and better organized defences ensured the eventual defeat of the attacking Danes; from 896 Wessex and England lay once more at peace.

Once able to walk and talk, the child Æthelstan apparently became a favourite of his grandfather, who elected at some point late in his own reign (certainly before his death in 899) to perform a formal ceremony on his grandson. Alfred thereby marked out the boy, if not as his designated future heir, at least as one who might in time prove worthy to accede to his grandfather's throne. At or around the time of his father's death in 899 and his own succession to the West Saxon realm, Edward remarried. Whether Æthelstan's mother had died, or Edward had tired of her and wanted a new wife, we cannot know; whatever the underlying reasons for the remarriage, it had a significant impact on Edward's first-born son. Ælfflæd proved a fertile mother, producing not just several daughters but also two further sons, Ælfweard and Edwin, whose future claim to succeed their father on the West Saxon throne was bolstered by the fact that (unlike their eldest half-brother) they had been born to a ruling king. Æthelstan's presence at Edward and Ælfflæd's court scarcely benefited the future royal careers of his younger brothers, and William of Malmesbury tells us that Æthelstan was thus sent away to be reared by his aunt Æthelflæd (Edward's sister) and uncle, Ealdorman Æthelred in Mercia.[3]

We know no more of Æthelstan's supposed education in Mercia than of his early years in Wessex. Once old enough to bear arms Æthelstan assisted his uncle and, after Æthelred's death in 911, his aunt, in their conquest of northern Mercia from the Danes, and the fortification of a network of *burhs* over their newly acquired territory. In that process the Mercian leaders acted as deputies under King Edward's overall authority, playing their part in his wider vision for the conquest of the Danelaw. As Æthelstan, and the eldest of his brothers Ælfweard, came to maturity they, too, shared in the military campaigns to drive out the Scandinavian rulers and settlers.

EDWARD THE ELDER AND THE CONQUEST OF THE DANELAW

Recording the death of Æthelstan's grandfather Alfred, six days before All Saints' Day, the Anglo-Saxon chronicler noted that Alfred had ruled as 'king over the whole English people except for that part which was under Danish rule'.[4] His son Edward proved a more than worthy successor to the newly created kingdom of the Anglo-Saxons: even though his successes found less celebration in the historical memory, his reign saw the bounds of Wessex pushed securely not just deep into the hitherto independently ruled Mercia, but also east into East Anglia, where West Saxon kings had never formerly held power.

Despite his clear designation as Alfred's heir long before his death, his probable appointment as sub-king in Kent and his leading of armies in battle against the Danes successfully before his father's death,[5] Edward did not accede to the West Saxon throne unchallenged. His father's brother's son, Æthelwold, the son of Æthelred, Alfred's next eldest brother, laid claim to the kingship, first mounting a challenge in Wessex before fleeing to Northumbria, where the Danish army accepted him as their king and swore him allegiance; the people of Essex accepted his rule two years later.[6] The Winchester version of the Chronicle, which consistently presented Alfred and Edward in a favourable light, tended to play down this episode, but that the rebellion found mention at all in the West Saxon Chronicle indicates its importance. Having induced the East Anglians to

[3] *GR*, ii, 133 (pp. 210–11). No other source supports William's assertion here; see further below, 34–7.

[4] ASC 900.

[5] Æthelweard, 49. Barbara Yorke, 'Edward as Ætheling', in H&H, 25–39.

[6] ASC 900C. JW, *s.a.* 901, 356–7; see fig. 1: The West Saxon Royal Family.

break their peace with Edward, Æthelwold harried Mercia and Wessex; in response Edward sent an army into the southern Danelaw, meeting his cousin at the battle of 'the Holme' (the precise site has never been identified). Edward won a decisive victory, although at heavy cost.[7] Had Edward lost to Æthelwold's forces, the history of England in the tenth century would have developed quite differently as of course would the fate of his young son, who was then only about nine years old.[8] Under the rulership of the heirs of Æthelwold whose power base lay in the north, and who enjoyed active Danish support, a genuinely Anglo-Scandinavian realm might have emerged.[9]

Following the battle of the Holme Edward maintained an uneasy truce with the Danes, making peace when necessary and also fortifying key strategic towns such as Chester in 907. He began a more concerted campaign against Danish forces in England in 909, and a combined West Saxon and Mercian last – quite possibly including the king's son Æthelstan, now in his mid-teens – won a major victory against a Danish army at Wednesfield near Tettenhall in 910.[10] In defeat, the Northumbrian Danes stayed north of the Humber leaving Edward with his sister Æthelflæd and brother-in-law Æthelred, ealdorman of the Mercians, assisted by their nephews Æthelstan and Edward's second son Ælfweard, to confront the Scandinavian forces of the southern Danelaw. Over the next few years, the English used fortified *burhs* as centres from which to advance against the settled Danes. A collection of forts across north-western Mercia cut off the Scandinavians settled on the Wirral from their counterparts in eastern England, particularly from the newly established King Rægnald at York.[11] A parallel building programme in the south-east had a similar purpose, the effectiveness of the new *burhs* being demonstrated on several occasions on which they withstood Danish attack.[12] English forces also attacked Danish strongholds; in 917 in a two-pronged attack Æthelflæd took Derby (one of the Five Boroughs) while Edward's host besieged the Danish fort at Tempsford, near Huntingdon and killed the last Danish king of East Anglia before going on to take Colchester and Huntingdon.[13]

---

[7] ASC *s.a.* 903; the battle probably took place at the end of the calendar year 902, but the Chronicle's year began in September, so events occurring in the autumn are recorded under the next AD date. Æthelweard, 52, also named the battlefield, as did Henry of Huntingdon, who reported its outcome as uncertain: HH, v. 16, 304–5.

[8] Cyril Hart, *The Danelaw* (London and Rio Grande, 1992), 514 argued that historians have underestimated the potential seriousness of this engagement.

[9] James Campbell has explored the significance of this rebellion and the influence Æthelwold had in uniting separate English regions: 'What is not Known about the Reign of Edward the Elder', in H & H, 21–2.

[10] ASC 910; Æthelweard, 52–3 (Æthelweard seems to date the battle to 909); JW *s.a.* 910, 362–5.

[11] F.T. Wainwright, 'North-West Mercia AD 871–924' (1942), reprinted in *Wirral and its Viking Heritage*, ed. Paul Cavill, Stephen E. Harding and Judith Jesch (Nottingham, 2000), 25–6.

[12] ASC 911, 912, 914, 916, 917.

[13] ASC 917.

At the end of 917 all the Danes in East Anglia and Essex submitted to Edward, as did the Danish armies of East Anglia and Cambridge.[14] Only the Danish forces at Leicester, Stamford, Nottingham and Lincoln now remained; all the others had by the end of that year submitted either to Edward or to his sister. While Edward obtained the submission of Stamford in 918, Æthelflæd gained peaceful control of the *burh* at Leicester and the people of York also submitted to her but, 'very soon after they had agreed to this', the anonymous writer of the Mercian Register reported, Æthelflæd died in Tamworth on 12 June.[15] Edward moved rapidly on his sister's death, going straight to the *burh* at Tamworth (a long-standing Mercian centre) and occupying it. In the words of the West Saxon chronicler, 'all the people in the land of the Mercians which had been subject to Æthelflæd submitted to him; and the kings in Wales, Hywel, Clydog and Idwal, and all the race of the Welsh sought to have him as lord.'[16] Next, Edward went to Nottingham, captured the Danish *burh* and ordered it to be repaired and manned with both English and Danes. Although not specifically mentioning Lincoln here, the chronicler implied that it, too, the last of the Five Boroughs, submitted at this time, for the record for 918 ends: 'And all the people who had settled in Mercia, both Danish and English, submitted to him.'[17]

York's submission to Æthelflæd might have heralded a new phase in the campaign against the Danes in England had she not died so shortly thereafter.[18] Edward's swift action in capitalizing on his sister's death gave him direct rule over her Mercian dominion. Mercia had probably enjoyed only a limited genuine independence from West Saxon rule between *c.*893 and 918, yet any self-determination that the old kingdom had retained under Æthelred and Æthelflæd's rule it now lost entirely on the latter's death.[19] West Saxon and Mercian chroniclers offer us different narratives at this point. While the West Saxon Chronicle reported the general submission in 918 and the next year Edward's strengthening of the Mercian border in the north-west, the building of a *burh* at Thelwall and the sending of a Mercian force into Northumbria to Manchester to repair and man a fort, the Mercian Register focused exclusively on family politics. After the report of Æthelflæd's death it gave notice of her burial at Gloucester; in the annal for 919 (perhaps a continuation of the entry for the previous

---

[14] ASC 917.

[15] F.T. Wainwright, 'Æthelflæd, Lady of the Mercians', in *Scandinavian England*, ed. H.P.R. Finberg (Chichester, 1975), 305–24. For the fascinating suggestion that the author of the Mercian Register (MR) was Alfred's youngest son, Æthelweard, see David A.E. Pelteret, 'An Anonymous Historian of Edward the Elder's Reign', in *Early Medieval Studies in Memory of Patrick Wormald*, ed. Stephen Baxter *et al.* (Farnham and Burlington, VT, 2009), 325–30.

[16] ASC 918A.

[17] Ibid.

[18] Michael Davidson, 'The (Non)submission of the Northern Kings in 920', in H&H, 203.

[19] S. Keynes, 'Edward, King of the Anglo-Saxons' in H&H, 42–4.

year), the Register reported, 'in this year also the daughter of Æthelred, lord of the Mercians, was deprived of all authority in Mercia and taken into Wessex, three weeks before Christmas. She was called Ælfwynn'.[20]

In comparison with the military skill of the mature Edward, backed by his adult sons Æthelstan and Ælfweard, a young female claimant with no political experience could have had little credibility with the lordship of Mercia, even if she had ruled under her uncle's overall authority. That a Danish king, Rægnald, grandson of Ímar, had recently taken over York further explains Edward's actions. His conquest of Northumbria in 918 'introduced an entirely new dynamic into the political alignment of eastern England', unsettling the delicate balance of loyalties of the Anglo-Scandinavian population of the region.[21] Against that new threat, Edward built fortresses along the northern edge of his realm at Nottingham and at Bakewell in Derbyshire, trying to ensure that he covered all possible access routes into Mercia. These efforts sought to prevent Rægnald from threatening his newly acquired (and perhaps still rather fragile) superiority over the Anglo-Danish population of the east midlands, or destabilizing it by coming to 'liberate' those peoples from West Saxon rule. Others in the region had reason to look equally warily at an emergent Northumbria under Scandinavian rule and Edward capitalized on his own unquestioned domination of the south of the island by brokering an arrangement of mutual protective benefit to all parties, while asserting his own superior status. As the West Saxon Chronicle recorded it: 'And then the king of the Scots and all the people of the Scots, and Rægnald, and the sons of Eadwulf and all who live in Northumbria, both English and Danish, Norsemen and others, and also the king of the Strathclyde Welsh, chose him [Edward] as father and lord.'[22]

This submission of all the other rulers of the island of Britain to Edward in 920 did not equate to an assertion of the same level of control that his son Æthelstan would enjoy after 927 (and later reinforce with conclusive military victories in 934 and 937). Edward's election as father and lord (the Old English words are *fæder* and *hlaford*) not just by the rulers of the Scots, Danes and Norsemen but by the people of the Scots and all those who live in Northumbria does not remotely diminish the greater achievement of his son, or challenge Æthelstan's claim to have been the first king to rule over all the English in the island. Since the twelfth century, historians have wanted to interpret Edward's treaty as marking the start of English

[20] MR 919. Quite what happened to Ælfwynn hereafter is unclear; see below, 59. Henry of Huntingdon's account neatly characterized Edward's motives, reporting that he acted with regard to expediency rather than to justice when he disinherited his niece of the lordship of the Mercians: HH, v. 17, 308–9.

[21] Alex Woolf, *From Pictland to Alba 789–1070* (Edinburgh, 2007), 145. F.T. Wainwright, 'The Submission to Edward the Elder' (1952), reprinted in *Scandinavian England*, ed. H.P.R. Finberg (Chichester, 1975), 352. A.P. Smyth, *Scandinavian York and Dublin*, 2 vols (Dublin 1975–9), i, 93–9.

[22] ASC 923A (*recte* 920).

hegemony over Scotland, an appealing notion when one considers that this is the first recorded occasion of diplomatic exchange between realms that might legitimately be considered the direct ancestors of the later Scotland and England.[23] Yet, bearing in mind the strength of Rægnald's kingdom in York, it seems unlikely that Edward's territorial control extended as far as Scotland, nor can he have exerted any direct authority over either Constantín or the king of the Strathclyde Welsh, whom Edward seems to have treated as his equals.[24] Edward needed most urgently to ensure that the Danish king of York did not attempt to assume possession of the formerly Scandinavian lands south of the Humber, or incite the population in the eastern Danelaw to rebel against him. For Rægnald, ruling a kingdom sandwiched uneasily between the Scots and Edward's expanded West Saxon realm, his northern neighbours may have posed the greatest threat. Both Edward and Rægnald had much to gain from an alliance of mutual co-operation and that is how we should interpret the agreement of 920.[25] Each party accepted the other's rule over the whole population – English and Danish or part-Danish – in his own territory; the northern kings accepted Edward's arbitration in this arrangement and to a degree thus, as the chronicler claimed, his lordship. But Æthelstan's hegemony would extend further, encompassing direct rule over the Northumbrian population and the genuine submission of the kings of the Scots and of Strathclyde.

Beyond the agreement of mutual co-operation asserted in this treaty, Edward exerted no direct authority north of the Humber in the last years of his reign. The sole chronicle reference for the period before Edward's death in 924 refers to his building of a *burh* at *Cledmutha*, probably on the Clwyd estuary to defend against the Norse in Dublin.[26] When Rægnald died in 920 or 921, his kinsman Sihtric Cáech succeeded him immediately in the kingdom of York; this gave Edward no chance to interfere in the York kingdom, and the fact that Sihtric minted coins in Lincoln rather suggests that his realm had incorporated parts of Lincolnshire before Edward's death. [27] Significantly, the reunited Northumbria now lay in the hands of a dynasty that also controlled the Isle of Man and the Scandinavian ports in Ireland, whose people remained pagan. The York–Dublin axis presented a direct threat to Mercian territory (and thus

[23] Davidson, 'The (Non)submission', 201; Woolf, *From Pictland*, 145–7.

[24] Wainwright's suggestion ('The Submission') that this was an anti-Viking alliance is weakened by the fact that those who 'submitted' included the Danish king Rægnald, grandson of Ívarr the Boneless; see Davidson, 206.

[25] Woolf, *From Pictland*, 147.

[26] MR 921.

[27] Smyth, *Scandinavian York and Dublin*, ii, 6–9; for the St Martin coins of Scandinavian design minted at Lincoln, possibly by the same moneyer who was working for Sihtric in York, see Ian Stewart, 'The St Martin Coins of Lincoln', *British Numismatic Journal*, xxxvi (1967), 49–54.

potentially to Wessex, further to the south) but promised equally to endanger the Welsh and potentially the Scots.[28] Æthelstan and his brother Ælfweard both came to maturity during this period and gained military experience in their father's wars against the Scandinavian settlers. Once his aunt Æthelflæd had died in 918, and Edward claimed hegemony over all of Mercia and East Anglia, Æthelstan continued in the defence and consolidation of the northern part of this extended realm, while Ælfweard seems to have built a power base for himself south of the Thames in Wessex, above all in the cathedral town of Winchester. Both thus laid claim by birth and by proven military capacity to succeed their father on his death.

ÆTHELSTAN'S ACCESSION AND HIS CONQUEST OF THE NORTH

Only one thing is certain about Æthelstan's succession to Edward the Elder's throne: it did not occur smoothly. Edward died on 17 July 924 at Farndon in northern Mercia (near Chester). Whatever arrangement King Alfred might once have envisaged for his eldest grandson, that plan had now been superseded by a scheme which included Æthelstan's eldest half-brother Ælfweard in the kingship. Despite Æthelstan's superior claims as the eldest surviving son, Edward apparently expected that Ælfweard, his second son, should succeed him, at least in Wessex, if not in the whole of his extended realm, but his precise intentions remain uncertain. At the time of Edward's death, Æthelstan seems to have been in Mercia with his father, while Ælfweard remained in Wessex. The physical location of the two princes as much as any prearranged plan of their father's probably explains why each separate historic kingdom elected its own ætheling as king. We can only speculate as to what might have happened had this proved a permanent division of Edward's realm, for Ælfweard died at Oxford soon after his father. Perhaps he had travelled north to meet his older brother and negotiate some mutually acceptable arrangement for power-sharing. But Ælfweard's death changed everything.[29]

Æthelstan thus succeeded in August 924 to the throne of a Wessex extended by his father far north of its traditional boundary at the Thames, to encompass the midlands as far as the River Humber as well as East Anglia. In Mercia, where Æthelstan had become a familiar figure, thanks partly to his involvement in military campaigns against the Danes, we may imagine that the young king met with the warm approval of the population, but his welcome in Wessex appeared far less certain. This may explain why his coronation did not take place until 4 September 925. His decision to be crowned at Kingston-upon-Thames, at the boundary of the

[28] *HSC*, chs 22 and 24; F.T. Wainwright, 'The Battles at Corbridge', *Saga Book of the Viking Society*, xiii (1950), 156–73; *HSC*, 105–7.

[29] Keynes, *Liber Vitae*, 19–22.

old kingdoms of Wessex and Mercia, speaks volubly to the new king's
aspirations to govern a genuinely united realm. Archbishop Æthelhelm
of Canterbury consecrated the young king using a revised coronation
ordo that celebrated the king's election to rulership over two peoples and
bestowed on him new royal regalia: a crown (not, as for earlier kings,
a helmet), a ring, sword and rod of office.[30] Despite the archbishop's
prayers that Æthelstan might 'establish and govern the apex of paternal
glory unitedly' and 'hold fast the state which you have held by paternal
suggestion', the king remained something of an outsider in Wessex,
maintaining for much of the rest of his life frosty relations with the
New Minster at Winchester, guardians of his father's and his eldest
half-brother's remains.[31]

Dealings with his neighbours, especially in Britain with the kingdom
of Northumbria and with Frankia across the Channel, preoccupied
Æthelstan at the start of his reign, as did the necessity to make suitable
provision for the future of the remarkably large number of sisters and
half-sisters with whom his father had thought fit to provide him. Just five
months after his coronation, in January 926, Æthelstan arranged for his
only known full sister to marry Sihtric, the Danish king in York. They met
to contract the marriage at the Mercian capital of Tamworth, deep in
Æthelstan's realm, not on a border, where treaties were more conventionally negotiated. Sihtric's willingness to travel so far into English lands need
not appear a sign of his relative weakness in these negotiations; he dealt
with Æthelstan on equal terms as king of the Northumbrians, and each
agreed not to invade the other's territory, or to support the other's
enemies.[32] Since the treaty served to secure the northern Mercian border
and promised to reduce the risk of renewed attack from Dublin, the political and military alliance was as important as the personal bond made
between the two kings. In the same year, while his court met at Abingdon,
Æthelstan received an embassy from his cousin Adelolf of Flanders on
behalf of the Robertian Hugh, duke of the Franks. Æthelstan agreed to
give his half-sister Eadhild to Hugh in marriage in return for a huge quantity of splendid gifts and relics.[33]

These would prove fortuitous alliances. When Sihtric died the following
year, in 927, the presence of a widowed sister in now hostile territory
gave Æthelstan a valuable excuse to invade his brother-in-law's realm
that summer. In fact, he responded to the northern power vacuum not a

[30] Wormald, *MEL*, 447, n. 114; Janet Nelson, 'The First Use of the Second Anglo-Saxon
Ordo', in *Myth, Rulership, Church and Charters*, ed. Julia Barrow and Andrew Wareham
(Aldershot, 2008), 124–5; for further discussion of the new *ordo* see below, 75–7.

[31] Nelson, 'First Use', 124; Keynes, *Liber Vitae*, 19–20; Alan Thacker, 'Dynastic
Monasteries and Family Cults: Edward the Elder's Kindred', in H&H, 254.

[32] ASC 926D; Woolf, *From Pictland*, 149–50; Sheila Sharp, 'The West Saxon Tradition of
Dynastic Marriage: with Special Reference to Edward the Elder', in *Edward the Elder*, ed.
N.J. Higham and D. Hill (London and New York, 2001), 82–5.

[33] Discussed in detail in below, 192–8.

moment too soon, for the Danes also reacted speedily to the news of Sihtric's death and Guthfrith, another of the grandsons of Ívarr, led a fleet from Dublin and Anagassan (Co. Louth) across to Northumbria to try and take over his kinsman's realm.[34] Whether the two forces met in battle remains uncertain; from the bald record in the northern recension of the Chronicle that Æthelstan 'succeeded to the kingdom of the Northumbrians' we might assume that the West Saxon king prevailed without having to fight his Danish rival. He captured the city of York and demanded, and received, the submission of the Northumbrian people to his rule.[35] William of Malmesbury said that he went so far as to level to the ground the fortress which the Danes had built at York, so as to leave behind no possible defensive place for future insurgency. He may also have driven out another ruler from the north of the kingdom called 'Ealdwulf' who was in revolt.[36]

The language of a Latin poem written immediately after these events strengthens the presumption that this was a military takeover. A clerk in the king's retinue called Petrus addressed his verse (referred to by its first line: *Carta dirige gressus*, Letter, direct your steps) to the queen and prince in the royal *palacium* in Wessex, celebrating the military events that followed from Sihtric's death: 'He [Æthelstan], with Sihtric having died, in such circumstances arms for battle the army of the Saxons throughout all Britain.'[37]

The poem celebrated both Æthelstan's control of Saxon armies throughout Britain, and his creation of a single realm of the English. Extending his territory in this way gave Æthelstan's Wessex a set of new borders far to the north of anywhere his father or grandfather had once attempted to control. Displacing Sihtric's designated heir from York also,

---

[34] Guthfrith's brief reign left no trace in English sources and he does not appear to have minted any coins while at York: Woolf, *From Pictland*, 148–51.

[35] ASCD: the chronicler here used the standard Old English phrase denoting succession to a kingdom: 'Æthelstan cyning feng to Norðhymbra rice'. Compare also the statements of Simeon of Durham and John of Worcester that Æthelstan added Sihtric's dominion to his own realm, having expelled Sihtric's son, Guthfrith: *HR* s.a. 926, p. 124; JW, s.a. 926, pp. 386–7. Also ASC 927E: 'In this year, King Æthelstan drove out King Guthfrith'.

[36] For Ealdwulf, William may have meant to say Ealdred, son of Ealdwulf of Bamburh, or he might have been confused and conflated the events of 927 and 934; alternatively, Ealdred might have had a cousin or brother who had the same name as his father, a man who did not share Ealdred's willingness to submit to a southern ruler. It is not helpful that William provides two narratives of these years: *GR* ii. 131 and 134, pp. 206–9 and 212–17; Dumville, *HBC* 3, pp. 5–6.

[37] Lapidge, 'Poems', 83–93; W.H. Stevenson, 'A Latin Poem Addressed to King Athelstan', *EHR*, xxvi (1911), 482–7. Benjamin Hudson's argument that the reference to the approach of ships and the poem's emphasis on Æthelstan's survival point rather to a compositional date after the battle of *Brunanburh* does not convince; the association with the death of Sihtric seems firmly to pin these verses to 927: *Kings of Celtic Scotland* (Westport, CT and London, 1994), 75.

however, created new enemies for Æthelstan among the Scandinavian rulers in Dublin.

Prudently, therefore, the West Saxon king sought at the same time the submission of other rulers within Britain who might otherwise have thought to advance the Danish cause. At Eamont, near Penrith rulers from Wales (Hywel of the West Welsh and Owain of Gwent), from the northern English kingdom based at Bamburgh (Ealdred, son of Eadwulf) and Constantín of the Scots all accepted his overlordship. This event, widely recorded in contemporary and later chronicles, marked in formal ceremony the profound significance of Æthelstan's acquisition of direct rule over Northumbria and the change in his royal status from king of the West Saxons and Mercians to ruler over all the English peoples.[38] Having secured the north, Æthelstan went from Eamont to the Welsh border, where he compelled the Welsh princes to meet him, agree to surrender to his authority and to pay him a regular tribute at an exceptional level.[39]

No longer king, as his father had been, merely of Wessex and Mercia combined, Æthelstan now held sway over all the Anglo-Saxon peoples of Britain, having united the formerly disparate Anglo-Saxon lands into one: 'Whom he now rules with this *Saxonia* now made whole: King Æthelstan lives glorious through his deeds,' wrote the poet Petrus, who also noted Constantín's loyalty in the service of the Saxon king.[40] Furthermore, the agreement reached at Eamont and the subsequent submission of the Welsh fundamentally changed the nature of Æthelstan's relationship with the other rulers in Britain, making him not just king of all the Anglo-Saxon peoples but effectively an over-king of Britain, a claim articulated henceforward on his coins and in royal charters, whose witness lists in the period between 928 and 935 included British sub-kings.[41] The submission of 927 marked the beginning of a new era in the political culture of Anglo-Saxon England and inaugurated a period of peace in the north that would last until 934.

In those years of peace Æthelstan preoccupied himself with the governance of his extended realm. His activities attracted little attention from chroniclers but he was far from idle during this time, as the surviving texts of his charters and his law codes indicate. Those documents that enable us to see where, and on which days, the king issued charters show him to

---

[38] ASC *s.a.* 926D. Eamont is in Cumbria, south of Penrith; its name means 'at the confluence of the rivers': A.H. Smith, *English Place-Name Elements*, Part I, EPNS 25 (Cambridge, 1956), 143.

[39] *GR*, ii, 134 (pp. 214–17). While Welsh sources confirm the payment of tribute to Æthelstan and Welsh kings attested his charters from this time onwards, one can have less confidence in William's tales about Cornwall and Exeter; see below, ch. 6.

[40] *Carta dirige gressus*, stanzas 3 and 5; Lapidge, 'Poems', 98.

[41] Ibid., 91; H.R. Loyn, 'Wales and England in the Tenth Century: the Context of the Æthelstan Charters', in his *Society and Peoples* (London, 1992), 178–81. For Æthelstan's claims to rulership over Britain, see below, ch. 8.

have travelled widely across the southern part of his realm, but record few royal councils convened outside the bounds of greater Wessex.[42] In 929 he received an embassy from another continental court, this time from Henry the Fowler, king of Saxony, seeking a bride for his son Otto. Æthelstan sent two of his half-sisters back to Germany for the prince to choose which he preferred: Eadgyth, whom Otto married, and (probably) her full sister Ælfgifu, who married Louis, the brother of Rudolf of Burgundy.[43] Cenwald, bishop of Worcester, accompanied the two girls on their journey, taking the opportunity to travel around the monasteries of Germany and entering the king's name and his own into various monastic confraternity books.[44]

Although not at war during this time, Æthelstan's realm seems to have been a less than wholly peaceable place. In his law codes the king demonstrated a recurrent preoccupation with breaches of the peace and with theft, which he took as an index of disloyalty to his person, and thus to his office as king. His repeated efforts to maintain the peace and to weaken the influence of powerful local kindreds, whom he blamed for much of the disruption of his day, reflect how much importance he placed on personal loyalty and on the requirement for a man to keep his oath to his king.[45] In that light, tensions at court and even more so within the king's own family circle will have rankled particularly. A laconic statement in the Anglo-Saxon Chronicle that Edwin (Æthelstan's second half-brother, son of Ælfflæd) was drowned at sea in 933 finds elaboration in the report of William of Malmesbury that the prince had plotted with factions in Winchester unhappy with Æthelstan's accession to the throne of Wessex. Unwilling to accept his brother's denial of involvement in this plot, Æthelstan supposedly banished Edwin, sending him over the sea in exile and thus unwittingly causing his death when he drowned in a storm. In reparation for his part in his half-brother's death, William claimed, Æthelstan founded a monastery at Milton Abbas in Dorset. While the details of William's story cannot inspire confidence, Edwin did apparently die at sea while making a cross-Channel voyage, for the Flemish monastery of St-Bertin claimed to have care of his body.[46]

We may imagine that in these years of peace, at times when the burdens of routine government and administration permitted, Æthelstan pursued his own interests. Like his father and grandfather before him, he probably enjoyed hunting, hawking and honing his sword skills by day; the quantity of poetry to survive from this reign suggests that poetry recitation may have formed a part of evening entertainment at his court. Although

---

[42] Æthelstan's movements, such as they can be determined, are represented in tabular form in Appendix II, 'When King Æthelstan was where'. See further, below, 77–91.

[43] Look at fig. 2, The West Saxon Royal Family in Europe, and see also below, 48–52.

[44] Cenwald's visit is discussed fully below, 101–2.

[45] See below, 140–5.

[46] See below, 41–3.

Æthelstan never married – for a complex variety of reasons among which a vocation to chastity and the desire to ensure a smooth succession for his youngest brothers seem the most plausible – he spent neither a solitary nor a lonely adulthood. Æthelstan acted as foster-father to several young males from continental lines, among them Louis, son of Charles the Simple and Æthelstan's half-sister Eadgifu, who later ruled as Louis IV in western Frankia; Alain, son of Matuedoi, count of Poher in Brittany; possibly Hákon, son of Harald Fairhair of Denmark; as well as the son of Constantín, king of the Scots. The consistency with which Welsh kings attested Æthelstan's charters during the central years of his reign also suggests that their company may reliably have enlivened many a dull evening.

The king had serious interests, however, beyond those more typical of his class and gender. Æthelstan's book-collecting reflects his aesthetic enthusiasm for manuscript books and a desire for learning as well as an eagerness to espouse his grandfather's precepts about the intellectual attributes necessary for the holding of high office.[47] Far beyond British shores the king had a reputation for collecting the relics of saints, leading Breton clergy in exile in Frankia to send him relics from their homeland in the hope of his prayers, while other clergy sold him the bones of saints and some even stole them on his behalf.[48] Bishop Cenwald's visit to German monasteries may have brought back to Æthelstan's court information about the early stages of Benedictine reformed monasticism on the continent. The future archbishop of Canterbury, Dunstan, spent time in his youth at Æthelstan's court as did Æthelwold, future abbot of Abingdon and later bishop of Winchester, both notable supporters of the reorganization of the monastic life in the reign of Æthelstan's nephew, King Edgar (959–75); so did Ælfheah, later bishop of Winchester, known as 'the Bald' (perhaps on account of his tonsure). All arguably acquired in the king's circle an interest in the Benedictine life as well as – if we can believe the account given by Abbo of Fleury in his *Passio* of St Edmund – information about the martyrdom of the East Anglian king, Edmund, at the hands of the Danes in 869.[49] Charters and law codes issued in these years display a considerable concern for spiritual matters and the life eternal; it cannot be coincidental that a group of land grants issued in these middle years echoes language of the king's laws in imposing on monastic houses the obligation to say masses, sing psalms and give alms annually on the king's behalf. That a contemporary poet should have addressed verses to the king beginning 'Rex pius Æðelstan' articulated no empty epithet: Æthelstan's renown for piety and the support of learning had indeed spread widely, if not over the whole wide world

---

[47] Asser, ch. 106; David Pratt, *The Political Thought of King Alfred the Great* (Cambridge, 2007); explored further, below, 117–22.

[48] See below, 189–92.

[49] See below, 109.

(as the poet had it), at least across his own realm and that of his immediate neighbours.[50]

ÆTHELSTAN THE WARRIOR KING

In 934 the king took a combined land and sea force to Scotland. His motives for this expedition must remain unclear, for various different factors may have necessitated this course of action.[51] Militarily, the expedition was extremely successful, for the king managed to use his naval and land forces strategically to defeat the Scots king, ravaging according to one source as far north as Caithness and achieving a decisive victory, taking the son of the Scots king back to Wessex with him as a hostage.[52] By early autumn the royal court had returned to the south once more.

News of Æthelstan's military prowess travelled beyond British shores and led to requests for him to deploy his forces again, this time overseas in support of his exiled foster-sons. A Frankish embassy came to the English court in 936, seeking not a marriage alliance but the king's personal support and practical military assistance in the restoration of his nephew, Louis, to his throne in western Frankia. Further bolstering of his continental alliances came from Æthelstan's direct involvement in helping his Breton foster-son Alain to regain his ancestral lands in Brittany in the same year.[53] Later Scandinavian sources allege further that Æthelstan offered military assistance to another of his supposed foster-sons, Hákon, son of the Norwegian king Harald Fairhair, when he reclaimed his throne at around this time. His reputation as a successful warrior thus proved an important element in the forging of these international treaties. The peace he achieved at home in England after the Scottish expedition would prove transitory, however, for Æthelstan's enemies regrouped and in 937 he faced the most serious threat to the long-term stability of his expanded realm: a joint attack on English shores by Norse forces from Dublin led by Olaf Guthfrithsson and the combined armies of King Constantín of the Scots and Owain's Strathclyde Welsh.

Commemorated in verse in the Anglo-Saxon Chronicle, the ensuing battle at *Brunanburh* was the most decisive military engagement of Æthelstan's reign and the one which would serve to define his posthumous reputation as a king 'victorious because of God', as Ælfric of Eynsham described him.[54] Defeat at *Brunanburh* would not merely have ended the king's life: the Germanic heroic warrior code to which Anglo-Saxon kings subscribed rendered it impossible for them to walk away from a battle in

---

[50] Lapidge, 'Poems', 93–7.

[51] Discussed in detail in ch. 6.

[52] *HR, s.a.* 934, II, 124; JW, *s.a.* 934, pp. 390–1; ch. 6.

[53] Flodoard 18A (936); see further below, ch. 6.

[54] *The Old English Version of the Heptateuch: Ælfric's Treatise on the Old and New Testament and his Preface to Genesis*, ed. S.J. Crawford (London, 1922), 416–17.

any other capacity than as victor, just as their immediate bodyguard would expect to die with their lord rather than face the ignominy of a lifetime as beaten survivors. Worse than causing the king's death, defeat would have brought an end to the stability of the wider, pan-English realm that Æthelstan had created, returning Northumbria to Norse rule and imperilling the continued security of the midland kingdom of Mercia by potentially encouraging the Scandinavian settlers in the Five Boroughs to rise up against their English masters and reforge their connections with Northumbria. All the military achievements of Æthelstan's father, Edward, and his aunt Æthelflæd and uncle Æthelred in driving back the Scandinavians from English territory lay in the balance.

Historians continue to dispute the identification of the site of the battle of *Brunanburh*; on the balance of strategic, geographical and onomastic considerations, my own preference among the most plausible sites is for Bromborough on the Wirral.[55] Most of our information about the battle comes from the Chronicle poem. That depicts the sons of Edward (Æthelstan and his younger brother Edmund, the oldest of the only two still alive in 937) fighting harmoniously at the head of an army comprising both Mercian and West Saxon forces. Here are English heroes, born to an historic dynasty, defending their lands and peoples against foreign – and pagan – enemies. Their opponents the Scots, and a host of Northmen from the ships, who have come 'over the tossing waters' to fight, are from the outset doomed to die. At the end of the day, five young kings lay on the battlefield, 'stretched lifeless by the sword, and with them seven of Olaf's earls and a countless host of seamen and of Scots'. The Norse fled ignominiously back to their ships and Constantín to Scotland, leaving his son dead on the field of battle. A rousing conclusion to the poem emphasizes both the magnitude of Æthelstan and Edmund's victory, but also its historical significance:

> Never in this island before now, so far as the books of our ancient historians tell us, has an army been put to greater slaughter at the edge of the sword, since the time when the Angles and Saxons made their way hither from the east over the wide seas, invading Britain, when warriors eager for glory, proud forgers of battle, overcame the Britons and won for themselves a country.[56]

In an unequivocally decisive victory, Æthelstan had saved his united English kingdom, preserving to the end of his life his hegemony not just over the Mercian kingdom where he had spent his childhood, but also the Five Boroughs in eastern Mercia, East Anglia and Northumbria, all formerly occupied by the Danes. Further, his crushing of England's

---

[55] See below, 178–9.
[56] ASC 937; poem *The Battle of Brunanburh*, lines 65b–73.

external enemies would help to ensure the smooth succession of his brother Edmund in 939. It did not, however, prevent Olaf from overrunning Mercia almost immediately after Æthelstan's death, leaving Edmund with the task of recreating his brother's wider realm.[57]

We know little of Æthelstan's final years, other than that no further military engagement proved necessary. He died – too early, according to William of Malmesbury – on Sunday 27 October 939 at Gloucester, almost forty years to the day since the death of his grandfather Alfred. By his own request, his men bore the king's body to Malmesbury Abbey in Wiltshire, burial place of two of his cousins who had died at *Brunanburh*, and buried him there, close to the shrine of St Aldhelm.[58]

ÆTHELSTAN, KING OF THE ENGLISH

An eleventh-century scribe from the cathedral church of Exeter in Devon described Æthelstan as a 'king who ruled England alone which, before him, many kings had held among themselves'. The significance of his consolidation for the first time of all the formerly separate English kingdoms and his claim to kingship over all the Anglo-Saxon inhabitants of the British Isles occurred to him and his immediate circle of scholars and clerics with the same force as it would strike subsequent generations. Those claims were reflected in the royal styles adopted to describe the king in his written records which witness to a new language of kingly power, fit for England's first monarch.

Before the 880s, ninth-century kings of Wessex generally used the regnal style 'king of the West Saxons' in their charters, imagining Wessex as a single unit, even after the annexation of Sussex and Kent to the east and Cornwall to the west. In order to mark the new political order created by his extension of direct West Saxon rule north into the formerly independent midland kingdom of Mercia, King Alfred coined a new royal style. Charters of the later 880s (issued after Alfred's annexation of London in 883 and the general submission to his overlordship of all the English not in captivity under the Danes in 886) gave the king new titles: *Angul-Saxonum rex* or *Anglorum Saxonum rex* (both meaning 'king of the Anglo-Saxons'). This choice of words expressed Alfred's authority over a newly invented polity, a people not hitherto ruled as a single unit, despite their separate ethnic origins as (West) Saxons and (Mercian) Angles.[59] Asser chose to use this title to describe the king in the preface to his life of Alfred where he emphasized the other key factor that bound this fusion of two peoples together: their shared Christian faith. He addressed

[57] ASC 941D.

[58] *GP*, v, 247, pp. 594–5.

[59] Simon Keynes, 'The West Saxon Charters of King Æthelwulf and his Sons', *EHR*, cix (1994), 1147–9; Pratt, *The Political Thought*, 105–6.

Alfred as 'ruler of all the Christians in the island of Britain, King of the Angles and Saxons', language that hinted additionally, of course, at Alfred's lordship over subject Welsh kings, as well as at the contrast between this faithful people and the pagan Danes then occupying the north and east of Anglo-Saxon England.[60] Alfred clearly considered himself as more than just a West Saxon king, and coined this royal title to suggest his novel vision of a future kingdom of Angles and Saxons bound together under a single monarch. By contrast – as I have argued elsewhere – the political label he invented for the imagined community to which all of his newly united subjects might now belong – *Angelcynn* – looked to the shared past they had each separately enjoyed.[61]

Alfred's newly invented and highly distinctive polity, which Keynes has termed the 'kingdom of the Anglo-Saxons', continued in place throughout the reign of his son, Edward the Elder. Edward, described in charters as 'king of the Anglo-Saxons', ruled Mercia directly; only he could mint coins across his expanded realm. Æthelred and Æthelflæd acted under his authority, taking substantial responsibility for defence of the old Mercian kingdom, but always as Edward's deputies.[62] This was the realm that Æthelstan – eventually – inherited and he, too, in his earliest charters generally adopted his grandfather's and his father's regnal style: king of the Anglo-Saxons.[63]

That changed after 927 when Æthelstan had, as we have seen, conquered the kingdom of the Northumbrians and assumed direct power and royal rule over the whole of the Anglo-Saxon peoples of Britain, acquiring a realm that stretched from the English Channel to the Firth of Forth. Just as his grandfather's new dominion had required new political labels, so Æthelstan's enlarged kingdom needed recognition. For the title 'king of the Anglo-Saxons' had achieved sufficient currency since its first use in the 880s now firmly to denote a king who ruled West Saxons and Mercians (or, arguably in Edward's case, West Saxons, Mercians and East Anglians). Æthelstan held sway over all the Anglo-Saxon peoples of Britain; his greater achievement deserved its own ideological expression in fresh language. The poet who wrote in celebration of the submission at Eamont, and talked of *ista perfecta Saxonia* (this Saxon-land now made whole) had, as Simon Keynes has remarked, 'the right idea, but what proved to be the wrong end of the stick'.[64] Æthelstan had a vision not of *Saxonia* but a kingdom of the English; he envisioned – or his close

[60] Asser, preface.

[61] Sarah Foot, 'The Making of *Angelcynn*: English Identity before the Norman Conquest', *TRHS*, 6th ser. vi (1996), 25–49. The Old English noun conveyed the same meaning as did Bede's Latin formulation: *gens Anglorum*, the English people.

[62] Keynes, 'Edward, King of the Anglo-Saxons', in H&H, 40–66.

[63] S 394, 396, 397.

[64] Keynes, 'Edward', 61.

associates imagined for him – a new label, king of the English, *rex Anglorum*.[65] His rule extended over all those realms whose history the eighth-century monk the Venerable Bede had encompassed in his *Ecclesiastical History of the English People* (*Historia ecclesiastica gentis Anglorum*). As *rex Anglorum* Æthelstan now bound together under a single royal authority for the first time that collective community which Bede had imagined but never seen created.

A significant group of charters issued in the king's name between 928 and 935 and all produced by a single scribe known as 'Æthelstan A' almost without exception used that title to describe the king.[66] This scribe first called him *rex Anglorum* in two charters both dated 16 April 928 and issued at the royal palace at Exeter recording grants of land in Wiltshire, one to a king's thegn, the other to a woman called Ælfflæd.[67] The appearance of this new royal style so soon after the conquest of Northumbria suggests the king's inner circle rapidly developed a sense not just of its significance but of the potential it offered for ideological aggrandizement of the king's public standing. 'Æthelstan A' continued to use it, with minor variations and embellishments, until 21 December 935, the last occasion on which he certainly copied a charter, on this occasion a grant made in Dorchester by which the king gave land in Wiltshire to the abbey at Malmesbury.[68] This remarkable collection of documents witnesses to an awareness of the magnitude of what Æthelstan had achieved in conquering all the English lands and obtaining the submission of all the surrounding British rulers. Simon Keynes has argued that it cannot be coincidental that these charters appear so swiftly after Eamont: 'they must be seen, first and foremost, as the work of an individual scribe; but they are symbolic of a monarchy invigorated by success, developing the pretensions commensurate with its actual achievements and clothing itself in the trappings of a new political order.'[69]

---

[65] Æthelstan apparently first employed the style *rex Anglorum* in a charter that survives only as a cartulary copy in the archive of Burton Abbey dated 925 (S 395) drawn up afresh because the original had been lost. Whether this reflects an early aspiration on the new king's part to unify greater Wessex and all Mercia into a single realm, or rather an 'improvement' of the form found in the earlier version of the text, normalizing his royal style to the one used consistently from 927, onwards, is less clear. See Geoffrey Little, 'Dynastic Strategies and Regional Loyalties: Wessex, Mercia and Kent, *c.*802–939', PhD thesis, University of Sheffield, 2007, 339.

[66] For the charters of 'Æthelstan A' see ch. 3. Apparently authentic 'Æthelstan A' charters that describe the king as *rex Anglorum* are: S 399–400, 403, 405, 407, 412–13, 416, 418a, 418–19, 422–3. Later charters using the same style are: S 425–6, 434 and 458. Many of these (both the 'Æthelstan A' texts and the later ones) add to the title 'king of the English' other, more grandiose epithets; see ch. 8 below. On royal styles generally, see Harald Kleinschmidt, 'Die Titulaturen englischer Könige im 10. und 11. Jahrhundert', in *Intitulatio III: Lateinische Herrschertitel und Herrschertitulaturen vom 7. bis zum 13. Jahrhundert*, ed. Harald Kleinschmidt *et al.* (Vienna, Cologne Graz, 1988), 103–7.

[67] S 399–400.

[68] S 434.

[69] Simon Keynes, 'England, *c.*900–1016' in *NCMH* III, ed. Timothy Reuter (Cambridge, 1999), 470.

John of Worcester, the twelfth-century chronicler, apportioned epithets
to those tenth-century kings he thought had been most effective in uniting
and bringing glory to the kingdom of the English. Among them Æthelstan
merited the description '*strenuus et gloriosus*', vigorous and glorious.[70] An
anonymous early twelfth-century marginal note added to a manuscript of
John's Chronicle glossed that positive assessment further by referring to 'the
vigorous and glorious king Æthelstan who first ruled alone the kingdom of
the English over all England'.[71] Æthelstan's claim to the title of first English
monarch rests on his creation – out of the kingdom of the Anglo-Saxons
first built by his grandfather and expanded by his father – of a kingdom of
the English, over which he ruled as *rex Anglorum*. Before considering the
military achievements on which Æthelstan's posthumous reputation has
largely rested and exploring the king's public performance of his royal role
on national and international stages, we shall seek him first in the more
private spheres of his own family and his immediate court circle. We begin
at the beginning, with Æthelstan's birth and his childhood.

[70] JW, *s.a.* 925, 934 and 940, pp. 368, 388, 394. Julia Barrow, 'Chester's Earliest Regatta?
Edgar's Dee-Rowing Re-visited,' *EME*, x (2001), 90. Other kings thus described were
Æthelstan's father Edward – *invictissimus* (most invincible) – and John's own favourite,
Æthelstan's nephew Edgar, the peaceable, *pacificus*.
[71] Oxford, Corpus Christi College, MS 157, p. 52: 'Strenuus et gloriosus rex Athelstanus
solus per totam Angliam primus regnum Anglorum regnauit'; discussed by Cyril Hart,
'The Early Section of the Worcester Chronicle', *Journal of Medieval History*, ix (1983), 308,
and illustrated ibid., figure 6, 270.

Chapter 2

FAMILY

Concerning this king [Æthelstan] there is a vigorous tradition in England that he was the most law-abiding and best-educated ruler they have ever had; though it is only a very short time since I learned the extent of his education, from an ancient volume in which the writer was at odds with the difficulty of his material, finding it hard to express his opinions as he would have wished.

William of Malmesbury, *GR*, ii, 132.

Æthelstan was born into the West Saxon royal family in the last decade of the ninth century, while his grandfather, Alfred the Great, was king. By the time of his birth his father Edward, Alfred's eldest son, already played a direct role in West Saxon affairs, attesting charters regularly and leading armies into battle against the Danes. Edward had been formally designated his father's heir since the mid-880s when Alfred drew up his will, and he thus had an obligation to take a wife and produce sons in order to ensure the continuation of the West Saxon dynasty into future generations.[1] Edward first married and had two children – a son, Æthelstan, and a daughter – during his father's lifetime, but that marriage proved short-lived; Edward would go on to marry twice more, producing four further sons and eight or nine more daughters. William of Malmesbury tells us that Æthelstan was thirty at the time of his accession in 924, in which case we may assume that he was born around 894, five years before his grandfather's death in 899.[2] Almost all our information about the childhood and upbringing of the future king Æthelstan comes from the pages of William of Malmesbury's 'History of the English Kings', written in the second quarter of the twelfth century; William may have had access to early, perhaps even near-contemporary narratives of the king's deeds which have since been lost, but he also by his own account made use of popular songs and other legendary material, so his account needs to be treated cautiously.[3]

[1] Will of Alfred, trans. Keynes and Lapidge, *Alfred the Great: Asser's life of Alfred and other Contemporary Sources* (Harmondsworth, 1983), 173–8; Richard Abels, *Alfred the Great: War, Kingship and Culture in Anglo-Saxon England* (London, 1998), 86–7, 93, 179–80; Patrick Wormald, '*On þa wæpnedhealfe*: Kingship and Royal Property from Æthelwulf to Edward the Elder', in H&H, 268–9.

[2] *GR*, ii, 133, pp. 210–11; Æthelweard, iv. 3, pp. 49–50. Barbara Yorke, 'Edward as Ætheling', in H&H, 26, 31–2. See fig. 1: genealogy of the West Saxon Royal Family.

[3] The problems of interpreting William's narrative are discussed fully in Appendix I.

PARENTS

Marriage was an imperative for any royal prince but may, for Edward, have become a more urgent necessity in the 890s when his own right to succeed his father on the throne was apparently threatened by his cousins. Æthelwold and Æthelhelm, sons of Alfred's elder brother Æthelred (who had ruled Wessex from 865 until his death in 871), could challenge Edward's claim to power under the terms of their grandfather Æthelwulf's will; once one of them produced children of his own, Edward's need to secure the succession in his own branch of the family became yet more pressing.[4] Assuming Edward was born at some time between 874 and 877, he would have been old enough to marry in the early 890s and it is normally assumed that he did so in about 893. Nothing can be said with confidence about his first wife, Æthelstan's mother, Ecgwynn, whose name appears in no contemporary source. Reports of later writers suggest she did not come from a family of a status equivalent to that of Edward's second and third wives, who were both descended from prominent aristocratic families in southern England. Yet, given that Edward married while his father still ruled it seems unlikely that, as later sources would claim, Æthelstan was illegitimate, or that his mother could have seemed an unsuitable bride for a future king; more than one twelfth-century chronicler in fact described her as noble.[5] Others, however, cast doubt on Æthelstan's mother's rank. Hrotsvitha, a nun of Gandersheim, wrote a verse account of the deeds of Otto I of Saxony in c.967 at the request of her abbess, Gerberga II, Otto's niece. There she drew a sharp contrast between the lineage of Æthelstan's mother (whom she called an ignoble consort of inferior descent) and the nobility of his most illustrious stepmother, whose daughter Eadgyth married Otto c.930.[6] Hrotsvitha did not intend to denigrate Æthelstan or his mother, but rather to emphasize the status of the parents of Otto's future wife; she never implied that Æthelstan was illegitimate, or his mother a concubine yet, according to William of Malmesbury, that opinion had considerable currency in court circles in Wessex after Edward's death.

William located his comments on the dubiety surrounding Æthelstan's mother in the portions of his narrative that drew most heavily on

---

[4] Richard Abels, 'Royal Succession and the Growth of Political Stability in Ninth-Century Wessex', *Haskins Society Journal*, xii (2002), 96–7.

[5] *GR*, ii, 126, pp. 198–9; JW, *s.a.* 901, pp. 354–5. See Pauline Stafford, 'The King's Wife in Wessex, 800–1066', *Past and Present*, xci (1981), 13. Yorke, 'Edward as Ætheling', 26, 33. The dating of Edward's marriage depends, as we have already seen, entirely on William of Malmesbury's report that Æthelstan was thirty when he became king in 924: *GR*, ii, 133, pp. 210–11.

[6] Hrotsvitha, *Gesta Ottonis*, lines 79–82, ed. Walter Berschin, *Hrotsvit Opera Omnia* (Munich and Leipzig, 2001), 278–9: 'Fratre suo regni sceptrum gestante paterni; / Quem peperit regi consors non inclita regni, / Istius egregie genitrix clarissima domne, / Altera sed generis mulier satis inferioris.'

legendary materials. At one point he attributed the opposition of a certain Alfred to Æthelstan's rule to Alfred's belief that Æthelstan's mother was a concubine; later William offered a frankly incredible alternative narrative of the future king's birth to a shepherd's daughter. On neither occasion, however, did William equate the rumours of Æthelstan's mother's low birth with the name Ecgwynn. Legends about the low birth of Æthelstan's mother can best be understood in the context of the king's disputed succession in 924, rather than as an issue current in the later years of Alfred's reign.[7] King Alfred would have benefited from securing his family's future as much as did his son; we should not doubt Ecgwynn's nobility, or question that she and Edward were – by late ninth-century standards – legitimately married.

Edward and Ecgwynn had two children: Æthelstan and a younger daughter whose name is not known. Æthelstan was a good West Saxon royal name which Edward's first-born son shared with his grandfather's eldest brother, who had died prematurely some time after 851; his sister may have had a name with similar family associations. This marriage did not last long. Edward might have repudiated Ecgwynn in favour of another woman, but we should be cautious before placing too much reliance on those stories of her unsuitability; it is more likely that she died. For whatever reason, Edward had remarried by c.900, possibly even before his father's death. The sons born of his second union would later contest Æthelstan's title to the West Saxon throne.[8]

King Alfred apparently took a keen interest in his grandson, choosing, according to William of Malmesbury, formally to invest Æthelstan with outward symbols that might point to his future greatness:

> For his grandfather Alfred, too, had long before wished him a pros-
> perous reign, observing and welcoming the child's notable good looks
> and graceful movements, and had knighted him at an early age with the

---

[7] *GR*, ii, 131, pp. 206–7: *quod Ethelstanus ex concubine natus esset*; compare also ii, 136–7, pp. 222–5 and ii, 139, pp. 226–7: 'only Alfred, a man of overweening insolence, with his followers resisted in secret as long as he could, disdaining to submit to a lord who was not of his own choosing'. For the shepherd-girl see *GR*, ii, 139, pp. 224–5. Following a dream in which 'her belly shone with the brightness of the moon, and all England was illuminated by its brilliance', the girl was taken into the household of Edward's former wet-nurse. When visiting his nurse one day, the young man was so taken with the girl that they slept together and she became pregnant. William never troubled to explain how a son so-begotten might then have made his way to the royal court to benefit from the upbringing due to a royal heir, remarking merely that as the boy Æthelstan reached adolescence, 'he gave great promise of a kingly nature, and won renown by his distinguished record' (ibid., 226–7). See Thomson, *Commentary*, 109 and Yorke, 'Edward as Ætheling', 33.

[8] *GR*, ii, 126, pp. 198–9. Yorke, 'Edward', 33; Janet L. Nelson, 'Reconstructing a Royal Family: Reflections on Alfred, from Asser Chapter 2', in *People and Places in Northern Europe, 500–1000*, ed. I.N. Wood and N. Lund (Woodbridge, 1991), 64. No evidence supports Michael Wood's suggestion that Ecgwynn might have been Mercian: *In Search of the Dark Ages* (London 1981; 1991 edn), 129.

gift of a scarlet cloak, a belt set with gems, and a Saxon sword with a gilded scabbard.[9]

Several aspects of this story merit considerable caution, not least the anachronistic reference to 'knighting'. But that William 'improved' an earlier text in order to depict a ceremony to which his twelfth-century audience could more readily relate does not necessarily mean that we must reject the notion that any such formal ritual ever occurred. One text may witness independently to this event: an eight-line acrostic poem written for a prince Æthelstan, possibly by the person 'Iohannes', the name spelt out by the last letter of each line. The verse plays on the meaning of the name of the young nobleman (*triumvir*) whom the poet addresses – *æthel* (noble), *stan* (stone) – while in prophesying future greatness for his subject, comparison is made with the prophet Samuel, who foretold the reigns of Saul and David.

> You, prince, are called by the name of 'sovereign stone'.
> Look happily on this prophecy for your age:
> You shall be the 'noble rock' of Samuel the Seer,
> [Standing] with mighty strength against devilish demons.
> Often an abundant cornfield foretells a great harvest; in
> Peaceful days your stony mass is to be softened.
> You are more abundantly endowed with the holy eminence of
> > learning.
> I pray that you may seek, and the Glorious One may grant, the
> > [fulfilment implied in your] noble names.[10]

The context for writing such a praise-poem is, however, disputed.

Conventionally the poem has been seen as confirming William's statement about Alfred's involvement in a ceremony of investiture for his grandson. According to this interpretation, in planning a formal event for Æthelstan King Alfred drew on his recollection of events from his own childhood, specifically a visit he made to Rome at the age of about four or five when he was presented to the pope, received as his spiritual son (through confirmation) and vested with consular regalia. Although that ceremony did not consecrate the young Alfred as a future king, it did serve, as Janet Nelson has argued, 'to set the seal of throne-worthiness on him'

---

[9] *GR*, ii, 133, pp. 210–11. See plate 2. This passage falls in the section of William's narrative supposedly derived from the ancient book he had found.

[10] Lapidge, 'Poems', 72–9; Samuel's rock, erected defensively against the Philistines, is mentioned I Samuel 7:12. The author of this poem so constructed his short verse that the first letter of each line, read downwards, spelt the name of its dedicatee, Adalstan, while the final letters gave us the name Iohannes, possibly that of the poet; see plate 4. Lapidge has identified Iohannes with John the Old Saxon, a continental scholar at the court of Alfred; for a different interpretation, see further below, 110–12.

and to make Alfred a prospective and potential heir. His investiture as a consul (a ceremony for which there are Carolingian parallels), confirms that Alfred was destined for secular life in adulthood.[11] Modelling his investiture of his young grandson on his own childhood experience, Alfred chose the insignia he gave to Æthelstan (scarlet cloak, jewelled belt and Saxon sword with a sheath) to evoke his own designation at a similar age; following his father's example, Alfred here marked the child out as throne-worthy. The acrostic poem thus appears to commemorate that ceremony, which would explain its description of the young Æthelstan as '*triumvir*', a noun that in this context we take to have the simple meaning 'consul'.[12] Having bestowed suitable regalia upon the boy, Alfred then, according to William of Malmesbury, 'arranged for the boy's education at the court of his daughter Æthelflæd and Æthelred his son-in-law, where he was brought up with great care by his aunt and the eminent ealdorman for the throne that seemed to await him. There too, with the reputation won by his high qualities, he trod envy under foot and quite suppressed it.'[13]

Alternatively, we might, following Gernot Wieland, prefer to see the poem as a product of Æthelstan's maturity, perhaps written at the time of his coronation, prophesying fruitfulness for the new king's reign.[14] If we did, this would downplay the likelihood of Alfred's having formally marked the child Æthelstan out as throne-worthy, a story that, without the corroboration of the acrostic poem, would rest solely on William of Malmesbury's imaginative invention. That the Anglo-Saxon Chronicle failed to mention any such event, even though it had provided a (rather garbled) account of the ceremony of investiture for Alfred in Rome in 853 may be significant, although one might hesitate before placing too much reliance on its silence here.

If Æthelstan's future had looked promising while King Alfred was still alive and his parents remained married, it became markedly bleaker after his father took a new wife, especially once his stepmother wanted to advance her own sons in West Saxon court circles at Æthelstan's expense. In this context, William's suggestion that the prince spent much of his childhood away from Wessex with his uncle and aunt in Mercia looks

[11] ASC *s.a.* 853, Asser, 8; Janet L. Nelson, 'The Franks and the English in the Ninth Century Reconsidered', in *The Preservation and Transmission of Anglo-Saxon Culture*, ed. P.E. Szarmach and J.T. Rosenthal (Kalamazoo, MI, 1997); reprinted in her *Rulers and Ruling Familes in Early Medieval Europe* (Aldershot, 1999), no. VI, 145; Stafford, 'Succession and Inheritance: a Gendered Perspective on Alfred's Family History', in *Alfred the Great: Papers from the Eleventh-Centenary Conferences*, ed. Timothy Reuter (Aldershot, 2003), 255–7. Lapidge, 'Poems'; Thomson, *Commentary*, 119; Paul Hill, *The Age of Æthelstan* (Stroud, 2004), 198–9.

[12] W.H. Stevenson, *Asser's Life of King Alfred: together with the Annals of Saint Neots erroneously ascribed to* Asser (Oxford, 1904; 1959 edn), 184–5; Lapidge, 'Poems', 81.

[13] *GR*, ii, 133, pp. 210–11.

[14] Gernot R. Wieland, 'A New Look at the Poem "Archalis clamare triumuir" ', in *Insignis Sophiae Arcator*, ed. Gernot R. Wieland *et al.* (Turnhout, 2006), 178–92. See further, below, 110–12.

deceptively attractive. A West Saxon annalist constructing chronicle entries for the last years of King Alfred's reign after his son's accession might have thought it politic to omit all mention of a ceremony that seemed to designate for future rule a prince whose chances of succeeding suddenly looked markedly less secure.

AUNT

At the time of Æthelstan's birth, western Mercia lay under the direct control of King Alfred, and was governed as a West Saxon dependency by Ealdorman Æthelred, who had married Alfred's sister, Æthelstan's aunt, Æthelflæd. King Edward continued the same arrangement after his father's death. Not just in the political circumstances of the late ninth and early tenth centuries but also in familial terms it makes complete sense to follow William in arguing that the Mercian leadership brought up the young Æthelstan after his father's second marriage. Acknowledging the attractiveness of the Mercian explanation, Dumville has argued, 'much would be explained thereby, but we must not assume that a mediaeval scholar would be incapable of seeing that too. William is a treacherous witness: for all the praise heaped on him in modern times, we must nonetheless recognize that his attitude to evidence is mediaeval and not ours.'[15] One piece of entirely independent evidence may, however, suggest a direct connection between the young Æthelstan and his uncle-by-marriage, Ealdorman Æthelred.

A text from the reign of Edward I refers to a grant of privileges made by Æthelstan in the year of his coronation (925) to the church of St Oswald's, Gloucester, a gift made in accordance with 'the pact of paternal piety which formerly he pledged with Æthelred, ealdorman of the people of the Mercians'.[16] If preserving memory of an authentic donation, this text would suggest that Æthelstan supported his aunt and uncle's patronage of ecclesiastical houses in Mercia, among which St Oswald's, Gloucester was of particular political significance.[17] That Æthelstan was first accepted as king in Mercia and apparently faced some opposition at the West Saxon court after his father's death may further suggest that he came to royal power in Wessex as something of an outsider. This would add some support to William's assertion that his youth had been spent away from his father's court.[18]

[15] Dumville, *Wessex*, 146.

[16] See Michael Hare, 'The Documentary Evidence for the History of St. Oswald's, Gloucester to 1086 AD', in *The Golden Minster: The Anglo-Saxon Minster and Later Medieval Priory of St. Oswald at Gloucester*, ed. Carolyn Heighway and Richard Bryant, CBA Research Report 117 (York, 1999), pp. 36–7 and further, below, ch 7.

[17] Caroline Heighway, 'Gloucester and the New Minster of St Oswald', in H & H, 103.

[18] Thomson, *Commentary*, 119.

Beyond this, we know little about the details of Æthelstan's education and can only speculate about the closeness of the young prince's relationship to his aunt and her family. William of Malmesbury made much of a vigorous tradition current in England in his day that saw Æthelstan as the 'best educated ruler' the English had ever had, reinforcing (perhaps deliberately from his own knowledge of that text) the references in the acrostic poem to Æthelstan's 'abundant endowment with the holy eminence of learning'. In the poem which concluded the portion of William's history that included both his account of Alfred's investiture of his grandson and the statement about his education in Mercia, we find references to the fact that the boy's father had him handed over to be educated in a school (*in documenta scolarum*), where he feared stern masters and the cane, and also to Æthelstan's training in arms and the laws of war. At best this verse section reworks earlier material and in fact these stock remarks could apply to any early medieval nobleman's education; William's poem tells us only what we might have expected to hear and contributes nothing to our understanding of Æthelstan's own experience. Indeed, attributing responsibility to King Edward for decisions about Æthelstan's education runs counter to his earlier assertion that Æthelstan's aunt and uncle took charge of the prince's upbringing.[19] William's account here contrasts unfavourably with the markedly more detailed description of the education King Alfred arranged for his own children given by Asser, his biographer.

In light of the importance Alfred had placed on learning and on wisdom as an attribute for kings and all holders of authority, secular and ecclesiastical, we might imagine that his grandchildren would have experienced the fruits of his educational reforms, benefiting both from the schools he had established and the availability of texts translated into Old English at Alfred's instigation. According to Asser, Alfred's eldest son Edward and his daughter Ælfthryth had been educated at the royal court in the company of other children of noble birth under the instruction of male and female tutors. There they learned the courtly virtues of humility, friendliness and gentleness to all compatriots and foreigners as well as great obedience to their father. Although allowed to engage in noble pursuits, they were discouraged from idleness by a 'liberal education' that involved reading the Psalms and books in English as well as vernacular poetry (*Saxonica carmina*), so that both made frequent use of books.[20] This represented an education fit for a future king (or, in Ælfthryth's case, a

---

[19] *GR* ii, 132, pp. 210–13. For discussion of the relationship of the verse and prose sections of William's account of this reign, see Appendix I. Michael Wood has placed greater reliance on the information given in the poem than I am inclined to do, making comparison with other tenth-century texts about schools and their strict masters: 'The Lost Life of King Æthelstan: William of Malmesbury's Account of Æthelstan's Reign' (unpublished paper).

[20] Asser, ch. 75; Yorke, 'Edward as Ætheling', 27–9.

princess destined for a prestigious marriage); organized at court, their education remained under their father's eye and subject to his supervision. Alfred's younger son, Æthelweard, however, was sent away from the royal circle and apparently given a clerical education. Asser explained:

> as a result of the divine wisdom and the remarkable foresight of the king, [Æthelweard] was given over to training in reading and writing under the attentive care of teachers, in company with all the nobly born children of virtually the entire area, and a good many of lesser birth as well. In this school (*scola*) books in both languages – that is to say in Latin and English – were carefully read; they also devoted themselves to writing, to such an extent that, even before they had the requisite strength for manly skills (hunting that is, and other skills appropriate to noblemen), they were seen to be devoted and intelligent students of the liberal arts.[21]

This school (also mentioned later in Asser's *Life* as receiving a quarter of the king's revenues intended for charitable purposes) may have been at Glastonbury, where Dunstan was educated before he joined the royal court. As Alfred himself explained in his preface to his translation of Gregory's *Pastoral Care*, only boys destined for clerical careers needed to learn Latin, for English was sufficient for those who would remain in secular life.[22]

If we accept William of Malmesbury's statement that Æthelstan was sent away from the West Saxon court after his father's second marriage, we may assume that Edward did not arrange for his first son an education just like the one he himself had received, although that may have been what he planned for his other sons, who remained in Wessex. Æthelstan's education in Mercia may have been organized by tutors within the household of Æthelflæd and Æthelred, but equally his aunt may have delegated responsibility to a Mercian bishop, or sent him to an episcopal or monastic school in the region. Wherever he was taught, we might imagine him to have learned in the company of noble Mercian children (and perhaps his cousin Ælfwynn, Æthelflaed's daughter) a curriculum that began with the Psalter and moved on to reading works in Old English. Even though never destined for the Church, Æthelstan might like his uncle Æthelweard have learned Latin; he certainly showed an interest in Latin books after becoming king. As well as book-learning, Æthelstan would have been taught to cultivate the behaviour deemed appropriate for royal and noble circles, and engaged in a range of noble pursuits including hunting and hawking, as well as training in the use of arms and the conduct of warfare. In adulthood King Æthelstan encouraged learning at his own court,

---

[21] Asser, ch. 75.
[22] Simon Keynes and Michael Lapidge, *Alfred the Great* (Harmondsworth, 1983), 126.

surrounded himself with scholars and had a significant collection of books; these may have been habits acquired from his education in Mercia, but he could also in this have chosen to emulate his grandfather's example.[23]

BROTHERS

Æthelstan's formal education played a key role in his personal and emotional development, yet his immediate family also helped to shape the future man and determine some of the life-choices he would make in maturity.[24] Even by medieval royal standards Æthelstan belonged to a remarkably large family. Edward may have brought up his children from his different marriages separately, yet he cannot have kept his two eldest children completely apart from their half-siblings.

Edward's first wife we have already discussed; his second, Ælfflæd, was, according to William of Malmesbury, the daughter of an ealdorman Æthelhelm, perhaps the ealdorman of Wiltshire whose death the Chronicle recorded in 897.[25] Edward's new wife need have felt little affection for her stepson, particularly not once she had sons of her own: Ælfweard (whom William of Malmesbury erroneously but consistently called Æthelweard) and Edwin. Without having to cast doubt on the nobility of Æthelstan's mother, or on the genuineness of her husband's first marriage, Ælfflæd could use the advantage given to her two sons by the fact of their birth to a ruling monarch in order to claim for them a legitimacy superior to their eldest brother's.[26] Ælfweard began attesting his father's charters as *filius regis* as early as 901, where he was named ahead of his elder brother Æthelstan, but behind his uncle Æthelweard (Edward's younger brother).[27] By the time of Edward's death in July 924, any arrangement King Alfred had envisaged

---

[23] Below, 64–70, 94–9.

[24] For a discussion of the value to biography of locating the subject within his familial context, see Janet L. Nelson, 'Did Charlemagne have a Private Life?', in *Writing Medieval Biography, 750–1250*, ed. D. Bates *et al.* (Woodbridge, 2006), 15–28.

[25] This Æthelhelm should probably not be identified with King Alfred's nephew (son of his elder brother Æthelred) of that name; not only did æthelings seldom take on the role of ealdormen at this period, but contemporary adherence to the Church's teaching on consanguineous marriages would have ruled out a union between first cousins: *contra* Stafford, *Unification and Conquest* (London, 1979), 43–4 and Sheila Sharp, 'The West Saxon Tradition of Dynastic Marriage: with Special Reference to Edward the Elder', in H&H, 82. Compare Yorke, 'Edward as Ætheling', 33–4; and her 'Æthelwold and the Politics of the Tenth Century', in *Bishop Æthelwold*, ed. Barbara Yorke (Woodbridge, 1988), 76–80.

[26] Ælfflæd attested just one charter of Edward, dated 901, S 363, where she was described as 'conjux regis'; she never attested as queen. Edward's coronation took place on 8 June 900, but it now seems unlikely (contrary to Janet Nelson's earlier arguments) that Ælfflæd was consecrated as his queen on the same occasion: see her 'The First Use of the Second Anglo-Saxon *Ordo*', in *Myth, Rulership, Church and Charters*, ed. Julia Barrow and Andrew Wareham (Aldershot, 2008), 117–26; and further, below, ch. 4.

[27] S 365 and 366; on these witness-lists, see S. Keynes 'The West Saxon Charters of king Æthelwulf and his sons', *EHR*, cix (1994), 1120, n. 2, and 1142–3 and his 'Edward', 51.

for his eldest grandson had apparently been superseded by a scheme that included Ælfweard in the kingship.

Quite what Edward had intended should happen we cannot know, not least because the old king could not have foreseen that his second son would die so rapidly after his own demise. Information about events following Edward's death on 17 July 924 derives from a range of sources, not all of which sought to tell the same story. The West Saxon version of the Anglo-Saxon Chronicle (the A manuscript) reported baldly that King Edward died in this year and his son Æthelstan succeeded to the kingdom. More emerges from the version of events in the Mercian Register, which stated that Edward died at Farndon in Mercia 'and his son Ælfweard died very soon after at Oxford and their bodies are buried at Winchester. And Æthelstan was chosen by the Mercians as king and consecrated at Kingston'. In fact his coronation did not occur until 4 September 925, but we can readily comprehend how the chronicler's train of thought moved straight from accession to consecration.[28] More than one interpretation presents itself here and we should pause for a moment over the information the chroniclers provide about the whereabouts of the different protagonists.

Farndon, where Edward died, lay in northern Mercia. An ancient settlement in Cheshire, seven miles south of Chester, Farndon controlled a crossing of the River Dee and had an ancient church dedicated to St Chad; John of Worcester described the place as a royal vill.[29] Although none of the contemporary chroniclers explained why Edward was at the north-western extremity of his realm in 924, according to William of Malmesbury when Edward fell ill, he had just put down a rebellion of the men of Chester, who had allied themselves with the Welsh.[30] If we can trust this account, we might go further and imagine that Æthelstan was with his father on this campaign, given the strategic significance of the north-western frontier. The Mercians' swift election of Æthelstan as their king would support such an assumption. Æthelstan could have taken advantage of the presence of the army and at least some of the leading men of the realm to seek to secure his succession on the spot; those same nobles may well have thought the current military situation, so soon after the crushing of a rebellion supported by the Welsh, required swift and decisive action.[31]

[28] ASC 924A; MR, 924. The northern D manuscript of the Chronicle states that Ælfweard died sixteen days after his father.
[29] JW, s.a. 924, pp. 384–5; David Griffiths, 'The North-West Frontier', in H&H, 182–4. John might have been guessing that this was a royal estate; the ailing king could simply have chosen to take refuge with the church community at Farndon: N.J. Higham, *The Origins of Cheshire* (Manchester, 1993), 139.
[30] *GR*, ii, 133, pp. 210–11.
[31] While the preference of the Mercian nobility for the elder son might have arisen from their direct knowledge of a young prince brought up in their kingdom at the court of Æthelred and Æthelflæd (*GR*, ii, 133, pp. 210–11), this fact does not necessarily support William's statements about Æthelstan's education. Indeed, William could have invented the prince's Mercian upbringing as a means of accounting for what he may have thought

It would have taken several days for the news of the king's death to reach the rest of the West Saxon court in Winchester, where Ælfweard remained in nominal charge, with his own group of leading men to advise and support him. Ælfweard, too, might have reacted opportunistically after his father's death far from home, capitalizing on the equally pressing need for the West Saxon nobility to fill the power vacuum Edward's death had created. Perhaps, as Keynes has suggested, those nobles hoped or even expected to see the prince continuing as 'king of the Anglo-Saxons', following his father and grandfather's example. For, although none of the narrative accounts reports this, other sources suggest that Edward had nominated not his eldest son, Æthelstan, but Ælfweard as his successor.[32]

A West Saxon regnal list in the twelfth-century *Textus Roffensis* attributes to the West Saxon Ælfweard a rule of four weeks, which would place his death not, as the Chronicle had it, on 2 August but around 14 August.[33] That Ælfweard was regal (yet, in Simon Keynes's words, 'not quite a king') emerges also from a narrative of the founding of the New Minster, Winchester written in the 980s and preserved in the *Liber vitae* of that abbey.[34] This text states that after a glorious reign Edward died on 17 July 924 and was buried on the right-hand side of the New Minster's altar, beside his parents' tombs. It goes on to report that two sons of Edward followed their father to the grave, namely Æthelweard and Ælfweard. One was a *clito* (that is an ætheling, or king's son) the other was 'crowned with kingly badges' (*regalibus infulis redimitus*).[35] All these sources fail to explain whether Edward had meant thus to divide his realm into two discrete kingdoms, or if only the Winchester establishment had recognized Ælfweard as king. Nor can we speculate about any possible territorial arrangements made for Edward's third son, Edwin, whose disaffection in the 930s seemingly led him to rebel.[36] As suggested earlier, the separate elections of Ælfweard in Wessex and Æthelstan in Mercia may have reflected nothing more than each son's pragmatic reaction to his father's

a rather odd decision of the Mercians to choose this young man as their king, thus potentially reopening rifts between Wessex and Mercia that Edward had done so much to heal. Of course, we also only have William's word for it that there was a faction opposed to Æthelstan at Winchester; see Keynes, *Liber Vitae*, 19.

[32] Keynes, *Liber Vitae*, 19; see also Yorke, 'Æthelwold', pp. 69–73.

[33] David Dumville, 'The West Saxon Genealogical Regnal List: Manuscripts and Texts', *Anglia*, civ (1986), 29.

[34] BL Stowe MS 44, fo. 9v; see Keynes, *Liber Vitae*, 82; W. de Gray Birch, *Liber Vitae: Register and Martyrology of New Minster and Hyde Abbey, Winchester* (London and Winchester, 1892), 113.

[35] Æthelweard was not Edward's son but his younger brother, who died ?16 Oct. 922: *HBC 3*, 24. See Keynes, *Liber Vitae*, 81. Compare also the reference in the *Liber Monasterii de Hyda*, ed. Edward Edwards (London, 1866), 113, to a son of Edward named Elfredus (presumably for Elfwerdus) who was crowned during his father's lifetime, but died not long after.

[36] Charles Plummer, *Two of the Saxon Chronicles Parallel*, 2 vols (Oxford, 1892–9), ii, 121, suggested that there might have been a third allocation of Kent to Edwin.

death far from home, in which ambition each found support from different groups of local nobles. In the event, Ælfweard's premature death left Æthelstan as the sole heir to the united realms, albeit without a particularly strong personal power base in Wessex.[37]

Opposition to the new king seems to have continued in some quarters beyond Æthelstan's coronation in 925. William of Malmesbury dwelt at length on a rebellion led by a certain Alfred, whose objection to the succession rested on the supposed blemish in Æthelstan's origin as the son of a concubine. Alfred and his co-conspirators allegedly tried to blind Æthelstan in the city of Winchester after his father's death; this imaginative ploy would, if successful, have removed the new king from power on grounds of physical disability, but without making his opponents murderers. Whether they sought to replace Æthelstan with his younger half-brother Edwin, or whether Alfred himself sought the throne remains uncertain. In any event, the plot failed and after its exposure Alfred went to Rome to try and clear his name by oaths before Pope John.[38] To this point we might accept that, however gilded it had become in the telling, some essential truth underlay this story; other evidence also points to a muted reception of Æthelstan's rule at Winchester which might have developed into an attempt on his person when he first sought to enter the city.[39] But the assertion that at the very moment of swearing his innocence before the pope, Alfred collapsed seems implausible, even given the known dangers of the journey to Rome and of the Roman climate. Taken by his followers to the *schola Anglorum* (the heart of the English quarter in Rome), Alfred died on the third night and was, with the king's permission, granted Christian burial. His lands were, however, deemed forfeit to the king, who gave them to God and St Peter. Bath Abbey and Malmesbury, both dedicated to St Peter, claimed possession of Alfred's forfeit lands and the archives of both houses preserve charters supposedly recording their acquisition of that confiscated land and narrating the details of this plot.[40]

---

[37] Keynes, *Liber Vitae*, 19–22.

[38] *GR*, ii, 136–7, pp. 222–3. Pope John X reigned from 914 to 928 and John XI from 931 to 935. If any historical truth underlies this narrative, and if the rebellion occurred in the period before Æthelstan's coronation, then we must assume that the oath was sworn to the first of these two.

[39] Sean Miller, *Charters of the New Minster, Winchester* (Oxford, 2000), xxviii–xxx; Susan Kelly, *Charters of Malmesbury Abbey* (Oxford, 2005), 217.

[40] *GR*, ii, 131, pp. 206–7. Later, William reported that the king had had Alfred put to death: *GR*, ii, 139, 226–7. William constructed the earlier narrative on the basis of Malmesbury's charters claiming the abbey's acquisition of the lands forfeited by Alfred: S 415, 434, 435, and probably himself confected a fourth text which conflates all three: S 436; see Kelly, *Charters of Malmesbury*, nos 25–7 and the composite 28. See Kelly, 216–18 for discussion of Alfred's rebellion and Susan Kelly, *Charters of Bath and Wells* (Oxford, 2007), no. 5 (S 414) for the Bath claim to these forfeited lands. For a possible connection between these events and the last chapter of Æthelstan's law code issued at Grately, see Wormald, *MEL*, 307 and below, 145, n.76.

While some of the details of this account are questionable, it seems probable that its different versions attest to a genuine intrigue against the king at Winchester early in his reign.

In the portion of his account of Æthelstan's reign derived from popular songs, William speculated about the involvement of Æthelstan's second brother Edwin (full brother to Ælfweard) in this Winchester rebellion. According to that material, some at the king's court accused Edwin of plotting against his half-brother, a malevolent construction that the king proved unduly willing to believe. So powerful were the rumours that Æthelstan refused to accept his brother's denial on oath of his involvement in the conspiracy and drove him into exile. 'Even his cruelty took a form without parallel; for he compelled his brother, attended by a single squire, to go on board a boat without oars or oarsmen and, what is more, rotten with age.' Once far out at sea, the ship's sails failed to withstand the fury of the winds; Edwin, struggling to cope in the conditions, dived overboard into the water and was drowned. His squire hauled his body aboard and managed to get it back to Kent. King Æthelstan, appalled at having unwittingly caused his brother's death, undertook a seven-year penance and executed the informant who had condemned his brother, a royal cup-bearer.[41] In detail, this version of Edwin's fate has nothing whatever to commend it, and William himself remained deeply sceptical: 'This story of his brother's death, plausible though it seems, I am the less ready to affirm, inasmuch as he gave practical proof of his remarkable affection towards his other brothers.'[42] Yet other independent sources confirm William's central proposition that something unpleasant happened to Edwin.

For the year 933 the E version of the Anglo-Saxon Chronicle reported laconically 'in this year the ætheling Edwin was drowned at sea'.[43] Henry of Huntingdon used his imagination to expand that bald statement, although he added nothing new to our understanding: 'Not long after [his conquest of Northumbria], struck by adverse fortune, he sadly lost to the waves of the sea his brother Edwin, a young man of great vigour and noble nature.'[44] Simeon of Durham went further in declaring 'King

---

[41] *GR*, ii, 139, pp. 226–7; compare *GP*, ii, 85, pp. 292–3: Æthelstan's foundation of a church at Milton in reparation for his part in his brother's death is discussed further below, ch. 7. Plummer commented on Irish parallels for the consigning of someone to sea in a boat without rudder or oars, looking both at the folkloric element of the tale and at instances when it was used as a judicial punishment, the culprit's fate being left in the hands of God: *Two of the Saxon Chronicles*, ii, 103–5. See also Zacharias P. Thundy, '*Beowulf*: Date and Authorship', *Neuphilologische Mitteilungen*, lxxxvii (1986), 110–12, although Thundy erred in thinking Edwin older than Æthelstan.

[42] *GR*, ii, 140, pp. 228–9.

[43] ASC 933E. E is a manuscript of the northern recension of the Chronicle which was associated with Canterbury from the mid-eleventh century and eventually found its way to Peterborough.

[44] HH, v. 18, pp. 310–11.

Æthelstan ordered his brother Edwin to be drowned at sea'.[45] Simeon might simply have inferred this from the Chronicle's notice; alternatively he could have drawn on information derived from the same legendary material used by William of Malmesbury. More interestingly, a quite different account of Edwin's death, entirely independent of the English versions, survives in the house-history of the Flemish abbey of St-Bertin, completed in 962 by Folcuin the deacon. Folcuin sought to explain how a group of monks from his abbey had come to make their way across the sea to England in the mid-tenth century. He reported that they were received generously by King Æthelstan because his brother, Edwin, had been buried at St-Bertin and so the king retained a fondness for that abbey. There are some confusions in this narrative; Folcuin did not realize that by the time his fellow monks went to England in 944 Æthelstan had been succeeded on the throne by his third brother, Edmund, nor did he understand that Edwin had never ruled in Wessex, for he mistakenly described him as king. But one element of the story is worth remark: Folcuin hinted that Edwin found himself obliged to leave England in a hurry because of another failed coup in Wessex:

> In the year of the Incarnate Word 933, when the same King Eadwine, driven by some disturbance in his kingdom, embarked on a ship, wishing to cross to this side of the sea, a storm arose and the ship was wrecked and he was overwhelmed in the midst of the waves. And when his body was washed ashore, Count Adelolf since he was his kinsman, received it with honour and bore it to the monastery of St-Bertin for burial.

According to Folcuin, Æthelstan sent several gifts to St-Bertin's as alms for his dead brother and chose graciously to receive monks from that abbey when they appeared at his court, giving them the use of a monastery called Bath.[46] If we read Folcuin's narrative rightly as describing a further attempt to undermine Æthelstan's hold on the West Saxon throne in 933 (this time to supplant him by Ælfflæd's other son), we might see how the memory of the events of that year could later have been retold in verse (such as the *cantilena* to which William of Malmesbury referred[47]) and so grown into the legendary narrative that William chose to repeat. Folcuin's narrative would suffer little if Edmund's name were substituted for Æthelstan's as that of the West Saxon king who donated Bath to the fleeing

---

[45] *HR*, §107, AD 933, p. 124.

[46] Folcuin, *Gesta Abbatum S. Bertini Sithiensium*, ch. 107 (ed. O. Holder-Egger, M.G.H., Scriptores, xiii, Hanover, 1881), 629. Adelolf, as already mentioned, was Edwin's (and Æthelstan's) first cousin; son of Ælfthryth and Baldwin II of Flanders he bore the name of his grandfather, Æthelwulf of Wessex.

[47] *GR*, ii, 138, pp. 224–5; see below, Appendix I.

monks, for Edmund, too, would have felt affection for the community responsible for praying for the soul of his dead brother. Yet, Folcuin may not have been mistaken when he described Æthelstan as a benefactor of his own abbey, for monasteries normally preserved such information with some care and accuracy.[48]

What part, if any, Æthelstan's two youngest half-brothers played in these events of the 930s remains unclear. Edmund and his younger brother Eadred were the sons of Eadgifu who married the king in *c.*919 after he had put his second wife aside, probably into the nunnery at Wilton where she was buried.[49] Much younger than the offspring of both Edward's earlier marriages, Eadgifu's children were still small when their father died. Edmund, the elder of the two boys, was eighteen years old at his accession in 939; he was thus probably born in 920 or 921 and Eadred at some point in the last two years of his father's lifetime. Both the boys apparently maintained close relations with their eldest brother, at least after he had become king. According to William of Malmesbury, Æthelstan showed remarkable affection towards his younger brothers, 'mere infants at his father's death, he brought them up lovingly in childhood, and when they grew up gave them a share in his kingdom'. One version of William's text goes further and asserts that out of respect for them the king never turned his thoughts towards marriage.[50] The inclusion of the young princes' names in their brother's charter witness-lists might suggest their participation in his royal councils, but most of the transactions to which the æthelings supposedly attested are spurious in the form in which they have survived, so this is not the most promising line of enquiry.[51] More securely we know that Edmund fought alongside his elder brother at the battle of *Brunanburh*, for the poem that marked that event in the Anglo-Saxon Chronicle celebrated his deeds together with the king's. Æthelstan had probably already designated him as his heir before 939; certainly Edmund succeeded to the kingship immediately without facing any apparent opposition. Whether by design or good fortune Æthelstan contrived to spare his younger brother the disputes that had marked his own and his father's accessions. No other heir, legitimate or otherwise, emerged on Æthelstan's death to contest Edmund's right to rule his brother's realm; the problems Edmund faced all related instead to his continuing hold on Northumbria. Other factors than a desire to ensure a smooth succession could also have led Æthelstan towards celibacy,

---

[48] Nor does it seem likely that it was Æthelstan's reputation for generosity to the monastic life that led to his being claimed a benefactor by St Bertin's (for such an assertion would have carried little weight in Flanders).

[49] *GR*, ii, 126, pp. 200–1.

[50] *GR*, ii, 140, pp. 228–9.

[51] Edmund appears among the witnesses to a series of charters in Æthelstan's name forged at Exeter in the eleventh century: S 386–90, 414–15, 433, plus 454. Eadred's name is found among the witnesses to S 414, 415 and 446.

however, in which context we should consider his relationships with his numerous sisters.

SISTERS

Any man whose parents managed to provide him with eight or even nine sisters deserves our sympathy. The size and gender balance of his family will have coloured Æthelstan's personal and emotional development in childhood and adolescence even if, as seems likely, the young prince lived apart from the households of his two successive stepmothers. In infancy, Æthelstan had only one sister with whom to vie for his parents' attention, but the proportion of girls to boys in his own generation increased steadily as he grew older, affecting the dynamics of the whole family. According to William of Malmesbury, Edward's second wife, Ælfflæd, had six daughters, and his third, Eadgifu, possibly produced two more, although, as we shall see, William may have counted one girl too many. Contemporary sources provide names for only some of Æthelstan's sisters and reveal nothing about their ages or birth order; once more, we depend for much of our information about the identities and ultimate fates of these women on William of Malmesbury.

As the girls approached adulthood their particular needs increasingly preoccupied their father and eldest brother; the women's future security was of course a key concern, but political issues played their part, too. Royal princesses had a value greater than their noble counterparts, for they could transmit their royal blood to their own children and so convey a potential right to future rule to their sons. Edward and Æthelstan were both sensitive to the dangers of dynastic competition and the necessity to restrict the number of possible claimants to the family's estates as well as to its future hold on royal power. Although at least two, quite possibly all three, of Edward's wives came from noble English families whose members played key roles in royal administration, neither he nor his son sought husbands for any of Æthelstan's sisters from within that same pool of possible suitors; instead they both looked to marry these princesses outside Wessex. Æthelstan's unprecedented intimacy with the leading western European rulers of his own day results directly from this policy.[52]

Marriage represented only one of the possible options open to a royal princess as she approached maturity. The Church had provided an effective and popular career for royal and noble women since the earliest days of its foundation in Anglo-Saxon England. In the middle and later tenth century, the West Saxon royal house proved a notable promoter both of monastic ideals in general and royal women's convents in particular; it

---

[52] Yorke, 'Edward as Ætheling', 34. F.M. Stenton, *Anglo-Saxon England* (3rd edn, Oxford, 1971), 333–4; Sarah Foot, 'Dynastic Strategies: the West Saxon Royal Family in Europe', in *England and the Continent in the Tenth Century*, ed. David Rollason *et al.* (Brepols, 2011), 241–57.

played a central role in the revolution in monastic organization that reached its climax in the reign of Æthelstan's nephew, King Edgar (957/9–975).[53] Earlier in the century, few female religious houses flourished in any part of England. In Wessex devout women could choose between Shaftesbury (founded by King Alfred for his daughter), the Nunnaminster at Winchester, begun by Alfred's widow Ealhswith, and apparently a new community at Wilton.[54] All three houses retained close links with the West Saxon royal house beyond Æthelstan's day, helping to maintain the cult of the family's dead. That some of the many women in Æthelstan's generation could serve the royal family's immediate and longer-term needs through their prayerful devotion will have escaped neither Edward and his son, nor their advisers; male pressure may have encouraged three of these sisters to enter the cloister. Eadflæd and Æthelhild, both daughters of Ælfflæd, apparently joined the community at Wilton, the former in a monastic, her sister in a lay habit; with their mother they were buried at Wilton. King Æthelstan made two grants of land to a congregation at Wilton in the 930s, one in 937 specifically for the remission of his own sins and those of his sister Eadflæd.[55] Eadburh, daughter of Eadgifu and thus one of Edward the Elder's youngest children, showed such precocious signs of devotion that her father supposedly consigned her to the Nunnaminster in infancy, where she assumed a nun's habit. Despite her royal birth, she proved popular with her companions, among whom she was remarkable for her humility as well as her piety and miracle-working.[56] A fourth sister of King Æthelstan's apparently became a nun after her husband died when she remained childless.[57] Entry to the cloister did not render royal princesses any less relevant to family dynastic politics than matrimonial alliances; their petitionary prayer contributed as effectively to the future security and prosperity of the royal line as did the marriage and child-bearing of their sisters in the world.[58]

Even with three of his daughters safely tucked away in cloistered homes, Edward still had the future of five or six more girls to plan. Edward must take much credit for initiating the policy that Æthelstan would continue and develop to excellent effect of locating husbands for

[53] For the attraction of the religious life to early medieval Englishwomen, see my *VW*, i.

[54] Shaftesbury: Asser, ch. 98; *VW*, ii, 165–6. Æthelstan made a grant to Shaftesbury in 932 in return for liturgical privileges: S 419. Nunnaminster: Birch, *Liber Vitae*, p. 5; JW, *s.a.* 905, pp. 360–1; *VW*, ii, 243–52; Wilton: S 799; *VW*, ii, 221–31.

[55] *GR*, ii, 126, pp. 198–201; S 424 and 438.

[56] *GP*, ii, 78, pp. 274–5; Susan Ridyard, *The Royal Saints of Anglo-Saxon England* (Cambridge, 1988), 16–37, 96–139.

[57] *GR*, ii, 126, pp. 196–9; the last mentioned was Æthelstan's full sister, who married Sihtric of York; see below.

[58] For a comparative perspective on the value of nunneries to Saxon dynastic politics, see Karl Leyser, *Rule and Conflict in an Early Medieval Society: Ottonian Saxony* (London, 1979), 64.

these women across the political divides of contemporary Europe. These
expedient alliances served the West Saxon royal family's wider interests
well, for they assured its kin a stake in the futures of several of the
emerging rival families of the Frankish realms, a strategy that Æthelstan
further advanced through his fostering arrangements. Earlier kings of
Wessex had looked across the Channel in the hope of securing prestigious marriage alliances. Edward's grandfather, Æthelwulf, and uncle
Æthelbald each in turn married Judith, daughter of Charles the Bald; his
sister Ælfthryth married Baldwin II, count of Flanders (son of the same
Judith and her third husband, Baldwin I). We have already encountered
Judith and Baldwin's son Adelolf, count of Boulogne and Ternois, who
took an interest in the cult of the dead ætheling Edwin at St-Bertin's.[59]
Good historical precedents thus lay behind the first alliance Edward made
on behalf of one of his elder daughters, Eadgifu (born to his second wife),
whom he married to the king of the West Franks Charles 'the Simple',
probably between 917 and 919.[60]

Anxiety on both sides of the Channel about the increasing level of
Viking activity in Brittany may have persuaded the parties of the benefits
of this new alliance, but the foreign match did the Frankish king little good
domestically, for he was deposed from his realm in June 922, when Robert,
margrave of Neustria was anointed king. Although Robert's reign proved
short-lived, Charles failed to regain his nobles' support, being captured,
deposed from power and imprisoned in 923. Charles and Eadgifu's small
son Louis (born in 920 or 921) was promptly sent to the court of his uncle,
Æthelstan for his own protection.[61] His mother may have fled home to
Wessex immediately on Charles's imprisonment, taking the child with her,
but Janet Nelson has wondered whether Eadgifu might have remained in
Francia until her husband's death in 929, sending Louis back alone to the

---

[59] Philip Grierson, 'The Relations between England and Flanders before the Norman
Conquest', TRHS, 4th ser., xxiii (1941), 83–4; Pauline Stafford, 'Charles the Bald, Judith
and England', in Charles the Bald: Court and Kingdom, ed. Margaret Gibson and Janet L.
Nelson (2nd edn, Aldershot, 1990), 139–53; Janet L. Nelson, 'Alfred's Carolingian
Contemporaries', in Alfred the Great, ed. T. Reuter (Aldershot, 2003), 293–310; Sharp, 'The
West Saxon Tradition', 80.

[60] Flodoard, 926 (8E); Æthelweard, prologue, 2, and see A. Campbell, The Chronicle of
Æthelweard (London, 1962), xix; Stenton, ASE, 344–5; Sharp, 'The West Saxon Tradition',
82. Charles the Simple was the son of Louis the Stammerer (d. 879) and so grandson of
Charles the Bald. His first wife, Frederuna, died in 916 or early in 917. It seems likely, as
Poole observed, that the marriage occurred before 919, because Flodoard, who began
writing in that year, did not mention it: R.L. Poole, 'The Alpine Son-in-Law of Edward
the Elder', EHR, xxvi (1911), 312. Karl Ferdinand Werner, Histoire de la France, I: Les origins
(avant l'an mil) (Paris, 1984), 449–51.

[61] Flodoard, 923 (5EF); Richer, Historiae, ii. 1, ed. H. Hoffmann, MGH Scriptores 38
(Hanover, 2000), 97; Stenton, ASE, 344–5; Simon MacLean, 'Making a Difference in
Tenth-Century Politics: King Æthelstan's Sisters and Frankish Queenship', in Frankland, ed.
Paul Fouracre and David Ganz (Manchester, 2008), 173. For a general discussion of the
internal Frankish politics here see Werner, Histoire 451–61.

safety of her own family.[62] Such a decision would have left her son's immediate needs and the arrangements for his future education firmly in the hands of her male kin: her father while he still lived and her brothers after his death. Edward's youngest children were much the same age as Louis, and we may imagine that the Frankish child joined his cousins' nursery and later shared their princely education, under his uncle Æthelstan's benevolent care.

Reports of the contracting of Eadgifu's marriage to Charles 'the Simple' gave no role to Æthelstan, nor did he apparently initiate the negotiations that saw another of his sisters marry into a Frankish ducal house. The Frankish annalist Flodoard of Reims reported under the year 926 that 'Hugh, son of Robert, married a daughter of Edward the Elder, the king of the English, and the sister of the wife of Charles'.[63] Hugh was count of Paris and had recently assumed the title *dux Francorum*, duke of the Franks. For him, the wisdom of making an alliance with the West Saxon royal family will have appeared the more pressing once its members were protecting the Carolingian heir to the Frankish throne.[64] A more lavish account of the marriage suit appears in William of Malmesbury's *Gesta regum*, in the part of his narrative of Æthelstan's reign that he claimed to have obtained from a certain very old book. Having briefly described the marriages of three of the king's sisters, William reported that the fourth, 'in whom the whole mass of beauty, of which other women have only a share, had flowed into one by nature', was demanded in marriage from her brother through envoys by Hugh 'king' of the Franks.[65]

By William's account (which finds no support elsewhere), Æthelstan's cousin Adulf (Adelolf, son of Baldwin of Flanders) led the mission and presented Hugh's requests, producing gifts 'on a truly munificent scale' for the West Saxon king. These included not only numerous precious objects but various holy relics, which had associations with the Carolingian royal family. Delighted with presents of this quality, Æthelstan apparently responded with gifts of similar worth 'and comforted the passionate suitor with the hand of his sister'. Æthelstan had a reputation for relic-collecting outside England even before he became king, yet kingly gifts on this scale

---

[62] Janet L. Nelson, 'Eadgifu (d. in or after 951)', *Oxford Dictionary of National Biography* (2004), quoting Folcuin, *Gesta abbatum*, ch. 101, p. 626, where Folcuin reported that Eadgifu had suffered many persecutions at this time but also clearly stated that she had sent her son to the English, lest anyone finding him should kill him. For Eadgifu's role in the marriages of her other sisters and in assisting her brother Æthelstan to restore her son to his throne see Flodoard, 956 (33G) (951), and further below, 56–8.

[63] Flodoard, 926 (8E). Compare Æthelweard, prologue 2. Nelson has wondered whether Queen Eadgifu might have helped to broker this alliance, since it served her own interests by breaking the bond between Hugh and Count Heribert: 'Eadgifu'.

[64] Stenton, *ASE*, 345.

[65] *GR*, ii, 135, pp. 218–19; William erred in calling Hugh king; cf. Jean Dunbabin, *France in the Making, 843–1180* (Oxford, 1985), 47.

would have done more than satisfy his passion for the sacred: they would have placed him on a par with Charles the Great, who had formerly owned some of the objects. At this early point in his reign, Æthelstan had yet to attain the renown for military prowess on which his later reputation would rest and we might prefer not to accept William's testimony unquestioningly. Since other sources corroborate it we need not doubt, however, that Hugh and Eadhild were married, nor question that the making of that union was marked by the exchange of gifts on both sides.[66]

Earlier in the same year (926) Æthelstan had made an alliance of arguably greater immediate strategic significance. Then he arranged for his only full sister to marry Sihtric, king of Northumbria, meeting the northern king at Tamworth on 30 January 926 to cement the agreement.[67] Unfortunately, we know little about the terms of this alliance, other than that it would have benefited both sides equally. Sihtric did not long survive his wedding, dying in 927, after which his widow's fate is unclear. A thirteenth-century writer from St Albans, Roger of Wendover, was the first to name Sihtric's widow, identifying her with the St Eadgyth culted at the abbey of Polesworth in Warwickshire. Roger may have confused this woman with Æthelstan's half-sister of the same name, but he need not have erred in imagining her to have entered the cloister in widowhood.[68]

Of greater political and strategic magnitude than any of the alliances discussed thus far was Æthelstan's negotiating of a treaty with the ruling house in Saxony. The marriage of Eadgyth (daughter of Edward's second wife Ælfflæd) to Otto, son of the East Frankish king Henry the Fowler in 929 or 930, conferred substantial benefits on both parties. For Æthelstan it offered another means of brokering an alliance between legitimate European rulers in the difficult period following the death of Charles 'the Simple' and the arrival of Louis, his baby son, at the West Saxon court. A prestigious alliance also helped to establish Henry's status as king; he probably conferred royal status on Otto at about this time. The marriage took place after a major Saxon military triumph over the Slavs in the late summer of 929, a royal wedding enhancing the victory celebrations,

---

[66] *GR*, ii, 135, pp. 218–21; discussed fully below, ch. 7. For the involvement of the comital family of Flanders in brokering this arrangement, see Heather J. Tanner, *Families, Friends and Allies: Boulogne and Politics in Northern France and England c.879–1160* (Leiden and Boston, 2004), 31–2 and MacLean, 'Making a Difference', 175.

[67] ASC 926D. John of Worcester provided a less clear account; he described Sihtric's wife as the 'third' daughter, but may not have ordered the girls by age, for he described the marriages made by three of Edward's daughters in order of the status of their husbands: the first married Otto of Saxony, the second Charles, king of the West Franks and the third Sihtric: JW, s.a. 901, 354–5.

[68] Roger of Wendover, *Flores historiarum*, s.a. 925, ed. H.O. Coxe, 5 vols (London, 1841–4), i, 385–6; trans. Whitelock, *EHD*, no. 4. Precisely the same statement was made by Matthew Paris, *Chronica Majora*, ed. H.R. Luard, 7 vols (London 1872–80), i, 446–7. For discussion of this princess's fate see Pauline Stafford, 'Sons and Mothers: Family Politics in the Early Middle Ages', in *Medieval Women*, ed. D. Baker (Oxford, 1978), 97.

according to Widukind of Corvey. Certainly the significance of the event struck a number of contemporary commentators.[69] Writing later in the tenth century Æthelweard explained the context of the marriage in his prefatory letter for his *Chronicle* addressed to his cousin Matilda; Æthelstan, he reported, sent two of his sisters to Otto, in order that he might choose the one who pleased him most. Otto selected Eadgyth, from whom Matilda herself was descended.[70] This same report, that Otto had the chance to select his bride from a choice of two West Saxon princesses, Hrotsvitha told more elaborately in her *Gesta Ottonis*.

Hrotsvitha went out of her way to assure her German audience of Otto's wife's royal lineage, contrasting the nobility of her birth with the doubt surrounding the origins of her brother, the king, with whom Eadgyth was living at court after her father's death. She laid considerable stress on Eadgyth's birth from 'the high quality seed of great kings' and from 'the seed of the saintly ancestors who produced her', including her supposed descent from the Northumbrian king St Oswald.[71] According to Hrotsvitha, Otto's father sent ambassadors to Æthelstan, who heard their suit and then urged the prince's case to his sister Eadgyth while he gathered treasures to send abroad for her new in-laws. When he had collected enough, the king dispatched the princess carefully with suitable attendants across the sea, sending with the girl her sister, a girl not only Eadgyth's junior but also her 'inferior in merit'. Thus, Hrotsvitha declared 'he bestowed greater honour upon Otto, the loving son of the illustrious king, by sending two girls of eminent birth, that he might lawfully espouse whichever one of them he wished'. As we might by now have anticipated, Otto only had to set eyes on Eadgyth to fall in love with her. Eadgyth made an entirely suitable wife for a Liudolfing prince, being beautiful, charming, queenly in her bearing and unanimously esteemed

---

[69] Widukind, *Res gestae Saxonicae*, i, 37, ed. P. Hirsch and H.-E. Lohmann, *Die Sachsengeschichte des Widukind von Korvei*, 5th edn, MGH SRG (Hanover, 1935) p. 54. Widukind mistakenly called Eadgyth's father Edmund, rather than Edward, and did not realize that Eadgyth and Æthelstan were only half-siblings, although he got the latter's name right: Karl Leyser, 'The Ottonians and Wessex', in *Communications and Power in Medieval Europe: the Carolingian and Ottonian Centuries*, ed. Timothy Reuter (London, 1994), 76. Timothy Reuter, *Germany in the Early Middle Ages c.800–1056* (London, 1991), 145. The copy of the collection of annals known as the Mercian Register broke off during the course of the entry for 924, reporting that in that year Æthelstan gave his sister in marriage without specifying to whom. This might have been a reference to the marriage of the king's full sister to Sihtric just discussed, but the author of the northern (D) version of the Chronicle for 925 made a different assumption and completed the Mercian Register's unfinished sentence by saying that the king gave his sister in marriage over the sea to the son of the king of the Old Saxons.

[70] Æthelweard, prologue, 2.

[71] Hrotsvitha, *Gesta Ottonis*, lines 79–82 and 95–8, ed. Berschin, 278–9; trans. Boyd H. Hill, *Medieval Monarchy in Action: the German Empire from Henry I to Henry IV* (London, 1972), 122. See above for the contrast Hrotsvitha made between the nobility of Æthelstan's and Eadyth's mothers. On the link with St Oswald, see below, 205–8.

in her own country; and so the two married and in time Eadgyth bore Otto a son, named Liudulf.[72] Bishop Cenwald of Worcester accompanied the two princesses on their journey to Saxony, going on to visit a number of German monastic houses. Both the account of Cenwald's visit (which is preserved only in a confraternity book from St Gallen) and Hrotsvitha's *Gesta Ottonis* make reference to the lavishness of the treasures that were sent with the wedding party to Germany, some intended for the king but others meant to reinforce Eadgyth's royal status.[73]

This alliance gave Æthelstan another powerful brother-in-law in Europe and, through the contacts forged by Bishop Cenwald, associations with various German religious houses. But we should not forget the second West Saxon princess whom Otto had rejected; she, too, had a role to play in cementing English alliances in Europe. Æthelweard did not know the second girl's name, but he thought she had married 'a certain king near the Alps'; since he had no information about that king's family, he hoped that his dedicatee Matilda might be able to find some for him.[74] Hrotsvitha never mentioned whom the additional sister married, but she did name her Adiva, by which she must have meant the Old English name Eadgifu. According to William of Malmesbury, Eadgifu was the name of a daughter of Edward the Elder's third wife who shared both her mother's name and that of one of her older stepsisters (wife of Charles the Simple). If Hrotsvitha named the extra sister sent to Germany with Eadgyth correctly and if we identify that Adiva with the Eadgifu whom William located among Edward's youngest group of children, then she could have been no older than ten or eleven at the time, for her parents did not marry until 917 or 918. According to William, this Eadgifu – a famous beauty – was given in marriage by her brother Æthelstan to Louis, prince of Aquitaine.

Yet William's testimony confuses this matter further, for he did not believe Eadgifu had accompanied Eadgyth to Saxony, but rather argued – as may seem more plausible – that Æthelstan sent with Eadgyth one of her full sisters, whom he called Ælfgifu. With Æthelweard, William thought

---

[72] Hrotsvitha, *Gesta Ottonis*, lines 110–24, ed. Berschin, 279–80, trans. Hill, 123. A different version of the story in the *Passio* of St Ursula, addressed to Gero, archbishop of Cologne (969–76), made a certain Count Hoolf leader of the embassy, his charge being to find a bride from the noblest lineage of that people as a fit companion for Otto, to whom the titles *magnus* and *imperator* were already attributed. Wilhelm Levison, 'Das Werden der Ursula-Legende', *Bonner Jahrbucher*, cxxxii (1928), 142–57 and commentary, 58–90. Leyser, 'The Ottonians', 79.

[73] Keynes, 'Books', 198–9; Leyser, 'The Ottonians', 81; for further discussion of Cenwald's trip and the various manuscripts exchanged between the royal courts at this time, see below, 101–2.

[74] Elisabeth van Houts has explored the role of women responsible for maintaining a family's memory: 'Women and the Writing of History in the Early Middle Ages: the Case of Abbess Matilda of Essen and Aethelweard', *EME*, i (1992), 53–68.

that the spare sister who travelled with Eadgyth and Cenwald had married a 'certain duke near the Alps'. That Alpine ruler has often been identified with Conrad the Peaceable, king of Burgundy (a match which would have given the Anglo-Saxon princess queenly status), but recently doubt has been cast on that suggestion.[75] Struggling with the complexities of disentangling Edward the Elder's offspring, William appears to have ended up by reckoning one girl too many, either giving a mythical sixth daughter to Ælfflæd or supplying Eadgifu with a spare daughter who shared her own name. It would be prudent, as Eduard Hlawitschka has suggested, to remove one of these from our reckoning. Æthelstan thus had just one further sister not yet accounted for, the one who went to Saxony with Eadgyth but failed to win Otto's hand. Our sources seem agreed that she married a prince near the Alps, and William might correctly have named that prince Louis, but he was not Louis prince of Aquitaine, nor Conrad of Burgundy, but Louis the brother of Rudolf II of Burgundy.[76] While we may reasonably assume that Louis's West Saxon wife was Eadgyth's full sister (and so of a similar age to Otto's queen, not a much younger child born of Edward the Elder's last marriage), her name remains uncertain. William's suggestion that she was called Ælfgifu does not square with Hrotsvitha's statement that her name was Adiva (Eadgifu). Hrotsvitha may, however, also have been confused here; she wrote some time after the events of 929–30 and could have muddled Eadgyth's sister up either with her stepmother, the mother of King Edmund, whose name is recorded in a confraternity book from Pfäfers, or with her elder half-sister who had married Charles 'the Simple'.[77]

All our authorities from Æthelweard onwards struggled to understand the continental marriage alliances made for Æthelstan's sisters. It appears from this discussion that Edward the Elder had in fact just eight daughters in his large family: quite enough, one might feel, for any eldest brother to

[75] *GR*, ii, 126, pp. 200–1. William also argued, yet more confusingly, that the one whom Otto had married was Ælfgifu not Eadgyth, but here he clearly erred. R.L. Poole, 'The Alpine Son-in-law of Edward the Elder', *EHR*, xxvi (1911), 314–15.

[76] Eduard Hlawitschka, 'Die verwandtschaftlchen Verbindungen zwischen dem hochburgundischen und dem niederburgundischen Königshaus. Zugleich ein Beitrag zur Geschichte Burgunds in der 1. Hälfte des 10. Jahrhunderts', in *Grundwissenschaften und Geschichte Festschrift für Peter Acht*, ed. Waldemar Schlögl and Peter Herde (Kallmünz, 1976), pp. 28–57 (at pp. 50–7). Leyser, 'The Ottonians', pp. 84–5. A notably clear account of these liaisons and their significance appears in MacLean, 'Making a Difference', 175–81. I am grateful to Dr MacLean for showing me a copy of this before its publication and for a useful discussion that helped me to reach a conclusion about the identity of 'Ælfgifu'.

[77] Together with King Æthelstan, King Edmund and Archbishop Oda, an *Odgiva* was named in a confraternity book from Pfäfers: St Gallen, Stiftsarchiv, MS Cod. Fabariensis 1, p. 33. This name could, if we believe Hrotsvitha, refer to Eadgyth's sister, but it seems more likely that the manuscript commemorates King Edmund's mother (Edward the Elder's third wife) not one of Æthelstan's or Edmund's siblings.

handle.[78] Four of them married into European families (all of them daughters of their father's second wife, who may indeed have been a significant driving force behind these alliances): Eadgifu, wife of Charles 'the Simple' of western Frankia; Eadhild, who married Hugh, duke of the Franks; Eadgyth, wife of Otto the Great of Saxony; and the fourth, possibly called Ælfgifu, who married into the Burgundian royal house. Nor did Æthelstan and his father Edward ignore the future spiritual health of the royal family, as we have already seen. We might also note, however, that none of Æthelstan's sisters seems to have remained unmarried at her brother's court to provide him with female company or to minister to his guests in the absence of a royal consort of his own. When thinking about Æthelstan's family and its role in his personal and emotional development, we should look beyond his blood kin to consider one other small group of young men who temporarily joined the king's immediate circle as his foster-sons.

FOSTER-SONS

Fostering, the rearing of children in another household of equivalent status (usually that of a friend or relative), was common in early medieval Celtic and Germanic societies, and particularly in aristocratic and royal circles. Kings typically sponsored other kings' sons at baptism or confirmation and not infrequently took the godchildren and other foster-sons into their own households for a part of their childhood and adolescence.[79] Many commentators have noted Æthelstan's willingness to offer support – both physical protection and military arms – to dispossessed foreign royals, notably to the child-sons of kings. His interest in these boys extended beyond the political into personal affection; non-contemporary sources report that all three of those to whom he allegedly offered shelter – his nephew Louis, son of Charles 'the Simple' and Eadgifu, Alain, heir to the Breton throne and Hákon, son of Harald of Norway – he brought up as his foster-sons. Further, Æthelstan reinforced the bond of mutual dependence with the two princes with whom he shared no blood tie, Alain and

---

[78] This conclusion is reflected in the West Saxon genealogy printed as fig. 1, which differs in this respect from those printed by Stafford, *Unification and Conquest*, 2; Sheila Sharp, 'England, Europe and the Celtic World: King Æthelstan's Foreign Policy', *Bulletin of the John Rylands University Library of Manchester*, lxxix (1997), 203 (and Sharp's table 6.1 in her 'The West Saxon Tradition', 83–4); and Veronica Ortenberg, "Aux Périphéries du monde carolingien: Liens dynastiques et nouvelles fidélités dans le royaume anglo-saxon', in *La Royauté et les élites dans l'Europe carolingienne (début IXe siècle aux environs de 920)*, ed. Régine le Jan (Lille, 1998), 517, all of which attempt to identify husbands for both Ælfgifu and the phantom Eadgifu.

[79] John Boswell, *The Kindness of Strangers: the Abandonment of Children in Western Europe from Late Antiquity to the Renaissance* (London, 1989), 206–9; Thomas Charles-Edwards, *Early Irish and Welsh Kinship* (Oxford, 1993), 78–82; Joseph Lynch, *Christianizing Kinship: Ritual Sponsorship in Anglo-Saxon England* (Ithaca, NY, and London, 1998), 222–4.

Hákon, by standing as godfather at their baptism. William of Malmesbury claimed that the king also acted as godfather to the son of King Constantín of Scotland following the submission of the Scots king and others at Dacre in 927.[80] John of Worcester also placed Constantín's son within Æthelstan's court circle, for he reported that among the terms agreed by the Scots following Æthelstan's ravaging of their country in 934, was that he took Constantín's son back with him to Wessex as a hostage. This information is unique to John's account and might of course be his own invention.[81] Æthelstan's cousin Arnulf of Flanders looked to Æthelstan's court for assistance with his own political rivalries when he tried to expand his territory southwards into the land held by Herluin of Ponthieu. After capturing Montreuil in 939, Arnulf sent Herluin's wife and sons for Æthelstan to hold them as hostages at his court.[82]

Brittany had suffered from particularly aggressive Scandinavian attacks during the second decade of the tenth century, which culminated in the overthrow of the realm, as Flodoard reported in 919: 'The Northmen ravaged, destroyed and annihilated all of Brittany in Cornouaille, which is located on the seashore. The Bretons were abducted and sold, while those who escaped were driven out.'[83] Later Breton tradition, preserved in the eleventh-century Chronicle of Nantes, reported that Matuedoi, count of Poher, found refuge from the Vikings at Æthelstan's court and that his infant son, Alain, became the king's godson. In fact Edward the Elder probably sheltered them first, and Alain may even, Dumville has suggested, have been born in England. Breton sources dwelt, however, on the boy's connection with Æthelstan, the Chronicle of Nantes reporting that 'Æthelstan, king of England, had lifted Alain from the holy font. The king had great trust in him because of this friendship and the alliance of this baptism.'[84] Known in adulthood as 'Crooked Beard' (Barbetorte), Alain was heir to the kingdom of Brittany; he was grandson through his mother of Alain the Great, king of Brittany 888–90. Spending his childhood at Æthelstan's court as foster-son to the king and foster-brother to his contemporaries, the king's youngest brothers Edmund and Eadred, Alain built close ties with the West Saxon royal house. The Breton prince forged a further connection in England with his fellow Frankish exile, Louis, son of Charles the Simple. Æthelstan clearly took his obligations to

[80] *GR*, ii, 134, pp. 214–15.

[81] JW, *s.a.* 934, pp. 390–1. Lynch, *Christianizing Kinship*, 222–3.

[82] Flodoard, 939 (21B); Richer, *Historiae*, ii, 12 (p. 146). Grierson, 'The Relations', 89; Tanner, *Families*, 35.

[83] Flodoard 919 (1).

[84] *Chronique de Nantes*, ch. 27, ed. R. Merlet (Paris, 1896), 82–3; *EHD*, no. 25; David N. Dumville, 'Britanny and "Armes Prydein Vaw"', *Etudes Celtiques*, xx (1983), 151; Julia M.H. Smith, *Province and Empire: Brittany and the Carolingians* (Cambridge, 1992), 196–7; Lynch, *Christianizing Kinship*, 223.

his nephew and foster-son seriously, offering practical and military support when requested to assist each to regain his inheritance.[85]

Although no contemporary Anglo-Saxon source reports the fact, several medieval Scandinavian texts, the earliest dating from the twelfth century, preserve a tradition that Hákon, son of Harald Fairhair of Norway was known by the nickname *Aðalsteins fóstri*, having been reared as a Christian at the king's court.[86] Two vernacular texts, *Fagrskinna* (*c.*1200) and *Heimskringla* (*c.*1230–35) tell the same tale of the circumstances behind the fostering. Æthelstan sent a fine sword as a gift to Harald Fairhair (the first king of Norway, d. 930) which the king accepted, only learning after having done so that he had thereby acknowledged Æthelstan's overlordship. Harald sent his son back to Æthelstan in return and when his ambassadors placed the child on the English king's knee they told him that he was thereby accepting Harald's lordship. Various established literary devices underpin this story, but in ignoring its details we need not also reject the suggestion that Hákon was brought up at Æthelstan's court.[87] Independent of the saga material is a Latin *Historia de antiquitate regum Norwagensium*, written 1177×1188 by a monk at Trondheim called Theodricus. He stated that Hákon had been sent to Æthelstan's court in order to be brought up and to learn the customs of the English people. These same Scandinavian sources report that Hákon was reared as a Christian (both *Fagrskinna* and *Heimskringla* state explicitly that he was baptized in England) even though his own country was pagan at this time.[88]

A different account appears in William of Malmesbury's *Gesta regum*, towards the end of the portion of narrative that he claimed to have derived from the ancient book he had found. Discussing Æthelstan's reputation in Europe, William talked of the foreign embassies sent to the king's court, including one sent by Harald, king of the Norwegians which came to the city of York to present its suit. According to William, 'A certain Harold, king of the Norwegians, sent him a ship with gilded beak and a scarlet sail the inside of which was hung round with a close-set row of gilded shields. The names of the envoys were Helgrim and Osfrith, and after a royal reception in the city of York, they wiped off the sweat of their journey with suitable rewards.'[89] If we accept that Harald did send this

---

[85] Flodoard, 936 (18A), 939 (21D); *Chronique de Nantes*, ch. 29, p. 83. For the military aspects of this see further below, 168–9 and 183–4.

[86] Gareth Williams, 'Hákon *Aðalsteins fóstri*: Aspects of Anglo-Saxon Kingship in Tenth-Century Norway', in *The North Sea World in the Middle Ages: Studies in the Cultural History of North-Western Europe*, ed. Thomas R. Liszka and Lorna E.M. Walker (Dublin, 2001), 113. Magnús Fjalldal, *Anglo-Saxon England in Icelandic Medieval Texts* (Toronto, Buffalo and London, 2005), 34–6. Harald Harfagri (Fairhair) was king of Norway, *c.*880–930; he died in *c.*933.

[87] R.I. Page, *Chronicles of the Vikings: Records, Memorials and Myths* (London, 1995), 30–4; Williams, 'Hákon', 113. For a more sceptical discussion, see Fjalldal, *Anglo-Saxon England*, 34–6. See also R.I. Page, 'The Audience of *Beowulf* and the Vikings', in *The Dating of Beowulf*, ed. C. Chase (Toronto, 1981), 113–16.

[88] Williams, 'Hákon', 111, 114.

legation (and he had a strong motive for so doing: to request the English king's assistance in eradicating groups of dissident Norwegians who had taken refuge in England), we would have to date this visit to before his death in c.933, in which case it might have coincided with Æthelstan's period in the north in 927.[90] On the other hand, the real purpose of the mission could have been, as the Scandinavian sources suggest, to ask Æthelstan to foster Harald's son, Hákon, a child born in the king's old age. Such an embassy could have come after Harald's death from the boy's maternal kin, keen to protect him from his older rivals to the throne, especially Erik Bloodaxe.[91] The legates might have found the king at York in 934 if he had paused at the city on his way either to or from Scotland in that year. However implausible their details, some historical truth probably underpins these accounts; we might thus wonder whether Æthelstan's interest in this scion of the Norwegian royal house reflected his awareness of the diplomatic significance of baptism, and so represented an attempt on his part to neutralize one potential external enemy by bringing its future leader into the Christian fold.

At one level Æthelstan's decision to take charge of the sons of some contemporary rulers from other parts of continental Europe and rear them in his own immediate circle was thus not unusual; Æthelstan stands out here only for the geographical breadth of the relationships he was able to make and the consequent multi-ethnic court he gathered around his person. Even so, the number of royal and noble scions whom he brought into his orbit may suggest that he took a particular interest in this form of royal diplomacy and perhaps actively sought out such connections. Some of these young men were related to him by blood; with others, the king reinforced his bond by acting not just as foster-father but also godfather, sponsoring them at the font at the time of their baptism. Given Æthelstan's childlessness, we might imagine these as his surrogate children, receiving the affection as well as the material and spiritual support that he would otherwise have bestowed on his own offspring. Through them we see a side of the king not otherwise much in evidence: a solicitous, caring and affectionate man who gladly took responsibility for vulnerable boys, seeking to provide not just sanctuary from political danger but a stable and loving home. Additionally, of course, they provided companionship for his youngest brothers, still small children at the time of Æthelstan's accession, for whom he clearly felt some quasi-paternal responsibility as well as fraternal affection. A group of young men, all much of an age, will have constituted a significant body within the royal court and done much to counterbalance the influence of the

---

[89] *GR*, ii, 135, pp. 216–17. Page, 'The Audience', 115–17. Page observes that not only was Æthelstan frequently in the north but that York was accessible to seagoing ships. The city was additionally a more obvious landing-point for Norwegian sailors than any West Saxon port.

[90] Stenton, *ASE*, 348–9.

[91] Page, 'The Audience', 113–17. Fjalldal, *Anglo-Saxon England*, 34–6.

king's many sisters. Having himself probably endured a rather lonely childhood, Æthelstan hereby provided not just a group of companions suitable for his brothers, but arguably a circle of like-minded friends for himself.

HOUSEHOLD

In one important respect, Æthelstan did not conform to the social (and royal) conventions of his day: despite his skill in arranging matrimonial alliances on his sisters' behalf, he himself never married. Without a queen, his household would have appeared distinctive among contemporary west European courts, and have differed from those of his immediate successors.[92] Although the West Saxons had not been in the habit of calling their kings' wives queens before the late ninth century, the wife of the king had a significant role within the royal household, the court and beyond. A decision to govern that family, and the wider family of the king's subjects, without a wife to be their queen was thus not one a king could take lightly. But Æthelstan scarcely lacked women in his family circle who could have taken on the administrative role in household management and the social duties of hospitality to visitors that would normally have fallen to the king's wife. If he had relied on his sisters in this respect, he did not do so for long but wasted little time in finding them suitable husbands; Eadgyth and her sister Ælfgifu were the last of those who would marry still to remain at home and they left for Germany in 929. When those who took the veil entered their respective cloisters cannot be determined; more than one of them might have remained at court for a part of her early adulthood, especially if she entertained hopes of a prestigious marriage of her own in due course. Nor should we forget the surviving women of the older generation. Æthelstan's mother had probably died before his accession, and his elder stepmother had already likely joined a nunnery, but Edward's third wife Eadgifu (aged only about twenty when she married the king) was still alive in 924 and would survive for a further forty years in widowhood.[93] Eadgifu proved active in the affairs of her sons Edmund and Eadred and remained a significant figure in the reign of her grandson Edgar. Could she also have run her stepson's household as a dowager queen? She did not attest any of Æthelstan's charters and

---

[92] On the roles of queens at early medieval courts, see Pauline Stafford, *Queens, Concubines and Dowagers: the King's Wife in the Early Middle Ages* (London, 1983); Simon MacLean, 'Queenship, Nunneries and Royal Widowhood in Carolingian Europe', *Past and Present*, clxxviii (2003), 3–38.

[93] Stafford, *Queens*, 145. William of Malmesbury's history of the abbey of Glastonbury hints that Ælfflæd was still alive during her stepson's reign but tells us nothing more: William of Malmesbury, *De antiquitate Glastonie ecclesie*, ed. John Scott, *The Early History of Glastonbury, An Edition, Translation and Study of William of Malmesbury's De antiquitate Glastonie ecclesie* (Woodbridge, 1981), ch. 54, pp. 112–13.

had apparently taken religious vows by early in 952 when her younger son Eadred made her a grant of land in which he referred to her as a servant of God (*famula Dei*). At least in the early years of Æthelstan's reign and perhaps for longer, she might have remained in Winchester to care for her own young children and possibly also to keep an eye on her rather older stepdaughters before they left court to marry or enter the Church.[94]

One contemporary source, already cited, mentions the presence of a queen at a royal palace in Æthelstan's day. Following the king's largely bloodless conquest of Northumbria and the consequent submission of all the other rulers in Britain to his authority at Eamont in 927, a clerk called Petrus in the king's entourage wrote a poem reporting Æthelstan's triumphs. Referred to conventionally by its first line, *Carta dirige gressus*, as noted above, the poem opens with an injunction that this letter should direct its steps over the seas to the king's *burh*, bearing good wishes to the queen, the prince, the distinguished ealdormen as well as the arm-bearing thegns. Conceivably the reference to a prince (*clito*) might allude to Æthelstan's second brother, Edwin, from which one might infer that the queen mentioned was Ælfflæd, Edwin's mother and Edward's second wife. Since other evidence suggests that Edward put Ælfflæd into a nunnery in order to marry his third wife, Eadgifu, it seems more likely that the poem refers to her, which would make the prince of the poem Eadgifu's elder son, Edmund, Æthelstan's future heir.[95] Further evidence associating Eadgifu with Æthelstan may come from an inscription added to the foot of the last leaf of the so-called Gandersheim Gospels.[96] This manuscript was written and illustrated at Metz in the middle of the ninth century (*c.*860) and may have gone to Germany among the gifts sent with Eadgyth on her marriage to Otto, either via England or alternatively from some monastic house on the continent where an Englishman could have added the marginal note recording the two names. The inscription, written in an unpractised Anglo-Saxon square minuscule, gives pride of place to Queen Eadgifu, whose name appears first, preceded by a cross; Æthelstan seems the secondary figure:[97]

+eadgifu regina:- æþelstan rex angulsaxonum
mercianorum:-

---

[94] S.E. Kelly, *Charters of Shaftesbury Abbey* (Oxford, 1996), xiii, 71–2. The charter is S 562; Kelly no. 17; Maggie Bailey, 'Ælfwynn, Second Lady of the Mercians', in H&H, 122.

[95] Lapidge, 'Poems', 83–93 and 98; for the suggestion that the queen was Ælfflæd, see Paul Hill, *Æthelstan*, 200–1, but see *GR*, ii, 126, pp. 200–1. For further discussion of the poem, see below, 112.

[96] Coburg, Landesbibliothek MS 1, fo. 168r.

[97] Keynes, 'Books', 189–93.

The unusual form of the regnal style given to the king here (king of the Anglo-Saxons and Mercians) suggests that its author had little familiarity with the language used in Æthelstan's charters, yet knew that his kingship amounted to more than that of his father and grandfather, for whom the title king of the Anglo-Saxons had become the norm.[98] Given my suggestion that Eadgifu remained at court after her husband's death, we need not share Simon Keynes's surprise that she should be associated with Æthelstan. If her role revolved principally around her own children, especially her sons, we would expect her to have stayed largely at Winchester or at some other West Saxon royal palace, and not to have trailed around the kingdom following the king's peripatetic court, which would account for her absence from his charters, but not make her a person of no consequence in royal affairs.[99]

We should also recall that one former queen joined Æthelstan's household for at least part of his reign. Eadgifu, widow of Charles 'the Simple' of Francia, lived in Wessex from at least 929 when her husband died until 936; then Louis, their son, regained his throne and she returned to Frankia with him. Such status as she had at her brother's court would have depended more on her position as mother to a future king than as widow of one who had so ignominiously been dispossessed of his throne.[100] We may doubt that the author of the inscription in the Gandersheim Gospels sought to associate this dowager queen Eadgifu with King Æthelstan. While there were thus plenty of women in Æthelstan's wider circle who could have shared the household duties of a queen, the king may have preferred to keep that group safely at home in Winchester and have moved around his realm with a tighter, exclusively male set of companions. This would not have made the king's immediate household unusual by the standards of an age in which the values of the war-band continued to predominate. But it would have distinguished Æthelstan's court from those of his uxorious father and monogamous grandfather.

That royal princes had an obligation to find suitably born wives and beget sons we held as axiomatic at the start of this chapter. Æthelstan's father, Edward, certainly took his responsibilities in this regard seriously, producing five putative male heirs to his dominions, but he apparently failed to arrange for his eldest son to marry. By the time of his accession Æthelstan was more than old

---

[98] This style would have appeared especially appropriate in the early part of his reign, before his acquisition of the kingship of Northumbria in 927, yet the uncertainties of the hand and the unconventional formulation may simply indicate that the author of the note was not close to the royal court; Keynes, 'Books', 190.

[99] Keynes's view of Eadgifu's obscurity in Æthelstan's reign rested centrally on her absence from the king's charters. He drew attention also to a charter in the archive of Christ Church, Canterbury that referred to some title deeds which Eadgifu had, during her husband's lifetime, withheld from a layman called Goda, but largely returned to him after Edward's death, when King Æthelstan interceded with her on Goda's behalf: S 1211 (SEHD, no. 23) see Keynes, 'Books', 190, n. 224. On Eadgifu, see also Stafford, 'The King's Wife', 25–6; Cyril Hart, 'Two Queens of England', Ampleforth Journal, lxxxii (1977), 10–14.

[100] Above, 43 Compare Keynes 'Books', 191–3.

enough to have fathered a family of his own, yet he remained unmarried and seemingly childless. Could Edward at one stage have planned to marry Æthelstan to his first cousin, Ælfwynn, daughter of Æthelred and Æthelflæd of Mercia? Although such a marriage would have been contrary to the Church's teaching on permitted degrees of marriage, it was not unheard of in this period for royal cousins to marry. Æthelstan's possible upbringing in Mercia might have brought the two close, but not necessarily close enough to want to marry. In fact, Ælfwynn disappeared from the historical record soon after her mother's death in 918, when according to the Mercian Register her uncle (Edward the Elder) deprived her of all authority and took her into Wessex, three weeks before Christmas. This would have been the time to contract such a marriage, when Edward had the strongest opportunity to exercise his authority as his niece's guardian. Instead, the king preferred the safer option of disposing of Ælfwynn into the cloister; no sources record that she ever married or produced children who might have laid claim to the English throne.[101] Appealing as the notion of a Mercian/West Saxon alliance might seem, we must dismiss it as mere speculation. Nor does any evidence suggest that Æthelstan, although formally unmarried, had liaisons with women which produced any illegitimate children. A single reference in the twelfth-century *Liber Eliensis* to a putative daughter of the king – 'Æðitha filia regis Æðelstani' – is probably an error for 'Eadgyth, sister of King Æthelstan'.[102]

Perhaps the very superfluity of available successors to his crown made Æthelstan reluctant to find a wife either during his father's lifetime or after his own accession. If he had doubted his father's plans for the kingdom after his death, Æthelstan might in youth have elected to remain without heirs until his own future status became clearer. Since in the event he struggled both to obtain and keep hold of that inheritance, we could see his decision to remain celibate as a deliberate, indeed carefully negotiated succession-strategy intended to restrict the number of potential heirs to his own younger brothers.[103] While bachelorhood was uncommon among secular European princes of his day, it was not a wholly inexplicable life-choice and need not be treated with particular suspicion. Yet for a modern readership another possibility arises which leads us to wonder if we should infer any more from the apparent encouragement this king gave to young

---

[101] MR 919. Alex Woolf, 'View from the West: an Irish perspective', in H&H, pp. 98–101; Bailey, 'Ælfwynn', 122. Edward might, of course, have had plans for his second son, Ælfweard, to marry, and indeed have contracted such a match, but Ælfweard's death so soon after his father's has ensured that no evidence of such a liaison now survives.

[102] *Liber Eliensis*, iii, 50, ed. Blake, p. 292. Yet more implausible are the claims in some versions of the legend of Guy of Warwick that Guy's son, Reynburn, married a daughter of Æthelstan with the unlikely name of Leonada, or Leonetta: William Dugdale, *The Antiquities of Warwickshire*, 2 vols (2nd edn, London, 1730), i, 376.

[103] J.L. Nelson, 'Rulers and Government', in *NCMH*, III, ed. T. Reuter (Cambridge, 1999), 103–4. William of Malmesbury indeed argued in one version of his *Gesta regum* that it was out of respect for Edmund and Eadred that he never turned his thoughts to marriage: *GR*, ii, 140 (pp. 228–9).

men in his court circle. Does Æthelstan's care for his younger brothers, his willingness to foster the exiled sons of kings and his enthusiasm for the presence of young male religious in his court suggest that he was happiest in a male environment, even that the company of young men was some-thing he actively sought out?[104]

Any attempt to talk about the sexual orientation of a tenth-century man is doomed to be anachronistic; early medieval views on sexuality and sexual mores were quite different from modern notions and were seldom expressed, in so far as they were articulated at all, in media that still survive for our consumption. The Church taught that homosexual relations were sinful; normative and prescriptive sources such as penitentials legislated for the punishment of those who indulged in such bodily sins. Kings were divinely chosen to rule and set as shepherds over their people; the obliga-tion to purity lay more powerfully on them than on their non-royal counterparts and their sins would bring divine vengeance not only upon their own heads but on those of a whole people. Æthelstan's anointing with holy oil at his coronation marked him out yet further from his peers: he became God's chosen vessel. In his own lifetime, Æthelstan had a reputa-tion for piety and devotion, which we might think an argument against his having given his contemporaries grounds for suspecting his sexual orienta-tion. Of course devotion was an attribute expected of all medieval kings, yet we have no reason to question the seriousness of Æthelstan's personal religious belief to which the interest he took in book- and relic-collecting and his patronage of religious houses both attest. Hypothetically, we could concede that, given both the vocabulary and the opportunity to express such desires, Æthelstan's interests might have tended towards same-sex relations, but we have no mechanism by which to test such a proposition.

A preference for the company of men need not have carried any sexual connotations, but could merely have expressed the king's predilection for male conversation and manly pursuits. Anglo-Saxon royal society still owed much to its Germanic, heroic origins; at tenth-century royal courts the affairs of war and of the hunt dominated proceedings, as they had in earlier eras. Alfred's court appears just as distinctively a masculine envi-ronment, where the king's officials rubbed shoulders with his leading clergy, ealdormen and nobles and a range of visiting foreigners. Young men were equally prominent there, too; Asser reported that despite his preoccupation with other affairs, Alfred did not cease to give instruction in virtuous behaviour and teaching in literacy to the sons of his leading men being educated in the royal household.[105] The presence of young males at Æthelstan's court is not remarkable; his apparently deliberate decision not

---

[104] Allen J. Frantzen, *Before the Closet: Same-Sex Love from Beowulf to Angels in America* (Chicago and London, 1998); Ruth Mazo Karras, 'Sexuality in the Middle Ages', in *The Medieval World*, ed. Peter Linehan and Janet L. Nelson (London, 2001), 290–1.

[105] Asser, ch. 76.

to take a wife is more noteworthy, but may prove readily explicable in terms that would have resonated with his contemporaries. Æthelstan might have had a religious vocation to chastity and so failed to marry because of a desire to preserve his virginity for the good of his soul. If he did, no contemporary or later commentators made such a claim on his behalf nor, interestingly, did any try to claim him as a saint; perhaps his established military reputation militated against any such possibility.[106]

Others have also found it profitable to scrutinize a king's private life through the lens of his immediate family circle. Æthelstan's position as the eldest of thirteen children remains the single most important factor in shaping his mature personality. His choices about the sort of company with which he would surround himself in adulthood, his plans for the futures of his sisters and above all his intentions for the succession to the West Saxon throne all arose directly from his own experience as the eldest, but not his father's favourite son. Æthelstan's debts to his grandfather are obvious. His childhood (especially if partly spent with his aunt, Alfred's daughter) may help to explain some of the ways in which he chose in adulthood deliberately to continue the Alfredian project, particularly in the promotion of learning (if not via translating, appealing as that notion may seem) and above all through the medium of law. A bookish and perhaps rather solitary childhood may have laid the foundations for his interest in relics of the saints and for book-collecting, which helped to give him a reputation for notable piety in adulthood. Given the complete absence of evidence, I have not dwelt on Æthelstan's relationship with his mother, who either died when Æthelstan was still young, or was removed entirely from royal circles (perhaps to a nunnery); psychologists usually have much to say about the impact on the developing psyche of separation from or loss of either parent, but a mother especially. Whether that has any bearing on the difficult question of Æthelstan's putative involvement in the death of his brother Edwin at sea remains unknowable. Childhood encounters might, however, go some way towards explaining why this king never married, although here, too, any answer should involve nuance, giving equal weight to spiritual as well as earthly motives. Tempting as it is to see his single status and childlessness as evidence of a

[106] Dumville, *Wessex*, 150–1; Nelson, 'Rulers and Government', 103–4. Contrast the example of Edward the Confessor who seems to have married with reluctance late in life and who wasted no time in disposing of his wife when her father, Earl Godwine of Wessex, fell out of favour. After his death his medieval biographer – admittedly trying to claim his subject as a saint – asserted that 'he preserved with holy chastity the dignity of his consecration, and lived his whole life dedicated to God in true innocence': *The Life of King Edward who rests at Westminster*, ii, ed. Frank Barlow (London, 1962), 60–1. See Barlow, *Edward the Confessor* (London, 1970), 81–5, 259 and for a more trenchant defence of Edward's deliberate choice of celibacy: Eric John, 'Edward the Confessor and the Celibate Life', *Analecta Bollandiana*, xcvii (1979), 171–8.

revulsion against the suffocatingly feminine atmosphere of his father's household, we should probably refrain from further speculation. That Æthelstan liked the company of young men and was genuinely fond of those around him seems an unexceptionable conclusion; we need not see the encouragement of boys and men at his court as an overt attempt to redress the balance in a household where women had formerly been in the ascendant.

Chapter 3

COURT

The great number of princes and *ministri* that attended Æthelstan's councils, the splendor of his palatial surroundings, the banquets and the festivals that his courtiers enjoyed, the great retinue that followed him about on his journeys, all these things testify to a magnificence far different from that which characterized the airy lodgings of his famous grandfather, where the wind extinguished the lighted candle on the king's table.

Larson, *The King's Household*, 194

All early medieval families, including royal ones, lived in social units larger than those created by ties of blood-kinship and marriage: these familial groups encompassed a wider collection of dependants as well as servants and slaves.[1] In royal circles, a range of court office-holders and servants augmented that body further, each of whom had his own area of responsibility; many of these men travelled round the kingdom as the court moved with the peripatetic king, serving his needs and those of his companions. Drawing distinctions between public and private within the royal court can prove difficult. Servants in Æthelstan's entourage ministered domestically to the king's person, cared for his clothes, books and treasures and ensured that he and his entourage were fed, watered and mounted. Yet their roles also extended into the public spheres of formal ritual and ceremony and to serving the king's guests, from home and abroad. Æthelstan's court appears to have differed significantly from those of earlier West Saxon kings both in size and in composition. Witness-lists to a group of diplomas from the middle years of his reign suggest that Æthelstan surrounded himself in his councils with a huge retinue of followers, not just West Saxon bishops, ealdormen and thegns but magnates from the more remote parts of his realm and independent rulers from other parts of Britain who had submitted to his rule. So distinctive do these assemblies appear that Sir Frank Stenton argued they represented

[1] For discussion of the language of family and household, see David Herlihy, *Medieval Households* (Cambridge, MA and London 1985), 2–3 and 57 and Thomas Charles-Edwards, 'Kinship, Status and the Origins of the Hide', *Past and Present*, lvi (1972), 3–33.

a new kind of royal council. The small, intimate and informal type of council common in Wessex until Edward the Elder's reign had, he asserted, been replaced by 'national assemblies'.[2] Shedding further light on the kind of company Æthelstan chose to keep at court may enable us to speculate a little about the king if not as a private man, at least as social being.

THE ROYAL HOUSEHOLD

Wherever physically located, the king's household represented the centre of the kingdom. Comprising the personal staff who served his own needs and officials with more public roles (ranging from the supplying of properly equipped horses for the king and his companions, through the provision of food and shelter for all travelling with the king, to the copying of documents on the king's behalf) the household was the largely invisible machine that made the process of royal government possible and organized the king's private life, both at rest and at play. In this intimate sphere of the king's personal household, we should also expect to find priests. In the second half of the ninth century, priests became for a brief time exceptionally prominent at the West Saxon court, in a way not repeated until the mid-eleventh century.[3] Because of the central role they played in Alfred's educational reform priests such as the Mercians Æthelstan and Werwulf frequently attended on the king and appear in records of his court; we also have Asser's testimony to the presence of royal chaplains (*capellanos suos*) in Alfred's entourage.[4] Edward's continued promotion of his personal clergy may surprise us more, yet early in his reign at least four priests appear among the witnesses to his charters.[5] Given Æthelstan's demonstrable debts to his grandfather's example especially in matters of education and learning, we should anticipate that he, too, would have priests and other religious in his inner circle and that these men would have had a significant impact on the king's thought and action. Although two priests witnessed a charter issued on the day of his coronation, thereafter priests did not appear in the lengthy witness-lists attached to many of his charters; we should not, however, assume that priests were any less prominent at Æthelstan's court than they had been at his father's and grandfather's.[6]

---

[2] Stenton, *ASE*, 352.

[3] L.M. Larson, *The King's Household in England before the Norman Conquest* (Madison, WI, 1904), 138–9.

[4] Asser, ch. 77; compare S 348 and Dorothy Whitelock, 'Some Anglo-Saxon Charters in the Name of Alfred', in *Saints, Scholars, and Heroes*, ed. Margot H. King and Wesley M. Stevens, 2 vols (Collegeville, MN, 1979), I, 77–98, at 79–80.

[5] Keynes, *Atlas*, xxxiv; S. Keynes, 'Regenbald the Chancellor (*sic*)', *ANS*, x (1987), 189.

[6] The failure to mention priests in later witness-lists could reflect a shift in diplomatic practice rather than, as Larson suggested, that the court had been reorganized to make priests less significant: Larson, *The King's Household*, 139; Keynes, 'Regenbald', 189.

Much of our evidence for the movements of the court around Æthelstan's kingdom and for the composition of the royal household derives from documents relating to the king's land grants. Charters (diplomas) record a king's gift of land or privilege to his followers, religious or lay; as a permanent record, often preserved in a monastic archive, they were intended to survive beyond the lifetimes and frail memories of the men present at the original conveyance. For a biographer of an early medieval king, such texts shed useful light on their subject's perception of the nature of his own royal power, through the language used in the main text of the donation and in the witness-list.[7] Here we are more concerned with the information charters provide about aspects of government in practice, specifically about the identities of the royal officials who travelled around the realm with the king whom they served, and the composition of the king's council of leading men. Kings made grants to their followers in public at meetings of their council (the witan, or witenagemot); the text of the charter recording a grant included ranked lists of the names of those who attended the council and so witnessed and assented to the donation, starting with the king and progressing in order through the bishops and clergy, ealdormen and finally thegns, including some from the king's inner circle. Copyists preserving charters in monastic cartularies often abbreviated those witness-lists for reasons of space, but where longer lists of witnesses do survive these constitute our most important evidence for the political culture of a king's reign as well as for the composition of his court.

One of the earliest texts produced in Æthelstan's name soon after his accession – a manumission granting freedom to a slave called Eadhelm, preserved in a gospel book belonging to the king – included among its witnesses members of the king's own household (*se hired*), among them Ælfheah and Beornstan, both described as mass priests, and some other, possibly secular office-holders: the reeve Ælfric, a certain Wulfnoth (known as 'the white') and Eanstan, described as provost (*prafost*) which could relate to either an ecclesiastical or a secular office.[8] A lease datable to the first decade of Æthelstan's reign provides additional evidence for the composition of the king's immediate entourage. By this deed the *familia* of the New Minster leased land in Wiltshire to a thegn called Ælfred for his own life, and for two lifetimes thereafter. Eighty-three people witnessed the transaction, their names arranged in the manuscript (an apparently contemporaneous single sheet) into two distinct groups, most plausibly explained as the royal household (supplemented with some

---

[7] For Æthelstan's regnal styles see above, ch. 1 and below, ch. 8.

[8] BL, Royal MS 1 B. vii, fo 15v; *SEHD*, no. 19; trans. Keynes, 'Books', 185, n. 201; see also 189–90 and plate 6. Ælfheah also witnessed a charter granted to St Augustine's, Canterbury on the day of the king's coronation (4 September 925): S 394; S.E. Kelly, *Charters of St Augustine's Abbey* (Oxford, 1995), no. 26.

men at the king's court) and the community of the New Minster.[9] First the king attested, followed by his younger brother the ætheling Eadwine (described as *clito*),[10] and then Wærulf, *sacerdos* (probably the Werwulf brought from Mercia to King Alfred's court to assist in the educational reform). Other individuals in this first group have no epithet, apart from two deacons Wigferth and Eadhelm.[11] Some further names near the head of this list that attract our attention may belong to men of continental origin including Petrus (an unusual name in Anglo-Saxon England, probably the continental royal clerk and poet, author of *Carta dirige gressus*),[12] and three men Walter, Gundlaf and Hildewine, perhaps scholars visiting from Europe.

This lease offers a snapshot of part of the king's household and of his wider court at a moment (perhaps one before his conquest of Northumbria, since the royal style used for Æthelstan is 'king of the Anglo-Saxons and the Danes') when the king must have been at Winchester, given that the New Minster *familia* appeared among the witnesses.[13] It was not granted at a meeting of the king's council, however, for the witnesses include no bishops, not even the bishop of Winchester, or any ealdormen. The laymen who have epithets are all described as *minister* (thegn); we might want to identify the Wulfnoth and Ælfric who had witnessed the earlier manumission among these men also, for the list included the names of two men called Wulfnoth and six Ælfrics (but no Eanstan).

Since a king's personal entourage always accompanied him as he moved around his kingdom, those responsible for transport and for provisioning the extended household on its travels played prominent roles in the court circle. One passage in the earliest of the lives of St Dunstan refers to officials going ahead of the king's retinue in order to ensure that there would be sufficient provisions when the king arrived; occasionally the

---

[9] S 1417; Sean Miller, *Charters of the New Minster, Winchester* (Oxford, 2000), no. 9. For a more cautious reading see Keynes, *Liber Vitae*, 20–1.

[10] Barbara Yorke suggests that the draftsman of this lease thus meant to imply that Edwin was Æthelstan's heir, *cliton* being synonymous with *ætheling*: 'Æthelwold and the Politics of the Tenth Century', in *Bishop Æthelwold*, ed. Barbara Yorke (Woodbridge, 1988), 72–3.

[11] Simon Keynes suggested – *Liber Vitae*, 58, n. 67 – that the same hand which had added the name *Aeðelstan rex* to the *Liber vitae* of the community of St Cuthbert (perhaps on the occasion of Æthelstan's visit in 934: BL, MS Cotton Domitian A.vii, fo 15r) had also added the names of Eadhelm *diaconus* and Ealhhelm *diaconus* to a different folio (fo: 26r) and thus that these two deacons belonged also to the royal circle. *The Durham Liber Vitae: London, British Library, MS Cotton Domitian A.VII*, ed. David Rollason *et al.*, 3 vols (London, 2007), i, 91 and 108 (text) and for comments, critical of Keynes's reading, see 235 and 242.

[12] The poem *Carta dirige gressus* was written by Petrus and addressed to the royal court after the victory over the Northumbrians and submission of the Celtic rulers of Britain at Eamont in July 927. Dumville, *Wessex*, 159, Miller, *Charters*, 53, *contra* Lapidge, 'Poems', 92–3, who argued that Petrus belonged to the *familia* of the New Minster.

[13] Keynes, *Liber Vitae*, 21.

sources permit us to identify some of these post-holders.[14] A Deormod *cellerarius* (cellarer) appears in charters of Alfred and also some from early in the reign of Edward the Elder; he had to ensure an adequate supply of provisions for the court and all the assorted people who followed the royal entourage around the realm. Old English texts describe this office-holder as *hordere* (storekeeper) and from the tenth century as *discthegn*, i.e. seneschal or steward. In the law code issued at Grately in Hampshire (convention-ally numbered *II Æthelstan*), the king imposed penalties on those who acted as accessories to theft, singling out his reeves and his *horderas*, stewards, for special mention.[15] We know the name of one of Æthelstan's stewards who held this office at the start of his reign: Wulfhelm, *discifer regis*, who witnessed one of the earliest of the king's charters.[16]

A more dubious charter from Exeter's archive gave the epithet *discifer* to two thegns among the witnesses, 'Oddo' (Odda) and 'Helpine'.[17] Helpine does not appear in any other surviving document, but Odda attested Æthelstan's diplomas regularly, usually as the first of his thegns, suggesting that he, too, belonged to the king's immediate circle. Odda's name occurs also in an undated grant by which the king gave to the burgesses of the town at Malmesbury five hides near his royal vill at Norton in Wiltshire in gratitude for the townsmen's help in his struggle against the Danes. The burgesses apparently obtained their charter through the good offices of the king's standard-bearer (*Godwinus qui fert vexillum regis*), who witnessed the deed together with Wolsinus (Wulfsige), described as the king's chancellor (*cancellarius*), and Odo (Odda), his treasurer (*thesaurarius*).[18] This text is entirely spurious and such formal titles are anachronistic for the early tenth century; presumably it was concocted in the late thirteenth century when Malmesbury was first given borough status and the townsmen felt the lack of an early royal charter that would bolster their standing. The charter may thus preserve some older traditions about

[14] 'B', *Vita S Dunstani*, ch. 10, ed. W. Stubbs, *Memorials of St Dunstan* (London, 1874), 17–18. J. Campbell, 'Anglo-Saxon Courts' in *Court Culture in the Early Middle Ages*, ed. C. Cubitt (Turnhout, 2003), 158–9. A charter of Alfred's granting land in Wiltshire to one of his thegns, named three officials in the king's household with the jobs they performed; S 348: Deormod, *cellerarius*, Ælfric, *thesaurarius*, and Sigewulf, *pincerna*; Whitelock, 'Some Anglo-Saxon Charters', 78–82.

[15] S 348, 342, 352, 355; *II As*, 3.2; Keynes and Lapidge, *Alfred the Great*, (Hamondsworth, 1983) 330, n. 15; Larson, *The King's Household*, 133–4.

[16] S 396; Larson, 133. Wulfhelm probably also witnessed the related S 397, but that has only an abbreviated witness-list, stating after the names of the attesting bishops: *et ceteri. duces. ministri et discifer* (and other ealdormen, thegns and the steward); see E.E. Barker, 'Two Lost Documents of King Æthelstan', *ASE*, vi (1977), 138–41. We cannot know whether he had held the same office under Æthelstan's father.

[17] S 450.

[18] S 454; S.E. Kelly, *Charters of Malmesbury Abbey* (Oxford 2005), no. 48. The charter has no dating clause and so could have been issued at any time in the king's reign, unless the reference to a battle against the Danes is to be taken to refer to *Brunanburh*, in which case it would have to be dated after 937.

the history of the town, where Æthelstan and two of his cousins were buried.[19]

Although the name Godwine, given here to the man who carried the king's standard, was recorded nowhere among the witnesses to Æthelstan's genuine charters, the king may have had standard-bearers among his military thegns; another putative holder of this office, Leofsige *signifer*, appears among the witnesses to a rather dubious charter of Æthelstan's from Abingdon.[20] Bede recorded that the seventh-century Northumbrian king Edwin had a standard carried before him wherever he went, so the office is well attested in Anglo-Saxon England.[21] As well as Odda, whom we have already met, we may also have some confidence in Wulfsige; three thegns of that name attested Æthelstan's charters at different times, one of whom did so through most of the reign, rising to fourth place by 939.[22] Perhaps the later medieval confectors of Æthelstan's grant to Malmesbury found the names of these men in another charter of the king's in the abbey's archive.[23] Either Odda or Wulfsige might, if we ignore these anachronistic titles, have held the post that gave them responsibility at court for the care of the king's possessions and wardrobe.

At this period, the king's treasures were stored in his bedchamber, so one court functionary had responsibility both for what the king would wear and for the safe-keeping of his valuables, documents, books and relics as well as his money. In Latin this official was called the *thesaurarius*, literally his treasurer, but better translated as the keeper of the wardrobe; the Old English term was *hræglthegn*, rail-thegn, thus wardrobe-keeper.[24] By the end of the Anglo-Saxon period the *cancellarius* had a well defined role in the royal household, taking responsibility for the safe-keeping of the king's documents and probably also his relic collection and perhaps also running a royal writing office, yet we cannot easily trace that role back into the earlier tenth century. We first find men clearly given that ascription

---

[19] Kelly, *Charters of Malmesbury*, 292.

[20] S 404; S.E. Kelly, *Charters of Abingdon Abbey* (Oxford, 2000), I no. 22. The witness-list to that document is particularly suspicious and probably not contemporary with the date of the supposed grant (930); Leofsige did not witness any of the king's other charters.

[21] *HE*, ii, 16.

[22] Keynes, *Atlas*, table xxxix (2).

[23] Perhaps the spurious S 415 (Kelly, *Malmesbury*, no. 25) which was witnessed by both Odda and Wulfsige; neither the one genuine Æthelstan charter in Malmesbury's archive (S 434) nor the other spurious ones (S 435–6) list the names of the thegns who attested the grants. Kelly has suggested that these names could equally have come from a charter of King Edmund's reign attested by Archbishop Oda of Canterbury and Bishop Wulfsige of Sherborne: *Charters of Malmesbury*, 293. There are several such charters – S 486, 490, 493–5, 497, 505, 508, 1497 – but none is preserved at Malmesbury.

[24] S 348 mentions an Ælfric, *thesaurarius*; compare also S 1445, where the same Ælfric is described as *hrælthegn*.

only in the reign of Edward the Confessor.[25] At least at the start of his reign, Æthelstan's already celebrated relic collection was apparently looked after separately from the rest of his possessions by his mass-priests, Ælfheah and Beornstan.[26]

A large and unwieldy institution with an ever-shifting membership, a royal household had to be sheltered, fed and watered as it made its cumbersome way around the king's realm, following his chosen itinerary. Since Æthelstan had neither wife nor children of his own, his court lacked the central domestic, familial focus that had characterized the courts of his father and grandfather and indeed that of his uncle and aunt in Mercia. But this did not make his court circle arid and impersonal, or the king an isolated and solitary figure within it. Æthelstan spent his time in the company of a small group of officials, a strong male fellowship, tied formally by bonds of loyalty and service to the lord their king and strengthened by the camaraderie that unites any group engaged over time in a shared endeavour and living constantly in close proximity. Odda, Wulfsige and Wulfhelm remain shadowy figures, but they and others whose names occur frequently near the top of the witness-lists, including Ælfric, Eadmund and Wulfgar, were the men consistently closest to the king. They had important duties on formal court occasions including major religious festivals, during meetings of the king's council, or when the court entertained foreign embassies. Yet to Æthelstan the man, their companionship will have mattered more in the daily routine of normal court life.

In this circle the king ate and drank, went riding, hunting and hawking and practised his sword skills. On dark, wet evenings he played dice and board games with them, listened to the harpist and shared the telling of stories, while his thegns mended and polished his armour and riding gear. Because of the proximity in which they lived, his men would perforce have had to share the king's enjoyment of poetry.[27] They would have learned to affect an interest in religious writings and narratives about the saints whose bones he loved to collect, even if such enthusiasm came less naturally to them than to their leader. Historians have focused on the famous members of Æthelstan's circle, the Welsh rulers who travelled in his retinue after their submission to his authority; the children of kings and princes and the boys who would one day become kings themselves whom Æthelstan fostered; or the future abbots such as Æthelwold and Dunstan who also spent time in this environment. The latter's recollections in maturity of his time at Æthelstan's court, for example his recounting of the tale he first heard there about the martyrdom of Edmund of East Anglia, offer

[25] Keynes, *Diplomas*, 145–53; Keynes, 'Regenbald'; and more generally H.R. Loyn, *The Governance of Anglo-Saxon England 500–1087* (London, 1984), 108–10.

[26] *SEHD*, no. 19; Keynes, 'Books', 143–4 and 185–9.

[27] We explore the king's interest in poetry in the next chapter, and will also discuss there a manuscript page illustrating how to play 'Gospel Dice', below 104–8.

some insight into this society,[28] yet we should not underestimate the depth of the king's own friendships. While abbots and princes came and went from his court, thegns like Odda and Wulfgar showed Æthelstan great personal loyalty, remaining in their king's service throughout his reign.[29]

Others in Æthelstan's household who remain anonymous fulfilled equally important roles in keeping the royal administration, and thus the government of the realm, functioning. The royal household provided permanent employment in three key areas: the production of written instruments (on behalf of the king in a personal as well as in a public capacity); the control of the financial affairs of the crown and hence the whole kingdom; and the administration of justice.[30] Each of these spheres of activity would become markedly more sophisticated during the later Anglo-Saxon period, to such a degree that some have written of the agencies of an Anglo-Saxon 'state'.[31] Æthelstan's reign generally predates these developments, but in one area of court activity we see inovations that appear to have laid the foundations for later developments: the centralization of document production. It may be that among his more specialized court officials were those charged with the production and preservation of documents.

A royal writing office?

Anglo-Saxon kings had long recognized the potential benefits provided by the use of the written word and capitalized on the availability within the Church of men with the linguistic education and scribal skill to create documents or write letters on their behalf. Æthelwulf, King Alfred's father, had a *secretarius* called Felix, and Alfred's court included a number of clergy, some of them brought there specifically to assist him in his programme of translations as part of his wider educational reform. These men and the royal priests of Alfred's household could all produce formal documents on the king's behalf if required, but so few genuine charters survive in Alfred's name that we can say little about the mode of their production. In his time, as in earlier periods, ecclesiastical beneficiaries of land grants played a key role in the production as well as the preservation

---

[28] Abbo of Fleury, *Passio S Eadmundi*, prologue, ed. Michael Winterbottom, *Three Lives of English Saints* (Toronto, 1972), 67.

[29] The same loyalty may have passed to their descendants also; the tenth chapter of the code conventionally known as *VI Æthelstan* reports pledges given to the archbishop at Thunderfield when Ælfheah Stybb and Brihtnoth the son of Odda attended the assembly at the request of the king; one wonders if this was the son of the king's thegn Odda: *VI As*, 10.

[30] Loyn, *The Governance*, 106.

[31] See for example the essays collected in James Campbell, *The Anglo-Saxon State* (London, 2000); and Patrick Wormald, 'Giving God and the King their Due: Conflict and its Regulation in the Early English State', *Settimane di Studio del Centro Italiano di Studi sull'Alto Medioevo*, xliv (Spoleto, 1997), 549–90.

of the documents recording those grants: royal charters.[32] Æthelstan's reign appears to mark a substantial departure from earlier practice, reflecting a centralization of charter production under more direct royal control. If the monastic life did, as many contemporary commentators suggested, fall into abeyance in the latter years of the ninth century, by the 920s few functioning minsters would have remained in southern England equipped with scriptoria and scribes capable of producing correspondence and royal documents.[33] A new system may have developed in Æthelstan's time out of necessity, therefore, rather than as a result of a deliberate policy to effect change. The centralized production of these diplomas makes them a particularly fruitful source for the study of government in his day.[34]

Between 928 and 935 one person (conventionally identified with a scribe responsible for two of the king's surviving single-sheet originals and known as 'Æthelstan A') apparently took over the drafting of all of the king's diplomas. The documents associated with this man conform to a distinctive model, using standardized formulas and a vivid linguistic style that owed much to the example of Aldhelm. Each has a remarkably detailed dating clause, and each indicates further the place where the council met to make the grant recorded, as well as supplying a witness-list of unusual length.[35] Clearly, one central agency had responsibility for the drafting and copying of charters in this period: the uniformity of these texts – the visible control exercised by one person over their form, language and layout on the manuscript page – points to the work of a single agency.[36] Quite what sort of organization the king might have

---

[32] F.M. Stenton, *Latin Charters of the Anglo-Saxon Period* (Oxford, 1955), 47–8; Susan Kelly, 'Anglo-Saxon Lay Society and the Written Word', in *The Uses of Literacy in Early Mediaeval Europe*, ed. Rosamond McKitterick (Cambridge, 1990), 43–5; Keynes, 'The West Saxon Charters of King Æthelwulf and his Sons', *EHR*, cix (1994), 1134–41; Keynes, 'Regenbald', 185–6.

[33] Sarah Foot, *Monastic Life in Anglo-Saxon England, c.600–900* (Cambridge, 2006), ch. 8.

[34] Keynes, *Diplomas*, 39–44; Keynes, 'England c.900–1016', in *NCMH III*, ed. Timothy Reuter (Cambridge, 1999), 469–70. Simon Keynes has made a detailed study of Æthelstan's charters and is currently preparing a book on tenth-century Anglo-Saxon charters; the discussion that follows owes much to numerous lively conversations with Professor Keynes on this topic. See also, Henry Loyn, 'Wales and England in the Tenth Century: the Context of the Æthelstan Charters', *Welsh History Review*, x (1980–1), 283–301; reprinted in his *Society and Peoples* (London, 1992), 185–90.

[35] The two originals are S 416 and 425, see Kelly, *Charters of Shaftesbury*, 32–3; Keynes, *Diplomas*, 44.

[36] Although they are conventionally treated as a homogeneous unit, Simon Keynes has demonstrated that they fall into four discrete groups: I, a pair from April 928: S400 and 399; II, a pair issued in April 930: S 403 and 405; thirdly, a larger group drawn up between March 931 and January 933, characterized by the use of an introductory paragraph (proem) beginning 'Flebilia fortiter detestanda'; and, fourthly, a group dated between May 934 and December 935 that all share a proem beginning 'Fortuna fallentis seculi'.

employed remains a matter of dispute. 'Æthelstan A' may have served as one of the first members of a royal writing office responsible for the production of the king's charters;[37] alternatively, he might have worked as a scribe attached to a monastic or episcopal scriptorium, only sometimes producing formal documents for the king.[38]

'Æthelstan A' charters stand out from earlier surviving royal diplomas, yet this one man's domination of royal charter-writing over a seven-year period does not alone constitute evidence for the existence of an early royal writing office. Although we can scarcely avoid the presumption that 'Æthelstan A' worked for at least some of this period as a king's scribe, we might perhaps better see him as *the* king's scribe. Perhaps he ran a solitary fiefdom, using his monopoly of the skills required to take sole control of the diplomatic output of the royal council, rather than supervising the work of a larger group of notaries. His apparent failure to delegate any of his burdensome responsibility becomes abundantly obvious when, for whatever reason, he gave up the role; for those who took over from 'Æthelstan A' show no signs of having learned at his side. Charters produced for Æthelstan from 935 onwards revert to a markedly more straightforward diplomatic form that owes more to earlier practice than to the elaborate detail of the 'Æthelstan A' texts.[39] We may get a hint of the scribe's identity from the fact that, in most of the documents produced by 'Æthelstan A', Ælfwine (also known as Ælle) bishop of Lichfield heads the list of witnessing bishops, even though his seniority within the episcopate did not justify so high a rank; perhaps he, or a member of his cathedral chapter, had some role to play in their production.[40] Another bishop, Cenwald of Worcester has been associated with a later group of Æthelstan's charters produced between 935 and the end of his reign. Whether we can go further and see any significance in this apparent 'Mercian' influence over the king's charter production throughout his reign is less clear.[41]

---

[37] R. Drögereit, 'Gab es eine angelsächsische Königskanzlei?', *Archiv für Urkundenforschung*, xiii (1935), 335–436; Keynes, *Diplomas*, 43–4 and 'England, c.900–1016', 470. See also Stenton, *ASE*, 353–4.

[38] Chaplais hesitated to associate 'Æthelstan A' directly with the Winchester scriptorium, but did observe similarities between his hand and the style of that house. That his texts sometimes mixed vernacular dialects and adopted a number of Kentish forms led him to wonder if 'Æthelstan A' were of foreign extraction but worked in Christ Church, Canterbury: 'The Royal Anglo-Saxon "Chancery" of the Tenth Century Revisited', in *Studies in Medieval History presented to R.H.C. Davis*, ed. Henry Mayr-Harting and R.I. Moore (London and Ronceverte, 1985), 47–9.

[39] There seems to have been some overlap between 'Æthelstan A' and his successors in 935, in which year charters in both styles were issued: S 434, 458 are Æthelstan A products, but S 430 and 429 are the work of a different draftsman.

[40] S.E. Kelly, *Charters of St Paul's London* (Oxford, 2004), 160.

[41] Keynes, 'Books', 157–9; P.H. Sawyer, *Charters of Burton Abbey* (Oxford, 1979), xlvii–xlix. Keynes, *Liber Vitae*, 22.

While 'Æthelstan A' had responsibility for producing the king's charters he would have had to travel with the king to the places where the royal council met, presumably doing so as a member of the king's immediate household. Whether he, let alone those who followed him, worked exclusively in Æthelstan's service remains uncertain; nor can we state confidently whether he joined (or created *de novo*) a formal royal writing office at the king's court, or if he worked largely alone. Yet this scribe's work is invaluable for the information his texts provide about the king's progress around his realm.

CORONATION

Æthelstan's movements in the months immediately after his accession to his father's realm point to the insecurity of his hold on power at the start of his reign and the need for him to build support among the West Saxon nobility. The rapidity with which Ælfweard's death followed his father's removed, at least for a while, the risk of sibling rivalry over the throne of Wessex, but it did not seem to bring the West Saxon counsellors round swiftly to accepting Æthelstan as king over them as well as the Mercians. The delay between Ælfweard's death in August 924 and Æthelstan's consecration at Kingston-upon-Thames on 4 September 925 might therefore have been significant. If he had to spend time winning round those magnates who had preferred his half-brother we might suspect that the young king's position remained insecure during that first year.[42]

Certainly during 925, Æthelstan behaved as a Mercian rather than as an 'Anglo-Saxon' king. Calling himself *rex Anglorum*, he gave one of his thegns Eadric land in Derbyshire, creating a new charter to replace an earlier 'book of inheritance' now lost. An enigmatic reference in that text to the king's 'investigating the matter of discussed obedience brought to notice by the careful sagacity of my faithful men', may suggest that a formal assembly had debated the succession rather than straightforwardly recognizing Æthelstan's right to rule. Only Mercian bishops witnessed this grant (the bishops of Lichfield, Dorchester, Worcester and Hereford) and the one abbot named was abbot of Evesham. Even though by this time already de facto king of Wessex (if not yet crowned), Æthelstan either could not, or chose not to involve the West Saxon bishops in confirming this grant.[43] The

---

[42] Keynes, 'Books', 187. George Garnett has noted, however, that significant intervals not infrequently separated an Anglo-Saxon king's constitutive royal accession from his coronation: 'Coronation and Propaganda: Some Implications of the Norman Claim to the Throne of England in 1066', *TRHS*, 5th ser. xxxvi (1986), 92.

[43] S 395 (preserved at Burton-on-Trent); Alfred P. Smyth, *King Alfred the Great* (Oxford, 1995), 439; see also Ann Williams, 'Some Notes and Considerations on Problems connected with the English Royal Succession 860–1066', *ANS*, i (1978), 144–67, at 151; but note that Williams dated this grant to 931. Discussed by Robinson, *TSD*, 42–5 and 49, where he suggested that this grant was made at a royal council held at Tamworth, the ancient Mercian capital. Also Keynes, *Liber Vitae*, pp. 19–20.

events surrounding Æthelstan's ultimate succession to the whole of his father's kingdom suggest that the Mercians evinced markedly greater enthusiasm for Edward's eldest son than did the West Saxons. Since in some West Saxon circles, particularly in Winchester, Æthelstan remained far from popular, he may not have held on to many of the key court officials who had served his father, but rather have needed to build up his own core of loyal servants, starting with those who had known him well during his time in Mercia.[44]

Æthelstan chose Kingston in Surrey as the site for his coronation, a place that lay symbolically on the River Thames at the border between the old kingdoms of Mercia and Wessex and the point where the Thames became tidal; an important church synod had met here in 838.[45] Later tenth-century kings also elected to be crowned here, but Æthelstan inaugurated the practice.[46] Quite apart from the presence of a party opposed to Æthelstan personally in the city, Winchester lay too far south and probably resonated unduly with memories of the West Saxon royal family to be suitable for a ceremony that would seal the unification of the historic kingdoms of Wessex and Mercia under a single crown. Alfred and Edward the Elder had acquired direct rule over Mercia through a combination of political circumstance and military conquest, and both had used the regnal style 'king of the Anglo-Saxons' to reflect their rulership over two peoples, but neither was inaugurated to that joint kingship at the start of his reign. Without speculating unduly about the extent of antipathy to his rule at Winchester, we can acknowledge the political significance of the choice of Kingston as a site for an inauguration ritual and recognize its reconciliatory potential.

Only the Mercian Register recorded Æthelstan's consecration at Kingston, adding that fact to its longer statement about the deaths of Edward and Ælfweard and the Mercians' choice of Æthelstan as king.[47] The much briefer notice in the West Saxon manuscript of the Chronicle

---

[44] Keynes, *Liber Vitae*, 20–22; see above ch. 2, for the rebellion of Alfred.

[45] J. Armitage Robinson, *The Saxon Bishops of Wells. A Historical Study in the Tenth Century* (London, 1918); 31–3; John Blair, *Early Medieval Surrey: Land Holding, Church and Settlement before 1300* (Stroud, 1991), 99. Julia Barrow, 'Chester's Earliest Regatta? Edgar's Dee-Rowing Re-visited', *EME*, x (2001), 85 and 87. See plate 5.

[46] It is not certain where Edward the Elder's inauguration on 8 June 900 took place; a twelfth-century chronicler, Ralph de Diceto (archdeacon of Middlesex and later dean of St Paul's, London, d. 1199/1200) located it at Kingston, but this could just have been surmise on his part, following the practice of later tenth-century kings. Edward might well have held the ceremony at Winchester. Since, as I argue below, I consider the second Anglo-Saxon coronation *ordo* (which introduced a crown for the first time into English king-making), to have been first used for Æthelstan, Edward would have been invested in 900 not with a crown but a helmet. After Æthelstan, Eadred (16 August 946) and Æthelred (4 May 979) were certainly crowned at Kingston and Edmund and Eadwig may have been: Keynes, *Diplomas*, 270–1.

[47] MR, *s.a.* 924; quoted above 38. This entry is found also in the BC and D manuscripts of the Anglo-Saxon Chronicle.

said only that Æthelstan succeeded to the kingdom after his father's death. West Saxon regnal lists attributed a rule of fourteen years, seven weeks and three days to Æthelstan, arriving at that calculation by counting from his coronation on 4 September 925 to his death on 27 October 939.[48] A charter of Æthelstan's confirms the date. This unusual text, closer in form to a memorandum of a gift than to a genuine charter, states that on 4 September 925, on the day of his consecration, the king – termed *rex Saxonum et Anglorum*, king of the Saxons and the Angles – restored fourteen hides of land at Thanet to St Augustine's, Canterbury.[49] Witnesses included the archbishop of Canterbury Athelm (for Æthelhelm) and seven other bishops; significantly the bishop of Winchester, Frithestan, chose to absent himself. The surviving text probably derives from a genuine contemporary record, perhaps one entered into a gospel book on the day of Æthelstan's coronation.[50]

Having struggled against familial and aristocratic obstacles to get to the point of his consecration, Æthelstan – with the support of his archbishop of Canterbury, Æthelhelm – chose to have his eventual consecration blessed with a new coronation ritual. The extended interval between Æthelstan's presumed assumption of the kingship of the whole realm after his brother's death late in the summer of 924 and the day of his coronation in September 925 presented an opportunity for crafting a fresh liturgical ceremony for the consecration of the new king in office. Designed to articulate a message of unity, this liturgy sought also to reduce the political tensions that had characterized the period since Edward the Elder's death. A new ritual provided the means for making important statements about the king's understanding of his power and responsibilities and for showing his uneasily united flock a novel conception of a single realm made up of two peoples.

The second Anglo-Saxon coronation *ordo* survives in no manuscript dating from earlier than the late tenth century, and scholars have long debated whether this rite was used first for Æthelstan in 925 or rather earlier, for the consecration of Edward the Elder and his queen, Ælfflæd. For this *ordo*, unlike the first English form in use from at least the mid-ninth century onwards, supplies a rite for consecrating a queen as well as the king.

[48] David Dumville, 'The West Saxon Genealogical Regnal List: Manuscripts and Texts', *Anglia*, civ (1986), 29.

[49] S 394; Kelly, *Charters of St Augustine's*, no. 26. Two charters of Æthelstan dated 16 April 928 (S 399 and 400) were dated to the third year of the king's reign, suggesting that the start of his rule was reckoned after 16 April 925 (Kelly, 100).

[50] Kelly, 100–1; Lapidge, 'Poems', 77, n. 74 suggested that the charter might have been drafted by a continental (perhaps an Old Saxon) scribe resident in England, since the king's name appears in the form Adalstan. For Archbishop Æthelhelm see Nicholas Brooks, *The Early History of the Church of Canterbury: Christ Church 597–1066* (Leicester, 1984), 214–16; Robinson, *Saxon Bishops*, 30–3. Adelard of Ghent reported that Archbishop Æthelhelm performed Æthelstan's coronation in his Life of Dunstan, ed. W. Stubbs, *Memorials of Saint Dunstan*, Rolls Series 63 (London, 1874), 55–6.

Revisiting the question recently, Janet Nelson has made a cogent case for the later date and for seeing Æthelhelm, the archbishop of Canterbury, as responsible if not for the composition of the *ordo*, then for organizing its compilation from a combination of English and Frankish sources.[51] That Æthelstan had no queen in 925 need not detract from this argument. Edward's decision to make his second wife his queen had radically – and permanently – altered the status of the king's wife at the West Saxon royal court, a state of affairs that would thereafter require liturgical recognition even if those prayers did not prove necessary on the occasion when the *ordo* was first used.[52] Part of Nelson's argument for dating the new *ordo* to the early 920s lies in the structure of the prayer of consecration and the wording of various new passages inserted into the form used previously; these appear to her judicious insertions reflecting Æthelstan's particular circumstances as a king of a united realm, elected 'on a Mercian ticket'.[53] In this context, she has argued, the repeated reference in the consecration prayer to the king's election to rule two peoples and the added words stressing that he ruled both those peoples together appear especially meaningful. The phrase about 'establishing and governing the apex of paternal glory unitedly, also makes sense in this context, evoking the intra-dynastic conflict that had delayed Æthelstan's election in Wessex'; resolution of that dispute would ensure the realm's future stability.[54]

Other innovations in the *ordo* have equal significance. Instead of vesting the new king with helmet, the second English *ordo* followed contemporary continental practice in having the anointed king crowned and given as symbols of his office a ring, a sword, a sceptre and a rod. The new prayer 'Omnipotens sempiterne Deus', based on a ninth-century Carolingian model pronounced just before the king's anointing, appealed to God to endow the new king with the qualities of Abraham (faithfulness), Moses (meekness), Joshua (fortitude), David (humility), and Solomon (wisdom). In its appeal to the living example of Old Testament kings the prayer evoked memories of King Alfred's court.[55] Sliding over recent, highly charged memories of disagreement between the political elites of Wessex and

---

[51] Janet L. Nelson, 'The First Use of the Second Anglo-Saxon *Ordo*', in *Myth, Rulership, Church and Charters*, ed. Julia Barrow and Andrew Wareham (Aldershot, 2008).

[52] On the wider issue of king's wives see Pauline Stafford, 'The King's Wife in Wessex, 800–1066', *Past and Present*, xci (1981), 3–27; and for Edward's marriage, Barbara Yorke, 'Edward as Ætheling', in H&H, 33–4.

[53] Nelson, 'First Use', 124, quoting Wormald, *MEL*, 447, n. 114.

[54] Nelson, 'First Use', 124.

[55] 'Second Anglo-Saxon coronation *ordo*', in *The Sacramentary of Ratoldus (Paris, Bibliothèque Nationale de France, lat. 12052*, ed. Nicholas Orchard (Cranbrook, 2005), ch. xxvi, p. 49. For the Alfredian connections see Richard Abels, 'Royal Succession and the Growth of Political Stability', *Haskins Society Journal*, xii (2002), 96; S. Keynes, 'Edward, King of the Anglo-Saxons', H&H, 49; David Pratt, *The Political Thought of Alfred the Great* (Cambridge, 2007), 75–8.

Mercia, the ceremony united the disparate factions by calling to mind their shared recollection of the wise and successful king who had first brought the *Angelcynn* together under a single authority.

Then the archbishop gave the king a ring, marking his acceptance of his responsibility to support the true faith, and a sword with which mercifully to help 'widows and orphans and restore things left desolated'. A sceptre was for him to defend the holy Church and Christian people committed to him; the rod so that he might 'understand how to soothe the righteous and terrify the reprobate, and teach the right way to those who stray, and stretch forth a hand to those who have fallen'. Prayers were said for his virtuous leadership, his victory over all his enemies.[56] The king was then enthroned and the archbishop prayed that he would 'hold fast the state which you have held by paternal suggestion . . .; remember to show honour to the clergy in due places, so that the mediator between God and men may strengthen you as mediator between clergy and people in the throne of this kingdom'.[57] An indication of the significance of Æthelstan's new regalia, especially his decision to wear a crown not a helmet, comes in the depiction of the king wearing his crown in both of his two contemporary manuscript portraits. Æthelstan further redesigned his coinage in the 930s, implementing a style that bore his crowned head and so disseminating his image to the widest possible audience.[58] This solemn ceremony thus involved a public acclamation of the king, his blessing and anointing with holy oil, the bestowal and blessing of these various new symbols of royal power – a ring, a sword, a crown, a sceptre and a rod – his enthronement and repeated acclamation. Visually it must have made an impressive spectacle for all able to get close enough to see the events unfold. The symbolism of a rite that set the new king on the throne of the Angles and the Saxons and included prayers that he be supported by the subjection of both peoples will not have escaped Æthelstan or his advisers.[59] The king's attitude to his newly united realm was reflected in his movements around his domain.

AN ITINERANT COURT

Early medieval Anglo-Saxon courts were, like their Carolingian and Ottonian equivalents, peripatetic.[60] Kings travelled widely and regularly over the entirety of their realms, mostly staying at royal vills, where they

---

[56] *The Sacramentary*, §§139–51, ed. Orchard, 50–2; Nelson, 'First Use', 125.

[57] 'Sta et retine', *The Sacramentary*, §154, p. 54; cf. Nelson, 'First Use', 125.

[58] See below, 216–19.

[59] *Sacramentary*, ed. Orchard, cxxix–cxxx. The new *ordo* is discussed in further detail below, ch. 4. For Æthelstan's depiction wearing a crown on his coins and manuscripts, see further below, 216–23.

[60] Disentangling the history of Anglo-Saxon royal courts remains very difficult: Campbell, 'Anglo-Saxon Courts', 155. Compare Frank Barlow: 'we know nothing about the ceremonial of the king's court, little about its staff and not much about its work. Its

ate their food-rents and tried to keep an eye on loyal (or not so loyal)
nobles and sub-kings in their own localities. Festal assemblies had historically met regularly at Christmas and Easter; Æthelstan introduced a
further such meeting at Whitsun, creating a regular pattern that would
persist into the twelfth century.[61] The royal itinerary combined the
symbolic with the practical; a king could assert his sacred, royal nature in
person while simultaneously performing useful political and judicial functions as judge, law-maker or generous donor (to secular as well as ecclesiastical beneficiaries).[62] While the royal *iter* (journey) played a key role in
maintaining a king's authority throughout his realm, most kings, in fact,
had their personal preferences among their various royal residences,
places that they visited more often than any other or where they regularly
celebrated key festivals every year. In Wessex, Winchester had a long
history not just as the seat of a bishopric from AD 660, but also as a traditional and ceremonial centre; it probably served as the site of one of the
seasonal residences of the itinerant West Saxon kings from the late seventh
century, if not before. During the reigns of King Alfred and Edward the
Elder Winchester became a more significant place in Wessex, growing in
military and economic importance and acquiring new monastic foundations with close royal links.[63] Many of Edward the Elder's charters
reflected his close association with Winchester, a town of central importance in the West Saxon polity; writing in the later tenth century
Æthelweard called it a royal city (*urbs regia*). Even if the court spent
increasing amounts of time there, especially in Edward the Elder's day,
this did not make Winchester the 'capital' of Wessex, or of the expanded
English realm. It remained just one of the West Saxon king's many royal
residences, albeit apparently a favourite one for the family in death as well
as in life.[64] Æthelstan did not, however, share his father's preference. His
difficult relationship with some factions in Winchester may in part have

organization, therefore, is a teasing problem', *The English Church 1000–1066* (London,
2nd edn, 1979), 119. The most comprehensive discussion remains Larson, *The King's
Household*.

[61] J.R. Maddicott, *The Origins of the English Parliament 924–1327* (Oxford, 2010) 12.

[62] John Bernhardt, *Itinerant Kingship and Royal Monasteries in Early Medieval Germany,
c.936–1075* (Cambridge, 1993), 48–9.

[63] Martin Biddle, 'Winchester: the Development of an Early Capital', in *Vor- und
Frühformen der europäischen Stadt im Mittelalter*, ed. Herbert Jankuhn et al. (Göttingen, 1973),
229–61, at 248–50. Martin Biddle, 'The Study of Winchester: Archaeology and History in
a British Town, 1961–1983', *Proceedings of the British Academy*, lxix (1983), 119–21.

[64] King Alfred, his wife Ealhswith, his sons Edward and Æthelweard as well as
Edward's second son, Æthelstan's rival Ælfweard, were all buried at Winchester in the
New Minster, which Edward and his mother founded in 901: S 365, 366, 1443. That
Winchester was coming to be thought of as a burial place for kings is further shown by the
fact that Alfred's father Æthelwulf's body, originally buried at Steyning in Sussex, had
been moved to Winchester by the end of the ninth century: Keynes, *Liber Vitae*, 16.
For the Winchester complexion of Edward's charters, see Keynes, 'West Saxon Charters',
1141–7.

accounted for his seldom spending time there, preferring to stay elsewhere, especially during the earlier part of his reign.

Earlier Anglo-Saxon kings who ruled small kingdoms perhaps no larger than a modern English county found it easy to traverse their realms keeping a close eye on affairs throughout their territory; the larger the kingdom, the more they had to delegate local matters to men on the ground. As the early eleventh-century homilist Ælfric explained,

> historians who write about kings tell us that ancient kings in former times considered how they might alleviate their burdens, because a single man cannot be everywhere and sustain all things at once, although he might have sole authority. Then the kings appointed ealdormen under them, as support for themselves, and they often sent them to many battles. . .[65]

Councils provided one mechanism for a king to remind his ealdormen in whose name they governed their own localities. Rather than meeting in one fixed, central court, councils assembled in different towns and vills across a king's realm. Considering that after his conquest of Northumbria Æthelstan ruled a territory of greater geographical extent and racial complexity than that held by any of his West Saxon predecessors, we might expect to find him regularly convening councils in the north and east of his realm. Yet the surviving documentary evidence appears to suggest that the king adopted a rather surprising solution to control over the regions.

Æthelstan's charters show him to have stayed predominantly in southern England and largely within the bounds of the old kingdom of Wessex, making his distant new subjects come to him.[66] The sources allow us to state confidently that the king travelled north of the Thames on only a few occasions: in 926 (to Tamworth for his sister's marriage to Sihtric) and in the same year to Abingdon (where, according to William of Malmesbury, he received an embassy on behalf of Hugh, duke of the Franks, to arrange his marriage to the king's sister, Eadhild); in 927 (to secure his hold on York and receive the submission at Eamont); in 934 (the Scottish expedition, on which occasion he stopped at Nottingham, probably visited the churches of Ripon, Beverley and Chester-le-Street and, on his way back, stopped in Buckingham); perhaps again to York in 936 (where, according to the Frankish annalist Flodoard of Rheims he received a second embassy from his brother-in-law Duke Hugh); and in 937 (to the site of the battle of *Brunanburh*). Otherwise he performed acts that left a trace in the written record only within Wessex, apart from an

---

[65] Ælfric, 'Wyrdwriteras us secgað', ed. J.C. Pope, *Homilies of Ælfric: a Supplementary Collection*, 2 vols, EETS (1967–8), ii, 728 (no. 22); trans. Loyn, *The Governance*, 101.

[66] Stenton, *ASE*, 351; Maddicott, *The Origins*, 16.

undatable occasion mentioned in legal provisions issued by the London peace guild when the king apparently addressed his council at Whittlebury in Northamptonshire on the subject of the capital punishment of juveniles, and visits to Colchester in Essex in March 931, to Cirencester in 935, and to Gloucester in October 939, where he died.

Witness-lists of Anglo-Saxon royal charters from the tenth and eleventh centuries give some indication, as has long been recognized, of who attended a king's assemblies.[67] In the case of the sequence of charters produced by 'Æthelstan A', we have not just unusually lengthy lists of the names of those who witnessed the king's grants but, even more unusually, a statement about precisely when and where each meeting of the king's council took place.[68] From this information we can determine something about the king's movements around his realm during the seven years when this one man had charge of creating diplomas in his name. Even this exceptionally detailed material is too patchy for it to prove possible to create a detailed itinerary of Æthelstan's movements during those years, still less for the rest of his reign. We should recall that information about where the king convened a council of which some written record has survived tells us nothing about his movements before or after that meeting, nor does it allow us to speculate about where he might have gathered his council together on other occasions for which no records now remain. It is equally impossible to guess how widely he might have ranged over his whole territory with only a small group of immediate companions around him; for most of the time we have no idea where Æthelstan was on any given day, or even in any particular month.

Æthelstan's early years

In the period before Easter 928 we can locate Æthelstan in a specific place on only a handful of occasions. We know that he was crowned at Kingston-upon-Thames in Surrey on 4 September 925 and that he went into Mercia early in the following year to arrange his sister's marriage to

[67] Charles Insley, 'Assemblies and Charters in Late Anglo-Saxon England', in *Political Assemblies in the Earlier Middle Ages*, ed. P.S. Barnwell and Marco Mostert (Turnhout, 2003), 51; compare Simon Keynes's close analysis of the huge body of charters issued in 956, on which basis a number of generalizations about the workings of the royal court can be made: *Diplomas*, 125–34.

[68] This discussion draws heavily on Simon Keynes's work on Æthelstan's charters; I have followed his lead and elected for the most part only to discuss the evidence of the king's authentic charters. Several of the dubious charters that survive in his name seem to have been forged on the basis of genuine instruments he issued, borrowing often witness-lists and the characteristic 'Æthelstan A' statements about when and where they were granted, but to include these in this discussion would be seriously to complicate the issue. Most charter witness-lists probably record only a proportion of the names of those who were present but, as already suggested, so large are the lists attached to the charters of 'Æthelstan A' that one has to wonder if these represent a fuller picture than normal.

the king of York. Where between those two events he spent his first Christmas as king we cannot say. Winchester had been one of his father's preferred residences, but Æthelstan would scarcely have chosen to spend the feast in the town most closely associated with opposition to his rule. On the other hand his advisers will probably have urged against a return to a favourite Mercian royal vill, recommending rather, on grounds of political expediency, that he look towards a West Saxon royal estate with good hunting.[69] In the New Year Æthelstan went north into Mercia, taking his sister with him to Tamworth in order to celebrate her marriage to the Danish king of Northumbria, Sihtric on 30 January 926.[70] In addition to the king's immediate court circle, other leading men from across the realm would have been invited to share in the marriage feast. Two apparently authentic and closely related charters survive from that same year, one from Abingdon's archive, the other from that of Burton upon Trent in Derbyshire, but neither indicates where the council in question took place. Those present included the archbishop of Canterbury and eight bishops of southern and midland sees (although interestingly the bishop of Winchester was again absent), four ealdormen and the king's *discifer* (Wulfhelm), together with eight of the king's thegns. Although the king could have made these grants while he and his council were at Tamworth for the wedding, especially since both charters relate to lands in the midlands formerly bought from the pagans, both could equally have been confirmed at a royal council meeting in Wessex later in the year.[71]

The year 927 marked Æthelstan's annexation of the kingdom of Northumbria on the death of his brother-in-law, Sihtric. Narrative sources tell only of the subsequent submission of the other rulers in Britain in July, but we might assume that the king secured his hold on the north by making a symbolic entry into the capital at York once he had disposed of his potential Danish rivals.[72] On 12 July the British rulers came to the king at Eamont, near Penrith, gave him oaths and established peace.[73] According to William of Malmesbury the king went straight from there to Hereford, where the Welsh submitted to him and agreed to pay him tribute. Afterwards, again according to William, he went on to the south-west, driving the 'Western Britons called the Cornish' out of Exeter, a city

---

[69] Perhaps one of the royal estates in the south-east mentioned in Alfred's will, or conceivably somewhere such as Bickleigh in Devon where Edward the Elder had visited his hunting lodge in 904: S 372 and 1286; Peter Sawyer, 'The Royal *tun* in Pre-Conquest England', in *Ideal and Reality*, ed. P. Wormald *et al.* (Oxford, 1983), 298–9. Æthelstan's liking for hunting is reflected in the tribute he imposed on the Welsh after their submission in 927, which according to William of Malmesbury included 'hounds that with their keen scent could track down the lairs and lurking places of wild beasts, and birds of prey skilled in pursuing other birds through empty air': *GR*, ii, 134, pp. 216–17.

[70] ASC 926D.

[71] S 396–7.

[72] This, indeed, is what William of Malmesbury assumed: *GR*, ii, 134, pp. 216–17.

[73] ASC *s.a.* 926D; see below, 160–3 for a full discussion.

the king then supposedly proceeded to fortify with some splendour.[74] If Æthelstan issued any authentic charters in this year, none has survived. Some members of the king's council would have travelled with him to the north, to serve in the army whose potential threat of force served to bring the Northumbrians to submission, but also to witness the English side of the negotiations with the northern and Welsh princes at Eamont and again at Hereford. If the king's council met again following his return to Wessex in the late summer – and surely the king would have had much he wished to report about the changed political landscape – it had other matters on its mind than the reallocation of land and so has left no trace of its deliberations. Once the king's charter series resumed in 928, it reflected the influence of the idiosyncratic draftsman, 'Æthelstan A'.

Æthelstan's whereabouts between 928 and 935

A sequence of royal charters all drafted by a single man sheds unprecedented light on the location of Æthelstan and his court on particular days between Easter 928 and Christmas 935 if not on his movements between those fixed points. Although Frankish annalists had long been in the habit of noting routinely in every annual entry where the king had spent Christmas and Easter, this was not a practice adopted by their English counterparts and the Anglo-Saxon Chronicle offers disappointingly little information about the itineraries of Anglo-Saxon kings. In trying to establish the movements of West Saxon kings, historians must depend on the vagaries of diplomatic practice; some draftsmen chose to record where a particular transaction had been made, but this was not universal practice.

The first charters produced by 'Æthelstan A' relate to grants made at a meeting of the council in the royal fortress (*arce regia*) in Exeter on 16 April 928. Æthelstan's decision to hold a council at Exeter, only recently brought within the West Saxon orbit, made a significant statement to the inhabitants of the south-west about the geographical extent of his power. Since the meeting occurred just three days after Easter (13 April), we may presume that the court had spent the sacred feast in the royal town in Devon. Æthelstan made two grants on this occasion, giving land at Odstock near Salisbury in Wiltshire to his thegn Byrhtferth and granting to a woman called Ælfflæd land at Winterbourne, also near Salisbury.[75] In the full witness-list attached to the grant to Byrhtferth we see for the first time a feature of these charters that we will come to recognize; after the name of the king (Æthelstan, *rex Anglorum*) and before that of the archbishop of Canterbury appear three men, all called *subregulus* (sub-king):

---

[74] *GR*, ii, 134, pp. 216–17; discussed in greater detail below, 164.

[75] S 400 (preserved in an archive copy from the Old Minster, Winchester) and 399 (a copy from Glastonbury's archive, which preserved only an abbreviated witness-list). Keynes observed (*Diplomas*, 43) that in several respects these two charters anticipate the features of the diplomas of Æthelstan issued over the next few years.

Howel, Juþwal (Iuthwal) and Wurgeat, the Welsh kings who had so recently submitted to Æthelstan's authority and agreed to pay him tribute. Not content to leave them within the borders of their own territories (where they might have fomented rebellion against their English overlord), Æthelstan had chosen expediently to keep his Welsh sub-kings in attendance on his person.[76] Their Welsh-speaking entourages would have given a different complexion to what had hitherto been a more uniform Anglo-Saxon (and to a lesser extent Anglo-Danish) court. A Welsh contingent brought not just their own language but different cultural practices and their own forms of entertainment, including music and verse to enliven dark evenings. Also present on that occasion were the archbishop of York and, in order of attestation, the bishops of Lichfield, Sherborne, Wells, Winchester, Crediton, Ramsbury, Rochester, Worcester, Hereford, and two other bishops from unidentifiable sees. Only three ealdormen witnessed: Osferth, Ælfwald and Guthrum; after their names came those of eighteen thegns, headed by Odda.[77]

Between Eastertide 928 and the fifth Sunday in Lent 930 we know nothing of Æthelstan's movements. It is extremely unlikely that his court failed to meet in these two years and of course quite possible that the king promulgated one or more of his law codes during this time.[78] On Saturday 3 April 930 at his royal vill in Lyminster in Sussex, the king granted land at Selsey to the bishop of that see, Beornheah.[79] While Æthelstan probably attended mass at Selsey cathedral the following morning, and there heard the bishop preach a Lenten sermon, we can only speculate about what he did next. Did he stay in Sussex for Palm Sunday, Holy Week and the festivities on Easter Day (18 April) or had he by then moved further west? At the end of the month he was in his vill at Chippenham, for on 29 April he gave an estate in Devon to the bishop of Crediton and his community.[80] Since the Welsh kings attested neither the Selsey nor the Crediton grants, we might imagine that the king had given them permission to spend Easter at home that year, for generally 'Æthelstan A' did note when they attended a council.[81] Even in the absence of the Welsh these were not, however, exclusively 'English' councils: several ealdormen with names of Scandinavian origin witnessed both grants, their names occurring as a block after the

[76] Loyn, 'Wales and England', 186–7.

[77] Keynes, *Atlas*, tables xxvi–xxviii. This is the first of Æthelstan's charters that Bishop Frithestan attested; if he had been one of those opposed to the king's succession, he would seem to have recovered from his pique (or to have been restored to the king's favour if his exclusion had been involuntary) by this time, for he attests fairly regularly from this point onward until his death in 931.

[78] See Wormald, *MEL*, 299 for the sequence in which Æthelstan's codes were issued.

[79] S 403.

[80] S 405.

[81] It is of course possible that on these two occasions he had decided not to name the Welsh kings, but since he did on both occasions include the names of northern and eastern ealdormen we might wonder at a deliberate omission of the Welsh.

English ealdormen and before the thegns. Presumably these men had responsibility for different localities in the former Danelaw areas of eastern England.[82] This group of charters displays graphically Æthelstan's preference for requiring his nobles to leave their own lands in order to attend on his person near the heart of the former West Saxon kingdom.

While the rest of the year 930 remains blank in the diplomatic record, the charter scribe 'Æthelstan A' copied fresh documents in the spring of 931, when the king made one of his rare recorded trips outside Wessex. On 23 March the royal council met at the royal vill in Colchester in Essex and confirmed the king's gift of land in Hampshire to an Abbot Ælfric.[83] What the court was doing at Colchester we cannot know. Perhaps Æthelstan wanted to visit the region and explore unfamiliar territory for himself. His father had refounded Colchester after sacking it in 916 and probably then rebuilt the royal vill there, with a chapel.[84] Alternatively, some local East Anglian problem may have arisen that made a royal visit to assert the king's authority seem politic. Otherwise one may wonder that no one in his circle advised against visiting the eastern seaboard in March and early April (Easter Day fell on 10 April in 931). Since East Anglia did not abound in monastic communities in Æthelstan's day and the local bishopric was vacant at the time (responsibility for the diocese falling to the bishop of London), it would have proved hard to find anywhere particularly suitable in the region for the court to celebrate Easter, even had the force (and chill) of the fenland winds not driven the king further inland.[85] Witnesses to the grant made in Colchester included again a collection of men of Scandinavian origin, but not the Welsh sub-kings. The latter, however, attended the king once more at Worthy in Hampshire on 20 June of the same year, when Æthelstan gave land in Berkshire to a thegn called Ælfric.[86] By July, the court – with all its

---

[82] See further below, 129–30.

[83] S 412; see Keynes, *Liber Vitae*, 22; and for the identity of Ælfric, ch. 4.

[84] P.J. Drury, 'Anglo-Saxon Painted Plaster Excavated at Colchester, Essex', in *Early Medieval Wall Painting and Painted Sculpture in England*, ed. S. Cather *et al.* (BAR, British ser. 216, 1990), 117–18.

[85] One possible site might have been Hoxne in Suffolk, where the bishop of London, Theodred is known to have had a residence (S 1526). Since this site had a connection with the cult of the East Anglian king, Edmund, who died at the hands of the Danes in 869 and was later commemorated as a holy martyr, it is appealing to wonder if interest in that cult had in part inspired Æthelstan's visit. There is, however, no evidence for the activities of the community at *Bedricesworth* that had charge of the saint's remains before the 940s. Æthelstan's brother Edmund made his namesake a grant in 945 (S 507) and the saint also benefited from the testamentary bequests of Ealdorman Ælfgar and his daughters (S 1483, 1486, 1494) and Theodred, bishop of London (S 1526).

[86] S 413. Howel (Hywel Dda), Iuthwal (Idwal, king of Gwynedd) and Morcant (Morgan ap Owain, king of Morgannwy and Gwent) witnessed as sub-kings (*subreguli*), as on this occasion also did Eugenius (Eogan/Owen, the Scottish sub-king of Strathclyde). All these had offered their submission to Æthelstan at Eamont in 927. Loyn, 'Wales and England', 187. Susan Kelly has discussed this charter and commented on the possibility that the witness-list, although long, is abbreviated, since only 18 thegns attest (in comparison with much larger numbers in S 416, 412 and 417): *Charters of Abingdon*, no. 23.

appendages – had moved on to a royal vill in Hampshire, either at East Wellow or one of the Wallops.[87] Since the charter issued at this council (granting land to one of Æthelstan's thegns and dated 15 July 931) closely resembled the text of the grant to Ælfric just discussed, the scribe of the Abingdon cartulary in which it survives apparently chose to abbreviate both text and witness-list. It is not clear whether we should assume from their absence from the attestations that the Welsh sub-kings had slipped back to their own lands in the interval since the June meeting. On 12 November in the same year two of them (Hywel and Idwal) attended the session of the king's council at Lifton in Devon. The charter drawn up on that occasion (in favour of Wulfgar, the king's thegn) is one of two drafted by 'Æthelstan A' that survive as original single-sheet charters.[88] If the king was in the south-west in mid-November, he may have stayed in that part of the country for Christmas, rather than face the difficulties of moving the court and its entourage through mud or frost on poor roads when winter days were short. Any of the several royal vills in the region could have offered him a temporary base; he might equally have divided his time between more than one without having to move any great distance.

During the first half of 932 we can say nothing about Æthelstan's movements or activities for he issued no surviving charters between November 931 and August of the following year. His council could of course have met, and may have discussed legal matters or have made land grants the records of which have failed to survive, but where it did so we cannot say. Diplomatically, the second half of the year saw greater activity, with councils meeting on 30 August at *Middletun*;[89] on 9 November in the town of Exeter in Devon (asserting once again the king's determination to keep the Cornish out of the south-western corner of his realm);[90] and on 24 December at the royal vill at

---

[87] S 1604; Kelly, *Charters of Abingdon*, no. 24.

[88] S 416; Loyn, 'Wales and England', 187 (where Luton is obviously a misprint for Lifton). My discussion ignores the evidence of S 450, a charter in Æthelstan's name granting land in Cornwall to the church of St Buryan supposedly at a meeting of the king's council on 6 October 943, four years after the king's death. This may have been based on a genuine Æthelstan charter, but it is not authentic in its current form and the witness-list – which includes neither the Welsh kings nor any of the Scandinavians from eastern England – bears little relationship to any genuine set of attestations from the early 930s, which gives one little confidence in the date or place of the meeting. Wormald thought that the original year of issue might have been 931 (*MEL*, 432) but this cannot be confirmed.

[89] S 417; the meeting place was either Milton Regis in Kent or Milton Abbas in Dorset; this charter records a grant of land in Hampshire, preserved in the archive of the Old Minster. It has a lengthy witness-list including four of the Welsh kings, 18 bishops, five abbots, 15 ealdormen (many men from northern and eastern counties), and 47 thegns. Loyn, 'Wales and England', 188.

[90] S 418a, a charter granting land in Essex. This is one of the recently discovered 'Ilford Hospital' charters, preserved at Hatfield House; obviously a product of 'Æthelstan A', it too has a distinctive and lengthy witness-list, including the names of three of the Welsh kings.

Amesbury in Wiltshire.[91] Having spent Christmas in Amesbury, the court had moved only a short distance to Wilton in the same county by 11 January 933, when the king granted land in Wiltshire to the New Minster.[92] Another short journey brought him at the end of the month to Chippenham, where on 26 January Æthelstan made two separate grants to Sherborne Abbey.[93] This pattern of movement reinforces my earlier suggestion that the king and his court stayed within a fairly confined area at midwinter, moving from one royal vill to another, sometimes, as in this case, without even crossing a shire boundary. The Welsh kings attested none of the grants made during this period. Whether they had departed to celebrate Christmas that year in their own courts, among their own people, or remained with Æthelstan but – contrary to 'Æthelstan A's' normal practice – were not included in these charter witness-lists must remain a matter of speculation. Frustratingly we can see nothing of how either their or Æthelstan's movements might have altered as the weather improved in the spring of 933. Considerable doubt surrounds the authenticity of the sole surviving charter from the remainder of that calendar year, supposedly issued at Kingston in Surrey on 16 December.[94]

Whether the king altered his planned itinerary in 933 on account of his brother Edwin's behaviour, we cannot know. Edwin, readers will recall, died after a shipwreck in the North Sea, having perhaps left England in something of a hurry following his involvement in a fresh, but again unsuccessful, rebellion at Winchester against his elder brother's rule.[95] Beyond the obvious point that one could hardly have hatched a putative plot against the king while he was resident in Winchester, this episode sheds no light on the king's itinerary during this year. If he chose to observe a period of formal court mourning in his brother's memory, we can only speculate about where he might have preferred to spend that time. Although some truth may underpin William of Malmesbury's report that the king built a church at Milton in memory of his brother's soul (if not necessarily in reparation for the part he had played in his death), the charter in favour of Milton Abbey that the king supposedly granted in a council at Dorchester meeting on the second day of Easter 934 (i.e. 7 April) has little to commend it.[96]

---

[91] Two closely related charters were issued on this occasion: S 418 and 419. The latter, in Shaftesbury's archive, has an abbreviated witness-list but was presumably originally supplied with a much fuller one, as for S418 (a list that does not, on this occasion, include the Welsh kings).

[92] S 379; the Welsh kings were again absent.

[93] S 422–3.

[94] S 420; although this charter may draw on genuine formulas in use at Æthelstan's court, we can have no confidence in the text as a whole and must therefore be sceptical about the dating-clause and thus the location of the court at Kingston just before Christmas in this year.

[95] Above, 40–3.

[96] GP, ii, 85, pp. 292–3. S 391. It is not helpful that the original charter is lost and we know of the text, in Latin and Old English versions, only from antiquarian transcripts. The witness-list may derive from some other Æthelstan charter of 931×934, but in diplomatic terms this is a highly dubious deed.

Æthelstan's expedition to Scotland, made either to quell a Scottish rebellion against the peace agreed in 927 or to capitalize on Scandinavian tensions in Northumbria following the death of Guthfrith the grandson of Ivart ruling in Dublin, dominates the historical record for the year 934. Wherever he had spent Easter (and in whose company), he chose to celebrate Pentecost in Winchester and to do so in some style. Three days later, on 28 May 934, Æthelstan granted an estate in either Sussex or Kent to one of his thegns, a man called Ælfwald. Recorded in a charter preserved in the archives of Christ Church, Canterbury, this survives as a single sheet and has one of this draftsman's characteristically long witness-lists, including the names of four of the Welsh princes: Hywel Dda, Idwal Foel, Morgan ap Owain and Tewdwr ap Griffri (of Brycheiniog) as well as a good selection of men with Danish names.[97] Can we connect the death of Edwin in 933 and Æthelstan's decision to convene his court at Winchester for the first time the following spring? If Edwin's removal had finally marked the end of opposition to Æthelstan's rule in Winchester, we could interpret this decision as marking Æthelstan's symbolic acquisition of the royal residence that had lain at the heart of the historic West Saxon kingdom in his father and grandfather's day, and so coming, after a long delay, into his full inheritance. That we do not know of an earlier stay in the town does not, however, prove that Æthelstan had not visited the place many times earlier in his reign without leaving any record of his presence. Even so, the removal of Edwin and his faction from influence in Winchester was highly significant. When Æthelstan left his family's lands to move rapidly north through England to launch his Scottish campaign, he did so knowing that – at last – the whole of the south was secure behind him.

The Scottish expedition required considerable advance planning by the officials of the royal household, for the king and his retinue moved north with impressive speed.[98] By 7 June the whole group – Welsh sub-kings, northern and West Saxon bishops and the Danes from eastern England – had arrived in Nottingham in the midlands, after travelling something over 160 miles in nine days. There the king made a grant of land in Lancashire to the newly appointed archbishop of York, Wulfhelm, saying that he had bought the land in question 'with no little money of my own'.[99] Æthelstan's route hereafter is hard to plot precisely. Poorer quality

---

[97] S 425; Loyn, 'Wales and England', 188.

[98] Sawyer, 'The Royal *tun*', 286–7.

[99] No abbots attested this grant, however, perhaps because they did not move far from their southern bases, or because this was essentially a military expedition in which, as non-combatants, they had no place. One charter, S 428, although bearing the incarnational date 930 would seem to have been issued in London on 7 June 934, but this is not an authentic diploma and the contrary evidence that Æthelstan was in Nottingham on this day seems overwhelming; see Kelly, *Charters of St Paul's*, 159. S 407. The text of the charter reports that the grant was made at the time of Wulfhelm's accession, i.e. in 930. It is possible that it was given then but the charter not drawn up until the king was on his way

roads in the north may have slowed the court's pace somewhat, but even
so by late June or early July the king and his entourage had probably
reached their next stopping point: the shrine of St Cuthbert, which then
lay 160 miles north of Nottingham at Chester-le-Street in the modern
County Durham. The *Historia de Sancto Cuthberto* records the text of a
charter Æthelstan supposedly issued to the community on this occasion,
giving them land at Bishop Wearmouth, a number of precious liturgical
items and some books.[100] We cannot determine Æthelstan's journey
further north with any precision although he was reported to have ravaged
as far as Caithness, and to have attacked by sea as well as land.[101]

All kings preferred to campaign in the summer months during the
better weather that made roads and waves easier to travel. As effectively
executed as it had been meticulously planned, Æthelstan's Scottish expedition was swiftly concluded and the king had brought the court back to
the south by early in the autumn; on 13 September 934 at his vill at
Buckingham he granted land in Wiltshire to one of his thegns.[102] The
Welsh kings did not appear in the abbreviated witness-list in Glastonbury's
archives; the copyist thought only to record one name beyond that of the
king: Constantín, the Scots king, described as *subregulus*. Clearly, having
quelled the Scottish rebellion, Æthelstan preferred to have Constantín
under his eye and leave nothing to chance. Beyond this meeting of the
council in September, we know nothing certain about the court's movements until the end of 935. Æthelstan and his circle probably took the
opportunity to spend a quiet winter in Wessex, riding to hounds, hawking
and generally recovering their strength after the gruelling campaign.
Perhaps they spent Christmas in Somerset; a dubious charter in the Old
Minster archive places the court at Frome on 16 December 934, but
whether the charter's dating clause derived from a genuine charter, now
lost, or the draftsman of this spurious text confected it himself on the basis
of a different 'Æthelstan A' product, cannot be determined.[103]

No extant texts shed any light on Æthelstan's movements during 935
apart from an extract from a now lost charter once recorded on a roll from
St Paul's in London, which probably relates to a genuine charter of

---

north, or that this phrase is an interpolation into the text of the charter which survives only
in a cartulary copy; *EHD*, no. 104. The *Chronicle of the Archbishops of York* (*Historians of the
Church of York*, ed. Raine, ii, 339), reported that Æthelstan had bought this land 'from the
pagans', implying presumably that it had been in the hands of a local landowner of
Scandinavian descent (or even a man of Hiberno-Norse origin, bearing in mind the proximity of the estate to Ireland).

[100] *HSC*, ch. 26. See further below, 119–24. Keynes suggested that the text of this charter
was based on two Old English records inserted into blank space in one of the gospel books
that the king gave to the community of St Cuthbert: BL Cotton Otho B. ix, a manuscript
that was badly burnt in the Cotton fire of 1731: Keynes, 'Books', 178.

[101] *HR, s.a.* 934, ii, 124; see below, 164–7.

[102] S 426.

[103] S 427; Wormald, *MEL*, 432.

'Æthelstan A'. In its abbreviated form, the text reveals only the year (935) from the dating clause, the location of the council (Cirencester in Gloucestershire) and the name of Æthelstan followed by the sub-kings Constantín, Owain, Hywel, Idwal and Morgan.[104] At Christmas in the same year the court found itself at Dorchester in Dorset, witnessing on 21 December to a grant to Malmesbury Abbey of land in Wiltshire. On this occasion the sub-king of Strathclyde, Owain (Eugenius), attested along with three of the Welsh sub-kings.[105] Other charters in Æthelstan's name from 935 reflect the changes in personnel at the king's court previously discussed.[106] 'Æthelstan A' may have died or retired at around this time; certainly production of the flamboyant charters associated with him ceased during this year.

Æthelstan's whereabouts between 935 and 939

In comparison with the wealth of detail about Æthelstan's councils available for the central years of his reign, we know less about the movements of the king and his court after 935. Genuine charters from this late period employ a simpler Latin prose style, never report exactly when or where the witan met and have briefer witness-lists. The changeover to the fresh format occurred at some point during 935 while 'Æthelstan A' remained at court, but the overlap is brief and from 936 we have only the simpler, shorter texts. Study of the king's earlier charters has taught us that the place at which Æthelstan issued charters bore little or no relationship to the location of the estates he donated or to the origin of the beneficiaries, where known. We may be on safer ground if we assume that the king continued to hold meetings of his council in the same sorts of place that he had chosen earlier, namely in royal vills easily reached by road or river.[107] That charter production was still based at the king's court seems probable, although the greater range of variation found in the formulas of the king's later charters suggests either that centralized control was more relaxed or that several draftsmen performed this role for the king. Strikingly, the bishop of Winchester appeared prominently in the king's

---

[104] S 1792. Kelly, *Charters of St Paul's*, no 11.

[105] S 434; Kelly, *Charters of Malmesbury*, no. 26. William of Malmesbury used this charter as the basis of a compound text he produced to safeguard the position of his abbey, including the Welsh sub-kings among its supposed witnesses and thus showing, as Loyn argued, that he accepted as commonplace the presence of these men at the great assemblies of King Æthelstan: 'Wales and England', 190. S 434 is the last full text of a charter produced by 'Æthelstan A' to survive; one other, S 458, preserved in the archives of Wilton Abbey, is incomplete, lacking both dating clause and witness-list. Although presumed to date from 935, it tells us nothing about the king's itinerary. The doubtful charters S 435 and 436 (both dated 21 December 937 and preserved in Malmesbury's archive) may perhaps have been based on authentic deeds issued at this same council in 935.

[106] S 429–30. See above 66–70.

[107] Compare Wormald, *MEL*, 437–8.

late charters. 'Æthelstan A' placed neither Frithestan (d. 934) nor Beornstan (934–5) high in any of the witness-lists he compiled, but Beornstan's successor Ælfheah witnessed all of the king's charters from 935 onwards in either second or third place among the bishops, sharing the privilege of coming immediately after the archbishop of Canterbury with Theodred, bishop of London. This might suggest that Ælfheah had a closer relationship with the king than that enjoyed by his predecessors, but it could also reflect a particular Winchester flavour apparent in diplomas from late in the reign.[108]

Without charters to indicate Æthelstan's whereabouts, we have only the sparse narrative sources for information on his movements during the later years of his reign. In 936, Hugh, duke of the Franks, sent an embassy to summon the exiled Louis (son of Charles the Simple and Æthelstan's sister Eadgifu) back to Francia to assume his rightful throne. Flodoard of Rheims reported this briefly in his annals, but writing a little later the historian Richer of Rheims gave a fuller account; according to him Hugh's envoys sailed from Boulogne and, driven by favourable winds, were rapidly taken to Æthelstan at York, where the king was deliberating the affairs of the kingdom with his nephew among his household (*apud suos*).[109] No contemporary English source suggests that Æthelstan ever convened a meeting of his council at York; whether this was indeed a full gathering of his council, or merely a visit made by the king's immediate circle we cannot say. If we could rely on Richer's version (which appears to suggest that the French sailed straight to the port at York, knowing that they would find the king in the north), we might wonder whether Æthelstan had taken his court to Northumbria because the truce agreed in 934 with the Scots had started to disintegrate. Alternatively, he may have wanted to make a second visit to the shrine of St Cuthbert, perhaps to hand over in person the book containing Bede's two *Lives of the Saint* that he had promised on his earlier visit, for which purpose a stopover in York would have made sense.[110]

In the spring or summer of 937 all of Æthelstan's energies went into quelling the resurgent Norse–Scots alliance and routing their combined army at *Brunanburh*, probably on the Wirral. The campaign apparently began in Mercia, where the English army first convened from the various southern shires. Neither Æthelstan nor his brother Edmund, who fought with him, is likely to have been in York at the time of the combined northern attack;[111] more plausibly both had spent the winter of 936–7 in western Wessex, as in previous years. After the battle Æthelstan's

[108] See Sawyer, *Charters of Burton*, no. 8.

[109] Richer, *Historiae*, ii. 2, ed. H. Hoffmann, MGH SS 38 (Hanover, 2000), 98; a briefer account appeared earlier, without mention of the meeting place in Flodoard's annals: 936 (18A).

[110] See further below, 119–24.

[111] See below, 169–72.

movements remain unknown until his death in 939. All versions of the Chronicle record that the king died in that year on 27 October; the northern version adds that his death occurred in the city of Gloucester, whence he was, according to John of Worcester, borne ceremonially to Malmesbury for burial.[112] Æthelstan's antipathy to Winchester seemingly persisted even in death.

A COSMOPOLITAN COURT

Æthelstan's court never stayed in one fixed place. Although he ended the growing prominence apparently attached to Winchester in the later ninth and early tenth centuries, Æthelstan continued the traditions of his West Saxon predecessors by focusing his movements predominantly on the kingdom of Wessex and spending the bulk of his time on his family's royal estates in the south. With so many gaps in the timetable of movements we have constructed, it is difficult to generalize, but the failure of the charter scribe 'Æthelstan A' to write diplomas at any meeting of the royal court held further north than Buckingham (other than that issued at Nottingham on the king's journey to Scotland in 934, which obviously stands outside the general pattern) appears significant. Armitage Robinson suggested that the king's court met often in Somerset, but in fact Æthelstan seems to have preferred royal estates in Wiltshire, where he chose also to be buried and rest eternally; he did not, however, forget the need to keep a weather eye on Devon and the newly subdued western frontier.[113] Where I would agree with Robinson is on the character of this ever-mobile court; it stood out among European courts of Æthelstan's day for its international character, partly because several foreign embassies brought 'magnificent presents to a king famed for his splendour and bounty'. The extent and variety of England's contact with the continent during Æthelstan's reign make his rule remarkable and certainly introduced the English to a range of contemporary continental ideas, as well as flooding the court and religious houses in England with texts, images and precious objects.[114] From the nature and value of the gifts made to the king we can determine the high value placed on his friendship by his European contemporaries: as William of Malmesbury observed, 'the whole of Europe sang his praises and extolled his merits to the sky'.[115] The munificence of those foreign kings made Æthelstan's court a place that literally glittered with wealth: according to William, the air was rich with fragrant spices, many never before known in England, courtiers admired gifts of 'noble jewels (emeralds especially from whose green depth

[112] ASC s.a. 940D; JW, s.a. 940.
[113] TSD, 83.
[114] TSD, 83–4.
[115] GR, ii, 135, pp. 216–17.

reflected sunlight lit up the eyes of the bystanders with their enchanting radiance)' as well as the solid gold of a crown, set with brilliant gems, and relics of Christ's Passion enclosed in crystal.[116] Other gifts equipped Æthelstan royally for battle: Harald, king of the Norwegians gave him a well-equipped ship; Hugh of the Franks' presents included swift horses with their trappings of gold, as well as weapons once linked to the emperors Constantine and Charlemagne.[117] Even though the king gave away many of these luxury presents – adorning churches and monasteries of his realm and generously bestowing on his own followers material possessions, whether those he was given or had inherited or the proceeds of his own victories – his personal treasure was still sufficient for many gold and silver objects to be carried before his body at his funeral.[118]

Another aspect of Æthelstan's court which distinguished it from those of his predecessors was, as we have already observed, the frequent presence of the Welsh sub-kings Hywel Dda, Idwal Foel, Morgan ap Owain and Tewdwr ap Griffri among the witnesses to Æthelstan's charters. The Scots king Constantín attested sometimes also (one wonders with how much enthusiasm) and so did Owain, sub-king of Strathclyde. Alfred the Great had made alliances with the rulers of Wales in his day, they having turned willingly to his lordship, Asser reported, because of fear of other powers, Scandinavian, northern Welsh or Mercian. Close bonds united Alfred to some of these men – Anarawd was accepted by Alfred as his spiritual son at confirmation – but even so, the surviving records note their presence only occasionally at Alfred's court.[119] In his relationship with the Celtic princes Æthelstan, king of the English added, as Henry Loyn argued, a quasi-imperial dimension to his kingship, as reflected in the grandiose titles accorded to him in his charters.[120] Not merely king of all the Anglo-Saxon peoples living on these shores, Æthelstan could claim in fact as well as in rhetoric to be overlord of other native kings in Britain. The presence of the Welsh kings in Æthelstan's charters shows, Loyn argued, how readily they proved able to fit into the 'new confident order of Æthelstan's world, side by side, but superior to the Danish ealdormen who were exercising their authority in the reabsorbed Danelaw'.[121] We could also reflect on how effectively their regular attendance at Æthelstan's peripatetic court witnessed to the extent and magnitude of his power.[122] That they accompanied the king at least as far as Nottingham on his

[116] *GR*, ii, 135, pp. 218–19.

[117] *GR*, ii, 135, pp. 216–19.

[118] *GR*, ii, 134, pp. 214–15 and ii, 140, pp. 228–9.

[119] Asser, ch. 80; David N. Dumville, 'The "Six" Sons of Rhodri Mawr: A Problem in Asser's *Life of King Alfred*', *Cambridge Medieval Celtic Studies*, iv (1982), 5–18.

[120] Loyn, 'Wales and England', 178.

[121] Ibid., 188.

[122] Ryan Lavelle, 'The Use and Abuse of Hostages in Later Anglo-Saxon England', *EME*, xiv (2006), 285.

journey north in 934 points to the king's reluctance to leave them to their own devices while he coped with a threat on a different frontier; they did not, however fight on either side at *Brunanburh*, but remained neutrally aloof from that conflict.

Foreigners from across the sea in Francia and also from Scandinavia had also frequently attended Alfred's court and we should not forget that the first of Edward the Elder's daughters to marry a continental monarch did so as a result of her father's diplomacy, yet the number and status of the non-English whom Æthelstan gathered around him is remarkable even in comparison with these precedents. Æthelstan's direct personal association with the various factions ruling parts of the former Carolingian realm came about through both marriage and the fostering of dispossessed heirs to the various territories. The first of Æthelstan's sisters to marry abroad, Eadgifu, met with mixed fortunes after her husband's loss of power, returning eventually to her brother's court where her son Louis lived in exile until Hugh, duke of the Franks organized his return to power in 936. Other unfortunates of high status shared that childhood, including Alain, heir to the Breton throne. Alain and Louis were more or less contemporaries and, having clearly struck up a friendship while in England, seem to have remained friends after each had regained his own realm; Alain was among those who acknowledged Louis's lordship in 942.[123] Æthelstan probably considered that connection with these different regimes in Europe could bring him domestic benefits – if only by enhancing his own reputation.

Attracted by the rumours of its riches and grandeur and by the king's own reputed interests especially in collecting manuscript books and relics, churchmen from across Europe flocked to Æthelstan's circle. That they would find, on arrival, so cosmopolitan, ethnically mixed and intellectually stimulating an environment may have surprised priests and monks accustomed to more monochrome and sober cloisters, or less cultivated (and more mono-ethnic) courts. The intellectual culture of Æthelstan's court had a significant impact on the minds of men such as the future monastic leaders Dunstan and Æthelwold, and thus did much to shape the path taken by the English Church in the middle years of the tenth century.

---

[123] Flodoard, *Annals*, 942 (24C); Richer, *Historiae*, II, 28, ed. Hoffmann, 118; Julia Smith notes that despite this renewal of contact between the two dynasties, Louis in fact played no role in Breton affairs: *Province and Empire* (Cambridge, 1992), 197–8.

Chapter 4

CHURCH

Holy King Æthelstan, renowned through the wide world,
  whose esteem flourishes and whose honour endures everywhere,
whom God set as king over the English, sustained by the foundation
  of the throne, and as leader of his earthly forces,
  . . .
Whosoever you are who looking into this book abounding in divine
  love, shining with light, read its excellent divine doctrines –
this book which the king, filled with the holy spirit,
  adorned with golden headings and places set with jewels,
and which, in his manner, he gladly dedicated to Christ Church
  and joyously made it accessible to sacred learning.[1]

The poem conventionally referred to by the first line of its Latin text, *Rex pius Æðelstan* (holy or pious King Æthelstan), indicates the honour with which contemporaries regarded the king. He found acclaim in his own day not only as a successful military leader and effective monarch but also as a man of devotion, committed to the promotion of religion and the patronage of sacred learning. Entered in a continental hand on the face of a blank leaf in a late ninth- or early tenth-century gospel book from Lobbes in Belgium, this poem was probably copied (and perhaps also composed) at the cathedral community of Christ Church, Canterbury, to which – as a prose inscription on the reverse of the same folio of the manuscript makes clear – Æthelstan had given the manuscript.[2] Apparently the book came to England as a gift made at the time of the negotiations over the marriage of Otto of Saxony to Æthelstan's half-sister Eadgyth in 929; at some later point (after Otto's accession in 936), an English hand added the names *Odda rex* and *Mihthild mater regis* to another folio, at the foot of the first page of Matthew's Gospel.[3] In many ways the sentiments conveyed in *Rex pius Æðelstan* have dominated perceptions of King Æthelstan from the tenth century onwards. The

[1] BL MS, Cotton Tiberius A. ii, fo. 15r; ed. and trans. in Lapidge, 'Poems', 95–6.
[2] Keynes, 'Books', 149–50. See plate 7–8.
[3] Lapidge, 'Poems', 93–7. Karl Leyser, 'The Ottonians and Wessex', in *Communications and Power in Medieval Europe: the Carolingian and Ottonian Centuries*, ed. Timothy Reuter (London, 1994), 43.

king's reputation for piety and demonstrable interest in matters relating to the practice of religion and the arts made him an important patron for the church. His widespread continental connections (forged by the various international marriage alliances he brokered, but also via contact with Breton, Frankish and German churches) had significant implications for the intellectual and spiritual life of his realm, especially for the growth of interest in reformed monasticism. This reign also stands out for the extraordinary outpouring of literature addressed to the king and couched in poetic form which emerged from his court.

KING ÆTHELSTAN AND HIS BISHOPS

The relationship between the crown and the Church grew noticeably closer during the reign of Æthelstan. Anglo-Saxon royal courts maintained intimate connections with the Church throughout the pre-Conquest period; bishops played key roles in the deliberations of royal councils, and royal palaces often lay near major religious centres. Church and court thus came together frequently both in formal meetings of the king's council and socially, too, especially for feasts.[4] The presence of a cathedral church and two other monastic houses close to the royal palace in Winchester strengthened Church–court bonds within Wessex yet further, ensuring that ecclesiastics had a significant place not just in court life but in decision-making and the governance of the realm. With the expansion of Wessex under Alfred and yet further in Edward's and Æthelstan's reigns, a wider potential circle of clerics from midland and northern dioceses could become involved in royal administration, creating new associations between West Saxon kings and senior clergy from the regions.

Most significantly, the relationship between West Saxon kings and the archbishops of Canterbury changed as a direct result of the territorial expansion of Wessex. The southern metropolitans came firmly into the West Saxon patronage system during Edward the Elder's reign. Marking a change in previous custom (and ignoring the prohibition on the practice in canon law), every archbishop of Canterbury from Æthelhelm (bishop of Wells, promoted in 923) came to archiepiscopal office from another English bishopric. To get round that canon-law impediment, each newly appointed archbishop from Wulfhelm in 926 onwards went to Rome to collect a pallium from the pope as a mark of his approval of their tenure of the metropolitan see.[5] Good relations between the king and his archbishops were central to the pursuit of royal secular and ecclesiastical

---

[4] James Campbell, 'Anglo-Saxon Courts', in *Court Culture in the Early Middle Ages*, ed. Catherine Cubitt (Turnhout, 2003), 164–5.

[5] Nicholas Brooks, *The Early History of the Church of Canterbury: Christ Church 597–1066* (Leicester, 1984) 216–17; Brooks, 'The Anglo-Saxon Cathedral Community 597–1070', in *A History of Canterbury Cathedral*, ed. P. Collinson *et al.* (Oxford, 1995), 20; Æthelhelm (Athelm) may also have travelled to Rome for a pallium, as Brooks observed.

policies and to ensuring that even bishops representing more distant sees promoted the ideals close to the king's heart. The significance of the closer bond between Æthelstan and his archbishop bore fruit at the very beginning of his reign, as we have already seen. Æthelhelm took on the task of inventing a new inauguration ritual that crowned Æthelstan king of his recently united realm and thus liturgically marked a distinct break with past tensions and dissent in court circles.

At the apex of the English ecclesiastical hierarchy stood the archbishop of Canterbury. His authority extended over the whole of the southern province of the English Church, from his inconveniently tangential location in the south-eastern corner of the island in Kent, westwards to the tip of Cornwall and north as far as the River Humber. During the period when northern and eastern England had lain under Danish rule, the eastern midlands and East Anglia had, perforce, fallen outside his remit. Episcopal provision in those areas became necessarily somewhat patchy in the later ninth century as bishops found themselves unable to operate in areas of Danish settlement. The see of Leicester had thus transferred to Dorchester at some time in the 870s or 880s and remained there throughout Æthelstan's reign; the diocese of Lindsey had no known occupant after c.870, nor after the same date do we know of any East Anglian bishops. In Æthelstan's day it appears that the bishop of London, Theodred, took responsibility for the spiritual care of the East Anglians, using as his base in the region an episcopal vill at Hoxne in Suffolk.[6]

Expansion of West Saxon rule not just as far as the Humber but, under Æthelstan, also into Northumbria, brought the northern Church for the first time under the sway of a southern English king, and potentially into the orbit of the archbishop of Canterbury, even though York had its own metropolitan see. The bishopric of Lindisfarne had moved with the community of Cuthbert to Chester-le-Street, but the other northern sees at Hexham and Whithorn had been vacant for years. A hint that Æthelstan took some interest in the supply of bishops in his new northern realm may come in a charter preserved in Worcester's archive. Not authentic as it stands, the witness-list of this document may derive from – or have been based on – a genuine witness-list compiled by 'Æthelstan A'. It gives to the archbishop of York, Hrothweard, four suffragans: Æsbyrht (who also witnessed other charters of Æthelstan), Wigred (bishop of Chester-le-Street), Earnulf, and Columban.[7] This might indicate a new policy of increasing the number of northern bishops and may well have been an idea promoted by the king himself; he did claim in a charter proem from early in his reign to be the 'supervisor of the whole Christian

---

[6] Dorothy Whitelock, *Some Anglo-Saxon Bishops of London* (London, 1975), reprinted in her *History, Law and Literature in 10th–11th Century England* (London, 1981), no. II, 18–19.

[7] S 401; see Keynes, *Atlas*, table xxxvii.

household as far as the whirlpools of the ocean surges'.[8] If Æthelstan took that view of his responsibilities literally, he will have wanted to see bishops working across his realm, right up to the far western shores of Galloway and the historical see at Whithorn.[9]

Closer to home, Æthelstan showed a preference for appointing men from his own immediate circle to vacant bishoprics in Wessex, a policy he may have adopted partly as a means of minimizing the influence of the bishop of Winchester, with whom his relations were frosty.[10] Among the priests who attended the young king Æthelstan at court and witnessed some early charters, the mass-priests Ælfheah and Beornstan both obtained higher preferment.[11] Ælfheah was appointed to the bishopric of Wells in January 926 (succeeding Wulfhelm) and Byrnstan (Beornstan) became bishop of Winchester after Frithestan in May 931. Another Ælfheah, described as priest and monk (*sacerdos et monachus*) when he witnessed a grant made on the day of the king's coronation, was also presumably a priest in the royal household; he went on to become bishop of Winchester after Frithestan in 934.[12] In a passage in his Life of St Oswald the chronology of which is rather confused, Byrhtferth of Ramsey indicated that a young priest of Danish extraction, Oda, who had recently revealed himself to have miraculous powers of healing while on a visit to Rome, came to Æthelstan's court early in the king's reign. 'Because of the miracle which had been performed, the king recognized Oda to be a true servant of God', and apparently encouraged him to join the royal circle briefly, before promoting him to the see of Ramsbury *c.* 926 (certainly before 929).[13] Cenwald, a monk perhaps from the monastery at Glastonbury, also appears to have belonged to the royal household for a time before he was appointed to the bishopric of Worcester in 929. Both Cenwald, described as *monachus*, and Oda, *presbiter*, appear in a list of names entered with King

---

[8] S 395; Michael Wood, ' "Stand Strong against the Monsters": Kingship and Learning in the Empire of Æthelstan', in *Lay Intellectuals in the Carolingian World*, ed. Patrick Wormald and Janet L. Nelson (Cambridge, 2007), 201–2.

[9] See Peter Hill, *Whithorn and St Ninian: the Excavation of a Monastic Town, 1984–91* (Stroud, 1997), 45–51 and 183–201, on evidence for the restoration of the minster at Whithorn in the late ninth century, and the reorganization of the site in the early tenth.

[10] Frithestan's name does not appear among the witnesses to S 394 (4 September 925) or the three grants of 926: S 395–7; Keynes, *Liber Vitae*, 20–1. For the king's difficult relations with Winchester, see above, ch. 2.

[11] Both had witnessed his manumission of a slave in his household called Eadhelm: *SEHD*, no. 19; and Ælfheah also the charter granted on the day of his coronation: S 394 above, 65.

[12] *TSD*, 82–3.

[13] Byrhtferth, *Vita S Oswaldi*, i, 5, ed. and trans. Michael Lapidge, *Byrhtferth of Ramsey, the Lives of St Oswald and St Ecgwine* (Oxford, 2009), 22–3. For the suggestion that Oda was a royal chaplain in Æthelstan's household, see E.E. Barker, 'Two Lost Documents of King Æthelstan', *ASE*, vi (1977), 139 and 143. For the problems of Byrhtferth's account, Michael Lapidge, 'Byrhtferth and Oswald', in *St Oswald of Worcester: Life and Influence*, ed. Nicholas Brooks and Catherine Cubitt (London and New York, 1996), 66–8.

Æthelstan's in the *Liber vitae* of the community of St Cuthbert, perhaps on the occasion of the king's visit to the north in 934.[14] Æthelstan thus elected to appoint priests from his own household circle to vacant West Saxon sees, so strengthening his personal ties with the ecclesiastical hierarchy in Wessex, probably at the expense of men who had formerly had his father's favour.[15]

In the early years of his reign, Æthelstan seems to have had a close relationship with one of his Mercian bishops, Ælle of Lichfield, for Ælle consistently attested the king's charters in a prominent position, witnessing immediately after the archbishops of Canterbury and York whose names head each list. If we have rightly seen Æthelstan's background and sympathies as predominantly Mercian before his accession, then we may wonder if Ælle had played a part in the king's education, and more confidently imagine that he and the king had already been intimates before Edward the Elder's death. Ælle might indeed have been 'Æthelstan A' who crafted the elaborate documents with lengthy witness-lists in the period 928–35; Ælle's name disappeared from charter witness-lists at precisely the point at which 'Æthelstan A' ceased to produce documents for the king.

When compiling witness-lists, 'Æthelstan A' did not rank the other bishops in any consistent order; at different times Eadwulf of Crediton, Sigehelm of Sherborne and Ælfheah of Wells occupied the fourth, fifth and sixth places in the list of witnessing bishops; Cenwald of Worcester often, but not always, attested around fifth place, also. Perhaps 'Æthelstan A' listed the prelates in the order in which they had articulated their assent to a donation on the occasion of which the charter represented the written record. That bishops from western Wessex and southern Mercia often consented early on in the proceedings may suggest that these were the men closest to the king, whose opinion he sought the most frequently. Such a supposition would fit well with what we can demonstrate about the king's movements, which appear to show some preference for the western part of the old kingdom of Wessex, especially Wiltshire.[16] On the occasions when he did attend the king's council, Frithestan, bishop of Winchester never attested in the prominent position among the witnesses to which his seniority (and the significance of his see) would in normal circumstances have entitled him. His successor, Beornstan, took a more prominent place beside the king, reflecting his long-standing close relationship with Æthelstan. Scribes in the royal writing office who produced the king's diplomas after 935 adopted a different strategy, listing the bishops consistently in the same order, reflecting their seniority. After Canterbury came in turn Winchester, London, Worcester, Selsey, Ramsbury, Wells, Rochester and Crediton. As

---

[14] BL, MS Cotton Domitian A.vii, fo. 15r; Barker, 'Two Lost Documents', 138–9.

[15] For some other, slightly more tenuous suggestions about members of this clerical circle round the king including two charter scribes, Benedict and Edward, a deacon, see Michael Wood, 'The Making of King Æthelstan's Empire: an English Charlemagne?', in *Ideal and Reality in Frankish and Anglo-Saxon Society*, ed. Patrick Wormald *et al.* (Oxford, 1983), 258.

[16] Illustrated in Appendix II and discussed above, 77–91.

already suggested, Æthelstan had good relations with Bishop Ælfheah of Winchester, another man appointed from his own circle in 934 or 935. Otherwise it would be unwise to read much about the king's relations with individual bishops into the order in which their names appear in his later charters.[17]

Bishops may have played a more prominent role than other clergy in assisting in the government of Æthelstan's realm, but they were not the only ecclesiastics who participated in the intellectual and social activities of his court. There the king's leading prelates encountered a more diverse group of learned men than had congregated at the court of Edward the Elder, many of whom had been attracted to England specifically by the growing reputation of Æthelstan as a discerning collector of books and relics, who had an informed interest in learning. Around him gathered a cosmopolitan and international ecclesiastical body, including not just people from different English kingdoms, but those of Welsh, Irish, Breton, Frankish and German extraction. Æthelstan's court sparkled visually with the precious objects such visitors brought as gifts from their own royal and noble patrons, but it also shone conversationally. Here the most up-to-date European learning – from Frankia, Germany, Ireland and the Greek East – found a receptive audience. In this polyglot, international environment, the seeds of new ideas about how best to regulate monastic life according to reformed principles now emerging in Frankia, Burgundy and Lotharingia fell on fertile ground.[18] Æthelstan's court served as the nursery for the first tentative shoots of the English monastic revolution that would reach maturity in the reign of his nephew Edgar.[19]

FOREIGN CHURCHMEN AT ÆTHELSTAN'S COURT

Æthelstan's continental connections, established through the marital arrangements he made for his various half-sisters and his fostering of continental princes, did not create entirely new bonds with the royal and noble families of western Europe, but through his energies previous connections were strengthened and new alliances made.[20] One consequence that the king and his father did not foresee when they first looked outside England for husbands for his sisters was the extent to which increased contact between Wessex and other parts of western Europe would lead to an influx of clerical and intellectual visitors to the West Saxon court. Marriage agreements

[17] Charter production and the role of 'Æthelstan A' were explored fully in ch. 3. For the evidence of the witness-lists, see Keynes, *Atlas*, table xxvii.

[18] In his study of *The Times of St Dunstan*, Armitage Robinson drew attention to the intellectual energy and creativity of Æthelstan's court as witnessed by the manuscripts collected and produced there, and by the diversity of the men who flocked to his circle: *TSD*, 51–71.

[19] Dumville, *Wessex*, 156–61.

[20] See above, 45–52 and compare fig. 2.

involved the exchange not just of people (the brides and their personal entourages, including clergy) but of gifts, frequently books, including illuminated manuscripts, and also precious objects, including liturgical vessels for the service of the altar or the adornment of sacred space. The potential for the exchange of ideas both via texts sent to England and through the conversation of those who carried correspondence between home and foreign courts is obvious. Yet beyond such visitors, a larger group of ecclesiastics and scholars gathered at the court of King Æthelstan, eager to share in the intellectual culture he fostered and to benefit from his patronage.

Before her forced return to England after her husband, Charles 'the Simple's' removal from power, Eadgifu might well have encountered some fruits of early movements to reform the conventual life on Benedictine principles promoted first by Abbot Odo at Cluny (in the diocese of Mâcon) in the 920s. Her sister Eadhild was even better placed, being married to Hugh, duke of the Franks, who took a substantial interest in the house of St-Benoît-sur-Loire at Fleury, reformed by Odo of Cluny in 930.[21] Clerics from both princesses' households had yet more information and specific examples of contemporary continental thinking to convey in their letters or visits home. Oda, bishop of Ramsbury and later archbishop of Canterbury, took the monastic profession at the newly reformed monastery at Fleury at some point in his career, according to Byrhtferth of Ramsey. Since we know him to have gone to Frankia to play a central role in the negotiations with Duke Hugh over the restoration of Æthelstan's nephew, Louis to the French throne in 936, he might have found an opportunity to visit Fleury on that occasion.[22] He had also, as we saw earlier, been on pilgrimage to Rome before joining Æthelstan's circle and so may have shared insights about issues current among the Roman clergy that he had acquired on that trip. Yet more significant for the spread of ideas about reformed monastic modes of living was the marriage contracted with Otto of Saxony, for this brought English clerics close to the reform movement in Lotharingia that had begun at Brogne, near Liège and at Gorze, near Metz, a monastery with close connections to the Saxon house.[23]

---

[21] At the time of Pope Leo VII's privilege for Fleury of 938, Eadhild had died, however, and Hugh was remarried, to one of Otto of Saxony's sisters: Donald Bullough, 'The Continental Background', in *Tenth-Century Studies*, ed. David Parsons (London, 1975), 21 and 34.

[22] Byrhtferth of Ramsey, *Vita S Oswaldi*, ii, 4, ed. and trans. Lapidge, *Byrhtferth of Ramsey*, 38–9. According to his hagiographer, Eadmer, Oda and Æthelstan became so inseparable that Oda accompanied the king on to the battlefield at *Brunanburh*: Michael Lapidge, 'The Hermeneutic Style in Tenth-Century Anglo-Latin Literature', in his *Anglo-Latin Literature 900–1066* (London and Rio Grande, 1993), 138; Brooks, *The Early History*, 222.

[23] J. Wollasch, 'Monasticism: the First Wave of Reform', in *NCMH* III, ed. T. Reuter (Cambridge, 1999), 162–85; David Rollason, 'The Concept of Sanctity in the Early Lives of St Dunstan', in *St Dunstan: His Life, Times and Cult*, ed. N. Ramsay et al. (Woodbridge, 1992), 262–3. For the bringing of books from Liège, Flanders and Lotharingia to England in this period, see Dumville, *Wessex*, 160 and n. 126.

When Æthelstan sent two West Saxon princesses, Eadgyth and her younger sister Ælfgifu, to the Saxon court in order that the young Otto might choose which he preferred for his wife, he instructed the newly appointed bishop of Worcester, Cenwald, to accompany them, to keep an eye on the girls and ensure that the whole process was conducted appropriately. Cenwald had served as a priest in Æthelstan's household before moving to Worcester in late 928 or 929 and so may while at court have got to know the princesses fairly well.[24] His mission had a wider purpose, too, for Cenwald sought on this trip to forge spiritual connections – bonds of confraternity – with monasteries in Germany. By having lists of English names inscribed in German confraternity books he ensured that houses throughout the Saxon realm would pray for the continuing good fortune of the English king, for his soul after his death, and also for the bishops, clerics and other people commemorated in these volumes.[25] Perhaps he hoped to acquire some relics to enhance the king's collection on the same trip (see below, Chapter 7) and books to add to the court's (and to Worcester's) library, as well as to learn about contemporary spirituality and coenobitic custom in German monasteries. He had gifts to bestow in return; the king gave lavishly to his new Saxon in-laws and Eadgyth herself had a number of treasures marking her royal origins.[26] Cenwald may further have tried to recruit some German ecclesiastics to come and work in the English Church. Certainly England and the Saxon realm became much closer in the years after the marriage alliance between Otto and Eadgyth, and various German names start to appear in English documents from this time onwards. Three Germans, as we saw in the last chapter, witnessed a lease given by Æthelstan to the New Minster;[27] another, the priest Godescealc (Gottschalk) supposedly received Abingdon Abbey from the king in 931, and various members of the household of Bishop Theodred of London had German names, although Theodred himself was probably not German, but English.[28] Germans appear also among Æthelstan's moneyers.[29]

[24] Barker, 'Two Lost Documents', 139 and 143; and for the suggestion that Cenwald wrote the inscription in the MacDurnan Gospels recording Æthelstan's gift of that book to Canterbury, see further below.

[25] Whether he had an interest in monasticism before he made this trip is not known, but he certainly did after his return; Cenwald later attested some charters of Eadred and one in the name of King Eadwig with the epithet *monachus* (S 544, 566, 569, 633), and John of Worcester described him as a man of monastic profession: JW, *s.a.* 957, pp. 406–7.

[26] Hrotsvitha, *Gesta Ottonis*, verses 107–11, ed. W. Berschin, *Hrotsvit Opera Omnia* (Munich and Leipzig, 2001), 279; Leyser, 'The Ottonians', 81–2; one of the manuscripts that came to Saxony at this time was Coburg Landesbibliothek, MS 1 (the Gandersheim Gospels); see above, 57–8.

[27] S 1417.

[28] S 409; Dumville, *Wessex*, 159–60; S.E. Kelly, *Charters of Abingdon Abbey* (Oxford, 2000–1), I, no. 25; this charter is spurious; on Godescealc, see ibid., 109 'a reference added as a flourish to give verisimilitude to a flawed text'. For Theodred, see D. Bullough, 'The Continental Background', in *Tenth-Century Studies*, ed. D. Parsons (London, 1975), 213, n. 40; *contra* Stenton, *ASE*, 444 and Whitelock, *Some Anglo-Saxon Bishops*, 17–21.

[29] Blunt, 'The Coinage', 81–2, 134–40.

Cenwald began his embassy at the monastery of St Gallen in the modern Switzerland on the eve of the abbey's patronal festival, 15 October 929, staying with them for four days to celebrate that feast. He had come, according to a note inserted into the St Gall confraternity book, in order to visit 'all the monasteries throughout Germany', with a substantial offering of silver entrusted to him by the king of the English for the purpose. Of that, he made a generous donation to St Gall, placing one portion on the altar and giving another for the use of the brothers. After he had participated in their patronal festival, the community granted him the allotted portion (*annona*) of a brother in their congregation and promised to say on his behalf in perpetuity the same prayer as they were accustomed to say for anyone of their own, whether alive or dead. There followed the names which he had asked to be recorded: King Æthelstan, Bishop Cenwald, a certain Wigheard and six others (some apparently Cenwald's relatives). That same list of names appears again in a second list in the same book, this time preceded by King Æthelstan, Archbishop Wulfhelm (of Canterbury, 926–41) and seven of his suffragans, all of whom were in post in 929, plus two abbots.[30] As part of the same journey, Cenwald visited Reichenau; the confraternity book of that monastery has an entry reading: 'In the name of Christ, we commend King Æthelstan to your service, together with Archbishop Wulfhelm and our friends both living and resting in peace. Wigheard.'[31] A slightly different group of English names in the confraternity book of the monastery of Pfäfers dates not from Æthelstan's reign but from Edmund's. That entry names King Æthelstan, King Edmund, 'Odgiua' (Eadgifu: either Edmund's mother or, less plausibly, one of his sisters), and Oda, archbishop; another longer group of mixed and unidentifiable English and German names was added to the same manuscript apparently on the same occasion. Both entries may arise from a German trip made by Oda, archbishop of Canterbury, perhaps on an occasion when he travelled through Germany on his way to Rome.[32]

Cenwald's German trip, along with the contacts made then and subsequently sustained by continuing correspondence, provide an important context for the transmission to Æthelstan's court of books and ideas, especially ideas about reformed monasticism. In seeking to forge agreements of

---

[30] St Gallen, Stiftsbibliothek, MS 915, p. 5; printed *C&S*, I, no. 10; trans. and discussed in Keynes, 'Books', 198–201. The bishops named are: Ælfwine of Lichfield, Edgar of Hereford, Wynsige of Dorchester, Sigehelm of Sherborne, Oda of Ramsbury, Frithestan of Winchester and Cyneferth of Rochester, and the two abbots, Cynath of Evesham and an abbot Ælfric, probably the same who attested several of the king's charters (S 412–13, 416, 418, 422 and 425). See also *TSD*, 35–40.

[31] Zurich, Zentralbibliothek, Rh. hist. 27, p. LXX; printed *Libri Confraternitatum*, ed. Piper, p. 238; trans. Keynes, 'Books', 200, n. 10.

[32] St Gallen, Stiftsarchiv, Cod. Fabariensis, I, p. 33; printed *Liber Confraternitatum*, ed. Piper, p. 363; Keynes, 'Books', 201 and compare also ibid., 190–1. J.A. Robinson, *The Saxon Bishops of Wells* (London, 1918), 60–2.

confraternity with foreign churches, Æthelstan followed his father's example. A letter addressed to Æthelstan from Radbod, prior of St Samson's of Dol reveals that King Edward had made a confraternity agreement with that cathedral church and the clergy, although in exile because of Norman attacks on Brittany, continued to pray for the soul of King Edward.[33] These contacts bore fruit beyond the king's acquisition of relics of Breton saints which Radbod sent him as gifts. Various fleeing political and ecclesiastical exiles from Brittany found their way to England during Æthelstan's reign, their presence reflected not just at the king's court, as discussed above, but in a number of Breton manuscripts known to have been in England since the tenth century, in a sudden growth of interest in the commemoration of Breton saints in English liturgical manuscripts (and the inclusion of a prayer for the English people in an early tenth-century Breton litany), and perhaps in the inclusion of Brittonic names on funerary monuments in Wessex.[34] Winchester particularly seems to have become a centre of Bretonism; enthusiasts in that community brought Breton liturgy, church music and musical notation to England.[35]

Among the Breton clergy who came to Æthelstan's court was a certain former *miles*, now an anchorite, who had travelled to England to seek the help of King Æthelstan and been installed by him in the religious life at a place called *Cen*. An anonymous continental figure wrote one of the only two surviving letters addressed to Æthelstan, seeking the king's help for the anchorite to go on pilgrimage. Although both the author and subject of this letter remain anonymous, the author – clearly the anchorite's superior – was seemingly an ecclesiastic who had either gained a church post in England or become head of a continental religious house that had links with the English Church. John, abbot of the Breton house at Landévennec, also had English connections for he may have engaged in the diplomatic negotiations to return the exiled Breton ruler, Alain, to his homeland. This John could conceivably have been the author of the letter written for the anchorite, even perhaps the same Iohannes who wrote an acrostic poem in praise of Æthelstan. Breton clergy brought different modes of expressing the religious life to English shores; the anchorite at *Cen* seems to have lived not within a community but as a solitary ascetic (even if he clearly retained contacts with some larger parent house). He

---

[33] *GP*, v 249, pp. 597–9; see below, 190–1 for a full discussion.

[34] David N. Dumville, 'Brittany and "Armes Prydein Vawr" ', *Etudes Celtiques*, xx (1983), 151; Julia M.H. Smith, *Province and Empire: Brittany and the Carolingians* (Cambridge, 1992), 197, n. 44; Dumville, *Wessex*, 157; also *TSD*, 74–5.

[35] Caroline Brett, 'A Breton Pilgrim in England in the Reign of King Æthelstan', in *France and the British Isles in the Middle Ages and Renaissance*, ed. Gillian Jondorf and D.N. Dumville (Woodbridge, 1991), 47–8; Dumville, *Wessex*, 157; Michael Lapidge, 'Israel the Grammarian in Anglo-Saxon England', reprinted in his *Anglo-Latin Literature 900–1066* (London and Rio Grande, 1993), 90.

should thus be compared with the various devout Englishwomen known to have behaved similarly in the same period.[36]

One further cleric, possibly another Breton, can be located at Æthelstan's court: a scholar noted for his learning in Greek and known as Israel the Grammarian. Tenth-century continental sources offer conflicting information about Israel's origins and early education (perhaps in Rome with an Italian scholar called Ambrose), although his later career is more certain. He taught Bruno, the future bishop of Cologne, brother of Otto the Great of Saxony, and later lived as a monk at St Maximin in Trier, under the patronage of Archbishop Robert of Trier; he died c.970. Flodoard of Rheims probably had the most accurate information about Israel, since he wrote as his direct contemporary; he refers to Israel as *Britto*, meaning either a Breton, or a Briton from Wales or Cornwall. That parents in tenth-century Celtic countries commonly gave their children Old Testament Hebrew names would explain Israel's name; he was not, as some have tried to argue, Jewish, nor an Irishman.[37] Two manuscripts associated with Æthelstan also have connections with Israel, thus placing him firmly within the intellectual nexus around the king.

A full page near the beginning of a twelfth-century Irish gospel book written in Bangor, County Down and now in Oxford contains a curious table described as the *Alea euangelii*, or Gospel Dice, accompanied by a lengthy textual explanation of how the table worked. Ruled horizontal and vertical lines create a large square with 324 smaller squares inside; at the points where the lines intersect, players place their men (*viri*) whom they will move around during the game.[38] Gospel Dice was an allegorized board game, a numerological treatise that attempted to correlate a complex arrangement of pieces on the board with canon tables (concordances for parallel texts of the Gospels).[39] The connection of this game with Æthelstan's circle confirms an earlier suggestion that the king and his friends played board games in the evenings. A note prefaces the board in the Oxford manuscript:[40]

---

[36] Brett, 'A Breton Pilgrim', 44–5 and 49–50. See further below, 111–12.

[37] Lapidge, 'Israel', 91–2. Lapidge's work thus invalidates the conclusions reached by David J. Wasserstein, 'The First Jew in England: "The Game of the Evangel" and a Hiberno-Latin Contribution to Anglo-Jewish History', in *Ogma: Essays in Celtic Studies in Honour of Próinséas ní Chatháin*, ed. Michael Richter and Jean-Michel Picard (Dublin, 2002), pp. 283–8. Michael Wood has suggested, alternatively, that Israel might have been an Irishman from Lotharingia: Wood, ' "Stand Strong" ', 206.

[38] Oxford, Corpus Christi College, MS 122, fo. 5v; described and discussed *TSD*, 69–71, 171–8. See plate 9.

[39] Martha Bayless, 'Alea, Tæfl, and Related Games: Vocabulary and Context', in *Latin Learning and English Lore*, ed. K. O'Brien O'Keeffe and Andy Orchard (Toronto, Buffalo and London, 2005), II, 9. A set of Eusebian canon tables precedes this diagram in this manuscript.

[40] 'Incipit alea euangelii quam Dubinsi episcopus bennchorensis detulit a rege Anglorum id est a domu Adalstani regis Anglorum depicta a quodam Francone et a Romano sapiente id est Israel.'

Here begins the Gospel Dice which Dub Innse, bishop of Bangor, brought from the English king, that is from the household of Æthelstan, king of England, drawn by a certain Frank[41] and by a Roman scholar, that is Israel.

In other words, this board game was brought back from the court of King Æthelstan to Bangor, where Dub Innse (died 953) was bishop; it remained there until it was copied into this mid-twelfth-century gospel book. The scribe copied and put into the third person an explanatory note that may well have been written by Dub Innse himself, not all of which the scribe seems fully to have understood.[42]

Other evidence also associates this Israel (called Roman because of the time he had previously spent studying with Ambrose in Rome, not because he was Italian by birth) with a period of time in England. Copies of a verse treatise by Israel (*De arte metrica*, dedicated to Robert, archbishop of Trier) made in England circulated with a dossier of texts relating to the study of Greek which Israel had probably also composed. That dossier included a Greek litany, a version of which survives – independently of the rest of the dossier – in another manuscript often associated with Æthelstan, the so-called 'Æthelstan Psalter'.[43] Although there is no certain link between this manuscript and the king, he may once have owned it (and perhaps later gave it to the Old Minster at Winchester). If it had once belonged to the king, the material added to the end of the manuscript in the second quarter of the tenth century (some Psalter collects, the Greek litany and a *Sanctus* in Greek) was presumably appended while the volume was in the king's possession. A strong case can be made that Israel obtained the litany and *Sanctus* which he added to his Greek dossier directly from the text in the Æthelstan Psalter, to which they are closely related. It follows, further, that Israel probably wrote his poem *De arte metrica* while still in England, sending it to the archbishop of Trier in a bid – ultimately successful – to win his patronage.[44] Israel provides a tantalizing link between the spheres of masculine camaraderie of a conventional royal court and the more rarefied, scholarly atmosphere that Æthelstan may have liked both his contemporaries and posterity to think he was keen to cultivate. Israel's fascinating career sheds further light on the prominence of Breton clergy and scholars in the circle around the king. These men brought to the

---

[41] Or, 'drawn by a certain [man called] Franco'.

[42] As Lapidge has explained ('Israel', 89, n. 17), the scribe struggled with the phrase *Romano sapiente id est Israel*, thinking it referred to a Roman Jew, not recognizing that Israel was a personal name. Others have made the same error: *TSD*, 70; Wood, 'The Making', 263; Wasserstein, 'The First Jew'.

[43] BL, MS Cotton Galba A. xviii. For the visual material added to this manuscript in England, perhaps during Æthelstan's reign see C.R. Dodwell, *The Pictorial Arts of the West 800–1200* (New Haven and London, 1993), 95–7, and below, 195 and plates 11–12.

[44] Lapidge, 'Israel', 99–103. For a full discussion of the manuscript and its putative link to the king, see Keynes, 'Books', 193–6.

English court their advanced learning in Greek, poetics and numerology, and shared these with the native clerics at Æthelstan's court, sharing also their own liturgical and monastic practices with their English counterparts.

An additional group of foreign clergy known to have stayed at Æthelstan's court deserves mention: the Irish. There had been Irishmen at Alfred's court, too, for example the three pilgrims mentioned in the Anglo-Saxon Chronicle, who sailed across the Irish Sea to Cornwall and made their way immediately to King Alfred.[45] In Æthelstan's day, as well as Bishop Dub Innse who took the Gospel Dice back to Ireland, another visiting Irishman, Dupliter, appears among the witnesses to the New Minster lease, named immediately after Eadhelm the Deacon. Previously thought to represent a tenth-century version of 'ditto' (i.e. to indicate that two deacons called Eadhelm witnessed the lease), this actually denotes the Old Irish name *Dub-liter* ('black letter'), common among Irish ecclesiastics from the eighth century onwards.[46] Inscriptions in manuscript books associated with King Æthelstan offer fascinating glimpses of some additional Irish scholars in the king's circle.[47] A ninth-century pocket gospel book known as the MacDurnan Gospels, now in Lambeth Palace Library, has a metrical inscription on the reverse of the third folio identifying the manuscript with King Æthelstan (who gave it to Canterbury) and with Mael Brigte mac Tornáin, an Irish cleric prominent in the late ninth and early tenth centuries: 'Mael Brigte mac Tornáin propounds this gospel book throughout the world, in a manner worthy of God, but Æthelstan, king and ruler of the Anglo-Saxons, gives it for ever to the metropolitan see of Canterbury.' Although the inscription does not say that the English king acquired the manuscript from the Irishman, we might reasonably assume that he did. Mael Brigte died in 927, however, so if he made the gift he did so either while Edward still ruled, or early in Æthelstan's reign.[48] Irish writers described Mael Brigte in hyperbolic terms; one obituary notice called him 'the head of the piety of all Ireland and of the greater part of Europe'. At least one Irish scribe thought equally highly of Æthelstan, describing him, after his death, as 'the pillar of the dignity of the Western world'. So in Ireland at least, the connection between the two did not appear implausible.[49] The inscription in the MacDurnan Gospels may have been written by Cenwald, bishop of Worcester, because of the similarities between the metre and language of inscription and a set of

[45] ASC, *s.a.* 891; Wendy Davies, 'Alfred's Contemporaries: Irish, Welsh, Scots and Breton', in *Alfred the Great*, ed. T. Reuter (Aldershot, 2003), 332.

[46] S 1417; Sean Miller, ed., *Charters of the New Minster, Winchester* (Oxford, 2000), 53; ASC 891; David N. Dumville, 'Mael Brigte mac Tornáin, Pluralist coarb (†927)', *Journal of Celtic Studies*, iv (2004), 97–116.

[47] *TSD*, 55–9.

[48] Lambeth Palace Library, MS 1370, fo. 3v; *TSD*, 55–9. The inscription has been printed, translated and discussed by Keynes, 'Books', 153–9.

[49] Dumville, 'Mael Brigte mac Tornáin', 97–116.

'alliterative' charters produced at Worcester in the 940s and 950s which should almost certainly be attributed to that bishop's authorship. Perhaps the king invited Cenwald to compose the verse for insertion in the manuscript late in his reign, when he wanted to give the book to Christ Church, Canterbury.[50] Another Irishman, Benedict, who had a prayer invoking St Cuthbert inserted into a now burnt gospel book given by Æthelstan to the community of St Cuthbert at Chester-le-Street, could also have visited the king's court; he might be identified with the *Benedictus episcopus* who witnessed one of the king's charters in 931.[51]

No concrete evidence locates Scottish or Welsh clergy in the king's court circle. Given the political circumstances of the submission of the Welsh and other British kings to Æthelstan's rule in 927, and the terms of the treaties he made with the Scots after English military successes in 934 and 937, it seems inconceivable, however, that such men were not represented in this multi-ethnic and multilingual environment, or indeed that they, too, would not have been attracted by the possibility of the king's patronage, given his known interest in learning.[52] This diverse body of international scholars – Franks, Germans, Scandinavians, Irish and above all Bretons – had a tangible influence on the intellectual development of English clerics in the king's circle. The dissemination of a wider range of texts, especially in Greek, and the sharing of new ideas about the practice of the communal religious life (ranging from the Breton and Irish solitary asceticism, to the recent promotion of Benedictine conventual living), all coloured the intellectual and spiritual development of churchmen in this circle and so fed, ultimately, into the institutional reforms of the Church witnessed in the second half of the tenth century.

Two key figures in the Benedictine revival of King Edgar's reign, Dunstan, abbot of Glastonbury and then archbishop of Canterbury, and Æthelwold, abbot of Abingdon and subsequently bishop of Winchester, both spent time as adolescents at – or at the fringes of – the court of Æthelstan. Æthelwold, who would in time prove the most energetic and passionate of the promoters of Benedictinism in England, served in a secular capacity at Æthelstan's court from the late 920s. Having attracted the king's attention as a young man, he found favour in his sight; 'he spent a long period there in the royal *burh* as the king's inseparable companion, learning much from the king's *witan* that was useful and profitable to him.'[53] The king saw him most valuably, however, not as a his secular adviser but as one

[50] Keynes, 'Books', 156–9.

[51] BL, Cotton Otho B. ix, fo. 1, lines 1–8 (prayer) and 9–10 (colophon naming Benedict): Keynes, 'Books', 170–3; S 413; Wood, 'The Making', 258.

[52] Dumville, *Wessex*, 156.

[53] Wulfstan of Winchester, *Vita S Æthelwoldi*, ch. 7, ed. and trans. M. Lapidge and M. Winterbottom (Oxford, 1991), 10–11. Æthelwold's name appears in charter witness-lists from the early 930s onwards; he could have joined the household rather earlier, perhaps in the late 920s: ibid., xliii.

of the clergy, commanding that he be tonsured by Bishop Ælfheah of Winchester into minor clerical orders and then, after a few years, that he be made a priest, supposedly on the same day as Dunstan. Æthelwold's adoption of the monastic life (at Glastonbury, under Dunstan), may post-date Æthelstan's death, but was arguably a decision that owed much to the ideas he had heard discussed in Æthelstan's circle.[54] Contacts forged especially by Cenwald through his German connections which brought knowledge of reforming ideas to England helped to inform Æthelwold's choice, but he would also have encountered scholars from West Frankish houses. For example Hilduin (his name anglicized to Hildewine), a Frank, appeared among the witnesses to the New Minster lease, and a certain Franco (or 'the Frank') had invented the Gospel Dice game with Israel, both of whom could have spoken of early essays in Benedictine life in Frankia. Æthelwold would later send one of his closest associates to Fleury to learn there the way of life according to the rule and teach it to his brothers at Abingdon on his return.[55]

Dunstan's connections with Æthelstan's court appear more tenuous, or at least prove harder to pin down, because of the lack of detail and loose chronology found in the earliest of his Lives. According to his first hagiographer, Dunstan had some kinship connection with the royal family, through his own kinswoman Æthelflæd who was supposedly of royal stock. If we may believe this account, the connection between Dunstan and the royal house came most plausibly through Æthelstan's mother, Ecgwynn.[56] A claim to royal lineage may exaggerate Dunstan's status somewhat; his father, Heorstan, was perhaps among the witnesses to the New Minster lease discussed above (it is not a common name), but he was not described there as a thegn. His brother, Wulfric, however, witnessed charters of Æthelstan's as a thegn from the early 930s onwards.[57] Dunstan himself only definitely became a member of the court circle of Æthelstan's successor, Edmund; he cannot certainly be placed in the immediate royal sphere before then. He spent his adolescence not at court, but as a tonsured cleric in the churches of the royal vill of Glastonbury, where his fellow *palatini* found his bookishness so irksome that they threw him out.[58] Thereafter, he joined the household of Bishop Ælfheah, bishop of Winchester, in

[54] Ibid., chs 7–9, pp. 10–15.

[55] Ibid., ch. 14, pp. 26–7.

[56] The earliest of the Lives of Dunstan said that the saint's kinswoman Æthelflæda was of royal stock (*regali ex progenie orta*) and related to King Æthelstan ('B', *Vita S Dunstani*, ch. 10, ed. W. Stubbs, *Memorial of St Dunstan* (London, 1874), 17–18). See Barbara Yorke, 'Æthelwold and the Politics of the Tenth Century,' in *Bishop Æthelwold*, ed. Barbara Yorke (Woodbridge, 1988), 66–7; Yorke, 'Edward as Ætheling', in H&H, 34.

[57] N. Brooks, 'The Career of Dunstan', in *St Dunstan: His Life, Times and Cult*, ed. N. Ramsay *et al.* (Woodbridge, 1992), 9; S 416–17, 425, 427.

[58] 'B', *Vita S Dunstani*, chs 5–6, ed. Stubbs, pp. 10–11; Brooks, 'The Career of St Dunstan', 5.

whose company he might have attended the royal court. Perhaps it was at this time that he supposedly heard the armour-bearer of King Edmund of East Anglia recount the details of that king's martyrdom at the hands of the Danes in 870.[59]

Dunstan owed his interest in professed monasticism to Bishop Ælfheah, whose epithet 'the Bald' probably relates to his adoption of a monastic tonsure. Ælfheah apparently persuaded Dunstan not to marry, as he had been intending, but to become a monk; a decision that clarified itself after a brief but severe bout of illness.[60] The bishop of Winchester clearly had a strong influence on Æthelwold and Dunstan, helping both towards realizing their vocation to the conventual life, yet we may give equal weight to the intellectual and spiritual character of the royal court during an impressionable period of these young men's lives and especially to the presence of foreign scholars in this circle. That environment would similarly have affected the personal development of other men later to hold senior office such as Beornstan of Winchester and Oda of Ramsbury (and later Canterbury), and other clerics close to the king, such as the deacons Eadhelm and Werferth and perhaps also Cynath, later abbot of Evesham.[61]

The king's charter scribe 'Æthelstan A' frequently included the names of abbots in witness-lists to the charters he drew up between 931 and 934, among whom an Abbot Ælfric always attested in first place. Ælfric might have been abbot of the Old Minster (which preserved a copy of a charter granted to Ælfric by the king), or of another Hampshire monastery. His prominence in the king's charters suggests that he was either the head of a community of some distinction or someone especially close to the king.[62] According to the *Passio* of St Ursula (the virgin saint whose cult was based in Cologne), an East Frankish count called Hoolf, sent to England to negotiate for a bride for Henry the Fowler's son, Otto, first heard of the story of the holy virgins of Cologne and St Ursula while in England, his source being St Dunstan. If the author of the text (written in the early 970s) has not simply added the name of the then archbishop of Canterbury to lend verisimilitude to an otherwise somewhat unlikely tale, we might imagine that Hoolf had encountered the young Dunstan in the circle of the English king.[63]

Study of the intellectual and ecclesiastical company gathered around the king has presented a picture of a royal court quite different from the sort of conventional warrior *comitatus* we might have envisaged assembling around a ruler with so great a reputation for military prowess as Æthelstan.[64] It may thus continue to surprise us that the contemporary

---

[59] Abbo, *Passio*, 67. Various aspects of this story fail to inspire confidence.

[60] 'B', *Vita S Dunstani*, ch. 7, pp. 13–15.

[61] *TSD*, 35–40.

[62] S 412; *TSD*, 82–3.

[63] W. Levison, 'Das Werden der Ursula-Legende', *Bonner Jahrbucher*, cxxxii (1928), 142–57 and commentary 58–90; see Leyser, 'The Ottonians', 79.

[64] A point made also by Dumville, *Wessex*, 167–9.

narrative sources for this king's reign are so few, for from this context prose composition in Latin and the vernacular could easily have emerged. Æthelstan had around him English men of the second generation able to capitalize on the benefits of the educational revival that his grandfather had launched in the 880s, as well as numerous educated scholars from continental Europe and the Celtic world, at least one of whom was adept also in Greek. The Anglo-Saxon Chronicle, of course, concerned itself predominantly with diplomacy and war; it tells us therefore about the three key military engagements of Æthelstan's reign and reports the deaths and successions of bishops, but its compilers had not previously considered cultural affairs to lie within their remit. Yet in the Chronicle's report of the greatest of this king's military exploits, his victory at *Brunanburh* in 937, we find a notable divergence from customary annalistic practice; that entry is written not in the laconic prose that characterizes the rest of the Chronicle from this period, but in verse.[65] And that recourse to poetry should give us pause. For far more remarkable than the paucity of prose to survive from Æthelstan's reign is the relative abundance of verse written for the king, or within his court circle.[66] Something in the atmosphere around this king clearly encouraged poetic expression. Perhaps descriptions of heroic deeds and accounts of particularly splendid diplomatic occasions were considered more suitable for poetic than for prose treatment.[67] Alternatively, the king may himself have encouraged the writing of poetry as a deliberate policy to differentiate the intellectual output of his own reign from the prose with which his grandfather was so closely associated; Æthelstan might thus have commissioned Israel the Grammarian to write his verse treatise on the metrical art during his time in England for the instruction and encouragement of other would-be poets in this circle.

ÆTHELSTAN PATRON OF POETS

Earliest of the surviving verses written in Æthelstan's honour was the acrostic praise-poem worked around the letters of his name. 'You, prince, are called by the name of sovereign stone,' it begins, punning on Æthelstan's Old English name, meaning 'noble stone'. The first letter of each line, read down the manuscript page, spells out the name ADALSTAN; the last letter of each line give us a second name, IOHANNES. The poem foretold the

---

[65] The *Brunanburh* poem is the first of five poems entered into the Chronicle in the tenth century; see Thomas Bredehoft, *Textual Histories: Readings in the Anglo-Saxon Chronicle* (Toronto, 2001).

[66] I owe this useful observation to David Luscombe. For the possibility that a contemporary life of the king once survived in the library of Glastonbury Abbey, see Wood, 'The Making', 265–7; Thomson, *Commentary*, 118. That text, too, could of course have been written in verse.

[67] James Campbell, *The Anglo-Saxon State* (London, 2000), 138.

great harvest that Æthelstan would garner because he was 'more abundantly endowed with the holy eminence of learning', and promised peace following victory against demons (perhaps to be understood as pagan Scandinavians).[68] If we follow the conventional reading of this verse as a product of the latter years of Alfred's reign, commemorating that king's investiture of his small grandson with symbols of hoped-for future greatness, we should locate its composition within the intellectual culture of that court. John the Old Saxon, the continental scholar in Alfred's circle, might have written it, or conceivably John, the abbot of the Breton house at Landévennec.[69] Assuming that its content amounts to more than bland and conventional panegyric, we could use the verse as evidence that even at this young age, the prince, already showing signs of intellectual ability, was being educated to a high level, 'groomed from the start as an intellectual'.[70]

Such an interpretation does, however, present a number of difficulties, not least the implausibility that such sentiments would be uttered to a small child. Although essentially prophetic, the poem assumes not a future marked out by scholastic excellence, but that its dedicatee *already* is 'abundantly endowed with the holy eminence of learning', something one would struggle to say of even the most precocious of five year olds. The prophecy came earlier – 'Often an abundant cornfield foretells a great harvest' – implying that the grain sown through the prince's education has already fallen on fertile ground and grown into a mature field of corn, from which the riches of a future harvest now seem clear. Offering a new interpretation of this verse, Gernot Wieland has argued that the poet wrote in praise of the adult king, specifically to celebrate Æthelstan's coronation in early September 925 (at which point of the year, metaphors about ripe cornfields would have come readily to the poet's tongue). As a prophecy inaugurating a new reign and celebrating the accession of a prince already marked out by his learning and with an existing reputation for prowess on the battlefield, the verse makes more sense. Further, Wieland has commented on the poet's reference not to one but to two names of Æthelstan: 'I pray,' the poet writes in the last line of this verse, that you may seek and the Glorious One may grant [the fulfilment implied in your] noble names.' He suggests that the name Iohannes which the terminal letters of each line spell out refers not to the author of the poem, but to a second name (the Hebrew name John meaning 'the favour of the Lord') either given to Æthelstan at his baptism, or assumed in adulthood, even perhaps at the moment of his consecration. The whole poem thus played on Æthelstan's given name, noble stone, but it also alluded to a second name by wishing on him the favour of the Lord, so that he might

---

[68] Above, 31. Lapidge, 'Poems' 72–83.

[69] Above, 33 for the possible identifications of Iohannes, see Lapidge 'Poems'; Brett, 'A Breton Pilgrim', 44–5 and 49–50.

[70] Wood, ' "Stand Strong" ', 194–9.

in war overcome devilish demons and in peace soften his stoniness and promote the learning in which he had already shown himself expert.[71]

The choice of a verse medium for the expression of these sentiments seems prescient in light of the later verses produced in Æthelstan's circle. As we have already seen, a clerk at the royal court, Petrus (probably of continental origin), wrote a longer set of verses in 927 celebrating the submission of other rulers in Britain to Æthelstan's authority at Eamont after his acquisition of power in Northumbria on the death of his brother-in-law, Sihtric of York. *Carta dirige gressus*, 'Letter, direct your steps, sailing across the seas and an expanse of land, to the king's *burh*', recounted recent events in Northumbria to the queen (Edward's widow, Eadgifu), the prince (probably the eldest of Æthelstan's surviving brothers, Edwin), and the ealdormen and thegns left behind at the court, presumably in Winchester. Assuming its author penned the verses while still in Cumbria, the swiftest route back to southern Hampshire would indeed have involved water, either by sea from Carlisle to the mouth of the Mersey and then by land south through Mercia and Wessex, or perhaps even all the way round Wales by sea to the northern coast of Devon and then by land to the royal *burh*. Petrus celebrated 'this Saxon land now made whole' (*ista perfecta Saxonia*) and lauded Æthelstan, 'who lives glorious through his deeds'.[72] Prose could have conveyed the same essential message, and arguably fleshed it out with extra supporting detail, but the choice of an elevated, more rhetorical verse form magnified the impact of the royal clerk's words. Great occasions demand higher modes of discourse. Detail could wait for the messenger carrying the poem to make an oral report.

Similar considerations governed the decision to celebrate Æthelstan's greatest victory at *Brunanburh* in verse not prose in the Anglo-Saxon Chronicle via a poem that may well have had an oral existence independent of its preservation with, the annals of the Chronicle. Although the poem does not rank among the greatest surviving examples of Old English poetry, and many have criticized its formulaic structure and the extent to which the poet depended on borrowing from pre-existing verse, it sheds important light on the cultural milieu of Æthelstan's court and it may in fact have been deliberately contrived to appear archaic and rhetorically mannered.[73] The poem shows in both language and poetic technique some debts to contemporary Norse poetry, and may thus reflect a familiarity with skaldic verse which its author had acquired at Æthelstan's court; its panegyric form fits well within contemporary traditions of

---

[71] Wieland, 'A New Look'.

[72] Lapidge, 'Poems', 83–93 and 98 for full text and translation. For the military context see below, 160–2.

[73] R.I. Page, 'A Tale of Two Cities', *Peritia*, i (1982), 336. Simon Walker, 'A Context for *Brunanburh*', in *Warriors and Churchmen*, ed. Timothy Reuter (London, 1992), 37. For the content of the poem, see the detailed discussion below, 170–1.

Old English and Old Norse praise-poetry. The poet's focus on the names of the protagonists in the battle – Æthelstan and his brother Edmund, the sons of Edward, and their foes Anlaf (Olaf) and Costontinus (Constantín) – corresponds typically to this genre; the poet heaps praise upon the West Saxon victors and triumphs in the unequivocal defeat of their enemies, who crawl away shamed, no longer having cause to exult, or boast or laugh.[74] Edmund plays so equal a part in the English success that some have wondered if the poem was in fact composed during his reign and not that of his elder brother, but it fits more obviously into the rhetorical milieu of Æthelstan's court.[75] Its author might have been a churchman from Æthelstan's circle; indeed, a case has been made for ascribing its authorship to Cenwald, bishop of Worcester (and that he apparently composed Latin verse celebrating Mael Brigte as well as the alliterative charters in the reigns of Edmund and Eadred would support such a supposition). The verses need not have reported his own personal views, still less those of the Worcester community. Despite no longer living as a member of the king's immediate circle after assuming the bishopric of Worcester, Cenwald may nonetheless have reflected attitudes to the significance of this battle current at the royal court.[76] Someone in the West Saxon court 'clearly thought the composition of panegyric verse a good idea' (and saw that it found inclusion in the Chronicle record);[77] that someone may well have been Æthelstan himself.[78] The poem's grandiose rhetorical language, appeal to historical precedent and focus on the dynastic claims to rulership of Æthelstan and Edmund all point to preoccupations of the royal circle and compare well with ideological statements adumbrated in Æthelstan's charters and on his coinage. The *Battle of Brunanburh* poem supports the king's claims to imperial sovereignty and to hegemony not just over the Anglo-Saxons, or the Anglo-Saxon and Anglo-Danish populations of the island, but to the whole of Britain.[79]

[74] John D. Niles, 'Skaldic Technique in *Brunanburh*', *Scandinavian Studies*, lix (1987), 356–66; Matthew Townend, 'Pre-Cnut Praise-Poetry in Viking Age England', *Review of English Studies*, n.s. li, 203 (2000), 352–4.

[75] Walker, 'A Context', 36–8; Donald Scragg, 'A Reading of *Brunanburh*', in *Unlocking the Wordhord*, ed. Mark C. Amodio and Katherine O'Brien O'Keefe (Toronto, 1998), 109–22. Above, ch. 4. Edward B. Irving has commented on the national sentiments evoked by the poem: Edward B. Irving, 'The Charge of the Saxon Brigade: Tennyson's *Battle of Brunanburh*', in *Literary Appropriations of the Anglo-Saxons*, ed. Donald Scragg and Carole Weinberg (Cambridge, 2000), 183.

[76] I have discussed this poem at length elsewhere: 'Where English Becomes British: Rethinking Contexts for *Brunanburh*', in *Myth, Rulership, Church and Charters*, ed. Julia Barrow and Andrew Wareham (Aldershot, 2008), 143; see also Walker, 'A Context', 21–39 for the suggestion that Cenwald was its author.

[77] T.A. Shippey, *Old English Verse* (London, 1972), 186.

[78] Townend, 'Pre-Cnut Praise-Poetry', 367.

[79] See my 'Where English becomes British', 127–44, and further below, 223–6.

Hyperbole also characterizes the poem set at the head of this chapter, *Rex pius Æðelstan*, a text which celebrates the multifaceted character of this pious warrior king. As already suggested, the poem was probably written at Christ Church, Canterbury, perhaps by the continental scribe who copied it into the manuscript, after Æthelstan had given the community the gospel book in which it survives. It honours Æthelstan as a king appointed by God to rule over the English people (*Angligenus*), and to lead his earthly forces

> plainly so that this king himself, mighty in war, might be able
> to conquer other fierce kings, treading down their proud necks.[80]

If these lines allude to Æthelstan's resounding defeat of Olaf and Constantín at *Brunanburh*, then we could date the verse to the last two years of the king's reign.[81] Yet this poem does not simply praise the powerful military man; it echoes the themes of the earlier acrostic, commending him equally for his promotion and celebration of learning, inviting those who read the verse to come and drink from the streams of learning within the volume. The poet claimed that the king himself, filled with the Holy Spirit, had had the manuscript adorned with golden headings and set with jewels, apparently in ignorance of its continental origins but showing perhaps some awareness of the richness of manuscript production in the king's circle. Its image of Æthelstan as a pious and serious-minded ruler is one that has had a marked influence on later historical readings of this reign from William of Malmesbury onwards, possibly unduly so.[82] Æthelstan also inspired the composition of verses after his own time; in addition to a late eleventh- or early twelfth-century poem in praise of the king, perhaps his own composition and from which William of Malmesbury quoted at some length in his *Gesta regum*,[83] we know other short verses were inserted into manuscripts associated with the king.[84]

Manifestly poetry was composed and we must assume recited in Æthelstan's circle; for praise-poetry was meant to be declaimed and thus remembered; an uncirculated praise-poem would have no value at all.[85] In such an environment we should not be surprised to find other verses composed in the king's honour by laymen as well as ecclesiastics. The thirteenth-century Icelandic *Egils saga* preserves poems attributed to its

---

[80] Lines 5–6, trans. Lapidge, 'Poems', 96.

[81] Lapidge, 'Poems' 97, n. 158; Keynes, 'Books', 150–1.

[82] Walker, 'A Context', 23. Compare the verse with which William began his account of Æthelstan's reign in his *Gesta regum*, which dwelt specifically on the king's education: *GR*, ii, 133, pp. 210–13; Wood, ' "Stand Strong" ', 197–8.

[83] Lapidge, 'Poems', 62–71; see further below, Appendix I.

[84] For example, the short poem 'Saxonidum dux' added, probably in the early seventeenth century as a title page to BL, Cotton Tiberius A. ii, a gospel book given by Æthelstan to Christ Church, Canterbury. Or the verses composed by Leland in praise of Æthelstan: Keynes, 'Books', 151–2, 164 and 168; Lapidge, 'Poems' 94.

[85] Townend, 'Pre-Cnut Praise-Poetry', 351–2.

eponymous hero, Egil Skallagrímsson and addressed directly to King Æthelstan. These Egil reputedly wrote during the winter after the battle of *Brunanburh* (*Vínheiðr* in the saga), which he spent at Æthelstan's court, where the king made him welcome and rewarded him generously. Some of these poems refer to the military campaign at *Vínheiðr* including one (stanza 17) which describes Egil's grief at the death of his brother, now buried under Vína's bank. The refrain to a long praise-poem in Æthelstan's honour of which the saga only quotes a few lines apparently ran: 'The highest path of the reindeer now lies in the power of the brave Æthelstan', in a seeming reference to his overlordship of the Highlands of Scotland. Although some remain sceptical as to Egil's authorship of some or all of these verses, this celebrated Norse poet may indeed have been among those laypeople who benefited from Æthelstan's patronage of learning and the creative arts.[86] It is further possible that the now lost account of the 'Wars of Æthelstan', which may have provided William of Malmesbury with the source on which he constructed his lengthy narrative of the king's reign, was written at least partly in verse; this may have been composed after the king's death, but could conceivably date from late in Æthelstan's reign, after his victory at *Brunanburh*.[87]

Could other known and surviving poetry have been composed at Æthelstan's court, even the most famous of all Old English poems, *Beowulf*? That poem now survives only in a single manuscript, dating from c.1000, but a case can be made for suggesting that it might first have been composed in Æthelstan's circle. Obviously, *Beowulf* is not just a lengthy, but a complex poem, perhaps originally more than one single poetic text. Given the richness of the cultural, social and historical repertoire on which it draws it can only have reached 'the literary form in which we have it after long gestation and sustained social thought. The traditions which contributed to this masterpiece were not welded to each other mechanically or quickly.'[88] Yet beyond the demonstrable popularity

---

[86] *Egils Saga*, chs 51–5, trans. and ed. Christine Fell (London, 1975), 74–86; A. Campbell, *The Battle of Brunanburh* (London, 1938), 74, n. 2; A. Campbell, *Skaldic Verse and Anglo-Saxon History* (London, 1971), 5–7; Magnús Fjalldal, 'A Farmer in the Court of King Athelstan: Historical and Literary Considerations in the Vínheiðr Episode of *Egils Saga*', *English Studies*, lxxvii (1996), 20–1.

[87] James Campbell, *The Anglo-Saxon State* (London, 2000), 138. See further below, Appendix I.

[88] R. Collins, 'Blickling XVI', in *Medieval Studies Conference, Aachen, 1983*, ed. W.-D. Bald and H. Weinstock (Frankfurt, 1984), 69; quoted by Audrey Meaney, 'Scyld Scefing and the Dating of *Beowulf* – Again', The Toller Lecture 1988, reprinted in *Textual and Material Culture in Anglo-Saxon England: Thomas Northcote Toller and the Toller Memorial Lectures*, ed. Donald Scragg (Woodbridge, 2003), 23–73, at 53. Multiple efforts to date the text have produced no consensus among scholars, and one might reasonably question the value of such an exercise, particularly attempts to date it on historical grounds: Hildegard L.C. Tristram, 'What's the Point of Dating *Beowulf*?', in *Medieval Insular Literature between the Oral and the Written, II: Continuity of Transmission*, ed. H.L.C. Tristram (Tübingen, 1997), 65–80. See also Roy Liuzza, 'On the dating of *Beowulf*', in *Beowulf Basic Readings*, ed. Peter Baker (New York, 1995), 281–302, which argues that many Old English poems may have been composed centuries before they were first compiled in manuscript texts.

of verse at Æthelstan's court, other factors might argue for *Beowulf*'s composition in his day.

Reference to a people called the 'Hugas' in *Beowulf*'s account of Hygelac's raid on the Merovingian kingdom might date from a period when men called Hugh controlled a Frankish realm. If so, the poem could date either from the time of Hugh the Abbot, who led the Neustrians from 866 until the 880s, or – more plausibly – from after the deposition of Charles 'the Simple' in 923, when Hugh, duke of the Franks, and Æthelstan's brother-in-law, ruled the western kingdom.[89] The prologue to the poem deals with the pedigree of the Danish kings and is closely related to the pedigree of Æthelwulf (grandfather of Alfred the Great) inserted into the Anglo-Saxon Chronicle under the year 858. While this could suggest a date of composition late in Alfred's reign,[90] the prologue also reflects the account of the funeral of Gildas in that saint's *Vita*, perhaps written in Brittany *c*.900. That text might have become available to the *Beowulf* poet if brought to England by Breton scholars who came to English shores in Æthelstan's (and his father's) reigns and whose presence in his circle we have already noted.[91] Another element in the case for dating the poem to the 920s or 930s rests on the presence of apparent allusions to *Beowulf* in the proems to some of Æthelstan's charters and even in his law codes.[92] Converted Danes living in the Danelaw could have been among the poem's intended audience and Æthelstan's annexation of Northumbria in 927 of course increased the number of those potential listeners to this verse in his own court circle.[93] Æthelstan showed his awareness of the significance of that racial group among his subjects in adopting the regnal style 'most glorious king of the Anglo-Saxons and the Danes' (*Angelsaxonum Denorumque gloriosissimus rex*) in the lease in favour of the New Minster granted early in his reign. Among those of Danish origin at his court we might mention the seven ealdormen with Scandinavian names who witnessed the charter Æthelstan issued at Lifton in Devon in 931 and Oda, bishop of Ramsbury, who was also of

---

[89] Walter Goffart, '*Hetware* and *Hugas*: Datable Anachronisms in Beowulf', in *The Dating of Beowulf*, ed. Colin Chase (Toronto, 1981), 83–100.

[90] As argued by Craig R. Davis, 'An Ethnic Dating of *Beowulf*', *ASE*, xxxv (2006), 111–29.

[91] Meaney, 'Scyld Scefing'.

[92] R.L. Reynolds, 'An Echo of *Beowulf* in Æthelstan's Charters of 931–933 AD', *Medium Ævum*, xxiv (1955), 101–3; Zacharias P. Thundy, '*Beowulf*: Date and Authorship', *Neuphilologische Mitteilungen*, lxxxvii (1986), 102–16. Thundy has proposed an identity for the poet, equating him with the thegn Wulfgar, who received a grant of land in Wiltshire from Æthelstan in 931, the bounds of which mention a piece of land belonging to one *Beow* and also Grendel's mere: S 416; Thundy, 115, and cf. Reynolds 103. Even though, as those familiar with the poem will recall, Wulfgar was the name of a counsellor of Hrothgar, this seems distinctly fanciful.

[93] R.I. Page, 'The Audience of *Beowulf* and the Vikings', in *The Dating of Beowulf*, ed. Colin Chase (Toronto, 1981), 113–22.

[94] S 416; 1417; Stenton, *ASE*, 347–8. Patricia Poussa, 'The Date of *Beowulf* Reconsidered: the Tenth Century?', *Neuphilologische Mitteilungen*, lxxxii (1981), 277; Alexander Murray, '*Beowulf*, the Danish Invasions and Royal Genealogy', in *The Dating of Beowulf*, ed. Colin

Danish extraction.[94] The *Beowulf* poet also demonstrates some familiarity with Scandinavian, skaldic verse, which those Danes may have helped to popularize in Æthelstan's circle, together with the king's foster-son Hákon.[95]

Unquestionably Æthelstan's court, where poetry was written and recited, could have provided the sort of intellectual milieu from which a poet such as the one (or ones) who composed *Beowulf* might have emerged. If we envisage this first as an oral piece commissioned by an English patron but designed for a mixed Anglo-Scandinavian audience, Æthelstan's international and cultured circle would constitute a suitable, even a likely setting for early recitations of this work.[96] Yet, to quote Roberta Frank: 'When after one hundred and fifty years of speculation we have reached no certainty regarding the date of *Beowulf*, certainty may not be attainable.'[97] A tenth-century date for the poem is entirely possible and one can even make a case for placing the text no earlier than the second quarter of that century and thus during Æthelstan's reign. Nothing in the political situation in England during his reign would preclude such an argument.[98] But this is not the same as arguing that the poem, or a version of it, did first emerge in this rather rarefied court environment or in a household a little removed from the king's own (such as that of one of the king's ealdormen, or a learned bishop). Appealing as it may seem to link this most famous early English epic poem with Æthelstan, to argue that *Beowulf* could have been composed in Æthelstan's reign, or even under his patronage, is not to demonstrate that it was.

Æthelstan's reputation for piety and education and for the keen encouragement of scholars and intellectual patronage of their activities is reinforced by the number of books associated with him, both those known to have belonged to him personally, and those he gave to various religious houses, for he saw patronage of the Church as an institution, as well as that of individual churchmen, as a central element of his role as king.

ÆTHELSTAN AS A PATRON OF THE CHURCH

Piety went hand in hand with generosity. Æthelstan's earliest legal pronouncements dealt with the necessity for all to pay tithes to support the Church and with the spiritual value of alms-giving; the proems of some of his charters also expounded the benefit of alms-giving for the remission of

---

Chase (Toronto, 1981), 109. Murray has further equated probable Mercian allusions in the poem with Æthelstan's known Mercian connections. Byrhtferth of Ramsey reported a popular belief that Oda's father had come to England in the army of Ubbe and Ivarr (who raided in England from 865–6 onwards): Byrhtferth, *Vita S Oswaldi*, i, 4, ed. Michael Lapidge, *Byrhtferth of Ramsey, the Lives of St Oswald and St Ecgwine* (Oxford, 2009), 16–17.

[95] Roberta Frank, 'Skaldic Verse and the Date of *Beowulf*', in *The Dating of Beowulf*, ed. Colin Chase (Toronto, 1981), 123–39.

[96] J.D. Niles, *Beowulf: the Poem and its Tradition* (Cambridge, Mass, 1983), 105, 112–13.

[97] Frank, 'Skaldic Verse', 123.

[98] Page, 'The Audience', 122.

sins.[99] That Æthelstan would prove a liberal benefactor to the Church of his day we might have anticipated, given what we have established thus far about his personality and interests; indeed his charters attest to his munificence to cathedral and monastic churches and to individual clerics and religious women, as do the various surviving books that contain inscriptions recording their donation by the king. Yet the fact of Æthelstan's pious reputation and his demonstrable enthusiasm for endowing churches with land, wealth, books and relics led later monastic scribes to claim that their institutions too had received his largesse. Just as we shall find some over-enthusiastic claims made by various monasteries about the acquisition of relics from this king (see Chapter 7), so a number of charters forged in monastic scriptoria purport to attest to Æthelstan's generous gifts of land and privilege. More secure evidence of the king's generosity comes from inscriptions in manuscript books recording his donations.[100]

Two gospel books given by the king to Christ Church, Canterbury and bearing inscriptions recording that gift we have already mentioned: the so-called MacDurnan Gospels with their verse inscription mentioning the Irish ecclesiastic Mael Brigte mac Tornáin,[101] and the continental gospel book (perhaps acquired by the king as a gift during his arrangement of one of his sisters' marriages) into which a scribe in the royal household copied an inscription recording Æthelstan's gift in terms reminiscent of the language of his charters. That text began, 'Æthelstan, king of the English and ruler of the whole of Britain, with a devout mind gave this gospel book to the primatial see of Canterbury, to the church dedicated to Christ. And may the archbishop and the community of this church, present and future, for ever regard the donation with diligent feelings, and in particular may they take pains to safeguard it . . .'.[102] Another continental gospel book, this one from Brittany, the king apparently gave to St Augustine's Canterbury. An inscription in a non-contemporary hand (perhaps one attempting to imitate Anglo-Saxon script) records: 'With a devout mind King Æthelstan gave this book to the church of Canterbury dedicated to St Augustine; and whoever reads this make prayers to the Almighty for him and for his [friends].' Despite the difficulties of interpretation, the inscription in imitative script probably copied a genuine contemporaneous text, perhaps because the original had been damaged, or removed from the manuscript.[103]

---

[99] Below, 133–4.

[100] Æthelstan's book-collecting and donation were studied by Armitage Robinson, *TSD*, 51–71, and have more recently been the subject of an exhaustive study by Simon Keynes: 'Books'.

[101] London, Lambeth Palace, MS 1370; Keynes, 'Books', 153–9.

[102] BL, MS Cotton Tiberius A. ii; Keynes, 'Books', 147–53, quoted the inscription in full, 149–50, n. 33. On the language of the inscription and contemporary royal charters, see below, 212–15.

[103] BL, MS, Royal 1. A. xviii, Keynes, 'Books', 165–70.

That inscription is closely related both to the one in the gospels he gave to Christ Church, and to another added to a copy of the Acts of the Council of Constantinople of 680 written on the continent in the late ninth century which the king gave to Bath Abbey, according to a tenth-century inscription recorded at the foot of one page: 'King Æthelstan gave this book to God and to the holy mother of Christ and to the saints Peter and Benedict in the monastery of the city of Bath, for the salvation of his soul. And may whoever reads these letters make prayers to the Almighty for him and for his friends.'[104] Reference to St Benedict in a text apparently pre-dating the Benedictine revival of the 960s may seem surprising, especially since it was to Bath that monks from St-Bertin fled in the 940s when they wished to escape the reforms being implemented in their own house by Gerhard of Brogne.[105] Perhaps a group of monastically minded men from the king's wider circle had established themselves together at Bath, having learned about the continental reforms either through their own direct experience or via conversations at the king's court. Bath had been the site of a religious community since the seventh century, although the estate may by the early tenth century have been in royal hands and perhaps was given to this congregation by the king himself. If he did give it to this group, it remains uncertain whether he also granted them any additional land for their support. Both the charter dated 931 claiming that Æthelstan donated land in Somerset and Gloucestershire to Bath and another later charter of Eadwig's which makes reference to that grant are spurious.[106] The sixteenth-century antiquary Leland reported that he had seen several other books at Bath with inscriptions reporting their donation by Æthelstan as well as this manuscript with the council's *acta*, into which he inserted a poem of his own, so the king may in fact have supported and indeed felt some affection for this congregation.[107] All of these gifts of books – to the houses in Canterbury, and to Bath – Æthelstan said he had made for the benefit of his own soul; the inscriptions served to remind the recipients not just of his generosity, but of their reciprocal obligations to pray for him and his soul in perpetuity, and also to remember his close associates through prayer. Further, as one inscription put it, the king hoped that a fine gospel book would 'provide in perpetuity an example of glory for those looking at it'.[108]

More than textual evidence associates King Æthelstan with literary and material gifts to the community of St Cuthbert. In the middle years of the tenth century this congregation had established itself at Chester-le-Street in County Durham, after some years of wandering following their abandonment of their island home on Lindisfarne in the face of Viking attack.

[104] BL, MS Cotton Claudius B. v, fo. 5r; Keynes, 'Books', 159–65.
[105] *TSD*, 62–4; Keynes, 'Books', 161–2; this episode was discussed fully above, ch. 2.
[106] S 414, 610, 643.
[107] Keynes, 'Books', 164.
[108] BL, MS Cotton Tiberius A. ii, fo. 15v; Keynes, 'Books', 149–50.

A full-page picture, the frontispiece to a manuscript copy of Bede's Lives of St Cuthbert now in the library of Corpus Christi College, Cambridge, depicts King Æthelstan in the act of giving the book to St Cuthbert, plate 1.[109] The two men both stand, the king on the left, the saint on the right, each contained within his own architectural frame. Cuthbert poses before his church, holding a small, closed book in his left hand and raising his right hand, palm towards the viewer. The crowned king stands inside an arch, intended perhaps to signify the entrance to the church through which the king progressed, climbing up steps towards the saint.[110] Bent forward, Æthelstan's eyes rest on the pages of the open book he holds in both hands. Although the two figures inhabit different spaces, these are not separate, discrete locations: they interconnect.[111] Cuthbert's right hand, raised perhaps in blessing, but also possibly in a gesture of acceptance or even of acknowledgement, intrudes into the king's frame, while the left-hand door jamb of Cuthbert's church partially obscures the right-hand pillar of the king's sheltering arch.

Conventionally understood to depict the king in the act of offering the book to the saint – for the composition of the whole image turns on the book in the king's hands – the picture has recently been differently interpreted by David Rollason. He has suggested that the fact that the pages of the book Æthelstan holds lie open and the bowed king's eyes are cast down on to the text, rather than directed up at the saint in front of him, indicates that he was not here donating the book, but rather engaged in a private act of devotion to the saint. The king reads and meditates on Cuthbert and his deeds, while the saint – standing apart in his own architectural space and looking out of the page, not across to the king – symbolizes Æthelstan's devotion to his memory.[112] Challenging that interpretation Catherine Karkov has argued that, despite the lack of inscription explaining the act, this portrait resembles more closely other early medieval presentation portraits than it does images of private or contemplative readers, who are normally shown seated.[113] That the book lay open may point observers to the extremely personal nature of the gift and remind them of Æthelstan's promotion of learning, implying that this was a book of as special relevance to the king as to the members of the community who preserved the cult of the saint whose deeds were described in its pages. The king's act of reading about the saint reminds those who look at the image of his

[109] Cambridge, Corpus Christi College, MS 183, fo. IV; Keynes, 'Books', 180–4. Mildred Budny, *Insular, Anglo-Saxon, and Early Anglo-Norman Manuscript Art at Corpus Christi College, Cambridge: an Illustrated Catalogue*, 2 vols (1997), i, 161–85 (no. 12).

[110] Richard Gameson, *The Role of Art in the Late Anglo-Saxon Church* (Oxford, 1995), 180–3.

[111] Catherine E. Karkov, *The Ruler Portraits of Anglo-Saxon England* (Woodbridge, 2004), 59.

[112] David Rollason, 'St Cuthbert and Wessex', in *St Cuthbert, his Cult and his Community to AD 1200*, ed. Gerald Bonner et al. (Woodbridge, 1989), 421; D.R. Rollason, *Saints and Relics in Anglo-Saxon England* (Oxford, 1989), 150; see also Gameson, *Role of Art*, 58–9, 118–19, 256.

[113] Karkov, *Ruler Portraits*, 59.

personal spirituality, showing himself as a 'brother of monks'.[114] Cuthbert held a book, too, and perhaps this was a reciprocal act of gift-giving, where books were exchanged. We might further note that this image of a figure standing to read resembles the picture of the standing, reading evangelist in a gospel book from Constantinople now in Paris dating from 964, which derives from the portrait tradition in Antiquity and Late Antiquity of depicting authors standing (slightly stooped, just as the king is here) and reading from the open page before them.[115] This, rather than Carolingian ruler-portraits, may have provided the model for the image of the king in the Bede manuscript. Æthelstan chose to present himself in that picture as a king cast in the mould recommended by his grandfather. King Alfred had made the ability to comprehend instructions sent in writing a precondition for holding positions of power and authority and threatened to remove from such positions ealdormen who failed in this respect. Æthelstan demonstrated through careful use of image that he, too, was a learned king, meditating after his grandfather's example on the meaning of the written word, as well as on the life and deeds of St Cuthbert. Humble, devoted and learned, he makes himself an entirely fit recipient of the saint's blessing.[116]

In composition and iconography the picture of Æthelstan and Cuthbert in the Bede manuscript appears superficially similar to a now lost miniature added to a Breton gospel book dating from the late ninth or early tenth century that Æthelstan also gave to the community of St Cuthbert. Antiquarian descriptions of that portrait made before it was burnt in the fire at Ashburnham House in October 1731, which damaged or destroyed much of Sir Robert Cotton's Library, permit its detailed reconstruction. Æthelstan appeared crowned there also, but rather than standing beside the saint, he knelt, a sceptre in his left hand as he held the closed book out to St Cuthbert with his right. Cuthbert did not stand either, but sat in his church, with a book in his left hand, as he blessed the king with his right. Unlike the picture in the Bede manuscript, the one in the gospel book had an inscription: 'To St Cuthbert the bishop, Æthelstan, pious king of the English (*Anglorum piisimus rex*), offers this gospel book.'[117] In that lost portrait, which may owe something to near-contemporary Carolingian representations, we cannot doubt that the king meant to present his book to the saint. It is usually argued that Æthelstan made that gift in 934, when we know he visited the shrine of St Cuthbert on his northward journey to quell the Scottish rebellion.[118]

[114] Gameson, *Role of Art*, 25.

[115] Paris, BN MS gr, 70, *Byzance*, no. 263, with colour plate on p. 352; see Kurt Weitzmann, *Ancient Book Illumination* (Cambridge, MA, 1959), 119–20; Gameson, *Role of Art*, 58–9.

[116] Asser, ch. 106; Gameson, *Role of Art*, 256. I am grateful to Richard Gameson for help in interpreting this portrait.

[117] BL, MS Cotton Otho B. ix; Keynes, 'Books', 174; Karkov, *Ruler Portraits*, 55–6.

[118] Below, 166.

Support for this interpretation comes in the mid-eleventh-century house-history of the Cuthbert community, the *Historia de Sancto Cuthberto*, which quotes from a signed *testamentum* (in the form of a charter) that King Æthelstan supposedly placed beside the head of the saint, when his coffin was opened for the visiting king.[119] According to this *testamentum* the king gave on this occasion three gospel books (one of which is normally identified as that manuscript burnt in the Cotton fire with its portrait of the king and the saint), a missal, and a copy of Bede's Lives of St Cuthbert (i.e. the manuscript with the surviving double portrait, now in Cambridge).[120] In fact the king may have given the Bede manuscript at some later point after 934, but the gospel book with the portrait he probably did have with him on that earlier occasion.[121] In addition to the books, the *testamentum* makes clear that Æthelstan's gift to Cuthbert included a number of vestments and other fabrics for ecclesiastical use: two chasubles, an alb, a stole and matching maniple, a girdle, three altar-coverings, three curtains and seven *pallia*.[122] He also, apparently, filled two silver cups with coin and ordered his whole army to give to St Cuthbert a large cash sum of more than 1,200 shillings, while instructing his brother Edmund, to whom he had already explained the significance of the saint and his shrine, to ensure that 'if anything sinister should befall him on this expedition to return his body to St Cuthbert and commend it to him for presentation on the Day of Judgement'.[123]

Among the items recovered from St Cuthbert's tomb when it was opened in 1827 were a stole and maniple which appear, from the identical inscriptions embroidered on the ends of each, to be those given by King Æthelstan. These texts identify Ælfflæd, Edward the Elder's second wife, as having commissed these objects, which she originally intended for

[119] *HSC*, ch. 26, pp. 64–5. That the original charter epitomized here was originally recorded in a gospel book is apparent from its opening sentence: 'I, King Æthelstan, give to St Cuthbert this gospel book . . .'. That book is customarily identified with the now burnt volume, BL Cotton Otho B. ix; Johnson South, *Historia de Sancto Cuthberto* (Cambridge, 2002), 109.

[120] Keynes, 'Books', 170–9.

[121] The manuscript containing these lives, prefaced by a portrait of the king presenting a book to St Cuthbert, cannot have been finished in time for Æthelstan to take it north with him in 934 because the episcopal lists it contains provide (in the hand of the main scribe, and the same ink) the names of bishops still alive in May 934. It could have been given to Chester-le-Street at any time between June 934 and the king's death in 939, and did not of course necessarily require the king to have made a second personal visit to the saint's shrine: Keynes, 'Books', 182–4.

[122] Normally identified as vestments, *pallia* can simply denote pieces of fabric; if so the fragments of seventh-century Byzantine silk found in the coffin in 1827 known as the 'Nature Goddess silk' might have been given by Æthelstan (although they could have been placed in the tomb at any time between 698 and 1103): Clare Higgins, 'Some New Thoughts on the Nature Goddess Silk', in *St Cuthbert and His Community*, ed. G. Bonner *et al.* (Woodbridge, 1989), 333. See plate 15.

[123] *HSC*, ch. 27.

Bishop Frithestan of Winchester, (*c*.909–31).[124] Stylistically, the ornamentation of the objects resembles the dedication miniature of Æthelstan and Cuthbert in the manuscript of Bede's Lives given by the king to the community of St Cuthbert, especially in the use of symmetrical tree-scroll foliage. Whether Bishop Frithestan designed the iconographic programme is unknown, although an ecclesiastic presumably did so; the embroiderers could have been nuns from the Nunnaminster, or women in the queen's retinue, official court textile-workers.[125] The survival of these vestments with Cuthbert's relics, but not in the cathedral church at Winchester, suggests that they still remained incomplete when Edward parted with Ælfflæd *c*.919 to marry his third wife; how long before Æthelstan planned his northern visit they became available one cannot know, but that they returned to the royal court which had paid for their manufacture seems certain. Royally commissioned and executed with considerable skill, these richly embroidered fabrics were more than fitting gifts for a saint as venerable as Cuthbert.[126] The third object made at the same time, sometimes called a second maniple and probably equivalent to the object described as a girdle in the testament in the *Historia*, may not originally have been ecclesiastical in purpose. Unlike the maniple and stole, this equally elegant and expertly finished garment was made as a reversible piece and may represent the only item of royal secular dress to survive from Anglo-Saxon England.[127] The gold and silver objects (secular and ecclesiastical) listed in the testament and the bells disappeared long ago.

Æthelstan attached substantial significance to his visit to St Cuthbert's community, desiring to advertise his generosity to the cult of this remarkable saint by having not one, but two separate – and subtly different – portraits depicting him at the moment when he made the donation. Inscriptions and portraits left 'visual and verbal reminders of the king's presence, authority, generosity and faith' on the books he gave to churches across his realm.[128] They provided a visual record of his gift. Yet more importantly, they reminded a Northumbrian audience of the significance of West Saxon expansion in the north of England. Here we might note the additional reference in the testament to two banners and one lance donated to the shrine by the king, although nothing in that text suggests that these were relics or even religious objects; the next items listed were gold armlets,

---

[124] At one end of each item the inscription reads 'Ælfflæd had [this made]' (ÆLFFLÆD FIERI PRECEPIT) and at the other end, 'for the pious bishop Frithestan' (PIO EPISCOPO FRIÐESTANO). See plate 15.

[125] Gameson, *Role of Art*, 119, 253.

[126] E. Plenderlieth, 'The Stole and Maniples. (a) the Technique', in *The Relics of St Cuthbert*, ed. C.F. Battiscombe (Oxford, 1956), 375–96; C. Hohler, 'The Icononography', ibid., 396–408. E. Coatsworth, 'The Embroideries from the Tomb of St Cuthbert', in H&H, 292–306; Maureen C. Miller, 'The Significance of Saint Cuthbert's Vestments', in *Studies in Church History* 47 (forthcoming).

[127] Coatsworth, 'Embroideries', 305–6.

[128] Karkov, *Ruler Portraits*, 53.

so perhaps they were pieces of royal military equipment that the king felt able to spare.[129] In leaving images of himself at the shrine, Æthelstan had himself portrayed as 'eternally present before the sainted recipient of his generosity, implying that his request for prayers, blessing and salvation had been heard and granted'.[130]

Varying degrees of authenticity attach to the charters in Æthelstan's name by which separate religious houses claimed to have received land and privileges from this famously pious king. Most significant among them in retrospect is, perhaps, none of the documents granted to religious institutions but the pair of charters issued in the last year of his reign to single religious women, both apparently following devout lives outside a nunnery.[131] Whatever the state of the organized, collective religious life in England in the second quarter of the tenth century – and we depend for our understanding of this in large measure on the highly partisan accounts written to justify the revolution in monastic observance effected in Edgar's reign – it seems clear that few opportunities existed for female religious to express their vocations collectively. Other than in the house established by King Alfred at Shaftesbury in Dorset, over which he had placed his daughter as abbess, and perhaps the historic community at Barking in Essex, most if not all of the nunneries of pre-Viking Age England (certainly all of those in Northumbria) had ceased to support female congregations by the 920s, although some may have housed men instead. Many women thus chose to take the veil and practise a life of religion on their own estates. One such was the widow Æthelflæd, supposedly a niece of King Æthelstan, who established a small community beside the male congregation at Glastonbury and had Dunstan to minister to her spiritual needs; on one occasion at least, Æthelstan paid a visit to this community.[132] Æthelstan's grants to the *religiosae feminae* Eadwulfu and Wulfswith initiated a series of donations to such women by his younger brothers.[133] The king also made a grant of land to one of his youngest sisters, Eadburh, a nun at Winchester.[134]

---

[129] *HSC*, ch. 26.

[130] Karkov, *Ruler Portraits, below,* 55. We shall return to discuss Æthelstan's devotion to St Cuthbert, below, 208–10.

[131] S 448 and 449.

[132] 'B', *Vita S Dunstani*, ch. 10, ed. Stubbs, 17–18; Brooks, 'The Career of St Dunstan', 7; *VW*, ii, 93–4. 'B' is our only witness to Æthelflæd's royal blood and kinship with Æthelstan; she could conceivably have been daughter of Æthelstan's eldest half-brother, Æthelweard, who died in 924, although he is not known to have married or had children. Edmund and Eadred were too young to have produced an adult, widowed daughter able to entertain kings and clergymen in the 930s. Perhaps her mother was one of Æthelstan's sisters who named her after her own aunt, King Alfred's sister, the lady of the Mercians. Alternatively, her kinship with the king might have been more distant than 'B' understood.

[133] For lists of these charters see Brooks, 'The Career of St Dunstan', 7, n. 24; Dumville, *Wessex,* 165–6 and 177; and my *VW*, i.

[134] S 446.

Even though Æthelstan did not initiate a reform of monastic organization in England, he did prove a significant patron of religious houses.
William of Malmesbury reported that he founded two new establishments
at Milton Abbas in Dorset, to which he also made substantial gifts of
relics, and at Muchelney in Somerset, and he also made grants to several
existing communities.[135] Not all the surviving charters in his name in
favour of ecclesiastical beneficiaries inspire confidence, but some – such as
the series of grants he supposedly made to Exeter – may draw on his
authentic deeds.[136] Among surviving charters that appear largely genuine
we find evidence that Æthelstan made grants to the bishops of Selsey and
Crediton, and to the cathedral church of St Peter's at York; on the day of
his coronation he made a symbolic grant to the community of St
Augustine's, Canterbury, in the presence of Archbishop Æthelhelm who
had just consecrated him king.[137] At different times he gave land also to
abbeys at Athelney, Malmesbury, Shaftesbury, Sherborne and Wilton, to
an Abbot Ælfric (possibly, but not necessarily, the abbot of the Old
Minster at Winchester), and to an Abbot Beorhtsige.[138] More problematical are the texts in favour of an Abbot Cynath, the various cartulary
copies of texts in Æthelstan's name making grants to Abingdon, Bath,
Beverley, Christ Church and St Augustine's, Canterbury, Chertsey, St
Buryan in Cornwall, St Paul's, London, Ripon, the Old Minster at
Winchester and the church of Holy Trinity in the same town, and a series
in favour of the church at Worcester.[139] That each of these congregations
should have sought to associate themselves with Æthelstan's generosity,
even if sometimes on rather flimsy grounds, indicates further the value the
Church placed on his patronage and the benefits each institution believed
it could accrue from connecting the name of so illustrious a patron with
its own past.

Many of the authentic documents demanded that their recipients sang
psalms and said masses for the king, just as some of Æthelstan's grants to

[135] Milton: *GP*, ii, 85, pp. 292–3; Muchelney: *GP*, ii 93, pp. 312–13. The charters in
Æthelstan's name in favour of Milton (S 391) and Muchelney (S 455) cannot be genuine in
the form in which they survive.

[136] S 386–90, 433; for these Exeter documents see Pierre Chaplais, 'The Authenticity of
the Royal Anglo-Saxon Diplomas of Exeter', *BIHR*, xxxix (1966), 1–34; reprinted with an
addendum in his *Essays in Medieval Diplomacy and Administration* (London, 1981), no. XV.
Æthelstan's other gifts to Exeter, particularly his substantial donation of relics, are
discussed below, 200–3.

[137] S 394.

[138] Selsey: S 403; Crediton: S 405; another grant in favour of Crediton, S 421, is more
problematical. York: S 407; Athelney: S 432; Malmesbury: S 434; Shaftesbury: S 419, 429;
Sherborne: S 422–3; Wilton: S 438; Abbot Ælfric: S 412; Abbot Beorhtsige: S 418a.

[139] Abbot Cynath: S 404; Abingdon: S 404, 408–10; Bath: S 414; Beverley S 451; Christ
Church and St Augustine's, Canterbury: S 398 and 394; Chertsey: S 420; St Buryan: S 450;
St Paul's, London: S 452–3; Ripon: S 456–7; Old Minster, Winchester: S 393, 439, 443–4;
Holy Trinity Winchester: S 427; Worcester: S 401–2, 406, 428.

laypeople required them to make offerings of food for the destitute in
return for the lands they acquired.[140] We should take seriously the statements made in the proems to these grants about the king's belief in the
spiritual efficacy of alms-giving, and treat as sincere his assertions that he
made donations to cathedral and monastic churches for the good of his
own soul. Expressions of his faith were central to Æthelstan's life and his
personal spirituality played a significant part in shaping his character. In
his generous acts of patronage to churches and monasteries, Æthelstan
fulfilled the promises he had made at his coronation to defend the Holy
Church and the Christian people committed to him and to honour the
clergy; he further demonstrated that he had not forgotten the widow and
the orphan.[141] Churchmen from England and farther afield in the king's
immediate circle did much to prompt, foster and support Æthelstan's spiritual development and encouraged his willingness to emulate his grandfather in the promotion of wisdom and learning. Those holding high
office in the Church also ensured the dissemination of the intellectual
agenda of the court to the wider Christian community in the shires. In
that process Æthelstan's bishops played a key role, above all his archbishops. These senior prelates collaborated with the king's ambitious plans
to achieve the administrative and legal unification of his enlarged
kingdom, ensuring that the Christian ideals promoted and discussed at his
court found expression in his legislative programme and that he governed
his united realm as a truly Christian monarch.[142]

[140] S419, 422–3 required the communities at Shaftesbury and Sherborne to sing psalms
for the king; S 418 and S 379 placed obligations to give alms on lay beneficiaries. See
further 133–4.
[141] Above, 77.
[142] Brooks, *The Early History*, 215.

Chapter 5

KINGDOM

Æthelstan's coronation in September 925 marked the formal beginning of his rule as king over two peoples: the West Saxons and the Mercians. Whatever the obstacles to his accession, the consecrated king henceforth stood above them, set apart from his brothers and the people over whom he was to rule by the holy sacrament of his anointing. Confirmation of his royal status at the hands of his archbishop gave Æthelstan both authority and enhanced responsibility. As shepherd over his people, he had to ensure their safety and prosperity; at the Last Judgment, he would answer at the highest throne for his discharge of that solemn duty. Fulfilment of these obligations took Æthelstan out from the intimate environment of his court on to the central, public stage of his kingdom. In the solemn and often highly formulaic official records from his reign, we see the king depicted in rather stereotypical fashion, yet the decisions he made about the governance of his realm reveal much about his personality. As convener and chair of royal councils he promulgated law, adjudicated in disputes, and made gifts to his followers; in council the king asserted his overall charge of the governance of the separate shires and regions of his wide realm, whose day-to-day administration he had delegated to men of his own choosing.

The wider cultural consequences of Æthelstan's political achievements were considerable. Having unified all the Anglo-Saxon areas of Britain, the king had not simply created a realm of new dimensions; he had brought together under one (largely) peaceful rule lands that had, in previous generations, suffered significant political disruption and consequent social collapse because of the Danish wars and later Scandinavian settlements. He thus directed much of his legal activity towards the repair and renewal of this fractured and damaged society.[1] The king therefore needed to devise new strategies for ruling a kingdom covering a much wider geographical area than that over which any previous Anglo-Saxon monarch had held sway; as well as legislating to tackle social breakdown, he had to find mechanisms for ensuring the continued loyalty of the nobility dispersed across his realm and those native rulers from his margins who had submitted themselves to his rule.

---

[1] H.R. Loyn, 'Wales and England in the Tenth Century: the Context of the Æthelstan Charters', *Welsh History Review*, x (1980–1), 284 and 300.

Central to the achievement of that goal was the king's treatment of his council of leading men and key advisers.

THE KING IN COUNCIL

No immediately obvious answer presents itself to the question: how did an early medieval king govern his kingdom? The Old English text known as *Maxims II*, which consists of a series of gnomic statements about the nature of the created world, the necessities of human society and the guidance of God, begins explicitly, but rather unhelpfully: 'A king must rule his kingdom' ('Cyning sceal rice healdan').[2] The verb *healdan* means literally to hold, so implying to rule, guard, keep, protect or govern; by opening with this statement the poet gives us an indication of the grandeur of kingship and its centrality to Anglo-Saxon society, but tells us nothing practical about how he should perform his central role of ruling and protecting his people in peacetime.

Given the size and disparate nature of his only recently united realm, we might anticipate that Æthelstan would have felt the need to assert his royal authority in person across the regions under his sway, yet he appears seldom to have transacted governmental business outside Wessex.[3] Recorded meetings of his peripatetic court show him to have convened his council mostly within the West Saxon heartlands, especially in their south-western corner; the evidence of his programme of meetings suggests that he made few concessions to the needs of his subjects travelling to the king's court from Mercia or the east. Although later tenth-century kings' recorded movements seem to reflect a gradual reorientation of the realm towards the Thames valley, this had not yet begun to happen in Æthelstan's day.[4] Obviously, Æthelstan would have made other journeys for different purposes of which no record has survived, and have stayed in additional places to those where we know councils met (probably at royal vills); we have no reason to believe that on those unrecorded travels he did not also gather councillors from across his realm to his side.[5] The royal

---

[2] *Maxims II*, line 1, trans. T. A. Shippey, *Poems of Wisdom and Learning in Old English* (Cambridge and Totowa, NJ, 1976), 76–7. I am grateful to Laura Ashe for advice on this gnomic text.

[3] We know of meetings of his council held at Eamont for the general submission of the British princes; at Nottingham in June 934 (on his way to Scotland: S 407) and at Buckingham in September 934 (presumably on his way back south: S 426); at Colchester (S 412), and at Cirencester (S 1792). One clause of a law code suggests a meeting convened at Whittlebury in Northamptonshire: *VI As*, 12.

[4] Timothy Reuter, 'Assembly Politics in Western Europe', in *The Medieval World*, ed. Peter Linehan and Janet L. Nelson (Routledge, 2001), 436. A similar pattern appears in the movements of the Ottonian kings, which centred on their Saxon homeland and in the Rhineland: James Campbell, *The Anglo-Saxon State* (London, 2000), 48–9.

[5] James Campbell, 'Anglo-Saxon Courts', in *Court Culture in the Early Middle Ages*, ed. Catherine Cubitt (Turnhout, 2003), 157–9.

council was the central governmental institution through which the king articulated his will and legislated to effect change; its composition thus sheds light on the way in which Æthelstan integrated representatives and local leaders from the regions into the process of decision-making for the whole kingdom.

In choosing to convene his council meetings mostly in Wessex, Æthelstan required many of his leading subjects from the midland, northern and eastern parts of England to travel substantial distances away from their own localities in order to attend. By insisting on their presence, Æthelstan created a royal council with a wider ethnic mix, one that was distinctively different from the smaller gatherings called by his predecessors who had ruled more homogeneous domains.[6] Mercian as well as West Saxon bishops regularly attested his charters and from 928 until 939 as well as the archbishop of Canterbury, the archbishop of York attended Æthelstan's council, attesting directly after the southern metropolitan.[7] In addition to the Welsh and Scottish sub-kings, a number of ealdormen whose names suggest Scandinavian parentage appear among the witnesses to several of the charters for which the scribe 'Æthelstan A' was responsible, listed as a group after the 'English' ealdormen and before the thegns.[8] While one cannot identify the localities from which such men came, one might agree with Stenton who argued, 'there is little doubt that they were the successors of the earls who had led the Danish armies of eastern England in the time of Edward the Elder'.[9] Æthelstan thus did not apparently seek to replace the local aristocracy of the former Danelaw areas after they had come under West Saxon control, but used men of Danish extraction as his representatives in the government of these newly conquered areas.[10] Assembling such a diverse body in council Æthelstan created, in Stenton's view, a 'new kind of assembly', contrasting sharply with the 'small, intimate and informal type of council common in Wessex

---

[6] J.R. Maddicott, *The Origins of the English Parliament 924–1327* (Oxford, 2010), 4–7.

[7] N. Brooks, 'The Anglo-Saxon Cathedral Community, 597–1070', in *A History of Canterbury Cathedral*, ed. P. Collinson et al. (Oxford, 1995), 22 and n. 64; Keynes, *Atlas*, table xxxvii.

[8] For example S 403, attested by Urum (for Thurum); Grim, Stircer and Regenwold; S 405: witnessed by Styrcær, Guþrum, þurferð, Fræna and Grim. See Keynes, *Atlas*, table xxxviii.

[9] Stenton, *ASE*, 351.

[10] Ibid. Alternatively, of course, these men might have been given charge over areas distant from their personal power base, in the same way that Carolingian kings from Charlemagne onwards used to assign counts to lands where they had no personal lands or followers and so could not easily foment rebellion against the king. The East Anglian ealdorman known as Æthelstan 'Half-King', for example, had personal estates in Berkshire and Somerset, although he served the king in the eastern provinces; Stenton, *ASE*, 351; Cyril Hart, *The Danelaw* (London and Rio Grande, OH, 1992), 569–604. In this Æthelstan may have continued a policy begun by his father, but the absence of any charters issued in Edward's name after 909 prevents us from making any statements about the composition of his council.

before the enlargement of the kingdom under Edward the Elder'; even for ordinary business, West Saxon representatives (bishops, ealdormen and thegns) were joined by lay and ecclesiastical magnates from all over the realm. To Stenton, these were 'national assemblies, in which every local interest was represented, and they did much to break down the provincial separatism which was the chief obstacle to the political unification of England'.[11]

Not the sort of primitive parliament in which the democratic voice of free Englishmen might be heard, meetings of the royal council or witan instead gathered the king's leading men – ecclesiastical and lay – those best able to advise him.[12] A witan assembled archbishops and bishops (and often also abbots), as well as ealdormen and thegns who owed allegiance directly to the king; these were the men who took day-to-day responsibility for defence, the administration of justice (and payment of legal fines) and the collection of regular payments to the crown from their part of the wider kingdom. After the ealdormen (historically the men of the highest status in each locality, given authority over an area larger than a single shire), much local administrative responsibility fell to the reeves, royal officials appointed from among the local noble landowners, often put in charge of a particular town or royal estate. The loyalty of reeves and ealdormen to the king depended in part on the rewards of land and privilege they received from him, but centrally on their personal bond of allegiance. In the shires, such men worked closely with their diocesan bishop and with leading abbots in the locality (who were themselves often substantial landowners). The fusion of church and state at royal councils merely reflected on a national scale the extent to which sacred and secular were united in early medieval societies.[13] Where Æthelstan's councils stand out distinctively is in extending the geographical range of local opinion represented in central decision-making, bringing laymen and clergy from across the whole of his extended realm so that Mercians and West Saxons rubbed shoulders and considered solutions to common problems with East Anglians and Northumbrians and with men of Scandinavian (or Anglo-Scandinavian) parentage.

Unification of the separate kingdoms into one English kingdom temporarily under Æthelstan (and more permanently once Edgar assumed sole rule after 959) removed the former clear geographical distinction that had existed between royal assemblies, convened by kings and attended by nobles and bishops, and ecclesiastical synods where all the bishops of a province (York or Canterbury) met under the authority of the metropolitan

---

[11] Stenton, *ASE*, 352; Maddicott, *The Origins*, 6–11.

[12] F. Liebermann, *The National Assembly in the Anglo-Saxon Period* (Halle, 1913).

[13] H.R. Loyn, *The Governance of Anglo-Saxon England, 500–1087* (London, 1984), 100–2, 131–5; Loyn, 'Church and State in England in the Tenth and Eleventh Centuries', in *Tenth-Century Studies*, ed. David Parsons (Chichester, 1975), 94–102; reprinted in his *Society and Peoples* (London, 1992), 162–3.

archbishop. The witan now took over the functions of a synod.[14] Meetings of the witan thus discussed matters requiring legislative solutions and issued law relating to both ecclesiastical and lay affairs, in addition to attesting royal grants of land and privilege, recorded in diplomas. Although all Æthelstan's law codes were promulgated in his name and some include statements uttered in the first person, reflecting oral pronouncements made by the king in council, the king did not always attend meetings that discussed law-making.[15] He did, however, have to be present in order to alienate lands and privileges. Texts drawn up on those occasions seldom reveal much about the deliberations of the council, still less about any voices of dissent that may have been heard, but the consensus to which they testify represents important evidence for the king's capacity to harness the resources at his disposal in order to provide for the well-being of his subject flock.[16]

In the Frankish realm, Carolingian kings held gatherings of their leading men at the major religious festivals of Christmas, Easter and Pentecost (Whitsun), as recorded in contemporary annals. We may assume that Anglo-Saxon kings did likewise, even though their regular assemblies found no mention in the Anglo-Saxon Chronicle. No English parallel exists for the Frankish system of the Marchfield (later the Mayfield) when the Frankish 'nation in arms' met annually and discussed the campaigns for the year to come.[17] However, a close correspondence between the dates on which English kings granted charters and these major church feasts, especially Easter and Pentecost, suggests that the liturgical festivals frequently occasioned the summoning of the king's witan. Study of Æthelstan's surviving charters shows that the king held at least one assembly every year; in some years we know of his convening as many as four. Which factors beyond the cycle of the Church's year dictated the calling of the witan we find harder to establish, nor can we determine how large an assembly the king gathered round him on each occasion.[18] Regular meetings were easier to plan than sporadic ones, for councils of this nature required considerable prior preparation. Since we know from the code conventionally referred to as *II Æthelstan* that even the regular four-weekly local assembly (*gemot*) called by a reeve had to be announced seven days in advance, we may imagine that rather more notice than this

---

[14] Brooks, 'The Anglo-Saxon Cathedral Community', 21.

[15] First-person pronouncements are found, for example, in the Grately code, *II Æthelstan* and that issued at Exeter, *V Æthelstan*: Wormald, *MEL*, 299.

[16] Charles Insley, 'Assemblies and Charters in Late Anglo-Saxon England', in *Political Assemblies in the Earlier Middle Ages*, ed. P.S. Barnwell and Marco Mostert (Turnhout, 2003), 48. Compare Janet L. Nelson, 'Legislation and Consensus in the Reign of Charles the Bald', in *Ideal and Reality in Frankish and Anglo-Saxon Society*, ed. P. Wormald *et al.* (Oxford, 1983), 202–27.

[17] Timothy Reuter, 'Assembly Politics in Western Europe', in *The Medieval World*, ed. P. Linehan and J.L. Nelson (Routledge, 2001), 435.

[18] Ibid., 434.

was required for a full meeting of the king's council.[19] It would greatly
have simplified the organization required if the king had always convened
his council at certain fixed points in the year, even though in the absence
of fixed royal capital or regular pattern to the king's itineration, he would
still have had to announce well in advance where those meetings would
take place.

Sometimes events caused the king to disrupt pre-existing arrangements
and convene his council unexpectedly. Æthelstan clearly gathered his witan
before setting off on the expedition to Scotland in 934, taking the same
body at least some of the way on his northward journey;[20] presumably he
thought it prudent to confer with his leading men and discuss strategy in
advance of imminent military conflict or planned aggression. A need to
legislate on a specific, perhaps a local issue may have caused Æthelstan to
call an unexpected meeting of his council, as when he convened a meeting
in Colchester in March 931.[21] Alternatively, he may have seized the opportunity presented when many were already gathered together in order to
make a new legal statement. Such a circumstance may account for the
addition of a clause to the final chapter of the ordinances agreed on by
the bishops and reeves of London, which arose apparently from a time
when the king addressed his councillors gathered at Whittlebury in
Northamptonshire. This explained his views about the capital punishment
of juveniles, declaring his objection to the execution of children under the
age of fifteen for minor offences. A royal council meeting at Whittlebury
(which lies on a Roman road running north–south through the county)
could have assembled when the king was on one of his journeys from
central Wessex into northern England, or perhaps when the king was in the
middle of an otherwise unattested general tour of his midland territories.[22]

While we can establish something of the composition of the king's
council and see how much he gathered representatives from the regions
around him, determining what the witan discussed remains more difficult;
did these meetings address matters of national, rather than local concern,
issues that related to the kingdom as a whole, not just to individual localities? Charters offer limited evidence as to the matters discussed at a royal
council beyond the question of the land or privilege whose conveyance the
diploma recorded.[23] We should remember that the whole of a diploma
and all of its features, both internal and external, carried political
meaning which those present on the occasion of its granting would

---

[19] *II As*, 20.

[20] S 425, 407.

[21] S 412; discussed above, 84.

[22] *VI As*, 12. Wormald, *MEL*, 440.

[23] The markedly more discursive charters of Æthelred 'the Unready' represent much
more fruitful lines of enquiry since they frequently make public statement about good kingship (and its reverse) and the role of noble counsel; see Keynes, *Diplomas*, 198–202; Pauline
Stafford, 'Political Ideas in Late Tenth-Century England', in *Law, Laity and Solidarities*, ed.
Pauline Stafford *et al.* (Manchester, 2001), 68–82.

understand.[24] Yet, much of that significance was not conveyed orally (and so preserved in the written record) but was enacted through action and gesture. The rituals, often highly visual as well as deeply symbolic, that surrounded the conveyance of land encompassed everyone present. All the witnesses could understand the symbolism of placing the document (or an emblematic piece of parchment) together with a sod of earth cut from the estate in question on the altar. Equally, most would make reasonable sense of a recitation of the bounds of the donated land in Old English, even if they had not been among the group that had walked the whole circuit in advance to confirm precisely where its boundaries lay. We might question, however, how much of the Latin of the main text, especially the hermeneutic and elaborate Latin with its Graecisms and neologisms beloved of 'Æthelstan A', even the more learned among the bishops grasped on first hearing. As for the ealdormen and thegns, they would have struggled to get much beyond the general meaning that the rituals of donation articulated so much more comprehensibly. When 'Æthelstan A' reminded his hearers of the transitory nature of earthly life and the fickleness of earthly fortune and urged them to turn their minds to matters eternal, or execrated earthly sin and commended the merits of alms-giving (both themes common to the charters for which he had responsibility), many of the audience must have struggled to keep up with his long periods.[25] For the majority of the witnesses, the predictability of a charter's essential shape may have offered some relief. Even the most extravagant proem (the lengthy preamble to a charter) must ultimately give way to a straightforward statement of donation; we can envisage those among his ealdormen less confident about their Latin craning forward to listen desperately for the familiar 'ego Æthelstanus', which presaged the announcement of the gift itself.

What remains unknown is whether the sentiments of the proems reflected this scribe's own particular preoccupations and desire to display his erudite vocabulary, or whether in his choice of subject-matter and language he encapsulated (or, perhaps better, elaborated) ideas emanating directly from the king, and topics discussed recurrently at his councils. For all the complexity of their expression, the views promulgated in Æthelstan's charters were scarcely novel ones. The transitory nature of earthly life and the fallibility of human memory featured frequently as themes in charters from earlier eras and the Church had expounded the spiritual benefits of alms-giving for centuries. Certainly Æthelstan seems to have had strong views on each subject, and probably also understood

[24] Herwig Wolfram, 'Political Theory and Narrative in Charters', *Viator*, xxvi (1985), 39–51, at 42.

[25] On these themes in the proems (introductions) to the charters of 'Æthelstan A' and the scribe known as 'Edgar A', see Charles Insley, 'Where Did All the Charters Go?', *ANS*, xxiv (2001), 115–16.

enough Latin to grasp the essential meaning of the lengthy preambles to his grants; we can only speculate as to whether the draftsman took the king's personal interest into account when creating his texts, or even tried deliberately to couch their language in terms of which his master would have approved. As for the potential involvement of the rest of his council, we may imagine that even if the whole textual content of each charter was accessible only to some of those present, its content and the rhetoric in which it was articulated would have reflected (and echoed) a dialogue in which all those attending participated. Issues about the nature of royal power, the state of the Church, problems of inheritance, and the necessity to provide for the poor affected all of the Anglo-Saxon elite, not just the king or those in his immediate circle.[26] Consideration of these social problems will of course have occurred in local settings also, but the gathering of representatives from across the shires provided the occasion to discuss these matters collectively and determine national policies for their remedy.

Thus, when the king's charters reflect similar concerns to those articulated in his law codes, we may reasonably conclude that the king's councils had discussed, or at least touched on, these matters. When those issues turn out to mirror closely the concerns for promoting Christian living, alms-giving and the care of the widow and the orphan that we already saw to be close to the king's heart, we may again associate the king with their articulation. A group of charters all issued within a short period of time (between Christmas Eve 932 and late January 933) obliged their recipients to provide food for the poor or to recite psalms regularly for the king. For example, making a grant to Shaftesbury Abbey on Christmas Eve 932, Æthelstan required that the community sing fifty psalms after prime every day for the excesses of his soul and that they should remember him at the morning mass, enjoining the community to do this until the Day of Judgment.[27] On these occasions at least, it would seem that the topics for discussion at meetings of the king's council included items about alms-giving, care for the poor and co-ordination of weekly liturgical recitation of the psalms for the king. To go further and suggest that Æthelstan himself cared sufficiently about these issues to push for their discussion and for the making of a record of his views in charters as well as legislating formally for their performance seems equally plausible. Conceivably, that

---

[26] Insley, 'Assemblies and Charters', 57–8.

[27] S 419, Shaftesbury, 8; see S.E. Kelly, *Charters of Shaftesbury Abbey* (Oxford, 1996), 33. Compare S 418, 379, 422–3. The *Regularis concordia*, the customary which regulated reformed Benedictine monasteries from the 970s onwards, designated the 'morning mass' (said after the office of terce) for prayer for the king or for any pressing need; *Regularis concordia*, chs 20, 27 ed. T. Symons (London, 1953), 23–4. Whether Æthelstan initiated this custom or it had been in use previously, his stipulations to Shaftesbury interestingly prefigure the later requirement that religious communities daily remember their king. See Helen Foxhall Forbes, 'The Development of the Notions of Penance, Purgatory and the Afterlife in Anglo-Saxon England', PhD thesis, University of Cambridge, 2009, 166–7. For similar provisions in the king's law codes, see below, 139.

royal preoccupation with charitable giving arose from the king's reflection over that Christmas feast in 932 on the Gospel narratives of the birth of the Saviour in poverty.

Beyond the rhetorical language of diplomatic form, charters issued at the meetings of Æthelstan's councils show which lands the king alienated from his own possession for the benefit of ecclesiastical and lay beneficiaries and might, therefore, enable us to say something about the politics of donation. Assemblies, essential elements of the consensual apparatus of royal government, provided a stage for the distribution of patronage, replacing one of the earlier functions of royal itineration.[28] Looking only at essentially genuine examples of surviving diplomas in Æthelstan's name, it seems that the king continued to follow his predecessors' habit of giving away predominantly lands from the West Saxon heartlands.[29] Of thirty-nine apparently genuine grants of land made by the king between 925 and 939, ten related to lands in Wiltshire, seven to Hampshire, five to Dorset and four to Somerset; he made two grants of land in Kent (perhaps three), and one, possibly two, grants of Sussex estates.[30] In Bedfordshire, Berkshire, Derbyshire, Devon, Essex, Huntingdonshire, Lancashire, Staffordshire and (possibly) Suffolk, he granted away land on just one occasion. As argued in Chapter 3, the site at which a council met frequently had no bearing on the location of the land whose alienation it confirmed, nor does the distribution of the estates donated generally shed much light on the politics of Æthelstan's reign. It reflects rather the fact that the royal demesne remained predominantly in Wessex; so when looking for estates with which he could afford to part, Æthelstan had only West Saxon estates at his disposal. If the king acquired any of the former Mercian royal lands, he seemingly did not choose to alienate them to his followers, perhaps not wanting to disturb the delicate balance of power in the midlands either by enhancing some local lords' landholding to the detriment of their neighbours, or introducing entirely new lords of West Saxon origin. As for the lands of the kings of East Anglia or Northumbria, those had presumably long since fallen into the possession of the settling Scandinavians. Equally relevant in determining the king's policy of donation to religious houses was the paucity of active religious communities in northern and eastern England. We have already noted that Æthelstan's

---

[28] Maddicott, *The Origins*, 26.

[29] This analysis draws heavily on Simon Keynes's register of the charters of Æthelstan which distinguishes essentially genuine from clearly spurious texts: 'The Charters of King Athelstan and the Kingship of the English', Toller Lecture, University of Manchester, 2001. This may not be an entirely representative sample of the whole corpus of charters once issued by the king (there were, for example, eleven charters of Æthelstan recorded in the lost cartulary of Glastonbury Abbey, the so-called *Liber terrarum*, of which four related to lands in Wiltshire, and six to Somerset estates; the location of the eleventh estate granted is not known). However, it seems unwise to base any conclusions about the extent of the king's patronage on charters of dubious authenticity.

[30] The uncertainty arises when a charter place-name might be identified with a place of the same name located in a different county.

support of monasticism as an idea did not extend to a policy of trying to restore the religious order among the English. He gave no lands anywhere in his realm for the endowment of new monastic houses, nor did he attempt to restore to active observance any of those former communities in the eastern midlands or northern counties that had fallen into desuetude during or after the Viking wars. As a means of answering our question about what was discussed at meetings of the king's council, his charters help to a limited degree; they certainly do not assist in establishing whether the counsellors devoted much attention to consideration of national affairs as a whole. Looking at his law codes may prove more profitable.

THE KING AS LAW-GIVER

So far we have explored the communication of ideas at Æthelstan's councils through the medium of texts written in Latin. Latin was, however, neither the language in which the king discussed matters of government with his councillors, nor necessarily the language of record. The Anglo-Saxons were the first peoples in northern Europe to use the written vernacular – Old English – in the work of government, producing increasing numbers of administrative documents of different sorts in the later part of the pre-Conquest period.[31] The promotion of education in Old English played a significant role in King Alfred's programme for the regeneration of his people after the Viking wars of the 870s and the king insisted that ealdormen should be able to follow his written instructions if read aloud to them, even if they could not read themselves. One of the texts Alfred expected his ealdormen to use was his law code, a text designed to serve practical as well as ideological purposes, for which the vernacular was well suited.[32] Unlike their continental counterparts, Anglo-Saxon kings from Æthelberht of Kent (c.585–616) onwards chose to codify their legal statements in Old English rather than the Latin with which their clerical scribes might have felt more comfortable.[33] While the process of law-making throughout the Anglo-Saxon period had obvious oral elements (visible to varying degrees in the surviving record), the codes themselves represent

[31] Jean Philippe Genet, 'La Monarchie anglaise et l'écrit: public ou privé?' in *L'Écriture publique du pouvoir*, ed. Alain Bresson *et al.* (Bordeaux, 2005), 89–102. James Campbell has listed many of the sorts of administrative record that survive, observing that these represent only a small proportion of what was originally a much more extensive body of material and that English was the ordinary language for much written business: 'Observations on English Government from the Tenth to the Twelfth Centuries', in his *Essays in Anglo-Saxon History* (London and Roncerverte, 1986), 157–8.

[32] Asser, ch. 106; Simon Keynes, 'Royal Government and the Written Word', in *The Uses of Literacy in Early Mediaeval Europe*, ed. R. McKitterick (Cambridge, 1990), 231–2.

[33] Patrick Wormald, '*Lex Scripta* and *Verbum Regis*: Legislation and Germanic Kingship from Euric to Cnut', in *Early Medieval Kingship*, ed. P.H. Sawyer and I.N. Wood (Leeds, 1977), 115; Susan Kelly, 'Anglo-Saxon Lay Society and the Written Word', in *The Uses of Literacy*, ed. McKitterick, 57–8.

more than mere ecclesiastical records of legislative decisions made orally; they provide important evidence for the role of the written word in government.[34] Edward the Elder's legislation referred specifically to written injunctions made to his reeves, suggesting that Alfred's strictures about the education of the lay nobility had started to bear fruit. The ordinances of the London peace guild (*VI Æthelstan*) indicate that Æthelstan, too, sought to convey his will to his reeves in written form; one clause specified the penalties that would follow if 'any of you is unwilling to attend to the duties of government, in accordance with what I have commanded and set down in writing'.[35] Decision-making remained an oral and consensual process, but the communication of those decisions to a wider population than the king's immediate circle relied increasingly on the use of written instruments, presupposing the existence of a functionally literate class able to comprehend their meaning and disseminate it yet further.

The various legal texts to survive from Æthelstan's reign cannot be dated precisely, but contain sufficient internal evidence to establish a relative chronology for their production. *I Æthelstan* (his tithe edict) and the so-called 'Ordinance on Charities' appear to be the earliest and both take the form of injunctions addressed in the first person by the king directly to his reeves. His other codes are more heterogeneous and need not have been agreed after discussions in the king's presence, yet they seem to have emerged from a series of councils convened by the king first at Grately in Hampshire (*II Æthelstan*), then at Exeter (*V Æthelstan*), Faversham and finally at Thunderfield in Surrey (*IV Æthelstan*).[36] Only two of them (those issued at Grately and Exeter) appear to record and publish specifically for wider dissemination legislation originally articulated orally and enacted at meetings held between the king and his councillors, but the similarities between the wording of the Grately code and that issued at the royal vill of Thunderfield are such that it seems likely that the king presided on the latter occasion also.[37] Collectively they do not constitute a coherent sequence of planned legal pronouncements, yet they do reflect different but complementary aspects of a fully functioning administrative system. The king's codes show the working of a partnership between the king and his leading men and derive their authority from the joint responsibility of both parties in their making.[38] In these texts lie traces of the

---

[34] *Contra* P. Wormald, Literacy in Anglo-Saxon England and its Neighbours', *TRHS*, 5th ser., xxvii (1977), 112; see Keynes, 'Royal Government', 235.

[35] *VI As*, 11; Keynes, 'Royal Government', 235–6.

[36] Keynes, 'Royal Government', 240–1; David Pratt, 'Written Law and the Communication of Authority in Tenth-Century England', in *England and the Continent in the Tenth Century*, ed. David Rollason *et al.* (Brepols, 2010), 340. Provisions agreed at a meeting of the king's council at Faversham have not survived, although reference is made to them (and to the fact that the king was present on that occasion) in other codes: *III As*, 2–3; *IV As*, 1; *VI As*, 10.

[37] Pratt, 'Written Law', 340; *contra* Wormald, *MEL*, 299.

[38] Maddicott, *The Origin*, 28–30.

reports sent from the centre to the localities and indeed from the regions back to the centre, directives that offer an unprecedented insight into the workings of a literate government machine in which the vernacular played the central role.[39] So, while in between the occasions when the king convened his council and issued law, local gatherings met to consider some of the issues that the larger body had tackled. As, for example, when the bishops, thegns, nobles and commoners of Kent assembled and addressed their views about how to preserve the public peace to the king (*III Athelstan*); their report, perhaps originally written in letter form, expresses the Kentishmen's gratitude for the king's previous legislation.[40] The meeting of a London peace guild, whose pronouncements are known as *VI Æthelstan*, similarly represent a local response to legal provisions issued centrally. Even those pronouncements made by the king in the first instance to a select group may ultimately have acquired a wider audience if the officials who heard him speak took copies of the written record in the form of laws into their localities and read them aloud to their neighbours, perhaps glossing those rather stark statements with a narrative of the conversations from which they had arisen. Wulfhelm, archbishop of Canterbury, could have played a key role in the promulgation of some of these and perhaps also have helped to ensure their preservation.[41]

Through his law-making we see more of Æthelstan's own view of his responsibilities in government and his attitudes to his subject people and their transgressions. Clerical concerns appear to dominate the earliest two legal texts surviving from his reign in which the king claimed to act on the advice of Wulfhelm, and his bishops, yet these were matters close to the king's own heart, too, as we have already seen, and reflect his agenda as much as theirs. Speaking in the first person, Æthelstan in his 'tithe ordinance' asserted the importance of paying tithes of livestock and agricultural produce to the Church, using both biblical allusion (from Genesis and Exodus) and quoting a sermon-text about the consequences of non-payment probably derived from a Carolingian source.[42] He directed his injunctions specifically to his reeves in the boroughs, urging them to ensure they rendered the tithes from the king's property, but also instructed all bishops, ealdormen and reeves to

---

[39] Keynes, 'Royal Government', 235. Much the fullest discussion of all aspects of these codes is that provided by Patrick Wormald in his *Making of English Law*, especially pp. 290–308 and 430–49. For a recent survey of Æthelstan's legislation, see Pratt, 'Written Law'. On the role of the vernacular as the language of government compare also Patrick Conner, 'Parish Guilds and the Production of Old English Literature in the Public Sphere', in *(Inter)Texts: Studies in Early Insular Culture presented to Paul E. Szarmach*, ed. Virginia Blanton and Helen Scheck (Tempe, AZ, 2007), 257–73, at 270–1.

[40] Pratt, 'Written Law', 340.

[41] Wormald, *MEL*, 299–300.

[42] *I As*, 3: 'it behoves us to remember how terrible is the declaration stated in books, "If we are not willing to render tithes to God, he will deprive us of the nine [remaining] parts, when we least expect it, and moreover we shall have sinned also."' That the ultimate source here (a sermon attributed to Augustine closely based on one of Caesarius of Arles) might have come to the West Saxon court via a Carolingian connection was argued by Wormald, *MEL*, 305.

do likewise with their own possessions. In the same code, the king instructed his reeves to ensure that church dues, payments for the souls of the dead and 'plough alms' (that is dues paid from each plough team) were paid regularly for the support of churches. He justified these injunctions with the comment 'for the divine teaching instructs us that we gain the things of heaven by those of the earth, and the eternal by the temporal'.[43] Failure to act on his instructions would bring punishment and the king drew a direct parallel between the obligation to the heavenly king and his own subjects' responsibilities to God's representative on earth, saying:

> Now hear what I grant to God and what you must perform on pain of forfeiting the fine for insubordination. And see to it also that you grant me that which is my own and which you may legally [have] acquired for me . . . And you must guard against the anger of God and insubordination to me, both yourselves and those whom it is your duty to admonish.[44]

The spiritual benefits of alms-giving, through which the soul might obtain 'treasure in heaven', were widely commended in early Anglo-Saxon penitential literature and reinforced via the prescriptions of church councils, which warned that alms should be given for the right reasons; some of that teaching had clearly found a receptive audience in King Æthelstan.[45]

A similar theological tone underpinned the brief legal text usually known as the 'Ordinance on Charities' which laid an obligation to feed the poor on the king's reeves, specifying the amount of charity payable from the rents of two of the king's estates and once more enumerating the penalties likely to befall reeves who failed to comply (in this case compensatory fines, to be divided among the poor where the reeve had failed in his charitable obligations). Reeves should supply the destitute with food 'for the forgiveness of [Æthelstan's] sins'; and arrange to free one penal slave annually, 'for the loving kindness of God and for the attainment of eternal life', the king declared. The religious and ideological foundations of both these early legal statements cannot be questioned, nor the explicit connection made between provision for the poor in this life and the hope

---

[43] *I As*, 4.1.

[44] *I As*, 5; see W. Chaney, 'Anglo-Saxon Church Dues: a Study in Historical Continuity', *Church History*, xxxii (1963), 268–77, at 269; Eric Stanley, 'Did the Anglo-Saxons Have a Social Conscience Like Us?', *Anglia*, cxxi (2003), 263. I owe both these references to Dr Martha Riddiford.

[45] For example, *Penitential of Ecgberht*, pref., ch. 1, in *Councils and Ecclesiastical Documents relating to Great Britain and Ireland*, ed. A. Haddan and W. Stubbs, 3 vols (Oxford, 1869–79), III: 418–9; Council of *Clofesho*, AD 747, ch. 26; ed. Haddan and Stubbs, III, 371–2.

of future salvation.[46] Given what we already know about Æthelstan's religious views we need not necessarily assume that the bishops (and Archbishop Wulfhelm in particular) had put these sentiments into the king's mouth, although they would surely have encouraged such a Christian approach to the obligations of kingship. Since these texts mirror the prominence given to alms-giving in the proems to some of Æthelstan's charters, we may conclude that the king's immediate circle and larger meetings of his witan spent time debating how best to relieve the sufferings of the poor.[47] Laws and charters together reinforce a presumption that questions about the provision of charity and the alleviation of poverty lay close to the king's own heart.

Collectively, his later law codes suggest that Æthelstan had clear ideas about what he wanted to achieve for the better governance of his realm through legislation, specifically which social problems he sought to ameliorate. In these texts, we see the king tackling directly issues that arose from the recent unification of heterogeneous peoples and devising strategies to repair the ills left in parts of the country following decades of warfare. Æthelstan may well have had the councils of Charlemagne and his successors in mind as models.[48] To the king's mind, theft constituted the greatest single problem and represented the most significant manifestation of social breakdown across the realm. He legislated repeatedly – even disproportionately – in his law codes for the prevention of thievery, making this topic one of the most striking features of his legal pronouncements: together, his codes contain one third of all the occurrences of the noun *þeof* (thief) in the entire corpus of Anglo-Saxon law.[49]

The earliest of his 'official' codes (*II Æthelstan*, issued at Grately in Hampshire), was dominated by the problem of stealing, opening with severe statements about the fate thieves could anticipate: 'First, no thief shall be spared who is seized in the act if he is over twelve years old and if the value of the stolen goods is more than eight pence.'[50] Æthelstan's concern about theft extended much further than to the problems occasioned by the victims of the crime from the loss of their property, for this issue went to the heart of the king's conception of his relationship with his subjects. Robbery represented a significant disruption to the peace in that it threatened the maintenance of order at local level. By legislating for the protection of livestock, especially cattle, and of moveable property, and imposing ferocious penalties on thieves and those who tried to shelter them and protect them from justice, Æthelstan sought to restore peace to

[46] Wormald, *MEL*, 302.
[47] Ibid., 306. Above, 125–6 and 133–4.
[48] Maddicott, *The Origins*, 31.
[49] Wormald, *MEL*, 301.
[50] *II As*, 1. The next clauses (1.1–1.5) make further recommendations about controlling thieving.

1 King Æthelstan stands holding a copy of Bede's *Lives of St Cuthbert*. His eyes are cast down reverently on the page as if he is reading about the deeds of the saint to whom he is about to present the book. Cuthbert stands in the doorway of his church, a book tucked under one arm while his right hand is raised, either in blessing or to take the king's gift from him.

2 King Alfred and his wife Ealhswith present a red royal cloak and a sword to their young grandson, Æthelstan, marking him out as a worthy future king. Æthelstan's parents, Edward and Ecgwynn (seated), and his aunt, Abbess Æthelgifu, look on.

3 Statue of Æthelflæd, lady of the Mercians, outside Tamworth Castle, Staffordshire; in her right hand she holds a sword, symbolising her involvement in campaigns to conquer Danish-occupied Mercia; her left arm shelters her young nephew Æthelstan, brought up at her court.

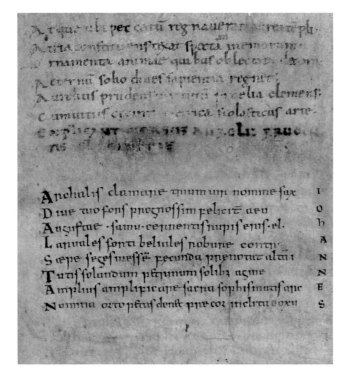

4 Acrostic poem addressed to Æthelstan perhaps at the time of his coronation. Reading down the poem, the first letter of each line spells out the king's name; the last letters spell 'Iohannes' (John), representing either the poet's name or possibly a name taken by the king in religion.

5 Coronation stone from Kingston-upon-Thames, Surrey, believed to be the stone on which six or seven Anglo-Saxon kings, starting with Æthelstan, were crowned. Now outside the Guildhall in Kingston, this once stood in the market place, where it was erected with a Masonic ceremony in 1850.

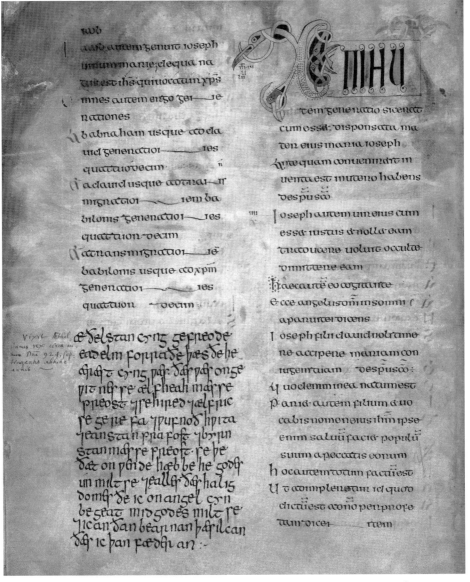

6 A record of one of Æthelstan's first acts after his accession: the manumission of his slave, Eadhelm, made 'when Æthelstan first became king' in the presence of members of his household. The Old English record is added in an early example of square minuscule script to a blank space in the bottom left-hand corner of the page. The rest of the text (written in Northumbria in the first half of the eighth century) is from the Gospel of St Matthew (ch. 1, vv. 16–22).

7 Poem *Rex pius Æthelstan*, written in Æthelstan's honour to mark his contemporary reputation for personal piety and notable religious devotion; added to a gospel book which the king gave to Christ Church, Canterbury.

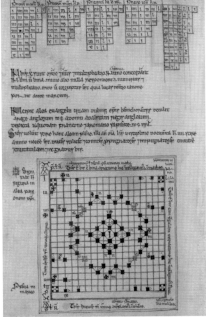

8 Inscription recording Æthelstan's donation of this late ninth- or early tenth-century gospel book to Christ Church, Canterbury.

9 Gospel dice. Text and diagram added to a twelfth-century Irish gospel book explaining how to play gospel dice (*alea evangelii*), and associating the game with the circle of King Æthelstan. This was an allegorized board game; players used canon tables to determine where to move their pieces on the illustrated board.

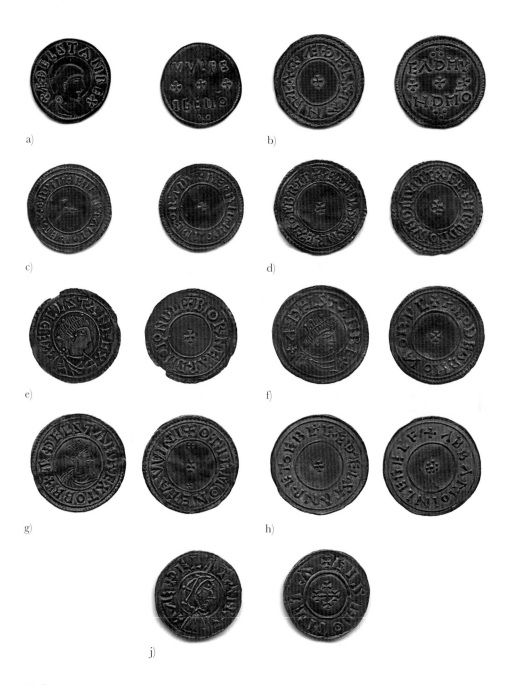

10 Coins. A selection of coins showing the different types issued during Æthelstan's reign. a) and b) are early types, similar to those issued by Æthelstan's father Edward the Elder, with the moneyer's name in two lines on the reverse. c) and d) illustrate his 'Circumscription Cross' type, bearing a legend that identifies Æthelstan as king of all Britain (*rex tot Brit*). e), f) and g) show the king wearing not a diadem (as in (a)) but a crown. h) illustrates the circumscription rosette type issued in Mercia when other regions showed the king crowned. j) was minted in the north east and shows the king with a crowned helmet.

11 'The Great Battle of Brunanburh', showing hand-to-hand fighting in the foreground, with the Norse ships, to which the defeated forces would flee, anchored offshore in the background; illustration for *Hutchinson's History of the Nations*, vol 1 (1914).

12 Æthelstan Psalter, possibly the king's personal copy of the Book of Psalms. We see here one of a cycle of paintings added to the book in tenth-century England. It shows Christ, seated in majesty (or possibly in judgement) surrounded by a chorus of angels and prophets. He holds a book and behind him are shown symbols of His passion including the holy lance, the cross and the sponge, reminding the viewer of the gifts of Hugh of the Franks.

13 Æthelstan Psalter: a second image added in tenth-century England (but by a different artist from plate 12). Christ is seated in Majesty, surrounded by choirs of martyrs and virgins; holding a cross, he pulls his garments back to reveal the wound made to his side by the centurion's lance.

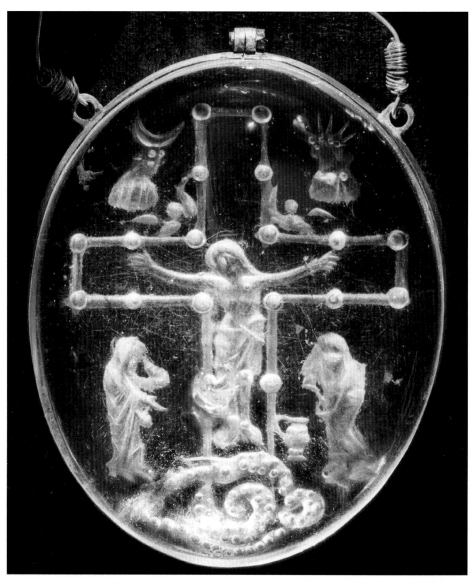

14 Carolingian rock crystal engraved with the Crucifixion; conceivably given to Æthelstan by
Hugh, duke of the Franks.

a)

b)

c)

d)

e)

15 Vestments found in the tomb of St Cuthbert on its opening in 1827 that are assumed to be those given by Æthelstan to the saint on his visit in 934. The inscriptions on the reverse ends of the stole and maniple show that they had originally been commissioned by Ælfflæd, Edward the Elder's second wife, as gifts for Bishop Frithestan but clearly never passed to his church at Winchester. The ornamentation resembles that of the double portrait miniature of Æthelstan and Cuthbert (1).

16 Fifteenth-century tomb chest in Malmesbury Abbey, with the reclining figure of King Æthelstan. Æthelstan was a generous patron of Malmesbury in life and chose to be buried there, near the tomb of St Aldhelm. In the twelfth century, William of Malmesbury saw the king's remains and remarked on his fair hair. At the Reformation, his bones were lost and the tomb is now empty.

17 Silver ring found at Beverley with inscriptions dating from the immediate post-Conquest period. The worn text on the outside may have read AĐELSTAN . R. ↑G. GIFAN (for 'Æthelstan Rex Anglorum gifen'); and the internal text probably reads IOHNSE BEVERIY ARCEB. 'Æthelstan, king of the English [has] given [this ring] to Johannes Beverlaiensis the archbishop'. The double inscription reflects the memory at Beverley that Æthelstan had once given privileges to the town and to Bishop John's church.

18 Life-size statue of King Æthelstan in Beverley Minster, cast in lead by William Collins, 1781, and added to an elaborate choir screen in mixed Classical and Gothic style set up in 1731 (perhaps to a design by Hawksmoor). Æthelstan stands holding a sword in one hand, symbolizing his military prowess, and in the other the charter of privileges he supposedly gave to the town of Beverley. On the other side of the archway leading into the choir is a similar statue of Bishop John of Beverley.

19 Engraving of Æthelstan asking that the Bible be translated into Saxon tongue. William Tyndale reported in 1528 on the authority of the 'Old English Chronicle' that Æthelstan had ordered the gospels to be translated into the vernacular; Thomas Tanner's *Bibliotheca Britannica*, published in 1748, dated the work to 930 and asserted that it was done 'from the purest founts of the Hebrews by certain Hebrews converted to Christianity in his kingdom'.

the localities throughout his wide realm. To Æthelstan, as to his grandfather, Alfred, crime (and for Æthelstan, especially thieving) led to the distur-
bance of the peace and hence to disloyalty against the king himself and to
his office. Breach of the peace became in his eyes tantamount to treachery,
the breaking of a man's oath to the king, his lord.[51] The whole Grately
code may indeed be read as an explicit statement of the king's intention
to tackle the social problems affecting his realm.[52]

Despite the strictness of his injunctions at Grately about theft, the king
appears to have made little progress on this front, for the third of his
codes (issued at Exeter and conventionally numbered *V Æthelstan*) opens
with a statement expressing his frustration at his incapacity to effect
change:

> I, King Æthelstan, declare that I have learned that the public peace has
> not been kept to the extent, either of my wishes, or of the provisions
> laid down at Grately. And my councillors say that I have suffered this
> too long.[53]

Æthelstan went on to explain why he felt compelled to legislate again:
'The cause which has led us to issue this decree is that all the oaths, pledges
and sureties which were given there [i.e. at Grately] have been disregarded
and broken, and we know of no other course which we can follow with
confidence, unless it be this.'[54] Can we detect a faint note of despair in the
king's voice here? Not merely exasperated by his subjects' collective failure
to heed his legal injunctions and keep their oaths (specifically the oaths to
keep the peace which all his subjects had given to his reeves who stood
proxy for the king in each locality),[55] the king sounds as if he is struggling
to find fresh ideas. So, rather than merely repeating the previous statements, or issuing yet more punitive directives, Æthelstan's council adopted
a different strategy against theft at Exeter. That code offered a temporary
amnesty to thieves, letting them off payment of fines until the Rogation
Days (perhaps those in May) if they paid compensation to injured parties
for every theft. In a later council meeting at Faversham in Kent, the king
went even further, promising a pardon for criminals 'for any crime what-
soever which was committed before the Council on condition that henceforth and forever they abstain from all evil doing' and before August
'confess their crimes and make amends for everything of which they have
been guilty'.[56] In his Exeter code the king also tried other methods to

[51] David Pratt, *The Political Thought of King Alfred the Great* (Cambridge, 2007), 235–41;
Pratt, 'Written Law', 344.
[52] Wormald *MEL*, 300; Keynes, 'Royal Government', 237.
[53] *V As*, prologue. Æthelstan's legislation is examined in meticulous detail by Wormald:
MEL, 290–308.
[54] *V As*, prologue, §3.
[55] *VI As*, 10; see further below, 143–4.

tackle powerful kindreds in the localities, decreeing that disturbers of the peace should be uprooted from their native districts and transplanted with their families and property to other parts of the realm, where they could do less harm. Any who returned thereafter to their homes would be treated with the severity meted out to thieves caught in the act.[57] Further, he attempted to eradicate corruption and neglect of the law by his reeves, by threatening both the imposition of fines and removal from office for such disobedience.[58]

The strategy adopted at Exeter and at Faversham of offering some amnesty to thieves did not last long; we find a tougher clampdown on thieves in the provisions of Æthelstan's next code issued when his council met at Thunderfield (*IV Æthelstan*). Thieves now found themselves facing the death penalty, whether or not they had been caught in the act (although Æthelstan did modify this blanket condemnation in the statement he made at Whittlebury that juveniles under the age of fifteen should not be executed 'because he thought it too cruel to kill so many young people and for such small crimes as he understood to be the case everywhere').[59] Any thief who took to flight was to be pursued to his death, and anyone who met him should kill him. Heavy fines were imposed on reeves who failed to carry out the king's command in this matter, who would also 'suffer such disgrace as has been ordained'.[60] In the same code the king tried once more to rein in powerful kindred groups, whose protection of family members accused of crime prevented their being brought to justice. Anyone so rich, or belonging to so powerful a kindred that he could not be restrained from crime should be exiled from his native area to another part of the kingdom of the king's choice; should he return home he would be treated as a thief caught in the act: 'and the reason for this is that the oaths and pledges which were given to the king and his councillors have been continuously violated, or observed less strictly than is acceptable to God or to the secular authority'.[61] Again we see that Æthelstan made a close mental association between disruptive behaviour and disloyalty.

Pronouncements collected in the ordinances of the London peace guild show that Æthelstan's preoccupation with these problems and his rhetorical device of associating theft with the language of disloyalty had communicated itself to his leading men beyond his court and galvanized them into action on his behalf. This group, responsible for policing the London

[56] *III As*, 3. We know of the Faversham provisions only from the account of them given in the decree of the bishops and men of Kent about the preservation of the peace known as *III Æthelstan*.

[57] *V As*, prologue 1–2.

[58] *V As*, 1.2–1.4.

[59] *VI As*, 12.

[60] *IV As*, 6–6.7; 7.

[61] *IV As*, 3.2; compare also *III As*, 6.

area, made arrangements also for the mutual help of the guild's members. Their legislation supplemented the king's laws issued at Grately, Exeter and Thunderfield, and addressed thieving at the outset in the prologue and at more length in the ninth clause, where they urged strict punishments for thieves and those who sheltered them. More interestingly, the eighth clause tried to articulate specific measures to weaken the potential for social unrest caused by powerful kindreds, using the collective force of members of the peace guild, officials in charge of groups of one hundred men, and those with charge over bodies of ten and the reeves to ride out together against wrongdoers.[62] Here we see the introduction for the first time in England of sworn associations of ten men, tithings, a custom already well known in continental Frankia.[63] Yet even this tight-knit association could not guarantee preservation of the peace; the guild turned to the king and his reeves rather plaintively to see if they could not between them invent a better solution:

> If our lord, or any of our reeves can devise any additional rules for our association, such suggestions shall not go unheeded, nor be passed over in silence; ... And if we are willing to act thus in all things, we may trust to God and our liege-lord that everybody's property will be safer from theft than it has been. But if we are negligent in attending to the regulations for the public security and to the solemn pledges we have given, we may anticipate – and indeed know for certainty – that the thieves of whom we were speaking will tyrannize over us still more than they have done in the past.[64]

Only from the provisions of this code do we learn the details of that new oath the king had imposed on all his men and see how closely it linked disruption of the peace and security of the realm with disloyalty to the king. A clause attached to the end of the provisions agreed by the London peace guild includes a statement about how the councillors, 'all in a body', had given their solemn pledges to the archbishop at Thunderfield, 'when Ælfheah Stybb and Byrhtnoth, son of Odda attended meeting at king's command'.[65] Although the precise occasion to which this alludes remains uncertain, it probably originated in a general meeting of all of the king's councillors which the two named men attended as representatives of the London guild; this clause may have arisen from their report back to their fellow guild members.[66] At that meeting all present agreed 'that every reeve should exact a pledge from his own district, that they would all observe the decrees for the public security which King Æthelstan and his

---

[62] *VI As*, 8.1–8.3.
[63] Pratt, 'Written Law', 341–5.
[64] *VI As*, 8.9.
[65] *VI As*, 10.
[66] Wormald, *MEL*, 298.

councillors had enacted, first at Grately, and afterwards at Exeter, and then at Faversham and on a fourth occasion at Thunderfield'.[67] The new oath imposed here required all the king's men to keep the peace; that those responsible for policing London recognized their failure to fulfil their part of this obligation emerges clearly from the passage quoted above, as does the fact that the danger of consequent social disintegration alarmed them as much as it did their king. We might compare here the other locally issued set of provisions, that produced by the men of Kent, who decreed that every lord should hold his own men in surety against theft, making reeves responsible for exacting the necessary oaths on larger estates.[68] In London and in Kent we see evidence, as David Pratt has argued, 'for a coherent reordering of local justice, with hatches truly battened down against thieves and disruptive king-groups. Both were now faced with the new tithing provision, with not only peace-keeping but now surety arrangements administered by lords.'[69]

Considered in this light, the king's own law codes and the other legal pronouncements made by different bodies during his reign do not appear like arid or rarefied statements made by dusty lawyers remote from the society for which they legislated, but seem to reflect more closely the immediate preoccupations of a king. Æthelstan has been criticized for his limited success in curing the ills he saw as rife within society; as Wormald asserted, 'the hallmark of Æthelstan's law-making is the gulf dividing its exalted aspirations from its spasmodic impact'.[70] Yet one can read his codes more sympathetically and see clear evidence of Æthelstan's own mind at work trying to devise novel solutions to his nation's ills: here was a monarch with a genuine concern for the well-being of his people, who could communicate his misgivings and disappointment with the failure of his remedies to a wide group of his subjects holding administrative responsibilities and instil in them similar anxiety. Other early medieval kings legislated about loyalty, especially the importance of swearing and keeping oaths, and several had also legislated to prevent theft and punish thieves.[71] King Alfred's lawbook, with its lengthy preface quoting extensively from the Book of Exodus, had made an ideological statement, creating his people,

---

[67] *VI As*, 10.

[68] *III As*, 7–7.2.

[69] Pratt, 'Written Law', 345.

[70] Wormald, *MEL*, 300. In the discussion that follows, I owe much to the work of my former student Dr Martha Riddiford and her analysis of Æthelstan's law codes in the context of a discussion about the treatment of 'deviants' in Anglo-Saxon society in: 'Social Exclusion in Anglo-Saxon Wessex', PhD thesis, University of Sheffield, 2008, ch. 3.

[71] The first substantive chapter of King Alfred's law code, for example, enjoined that each man should keep his oath and his pledge: S. Keynes and M. Lapidge, *Alfred the Great: Asser's Life of Alfred and other Contemporary Sources* (Harmondsworth, 1983), 164 and 306, n. 6; Pratt, *The Political Thought*, 232–5. Compare Charlemagne's injunctions about the fidelity owed to the Lord Emperor in his programmatic capitulary of 802: *MGH, Capit* I, no. 33, ch. 2, p. 92.

the *Angelcynn*, as a new people chosen in the sight of God. To Alfred, crime became an outrage against God, an ultimate act of disloyalty; punishment thus expressed the Almighty's anger.[72] The West Frankish king Charles the Bald had issued a capitulary in 853 at Servais which applied the obligation of oath-taking specifically to the question of theft as he sought to deal with the repression of violent crime and public disorder at grass-roots level, laying on the hundred men the responsibility to control theft, pursue the guilty and raise the hue and cry.[73] But the equation of theft with disloyalty to Æthelstan's person appears peculiar to him. His preoccupation with theft – tough on theft, tough on the causes of theft – finds no direct parallel in other kings' codes. Æthelstan also stands apart for his equation of breach of the peace, as symbolized by theft, as tantamount to oath-breaking. Loyalty mattered to Æthelstan; personal loyalty, the bond of a man's word to his lord, seemingly mattered very much indeed.

Theft and the problem of powerful local kindreds did not represent the only manifestations of social disorder in Æthelstan's realm and his law codes tackled other problems as well as thieves, their accessories and those who harboured thieves, in an attempt to ensure order and enhance social cohesion. For example, at Grately the king legislated on the problem of lordless men from whom it proved difficult to obtain legal satisfaction; offences committed by landless men who visited from another shire; abuses of justice whether by lords or the king's officials; plots against a man's lord; non-attendance at assemblies (deemed an act of insubordination); and swearing false oaths.[74] The same code addressed further causes of social ills relating to the minting of money, and the organization and control of trade and decreed that there should be no trading on a Sunday (a provision overturned by the council which met at Exeter, it presumably having proved unworkable).[75] A final clause – perhaps appended to the Grately code as an afterthought, since it fits oddly with what immediately precedes it – addressed the treatment of one who had sworn a false oath, stressing once more the fundamental significance placed by the king on the importance of keeping one's word.[76] In the light of the seriousness

---

[72] *MEL*, 416–29.

[73] Capitulary of Servais, 853: *MGH, Capit* II, no. 260, chs 4–8, pp. 272–3; see Patrick Wormald, '*Engla lond*: The Making of an Allegiance', *Journal of Historical Sociology*, vii (1994), 66–7; Pratt, *The Political Thought*, 234.

[74] *II As*, 2–4, 8, 26.

[75] *II As*, 24.1; *IV As*, 2. For the provisions about money and trade made at Grately, see below.

[76] *II As*, 26; Keynes, 'Royal Government', 237. It is difficult on the face of it to draw any direct connection between this provision and the narrative given by William of Malmesbury (and found also in some charters from Malmesbury) of the plot to blind Æthelstan at Winchester led by a certain Alfred discussed above, 40–1. One might see a possible link in the fact that after Alfred's death in Rome, where he had fled on the discovery of his plot, the pope, according to William, questioned whether he had the right to a Christian burial. Wormald was keener to link the two than am I: *MEL*, 307.

with which Æthelstan approached transgressions that threatened the maintenance of the peace, we might indeed have expected him to have used the secular law to enforce the imposition of heavy penalties on offenders. What is more surprising is the overtly ecclesiastical character of some of the judicial provisions enacted here.

As we have seen, the Grately code specified the death penalty for thieves over the age of twelve who stole goods worth more than eight pence; it also raised the possibility of imprisoning thieves for a specified period of time before they made recompense for their crime by the payment of a heavy fine. That option might have referred to the under-aged or to those who had stolen goods of lesser value.[77] Imprisonment as means of exacting society's retribution and causing the criminal to reflect on his misdeeds and turn towards a better life (as opposed to incarceration before trial) was a relatively new idea in Anglo-Saxon law. First introduced by King Alfred, it apparently owed a good deal to the Church's teachings on penance.[78] The forty days specified in the Grately code for which a thief should be imprisoned before, on his release, he paid a fine of 120 shillings, equated to a standard period of penitential observance. Similarly the period of 120 days' imprisonment imposed later in the same code on practitioners of witchcraft, arsonists or those who tried to avenge thieves, represented the long-established equivalent of a year's penance.[79] Penitential practice also featured in the final clause of this code, which denied burial in consecrated ground to perjurers unless their confessors could testify to their diocesan bishop that the perjurer had made the amends they had prescribed.[80]

Further indications of the Church's increased involvement in the legal process emerge in the importance placed on the ordeal in this same code. Æthelstan did not innovate in recommending the ordeal as a test of a man's innocence; the seventh-century West Saxon king Ine had referred to ordeals in his code, and Edward the Elder had also advised its use in case of alleged perjury, while forbidding the timetabling of trials by ordeal during periods of festival or fast.[81] Thoroughly ecclesiastical rituals, ordeal ceremonies were preserved from the tenth century onwards in pontificals

[77] *II As*, 1: 1–3.

[78] *Alfred*, 1.2 required an oath-breaker humbly to give up his weapons and possessions to friends for safe-keeping and remain forty days in prison at a royal manor, undergoing there whatever the bishop prescribed for him. *Alfred*, 1.3–7 covered various possibilities if the criminal failed to follow this instruction, imposing excommunication on anyone who succeeded in escaping from his prison.

[79] Compare the Penitential attributed to Archbishop Theodore, I. ii. 8 and I. xv. 4, where penance is prescribed for one year or three forty-day periods: *Medieval Handbooks of Penance*, trans. John T. McNeill and Helena M. Gamer (New York, 1990), 185, 198. I owe this point to Richard Sowerby: 'Punishment and the Transformation of Space in Anglo-Saxon Monasteries', MLitt. dissertation, University of St Andrews, 2008, 24–5.

[80] *II As*, 26–26.1.

[81] *Ine* 37, 62; 1 *Edward*, 3.

(liturgical books containing orders of service for rites performed by bishops). David Rollason has argued that their prominence in Æthelstan's legislation offers testimony either of the hold that the Church had gained over Anglo-Saxon society by the early tenth century, or of the growing and increasingly intrusive power of royal government.[82] Bearing in mind the earlier remarks made about Æthelstan's attitudes to remedies for poverty and his interest in monastic psalmody on his behalf, one might rather interpret his interest in the use of ordeals as part of a wider sacralizing of law apparent in his reign.

Æthelstan's Grately code made the first full, official statement of the judicial procedure of the ordeal, in terms which demonstrate clearly the extent to which this was a liturgical as well as a judicial ceremony. For the accused, the ordeal involved three days' preparation, in the company of a mass-priest, when the alleged wrongdoer had to eat a penitential diet, make a daily charitable offering and attend mass each day; all attending the ordeal whether on the side of accused or accuser were also required to fast in order to ensure both the purity of all participating and the justness and fairness of the judgment reached.[83] Those who denied an accusation of theft or who wished to contest a charge of minting lightweight coins faced the single ordeal (in the case of a moneyer, the ordeal by hot iron),[84] but those accused of plotting against their lords, church-breakers, people who caused death by witchcraft, sorcery or deadly spells, and arsonists or those who avenged a thief all faced the threefold ordeal.[85] If the accused failed at the triple ordeal, he faced imprisonment for 120 days before his kinsmen could bail him by paying a fine of 120 shillings to the king and the wergeld of the dead man (in the case of those who had caused death by witchcraft) to his relatives. The different fates awaiting those who could not deny such charges – who faced the death penalty – and those who did deny them but yet failed the ordeal (who were punished by imprisonment and severe financial penalties) rested on the significance placed on the formal denial. Failure at the ordeal did not equate to confession to the crime with which the accused had been charged; as Bartlett argued, this suggests that the verdict of ordeal was not absolute and might testify to some contemporary scepticism about the ceremony's worth.[86]

More significant for this argument is the evidence the regulations for the ordeal provide for the direct involvement of the Church not just in the enacting of legal provisions at Æthelstan's royal councils but in the administration of law and justice in practice in the regions, something which may reflect the king's own interests. These provisions all have a faintly

---

[82] David Rollason, *Two Anglo-Saxon Rituals: Church Dedication and the Judicial Ordeal* (Leicester, 1988), 12–17.

[83] *II As*, 28; Rollason, *Rituals*, 16.

[84] *II As*, 7, 14.1.

[85] *II As*, 4–6.3.

[86] Robert Bartlett, *Trial by Fire and Water: the Medieval Judicial Ordeal* (Oxford, 1986), 68–9.

clerical air. Other ecclesiastical features of Æthelstan's laws include the recommendation in the Exeter code that 'every Friday at every minster all the servants of God are to sing fifty psalms for the king and for all who desire what he desires'; the temporary amnesty from the requirement to pay fines for theft made at midwinter at Exeter to last until Rogationtide (late April); the pardoning of criminals for crimes committed before the Faversham council on condition that wrongdoers confess their sins and make amends; and the arrangements made about sanctuary in the Thunderfield code.[87] Yet rather than attribute these to the overt influence of the archbishop of Canterbury on the issuing and preservation of Æthelstan's legislation, one could see them as articulations of the fruits of the king's internal wrestling with the burdens of ruling in accordance with the Church's teachings. In that light, Æthelstan's announcement at Whittlebury that he would raise the age at which a thief might be executed from twelve to fifteen, and the value of goods whose theft would immediately incur the death penalty to twelve pence suggest a greater willingness to leave vengeance to the Lord than emerges from his earlier legislation.[88]

For all their formulaic nature Æthelstan's laws have thus shed a surprising amount of light upon the king's attitude to the maintenance of order within his extended realm, light that may go some way towards corroborating William of Malmesbury's unsupported statement that concerning this king, 'there is a vigorous tradition in England that he was the most law-abiding ruler they have ever had'.[89] We have seen how closely the king connected breaches of the peace with disloyalty to his own person, and attributed the increasingly religious undertow that character-izes some of this legislation to the king himself, albeit acting with the support and on the advice of his bishops. As a law-maker, Æthelstan took the responsibilities laid on him at his coronation to act as shepherd of his people extremely seriously; yet, as well as ensuring their safety, he had a charge to work for their material well-being and prosperity by the judicious management of his resources.

THE KING'S WEALTH

That an early medieval king's prestige depended in large measure on his possession and retention of wealth scarcely needs asserting. A king needed material possessions not just for the support of his own court and for his personal needs or the pursuit of his own interests but to fund the protec-tion and governance of his realm, whether through direct payment or the reward of those who would administer it on his behalf. We should remind

---

[87] *V As*, 3; *V As*, 3.1; *III As*, 3; and *IV As*, 6–6.2.
[88] *VI As*, 12.1, 12.3.
[89] *GR*, ii, 132, pp. 210–11.

ourselves once more of the increased size of Æthelstan's kingdom in comparison with the territory ruled by his ancestors and reflect on how much additional income that greater land mass could have brought to the royal purse, if well managed.[90]

The Anglo-Saxons honoured their kings above all for their military prowess. They prized their success in warfare because it testified to kings' royal lineage and reflected their heroic virtue; it also brought tangible rewards. A victorious king ensured peace for his realm, enhancing that security materially by the wealth he captured from the defeated (or demanded in tribute) and endowed upon his own followers. *Beowulf* expressed an image of the king as ring-giver which recurs frequently in Anglo-Saxon poetry as a reflection of the ideals and aspirations of the heroic Germanic age, already recognizably past at the time of the poem's composition. All early medieval kings needed to acquire treasure with which to reward their followers. By the early years of the tenth century, rings were given only metaphorically and commuted into the more permanent resource of land (perhaps a land grant augmented with an attractive sack of loot, or some cattle paid in tribute).[91] A king who proved so successful in battle that he added substantially to the landed realm over which he had dominion, found himself well equipped to reward his favourites, yet in his success Æthelstan took over a wider group of subjects for whose well-being he now had to provide. A king's wealth significantly affected the way in which he governed.

On his inheritance of the throne of Wessex, Æthelstan obtained all the royal demesne of the West Saxon royal family; the addition of estates in the south-eastern counties acquired on the expansion of Wessex in the second half of the ninth century enhanced the extent and value of the family's core holdings in central Wessex. Some of those estates belonged to Æthelstan personally (giving him a reasonable degree of control over their future disposal); others seemingly pertained to the West Saxon monarchy, and were intended to pass intact from one king to his successor.[92] The Anglo-Saxon realm to which Æthelstan succeeded extended, however, beyond Wessex north into Mercia and east into the lands of the eastern Danelaw brought under English control by his father, uncle and aunt.[93] Quite what had happened to the land formerly belonging to the ruling houses of other Anglo-Saxon kingdoms remains unclear. In English Mercia – west of Watling Street – the demesne may have stayed partly intact after Burgred's abdication in 874; if so, Edward would have

[90] This chapter will focus centrally on the king's use of money and the control of minting; consideration of the ways in which his coinage expressed Æthelstan's ideas about the nature of his own kingship are reserved for ch. 8, below, 216–33.

[91] Campbell, *The Anglo-Saxon State*, 242.

[92] As implied by Asser's description of King Æthelwulf's disposition of his inheritance: ch. 16, pp. 14–15.

[93] Above, 12–17.

succeeded in retaining a good deal of those former royal lands that his sister and brother-in-law, Æthelflæd and Æthelred, had enjoyed and so passed these on to his son. But where Danish lords had held former English realms since the Scandinavian settlements of the later ninth century – in East Anglia, north-eastern Mercia and in Northumbria – royal family land and its appurtenant privileges would long ago have been dispersed and passed into the hands of different, independent landowners. As ruler in York Sihtric would have enjoyed at least some of the lands of the Anglo-Saxon Northumbrian crown, and presumably the royal residence in its principal city; that fell into Æthelstan's hands on his acquisition of Sihtric's realm in 927. Yet the wider holdings of the Northumbrian royal house one must assume to have long since passed into other noble families, and so were available neither for the support of the new king of all England, nor for him to give away to reward his followers. We struggle, therefore, to assess just how much more personal wealth Æthelstan had at his disposal as a result of his acquisition of direct rule over all the English territories than his father and grandfather had enjoyed.

Each of the estates in the king's possession, however acquired, provided him with a nominal income, whether paid in monetary rent, food (or other produce) or in the form of labour; several royal residences are named among the places where Æthelstan spent time as he travelled around his realm, their produce supplying the resources necessary to support the king and his entourage during their stay.[94] In the study of royal residences we approach more closely the realities of early medieval kingship, for it was in these vills that contemporaries saw at first hand the routines of royal power: meetings and councils of the king's leading men; visits and embassies from foreign dignitaries; celebrations of solemn religious feasts; as well as the conviviality of entertainments such as feasting and hunting.[95] Although contemporary sources provide limited information about the running of royal palaces and their associated lands, later evidence (largely from the Domesday survey of 1086) suggests that a network of royal estates extended throughout England. Divided into manageable units for administrative purposes, these were organized by the king's reeves, through whom thegns living on the estate paid renders to the king (origi-nally in kind, arguably more often in cash by Æthelstan's day) and provided some customary services.[96] Yet, the king held land in more places than merely those where he had residences, and the location of such royal vills did not necessarily remain constant. Indeed the royal demesne constantly changed as a king alienated estates (or just portions of estates)

---

[94] See 'When King Æthelstan was where' Appendix II and associated map 4. Although the majority of the estates were in Wessex and southern Mercia, as discussed earlier, others farther afield may have been residences of other native royal lines.

[95] P.H. Sawyer, 'The Royal *tun* in Pre-Conquest England', in *Ideal and Reality*, ed. P. Wormald *et al.* (Oxford, 1983), 273.

[96] Ibid., 281–2.

and acquired others, by gift, sale or legal forfeit.[97] Still, royal lands served
a useful function throughout England as places where rents in kind and in
cash were collected and also acted more generally as centres of royal
government controlled by reeves.[98]

Lands other than those held directly by the king also contributed to his
wealth and that of the kingdom he governed, and here Æthelstan's possession of a larger domain produced tangibly greater financial rewards.
Detailed records about the workings of taxation are not available before
the eleventh century, but extrapolation back from that material suggests
the gradual evolution of mechanisms to assess land for taxation purposes,
relying on its division into units of nominal assessment (hides) and the
grouping of multiples of those units into larger areas both for assessment
and for revenue collection.[99] In the evolution of the shire (a defined territorial area based on a central shire town) as the central administrative unit
of an extended West Saxon and later English realm, the first half of the
tenth century proved a critical period. Much of the credit for the shiring
of Mercia and of the eastern Danelaw may belong, however, not to
Æthelstan but to his father.[100] While each West Saxon shire had its own
ealdorman, north of the Thames ealdormen acted for Æthelstan over
rather larger areas, more closely resembling older provinces. Reeves and
thegns served under those ealdormen in the fortified *burhs* that had acted
as defensive as well as administrative headquarters since the expansion of
West Saxon power northwards under Edward the Elder and Æthelflæd. A
large element of the role of these royal officials lay in the collection of
revenues on the king's behalf, not just dues from land but also profits from
the judicial process and from the minting of the coin in which those
monies were rendered. Mention of the coinage brings us back to the
person of the king. Control of the coinage offered a king more than the
opportunity to enjoy the profits from the dues payable by moneyers when
they received their new dies; it enabled him to disseminate ideas about the
nature of his kingship via the visual designs and written legends that his
coins bore.

The king's money

Coins provide one indication of the strength and sophistication of Anglo-
Saxon royal government in the tenth and eleventh centuries. As Henry
Loyn argued, 'payment of geld involved the handling of coinage, and it is
no coincidence that the well-taxed English should produce the most

[97] Ibid., 279–80.

[98] H.M. Chadwick, *Studies on Anglo-Saxon Institutions* (Cambridge, 1905), 228–39.

[99] Stenton, *ASE*, 286–7.

[100] Loyn, *The Governance*, 133–7. David Hill, 'The Shiring of Mercia – Again', in H&H,
144–59.

advanced currency in the Europe of its day – which is one of our best indications of the strength of royal government in England and of the general coherence of the English community'.[101] Although the most powerful arguments for using the coinage as an index of the extent and reach of royal power rest on the period after King Edgar's reform of the monetary system in the 970s, royal control over the minting of money appears to have increased during Æthelstan's reign. The king's coinage thus serves as one index of his attitude towards the governance of his realm.

Central to an understanding of the king's view of his coinage are the clauses in the code which Æthelstan issued at Grately (*II Æthelstan*), which make detailed provisions for various economic matters especially trading, but also the organization of the issuing of coin. As a group these clauses do not belong with the original text of the Grately code. The fact that they repeat and contradict some points made previously in the same code and have their own separate numbering implies that they were incorporated from somewhere else, most probably an earlier set of provisions, perhaps dating from the middle years of the reign of Edward the Elder. When they became part of the Grately code remains uncertain; if not at the Grately meeting, then probably soon thereafter.[102] After some provisions for the repair of *burhs* and a requirement that all buying should be done within towns,[103] there follows a series of detailed clauses about the minting of money, including the explicit statement 'that there is to be one coinage over all the king's dominion, and no one is to mint money except in a town' (*port* or *burh*). In other words, only the king's coin, properly minted, is to be accepted as legal tender.[104] After stipulating the penalties for those caught minting false coins, the text goes on to specify how many moneyers are to work in each town.[105] This interpolated collection of earlier provisions concludes with four more succinct directives concerning shield-making, the provision of mounted men for military service, bribery, and, seventhly, the sending of horses overseas.[106] Thereafter, the Grately provisions resume with a clause about the punishment for a slave convicted of theft in the ordeal.

Specifying at a level of detail unparalleled in any other royal legislation how many moneyers might mint on the king's or a bishop's behalf and at

---

[101] Loyn, *The Governance*, 122; compare Campbell, *The Anglo-Saxon State*, 32–3, 181.

[102] Mark Blackburn, 'Mints, Burhs and the Grately Code, Cap. 14.2', in *The Defence of Wessex*, ed. D. Hill and A. Rumble (Manchester, 1996), 160–75, at 167. The interpolated clauses are internally numbered from 13.1 (secondly) to 18 (seventhly); see also Wormald, *MEL*, 294.

[103] *II As*, 12; Blackburn, 'Mints', 167.

[104] *II As*, 14.

[105] *II As* 14.2. '14.2: In Canterbury there are to be seven moneyers; four of the king, two of the bishop, one of the abbot; in Rochester three, two of the king, one of the bishop; in London eight; in Winchester six; in Lewes two; in Hastings one; another at Chichester; at Southampton two; at Wareham two; at Dorchester one; at Exeter two; at Shaftesbury two; otherwise in the other burhs, one.' See map 3.

[106] *II As*, 15–18.

which fortified places in southern England, as well as asserting bluntly that there was to be only one coinage (*an mynet*) across the king's dominion, these clauses appear to make powerful statements about Æthelstan's desire to assert his authority through the visual symbol of his coinage. Only a strong king could have aspired to such control over so large and diverse a realm. But to read these provisions thus may be unwarranted.[107] Despite that statement about one coinage, the towns named as mint sites lay in a restricted area, running from east to west across Greater Wessex, starting with Kent and moving through London, Hampshire, Sussex and the rest of southern Wessex. None are specified for the northern most part of Wessex, for Mercia or indeed any of the other formerly English or Danish regions, beyond the bald statement that each *burh* not mentioned by name should have a single moneyer.[108] Only in part of Wessex did the king apparently seek to control the administration of coinage directly; in Mercia and Northumbria previous local arrangements, presumably controlled by the ealdormen, still pertained.[109] We should also recall that, although these clauses survive in a code in King Æthelstan's name, they probably date from his father's reign and thus refer to a time when the expanded West Saxon realm was distinctly smaller than that ruled by Æthelstan by the time he issued the Grately code. The provision for a single coinage must, therefore, have been intended as an unambiguous statement that only coins of the West Saxon king (and presumably of his predecessors) constituted acceptable currency; coins minted abroad, or in the name of former Danish rulers in York, would not be legal tender.[110] Æthelstan's decision (or that of his advisers who compiled this law code) to include these earlier discrete administrative directives about the minting of coins need not necessarily mean that this king sought to take direct control over all minting throughout his realm, determining the types issued and reserving the profits related to the process to himself. Like his father, Æthelstan may have sought to maintain closer control only within the West Saxon heartland, allowing coinage in the more distant parts of the realm still to fall under the control of local authorities.

In fact, the continuing degree of variety in the types of coin issued in different parts of Æthelstan's wider realm shows that the minting of English money continued to be organized on a regional basis long after Æthelstan's unification of the kingdom. The regional differences visible in the types issued in different parts of the country reflected both the former

[107] I am grateful to George Molyneaux of All Souls College, Oxford, for letting me read a chapter from his doctoral thesis on coinage in late Anglo-Saxon England which argues for a lesser degree of direct royal control in the period before Edgar's reform of the coinage in 973 than many historians have tended to assume.

[108] Blackburn, 'Mints', 169–71.

[109] Blunt, 'The Coinage', 114–16.

[110] Ibid., 41.

kingdoms of earlier Anglo-Saxon England and the division of England after Alfred's treaty with the Danish leader Guthrum, c.890.[111] While we can say something about the ways in which Æthelstan used his coins to articulate ideas about the nature of his rule, or about how he wished his subjects to imagine him, such images and written legends appear to have circulated within a more restricted sphere than we might at first sight have imagined from the assertion 'there is only to be one money over all the king's dominion'.

King Æthelstan's earliest coinage closely resembled that of his father, much of it issued by the same moneyers who had produced coin for Edward. On the obverse the king's name and title were written around a linear circle on the edge of the face, within which was a small cross, or a bust of the king wearing a diadem; on the reverse, the moneyer's name was given in two horizontal lines, with three crosses between them. In the first few years after 924, different styles of coin were issued in each of the English regions: southern England, English Mercia, York, the southern and the northern Danelaw, although no coins in Æthelstan's name were apparently minted in East Anglia until the last years of the king's reign.[112] After his conquest of York, acquisition of Northumbria and the submission of the other kings in the British Isles, Æthelstan introduced a coin of a new style bearing a fresh legend. Called by numismatists the 'Circumscription Cross' type, these coins bear on their obverse a central cross, with an inscription including the king's name and the new royal title – *Rex totius Britanniae* (variously abbreviated) – around the circumference; on the reverse the name of the moneyer (and sometimes the mint) appear around the edge, with again a cross in the centre. The new royal title adopted for this style indicated Æthelstan's newly acquired dominion and his status as 'king of the whole of Britain'. Examples of this type were minted in Wessex, English Mercia and York, although again not in East Anglia, nor anywhere in the Danelaw. We may read these coins as presenting similar images of the king, his power and authority to those statements articulated in his charters from the same period in which he laid claim to guardianship of the whole country of Britain.[113] Coins provide further evidence that Æthelstan sought to place his stamp on the newly exalted position in which he found himself by virtue of his conquest of all of Britain. His reiteration of the same claims in charters and on his coins suggests that Æthelstan would have liked to disseminate his

[111] Ibid., 114.

[112] Stewart Lyon, 'The Coinage of Edward the Elder', in H&H, 67–78; Blunt, 47. See plate 10.

[113] For example, charters S 429–31 and S 416 and S 445. Discussed further below, ch. 8. We might wonder whether a decision to include mint-signatures on some of his coins reflected any of the same impulses that had led the charter scribe 'Æthelstan A' to record so meticulously the location of each royal council whose decisions he recorded in charter form.

conception of his own power and status to his subject people beyond Wessex, even though this particular issue appears in fact to have had a limited circulation in that realm. For example, in an apparent statement of Mercian independence, asserting Æthelstan's *Saxon* roots instead of any title to rule over the whole island, some of the coins minted in Mercia in this style gave the king the rather different royal title, *Rex Saxorum*.[114] The same could not, however, be said of the new type that replaced the Circumscription Cross in southern England at some point early in the 930s and – with minor variations – came to be issued across almost all the English regions other than Mercia: the crowned-bust type.

Earlier Anglo-Saxon kings had modelled their coinage on that of classical Roman emperors, choosing to depict themselves in portrait busts drawn in profile, frequently wearing diadems.[115] In similar fashion on this new issue, Æthelstan's profiled bust looks fixedly to the right; the eye stares somewhat, but the rest of the head is well proportioned. His face is clean-shaven; the hair styled high on his head in the Roman fashion, and curled in the nape of his neck. The king wears a *paludamentum* (a Roman military cloak) about his shoulders, fastened at the neck on his right (so to the left of our image); as the fabric falls away from the clasp, the patterned braid round the neck of his tunic is sometimes visible. He does not, however, wear the conventional imperial symbol of the diadem. Instead, on his head, raised up by his hair, sits a crown of simple design: a plain circlet, from which protrude three vertical stalks, each with a small sphere at its tip.[116] Examples of this style where the bust was drawn small enough to lie wholly inside the inner circle on the obverse of the coin carry the legend *Rex Tot Brit* (or variants for *Rex Totius Britanniae*, 'King of all Britain'); where the king's shoulders intruded into the bottom border, the legend was normally just *Æthelstan Rex*.[117]

Within the royal circle the new image went hand in hand with a new rhetoric in charter styles: together they asserted the imperial quality of the king's rulership over all of Britain.[118] Quite what impact this image and associated legend had on those beyond the king's immediate circle who encountered it on his newly circulated coins we can only speculate. Dissociated from 'the constantly repeated ritualized activity of the court,

[114] Blunt 'The Coinage', 47; Maddicott, *The Origins*, 20–1.

[115] Anna Gannon, *The Iconography of Early Anglo-Saxon Coinage: Sixth to Eighth Centuries* (Oxford, 2003).

[116] W.J. Andrew, 'Evolution of Portraiture on the Silver Penny', *BNJ* ser. 1, v (1908), 363–80, at 366–7. Andrew suggested that the balls might have been pearls, but although one might make such an assumption from the numismatic images, the clearer manuscript portrait rules out such a suggestion. Blunt described them as 'globules': Blunt, 'The Coinage', 47–8. See plate 10.

[117] For the close association between Æthelstan's *Rex Totius Britanniae* type and the *burhs* see G. Williams, 'Military and non-Military Functions of the Anglo-Saxon *burh*, c.878–978', in *Landscapes of Defence in the Viking Age* (Turnhout, forthcoming).

[118] This point is developed further below, 216–23.

of its local representatives or of the church',[119] the king's portrait might in isolation have created different impressions from those originally intended by its designers. Even so, Æthelstan's coins were the most widely disseminated symbols of his power, an image of his authority encountered potentially across the entire breadth of his domain. In an age of what we might best term transitional literacy, the visual iconography of a king's coinage spoke much more directly to his subjects than a written legend only some could decipher (and, having expanded its abbreviations, understand). To us, however, the force of the message these coins sought to convey appears the more effective, both visually and textually, when considered in the context of the heightened rhetoric of charter styles adopted by the king at the same time in his reign and in comparison with the one surviving manuscript portrait of the king – where he gave a book to St Cuthbert – in which he wears a crown of the same design.[120]

We have already noted that the new coronation *ordo* drafted in the first months of his reign and used for the first time at his own coronation in 925 invested Æthelstan with crown and sceptre as symbols of his royal power instead of the traditional regalia of helmet and axe.[121] Here in his coins we see Æthelstan's use of arresting and unprecedented visual imagery to convey across his realm his own ideas about his hegemonic power. He had this crowned-bust type issued everywhere in England (including East Anglia) apart from Mercia. There, instead of the crowned bust, a 'Circumscription Rosette' type was used. The reluctance of Mercian moneyers to mint coins bearing an effigy of the West Saxon king suggests that the ideological implications of the new portrait style had not passed unnoticed. Their choice of a different style without a ruler portrait articulates strikingly the extent of Mercia's continuing self-perceived independence long after the merger of that realm with the West Saxon kingdom. Further, it indicates rather starkly that any affection subjects of the former midland kingdom might have felt for a West Saxon prince supposedly reared in their midst had not survived into his reign.[122]

Æthelstan's decision to repeat in the Grately code the provision first made by his father insisting that there be only one coinage throughout his realm suggests that he shared Edward's desire to keep foreign issues out of his kingdom and restrict circulating money to his own issues. But close study of the coins reveals that, just as was suggested by information

---

[119] Donald Bullough, ' "*Imagines Regum*" and their Significance in the Earliest Medieval West', in *Studies in Memory of David Talbot Rice*, ed. Giles Robertson and George Henderson (Edinburgh, 1975), 223–76, at 227.

[120] Cambridge, Corpus Christi College, MS 183, fo. 1; cf and plate I and II; Blunt, 47–8.

[121] For the liturgical form used at the king's coronation *ordo*, see ch. 4; Catherine E. Karkov, *The Ruler Portraits of Anglo-Saxon England* (Woodbridge, 2004), 67.

[122] Christopher Blunt *et al.*, *Coinage in Tenth-Century England: from Edward the Elder to Edgar's Reform* (Oxford, 1989), 109. We will explore the ideological implications of this coinage – and its possible iconographical models – further below, 216–23.

collected about places where he spent time, for all the rhetoric about a large single united kingdom implicit in that overarching statement, in practice Æthelstan continued to behave as a conventional West Saxon monarch, his attention focused firmly south of the Thames. The disjunction between the magnitude of the claims made visually and textually on his behalf to hegemony over the whole island and his movements in peacetime was to some extent diluted by the policy of bringing his subjects from the further regions to his court wherever it met, rather than frequently venturing into their home territory.

As Sir Frank Stenton remarked, Æthelstan is one of the few pre-Conquest kings of whose personality a faint impression can be formed; for Stenton the most revealing evidence about Æthelstan's character comes from those texts that show him fulfilling that maxim quoted at the start of this chapter, 'A king must rule his kingdom'. More unusual, or at least more rarely recorded than any of these qualities of an ideal ruler, is the touch of humanity shown in the pardon which he granted to criminals willing to make amends, and in his revulsion at the execution of young offenders. In character and cast of mind he was, for Stenton, the one West Saxon king who bears comparison with Alfred.[123] Æthelstan showed himself more than willing to emulate his grandfather's example and take inspiration from his policies. Yet, he had no doubt as to how far his own achievements had exceeded Alfred's and the need therefore to articulate novel statements about his perceptions of his power and the ways in which he wanted his subject peoples across his dominion to perceive him, especially via the highly artificial medium of the coinage. We shall return to explore further those hegemonic claims to rulership over all of Britain in Chapter 8. Meanwhile, we should turn to the sphere of action on which much of Æthelstan's posthumous reputation has conventionally rested: the battlefield.

---

[123] Stenton, *ASE*, 356.

Chapter 6

WAR

Athelstan King,
Lord among Earls,
Bracelet-bestower and
Baron of Barons,
He with his Brother,
Edmund Atheling,
Gaining a lifelong
Glory in battle,
Slew with the sword-edge
There by Brunanburh . . .
Tennyson, 'The Battle of Brunanburh'

King Æthelstan's greatest military triumph lay in his convincing defeat of a combined army of Dublin Norse, Scots and Northumbrians in 937 at a place called *Brunanburh* (probably in Cheshire on the Wirral peninsula). A contemporary or near-contemporary poem in the Anglo-Saxon Chronicle commemorated that victory, whose significance continued to ring in Victorian ears when Alfred, Lord Tennyson made the evocative verse translation quoted above.[1] A generation after Æthelstan's death the West Saxon chronicler Æthelweard still remembered *Brunanburh* as 'the Great Battle', a victory over barbarians that brought the submission of the Scots and Picts, united the fields of Britain and brought 'peace everywhere and abundance of all things'.[2] The king triumphed here resoundingly over the most powerful, and most feared, enemy armies of the island.[3] Although confirming Æthelstan's rule of all the Anglo-Saxon peoples of England and his dominance over the other British rulers, the battle of *Brunanburh* does not represent an isolated triumph. This victory marked the culmination of the final phase of a process begun much earlier in the king's reign, one that built on political and military foundations laid by the king's father and grandfather. Æthelstan's military strategies rested directly upon King

---

[1] ASC *s.a.* 937; Alfred Tennyson, *Ballads and Other Poems* (London, 1880), 178. For the location of the battle, see further below, 172–9.

[2] Æthelweard, iv, 5, p. 54.

[3] Compare the comments of the twelfth-century historian Henry of Huntingdon, quoted in the Epilogue below, 230.

Edward's efforts to increase the bounds of Wessex by bringing into English hands areas once settled by the Danes. Edward thereby succeeded in consolidating a kingdom of the Anglo-Saxons, whose origins lie in Alfred's reign,[4] yet we should not forget how precarious West Saxon superiority remained at Edward's death, or the fact that in earlier centuries the dominance of the kingdom of Wessex could scarcely have been predicted. The significance of Æthelstan's creation and subsequent successful military defence of a realm uniting all English peoples cannot be overemphasized.

For all of Æthelstan's life before he became king, the realm of Wessex if not always technically 'at war' remained in a state of perpetual preparedness for conflict. During his youth and early adulthood Æthelstan's father, Edward the Elder, together with the leaders of the Mercians (Ealdorman Æthelred and his wife Æthelflæd) had led active military campaigns to expand West Saxon and Mercian territory into those areas of the eastern midlands and East Anglia that had been settled by the Danes in the late ninth century. Whatever the precise circumstances of his upbringing, Æthelstan must from an early age have been aware of these wars, even if he were far too young to have had any first-hand understanding of the battles during the latter years of his grandfather, Alfred's reign. As the eldest of the king's sons, an ætheling marked out for future rule, Æthelstan's education involved as much training in arms and military tactics as book-learning.[5] On reaching manhood, he expected to play a direct role in current campaigns, perhaps increasingly so after his uncle's death in 911, when English armies faced difficulty on various fronts and King Edward needed others to lead some of his forces. In the context of the disputed succession after King Edward's death in 924, Æthelstan's proven experience in war would have counted in his favour among the Mercian aristocracy, beside whom he had fought to defend and consolidate that kingdom's bounds. The military context of the last years of Edward's reign and the particular situation to which Æthelstan acceded in 924 help to set the significance of his own later armed successes in wider perspective.

Although eclipsed by the greater achievements of both his father and his eldest son, Edward the Elder contributed substantially to the future forging of a kingdom of the English. Writing in the 1140s, John of Worcester had great admiration for him and celebrated his military and diplomatic triumphs:

> [Alfred's] son, Edward, surnamed the Elder, succeeded him, inferior to his father in the practice of letters but his equal in dignity and power,

---

[4] Simon Keynes, 'Edward, King of the Anglo-Saxons', in H&H, 40–66.

[5] David N. Dumville, 'The Ætheling: a Study in Anglo-Saxon Constitutional History', *ASE*, viii (1979), 1–33. William of Malmesbury quoted a poem about Æthelstan's youth that referred specifically not just to his school education but to his practice of the pursuit of arms and training in the laws of war: *GR*, ii, 133, pp. 212–13.

and his superior in glory, for, as will be made clear from what follows, he enlarged the confines of his realm much more widely than his father had, inasmuch as he built many cities and towns, indeed rebuilt some which had been destroyed; he wrested from Danish hands the whole of Essex, East Anglia, Northumbria, and also many areas of Mercia, which the Danes had long held; he took and held all Mercia after the death of his sister Æthelflæd; he received the submission of all the kings of the Scots, the Cumbrians, the people of Strathclyde, and of the West Welsh when he had conquered and slain many kings and leaders in battle.[6]

It was thus before Æthelstan's succession that the bounds of Wessex were pushed into the formerly independent Mercia and east into East Anglia as far north as the River Humber and Edward also achieved a degree of authority – or at least mutual recognition – from the other ruling powers in the north.[7] He brought new lands and economic opportunities into the West Saxon orbit on the back of substantial military success and strategic planning for defence. His firm annexation of Mercia on his sister's death had military dimensions; that show of force was directed not only at both the English and Danish Mercians, it made a strong statement of intent to the Danes in Northumbria and to the Welsh, who submitted immediately after Edward's capture of Tamworth. The tenth-century chronicler Æthelweard encapsulated the magnitude of Edward's achievements when in reporting his death he termed him king of the English (rex Anglorum) in contradistinction to the title he had awarded his grandfather, Alfred: 'king of the Saxons'.[8] With the exception of the sons of Bamburgh ruling in English Bernicia, Edward was, in the last years of his reign, the sole native king ruling in England, having direct royal authority over all the Saxon and Anglian areas in the south. He might thus reasonably be seen as king of the English in Britain, while Rægnald and then Sihtric ruled over the Danes, and Constantín the Scots. Building on that success, his son Æthelstan extended English rule further into the north and genuinely became, as already argued, the first king of all England.

THE ANNEXATION OF NORTHUMBRIA

In the immediate aftermath of Edward's death it had seemed for a time that the recently united Mercian-West-Saxon realm might be dissolved when the West Saxon and Mercian peoples each elected their own successor to the throne. Ælfweard's death only a few weeks later changed matters, forcing the West Saxons to accept Æthelstan as their king.[9]

---

[6] JW, s.a. 901, pp. 354–5.
[7] Above, 12–17.
[8] Æthelweard, iv, 4 (p. 54).
[9] Above, 37–9.

Strategically the new king benefited from having a secure power base in Mercia, especially given the situation north of the Humber; not having to worry about the solid support of English Mercia, Æthelstan could focus on the less certainly loyal population of the eastern Danelaw and look for means of nullifying the potential threat from the north. The speed with which he sought to enter into an alliance with the new Danish ruler Sihtric Cáech demonstrates the importance he placed on securing his northern border. He successfully contracted a marriage alliance between his sister Eadgyth and the Danish king in York in January 926; when Sihtric died the following year, he acted no less swiftly to annex his former brother-in-law's kingdom to his own.[10]

Æthelstan's acquisition of Northumbria shifted the balance of power in the north, making the West Saxon king suddenly the direct neighbour of the kings of the Scots, of Strathclyde and of Bamburgh. The king probably raised an army and marched in a show of military might to take over the northern kingdom; certainly the poem written back to the royal court after the event by the poet Petrus, *Carta dirige gressus*, presents this as a victory achieved by force of arms. The mere threat of his military power may, however, have been sufficient to persuade the Celtic kings elsewhere in the island to sue for peace before any battle was engaged. The Chronicle reported most succinctly what happened next:

> King Æthelstan succeeded to the kingdom of the Northumbrians, and he brought under his rule all the kings who were in this island: first Hywel, king of the West Welsh, and Constantín king of the Scots, and Owain, king of the people of Gwent, and Ealdred, son of Eadwulf from Bamburgh. And they established peace with pledge and oaths in the place which is called Eamont on 12 July, and renounced all idolatry and afterwards departed in peace.[11]

That the Chronicle failed to mention fighting is probably significant; while the West Saxon annals generally had little to say about Æthelstan's deeds, a northern annalist would hardly have concealed what would have been a significant victory had Æthelstan's forces confronted those of the British kings and defeated them.

However, the twelfth-century chroniclers Simeon of Durham and John of Worcester said that it was after Æthelstan had overcome the northern kings in battle and put to flight 'all the kings of Albion' that, seeing that they could not resist Æthelstan's might, these kings begged him for peace and so met him at Eamont to confirm a treaty with an oath. Both offered

---

[10] Above, 17–19.

[11] ASC *s.a.* 926D. Eamont is in Cumbria, south of Penrith; its name means 'at the confluence of the rivers': A.H. Smith, *English Place-Name Elements*, Part I, EPNS, 25 (Cambridge, 1956), 143.

the same list of names as did the chronicler, although they gave the name of the king of Gwent as Uuer, but John of Worcester added that Æthelstan had driven Ealdred, Eadwulf's son, out of Bamburgh, something no other source reports, which may reflect a confusion in John's mind; the Old English chronicle said that Eadwulf came 'from Bamburgh', not that he was ejected from there.[12]

William of Malmesbury maintained that Northumbria belonged to Æthelstan 'by ancient right no less than by modern connection', a contention entirely without historical foundation: the West Saxon royal family could lay no claim to kingship north of the Humber. More plausibly, he asserted that Æthelstan caused Sihtric's son Anlaf (Olaf) to flee to Ireland and his 'brother' Guthfrith to 'Scotia' (i.e. Strathclyde).[13] Hereafter Æthelstan immediately sent an embassy to Constantín, king of the Scots, and to Owain of the Cumbrians (the king of Strathclyde) demanding the return of the fugitive and threatening war if they failed to comply. In response to these threats, William said that the kings came to Dacre (a Cumbrian monastic house, near Eamont south of Penrith),[14] and put themselves in Æthelstan's hands; Constantín's son was baptized with Æthelstan standing as his godfather.[15] That Guthfrith, assisted by a certain Turfrith, managed for a time to lay siege to York and then escaped from another fortress where he had been surrounded explains why William of Malmesbury reported that Æthelstan levelled the Danes' fort at York to the ground 'in order to leave disloyalty no place of refuge'. According to his account, Turfrith was drowned in a shipwreck but, after some wanderings, Guthfrith eventually came to Æthelstan's court to surrender; laden with gifts he then returned to Dublin, where he continued to rule until 934.[16]

---

[12] *HR*, s.a. 927. JW, s.a. 926, pp. 386–7.

[13] *GR*, ii, 132, 134, pp. 210–11, 214–15; William's detailed and circumstantial account of these events is of questionable authenticity and probably draws on later legends as well as his own imagination. Thomson, *Commentary*, 120–2 sees much of this chapter as deriving from the lost book; others have been more cautious; see further Appendix I. Compare ASC s.a. 927E, H.R. Loyn, 'Wales and England in the Tenth Century: the Context of the Æthelstan Charters', reprinted in his *Society and Peoples* (London, 1992), 180.

[14] William might have been mistaken here. There was a seventh-century minster at Dacre, but Eamont (on the boundary between the later counties of Westmorland and Cumbria) is a more plausible place for a meeting of this kind, lying as it does at the junction of the Rivers Eamont and Lowther, near the old Roman road from York to Carlisle.

[15] In identifying the Owain who swore oaths near Eamont as king of the 'Cumbrians' (i.e. of Strathclyde) William might have had better information than the Chronicler; alternatively, if both were right there could have been two Owains. Owain son of Dynfnwal was active in Strathclyde in the 930s; there was also from 931 a king in Gwent called Morgan, son of Owain, who attested Æthelstan's charters. Alan MacQuarrie, 'The Kings of Strathclyde, *c.*400–1018', in *Medieval Scotland: Crown, Lordship and Community*, ed. Alexander Grant and Keith J. Stringer (Edinburgh, 1993), 14–15; A.P. Smyth, *Warlords and Holy Men: Scotland AD 80–1000* (London 1984), 201–4, 222.

[16] *GR*, ii, 134, pp. 214–15.

After the meeting at Eamont, the king compelled the princes of the Northwalians, i.e. the Northern Britons, to meet him in the city of Hereford and agree to surrender to him, paying tribute on a previously unimagined scale:

> He thus brought into effect what no king before him had presumed even to contemplate: they were to pay him by way of annual tribute twenty pounds of gold and three hundred pounds of silver, and to hand over by the count 25,0000 oxen, besides as many as he might wish of hounds that with their keen scent could track down the lairs and lurking-places of wild beasts, and birds of prey skilled in pursuing other birds through empty air.[17]

The Welsh submission can also best be explained by reference to Æthelstan's perceived military might and the potential threat presented by his army. Although no contemporary chronicler reported this event of which we know the details only from William of Malmesbury, other evidence also suggests that the Welsh did not submit voluntarily to King Æthelstan but were forced into submission. The Welsh prophecy poem *Armes Prydein*, probably composed around 930, acknowledged Æthelstan's greatness and referred to the need for the Welsh to pay tribute during his reign.[18]

A short anonymous legal text known as the *Ordinance concerning the Dunsæte* might also date from Æthelstan's reign. Agreed between the witan of the English people (*Angelcynn*) and the counsellors of the Welsh living in the Archenfield area of South Wales (south-west of Hereford) along the River Wye, the treaty addresses issues that occur also in other legal pronouncements from Æthelstan's reign including recovery of stolen cattle, the use of ordeals, theft, and the price of goods. Further, it tackles the question of hostages: a royal prerogative which the treaty limited to the West Saxon king (§9).[19] One could date this ordinance to around 930, reading it in the light of the king's imposition of such a punitive treaty on the Welsh at Hereford.[20] On the other hand, it appears that Æthelstan did not treat the Welsh with the sort of even-handedness to which *Dunsæte* bears witness, but viewed them as an entirely subject people, compelled to pay tribute and their kings forced to attend the English king's court. *Dunsæte* should probably be dated to the late tenth or

---

[17] *GR*, ii, 134 (pp. 214–17).

[18] *Armes Prydein: the Prophecy of Britain from the Book of Taliesin*, ed. Ifor Williams and Rachel Bromwich (Dublin, 1982), lines 17–22.

[19] F. Liebermann, *Die Gesetze, der Angelsachsen*, 3 vols (Halle, 1898–1916), I, 374–9; trans. Frank Noble, *Offa's Dyke Reviewed*, ed. Margaret Gelling, British Archaeological Reports, British Series 114 (1983), 105–9.

[20] Wormald, *MEL*, 381–2. Ryan Lavelle, 'Towards a Political Contextualisation of Peace-Making', in *Peace and Negotiation*, ed. Diane Wolfthal (Turnhout, 2000), 53.

eleventh century, in which case it can shed no further light on Æthelstan's Welsh policies.[21]

Æthelstan's thus far largely peaceful conquest of the British mainland was completed, according to William of Malmesbury, by an overtly military expedition into Cornwall; William had visited Exeter in the 1120s and reported that local people had much to say about Æthelstan, which clearly fuelled his otherwise unsupported statements. Æthelstan apparently went straight from his meeting with the Welsh at Hereford to the Western British called the Cornish; they, too, he attacked vigorously and forced to leave Exeter where they had formerly lived equably with the English and he fixed the boundary of their territory at the River Tamar, just as he had fixed the boundary of the Welsh at the River Wye.[22] The city of Exeter Æthelstan then supposedly rebuilt, fortifying it with towers and surrounding it with a stone wall. William remarked on the wealth and splendour of the city, its attraction to visitors and commercial success, noting: 'numerous reminders of Æthelstan are to be seen both in the city and in the country round'. Although probably accurately reflecting early twelfth-century popular folklore, the story has little to commend it. Wessex extended its control over Cornwall about a century before Æthelstan's time and the king's concern for the Church in Cornwall shows that he considered this securely part of his realm; it seems unlikely that there was a strong Cornish presence in Exeter in the 920s. Æthelstan may, perhaps, have strengthened Exeter's fortifications, but the city had walls strong enough to resist Viking attack in 894, so he cannot have built them from scratch.[23]

THE SCOTTISH CAMPAIGN OF 934

The peace made with the Scots in 927 did not prove permanent: in 934 the king had to plan a new campaign in the north. Quite what triggered this remains uncertain. Æthelstan may have assembled an army in response to an offensive move by the Scots; John of Worcester reported that Æthelstan set out for Scotland 'with a very strong fleet and no small mounted force' because Constantín, king of the Scots had broken the treaty he had made

---

[21] George Molyneaux, 'Non-Military Contacts between the English and Welsh in the Late-Tenth and Early-Eleventh Centuries', Master of Studies dissertation, University of Oxford, 2007, 22–33. I am grateful to Dr Molyneaux for showing me a copy of this dissertation and for discussing this matter with me.

[22] *GR*, ii, 134, pp. 216–17; D.P. Kirby, 'Hywel Dda: Anglophil?', *Welsh History Review*, viii (1976–7), 3.

[23] Nicholas Orme, *Exeter Cathedral: the First Thousand Years, 400–1550* (Exeter, 2009), 7–8. For another sceptical reading of William of Malmesbury's account of apparent 'ethnic cleansing' in Cornwall, see also Charles Insley, 'Athelstan, Charters and the English in Cornwall', in *Charters and Charter Scholarship in Britain and Ireland*, ed. M.T. Flanagan and J.A. Green (Basingstoke, 2005), 15–31.

with him.[24] The king might have wanted to capitalize on insecurity among the Danes in the north following the death in 934 of Guthfrith, grandson of Ímar.[25] Alternatively, if we believe the otherwise unsupported evidence of the Annals of Clonmacnoise, the death of the king of Bamburgh, Ealdred son of Eadwulf, could have persuaded Æthelstan to lead an army northwards. This might have been a pre-emptive move on the part of the West Saxon king, designed to prevent the raising of a coalition of forces against him.[26] We could also connect Æthelstan's decision to campaign far from Wessex with the laconic entry in the Chronicle for the year 933 about the death of his half-brother, the ætheling Edwin, if this represented the point at which the king finally rid the West Saxon court of factional elements still opposed to his rule.[27] Most credibly, however, we should seek to explain the expedition of 934 as a response either to a direct threat from Scotland (or conceivably Ireland), or to the new political climate in the north-east following the death of the only other remaining native English ruler. West Saxon dynastic politics resonated with markedly less noise in insular accounts of that year's fighting.

All the manuscripts of the Anglo-Saxon Chronicle report the key event of 934 with typical brevity: in that year 'King Æthelstan went into Scotland with both a land force and a naval force, and ravaged much of it'.[28] The significance of this expedition should not, however, be underestimated, nor the king's energy (and capacity for effective strategic planning) in organizing two forces, one travelling over land with him and the other proceeding independently but in a synchronized fashion, to attack by sea. Since King Alfred's early unsuccessful efforts at countering the Danish threat by building longships twice as long as theirs (which proved unnavigable and ran aground), West Saxon military technology and planning had obviously advanced substantially.[29] We can follow the movements of the king's court

---

[24] JW, s.a. 934, pp. 388–91. Æthelstan need not hereby have claimed any direct kingship over the Scots, contra Benjamin Hudson, Kings of Celtic Scotland (Westport, CT and London 1994), 78–9.

[25] AU 934: 'a most cruel (crudelissimus) king of the northmen'; Alfred P. Smyth, Scandinavian York and Dublin, 2 vols (Dublin, 1975–9), ii, 26.

[26] Ealdred's death was not reported in any English source, but for this year the Annals of Clonmacnoise (an early medieval Irish chronicle that survives now only in an English translation from 1627) reported s.a. 928 (recte 934), ed. Denis Murphy (Dublin, 1896 and Felinfach, 1993), p. 49: 'Adulf mcEtulfe king of the North Saxons died'; see Hudson, Kings of Celtic Scotland, 79.

[27] ASC 933; HR s.a. 933. See above, ch. 2.

[28] ASC 934; William inserted a slightly confusing statement at this point in his narrative saying that the king compelled Idwal, king of all the Welsh, and Constantín, king of the Scots, to abdicate. 'Not long after, however, yielding to pity, he restored them to their former status, to reign under his lordship, declaring it yet more glorious to make kings than to be one.' If we could rely on this statement, we might think it somehow related to the events of 934, but it could of course equally add extra information about the terms of the general submission of 927. GR, ii, 13, pp. 206–7; Kirby 'Hywel Dda: Anglophil?', 4.

[29] ASC 896.

as he advanced towards the Scottish border with a substantial entourage (including the Welsh kings) via the texts of his charters, which show him to have been in Winchester at Pentecost in May, but in Nottingham by 7 June.[30] On his way to the border he stopped also at the shrine of St Cuthbert at Chester-le-Street, making generous gifts to the saint, whose coffin he had opened in order that he might place a gift at his head.[31] The *Historia de sancto Cuthberto* remarked on the 'great army' which Æthelstan was leading from the south to the northern region (of Britain), taking it to Scotland, when he made this diversion. Quite how far north Æthelstan fought in person is contested; the Annals of Clonmacnoise recorded that Æthelstan ravaged Scotland as far as Edinburgh, but the Scots forced him to return without any victory.[32] Yet the northern annals preserved in the *Historia regum Anglorum* attributed to Simeon of Durham provide a fuller account, suggesting the king's forces engaged deep in Scots territory:

> King Æthelstan, going towards Scotia with a great army, came to the tomb of St Cuthbert, commended himself and his expedition to his protection, and conferred on him many and diverse gifts befitting a king, as well as estates, and consigned to the torments of eternal fire anyone who should take any of these from him. He then subdued his enemies, laid waste Scotland as far as Dunnottar and *Wertermorum* [the mountains of Fortriu] with a land force, and ravaged with a naval force as far as Caithness.[33]

Combined land and sea attack enabled Æthelstan to ravage the eastern districts between the Forth and Stonehaven, trapping the Scots' forces in a pincer movement. According uniquely to John of Worcester, after the king had laid waste a very large part of Scotland, the Scots king was forced to give up his son as a hostage. That the English armies seemingly ranged as far north as Caithness (part of the Norse kingdom of Orkney) hints at the beginning of the alliance between Scots and Norsemen that would find full expression in their attempted joint invasion of England in 937.[34]

---

[30] S 425, 407.

[31] *HSC*, ch. 26; see below, 208–100.

[32] Annals of Clonmacnoise, ed. Murphy, 159. For the translator's confusion here which led him to equate the Irish *Dunfoither* (Dunottar) with 'Edenburrogh', see Alex Woolf, *From Pictland to Alba 789–1070* (Edinburgh, 2007), 164.

[33] S 425; S 407; *HSC*, ch. 26. *HR*, *s.a.* 934, ed. Arnold, ii, 124. Stenton, *ASE*, 342; Loyn, 'Wales and England', 189. For the movements of the king's court see above ch. 3; and for the gifts the king made to the community of St Cuthbert below ch. 7.

[34] JW, *s.a.* 934, pp. 390–1. Hudson, *Kings of Celtic Scotland*, 77–8. The Annals of Clonmacnoise, *s.a.* 928 (=934), ed. Murphy, 149. The local place-name Athelstansford may preserve some memory of his army's crossing of the Forth. Twelfth-century collections of the miracles of John of Beverley claimed that the critical battle was at a site south of the Forth, it being the Scots' defeat there that enabled Æthelstan to ravage farther north: *Miracula S Iohannis*, ed. Raine, *Historians of the Church of York*, i. 263–4; 295–7. Hudson, *Kings*, 78.

It also demonstrates – should any further evidence be necessary – the strategic advantages to a West Saxon king of having acquired the kingdom of York. Only with that territory firmly within his grasp, could any king of Wessex have contemplated fighting with ships as well as on land so far from his natural power bases. Again we may remark on the impressive logistical planning evident in this campaign; we have not previously encountered the ships, which had presumably departed from a southern (or perhaps a south-eastern) port at around the same time as Æthelstan and his land army departed from Winchester in late May. Perhaps the two groups joined forces when Æthelstan reached the Firth of Forth and plotted the final stage of this concerted effort from there. In order to sustain so well co-ordinated an attack designed to cut off the Scots from flight over land or water, the king must have had a working system of communication between his land and naval forces as each moved north and after both had arrived in Scottish territory.

The victorious king's progress southwards can again be traced from his charters; by early autumn he was close to the West Saxon border, issuing a charter from a royal vill in Buckingham on 13 September.[35] These documents show that this time he had the Scots king Constantín firmly in tow. Æthelstan must have hoped through his strategy of keeping the Celtic rulers close by him to ensure their loyalty, something the regular payment of tribute would have reinforced. The arrangement offered them certain advantages, not least the protection Æthelstan provided for their realms as well as his own from external attack. Although that sense of security was to prove short-lived, it apparently allowed Æthelstan to feel able to turn his attention away from British shores and intervene in Frankish affairs. In 936 he assisted in restoring two of his foreign-born foster-sons to power in their native lands. According to Flodoard (the tenth-century chronicler from Rheims), the Bretons in exile across the sea (in England), 'with the support of King Æthelstan returned and took back their land'. Æthelstan sent an English fleet to assist his foster-son, Alain, son of Matuedoi, count of Poher to drive the Vikings out of Brittany.[36] A fuller account appears in the eleventh-century Chronicle of Nantes, which also stresses Alain's connections with Æthelstan:

> The city of Nantes remained for many years deserted, devastated and overgrown with briars and thorns, until Alan Crooked Beard, grandson of Alan the Great, arose and cast out those Normans from the whole region of Brittany and from the River Loire, which was a great support for them. This Alan was brought up from infancy with Æthelstan, king

of the English, and was strong in body and very courageous, and did not care to kill wild boars and bears in the forest with an iron weapon, but with a wooden staff. He collected a few ships and came by the king's permission with those Bretons who were still living there, to revisit Brittany.[37]

Another embassy from the Frankish court came to Æthelstan in the same year. Immediately after his account of the Breton expedition Flodoard reported that Hugh of the Franks (Æthelstan's brother-in-law) sent across the sea to England and summoned Louis, son of Charles 'the Simple', who had married Æthelstan's sister Eadgifu) to take up the rule of the kingdom of Frankia.

> Louis's uncle, King Æthelstan, sent him to Frankia along with bishops and others of his *fideles* after oaths had been given by the legates of the Franks. Hugh and the rest of the nobles of the Franks set out to meet Louis when he left the ship, and they committed themselves to him on the beach at Boulogne-sur-Mer just as both sides had previously agreed. They then conducted Louis to Laon and he was consecrated king, anointed and crowned by Lord Archbishop Artoldus (of Rheims) in the presence of the leading men of the kingdom and more than twenty bishops.[38]

A charter in the eleventh-century cartulary of the Breton house at Landévennec records a grant made by Alain, *dux* of the Bretons, to John, abbot of Landévennec, because the latter had called Alain 'and invited him to this side of the seas'; if we take this at face value, we might assume that John had played some role in the diplomatic arrangements to bring Alain back to his homeland, possibly visiting Æthelstan's court to argue for the young prince's return. The charter tells us that John had 'served the cause of reparation among the barbarians and among very many peoples of the Saxons and the Northmen and announced what was needful and peace, many times constantly beyond and on this side of the sea'.[39]

In a more elaborate account of Duke Hugh's embassy to Æthelstan to arrange for Louis's restoration to his throne, Richer stated that the envoys set sail from Boulogne and went straight to Æthelstan, who was then

---

[37] *La Chronique de Nantes*, ed. R. Merlet (Paris, 1896), ch. 29, p. 89; Smith, *Province and Empire*, 197.

[38] Flodoard, 18A (936); Smith, *Province and Empire*, 196–7. Brett, 'A Breton Pilgrim', 44–5; Karl Ferdinand Werner, *Histoire de la France, I: Les origines (avant l'an mil)* (Paris, 1984), 463–5.

[39] Brett, 'A Breton Pilgrim', 44–5, 50. Julia Smith wondered whether Æthelstan might have wanted to extend his hegemony over Brittany, just as he had done over Wales; in his interference in his foster-son's return to his homeland she saw all the conventions of hegemonic lordship represented: *Province and Empire*, 196–7.

staying in a town called *Euruich*, where he had his nephew with him.[40] If we could rely on Richer's version and locate the king securely at York in 936, this might give us an important clue to events leading up to the confrontation at *Brunanburh* the following year. Perhaps signs of the disintegration of the truce agreed in 934 caused an anxious Æthelstan to take his court into Northumbria in order to remind his reluctant subjects of his authority by a show of force. If so, he was sufficiently reassured by what he found in the north to part with an armed retinue in order to accompany his nephew back to Frankia, and send a naval fleet to take his Breton foster-son home. Had Æthelstan gone north because he feared the breakdown of the treaties of 934, one doubts whether he would quite so cavalierly have deployed his forces abroad. According to Richer, Oda, bishop of Ramsbury, played a key role in the negotiations to ensure Louis's safe return to France. Arnulf, count of Flanders arranged for Louis to land at the important Flemish port of Boulogne.[41] Another of Æthelstan's foster-sons, Hákon, son of the Norwegian king Harald Fairhair, may have reclaimed the kingdom of Norway, supposedly also with military help from his English foster-father, at about the same time, although these events cannot be dated with any confidence.[42] While the English king meddled on these foreign stages, his insular enemies took the opportunity to regroup.

THE BATTLE OF *BRUNANBURH*, 937

Individually Æthelstan's northern neighbours lacked the strength to counter the wealth and military capability of the enlarged English kingdom. Together, however, they might hope to check the northward expansion of Wessex or even reverse some of its more recent gains. Sheer

---

[40] Flodoard, 936 (18A); Richer, *Historiae*, ii. 2, ed. Hoffmann MGH SS 38 (Hanover, 2000), 98. Whether this refers to a formal meeting of the king's council (at which charters were issued or law discussed) or simply a stopping point on a journey of the king and his immediate household is unclear. Richer's phrase *apud suos* that I have taken to mean 'at his court' was translated more literally by Latouche as 'au milieu des siens', 'among his own': Robert Latouche, *Richer, Histoire de France*, 2 vols, (Paris 1930–37), i, 129. The embassy was discussed also by Philippe Lauer, *La Règne de Louis IV d'Outremer* (Paris, 1900), p. 12. See above, 46–7 for a discussion of how Louis came to take refuge at his uncle's court.

[41] Flodoard, 936 (18A), 939 (21D). For Oda's part in the negotiations, see Richer, *Historiae*, ii, 4, ed. Hoffmann, 100; N. Brooks, *The Early History of the Church of Canterbury* (Leicester, 1984), 222. For the Flemish angle, see Folcuin, *Gesta abbatum Sithiensium*, ch. 102, ed. O Holder-Egger, MGS SS XIII (Hanover, 1881), 626; Simon MacLean, 'Making a Difference in Tenth-Century Politics: King Æthelstan's Sisters and Frankish Queenship', in *Frankland*, ed. Paul Fouracre and David Ganz (Manchester, 2008), 175; Heather J. Tanner, *Families, Friends and Allies: Boulogne and Politics in Northern France and England c.879–1160* (Leiden and Boston, 2004), 34.

[42] Gareth Williams, 'Hákon *Aðalsteins fóstri*: Aspects of Anglo-Saxon Kingship in Tenth-Century Norway', in *The North Sea World in the Middle Ages: Studies in the Cultural History of North-Western Europe*, ed. Thomas R. Liszka and Lorna E.M. Walker (Dublin, 2001), 108–26.

necessity in the face of this apparently inexorable northward movement must have forced the Scots to turn to the York–Dublin Scandinavian dynasty with which they had previously been in conflict. A combined force of Dublin Norse led by Olaf Guthfrithsson (who had become king in Dublin on his father's death in 934), Scots under Constantín, and Owain's Strathclyde Welsh confronted the English in 937, meeting them in 'a great, lamentable and horrible battle', as the *Annals of Ulster* described it.[43] In stark contrast to the scanty, brief and allusive annals found in the Anglo-Saxon Chronicle for most of Æthelstan's reign, we have a wealth of circumstantial detail about this battle. The whole Chronicle entry for 937 consists of a seventy-three-line verse account of an engagement in which 'Æthelstan, lord of nobles, dispenser of treasure to men, and his brother also, Edmund ætheling, won by the sword's edge undying glory in battle around *Brunanburh*'.

Almost all that we know of the battle, who fought on which side, the extent of the casualties and the fate of the defeated, we know from this praise-poem. Its opening lines (1–10a) identify the poem's heroes – Æthelstan, 'lord of nobles, giver of treasure to men' and his younger brother, Edmund – and set them in their genealogical context (as the sons of Edward the Elder and the heirs of the West Saxon dynasty). From the outset the hearer is persuaded of this family's historic success in battle: the brothers fought valiantly with their hammered blades (swords) and so lived up to their dynastic reputation for always defending 'their country, their treasure and their homes in battle against every enemy'. Then the poet goes on (lines 10b–20a) to define the enemy as Scots (*Sceotta*) and the 'host from the ships', men of the North (*guma nor perna*); even before swords have been drawn, he stresses the extent of the slaughter to come and the inevitability of the enemy's defeat. A recurrent motif enumerates the fallen: the field flowed with the blood of men as the doomed warriors of the Scots and the host from the ships fell. The action he places within the span of a single day: all day long, the West Saxon troop of horse pressed against the enemy forces. Having given a description of the fighting, 'with swords sharpened on the grindstone', the poet lists the casualties: five young kings, seven of Olaf's earls and a 'countless' host of seamen and Scots (lines 20b–36b). On the winning side are the West Saxon horse accompanied by the Mercians, their triumph being contrasted with the despair and the dejection of the defeated. Olaf had come 'over the tossing waters' to fight (*ofer æra gebland*, line 26b) but ran away defeated; Constantín, 'the grey-haired warrior', also suffered ignominious defeat, bereaved not only of men and friends but of his young son, whom he left dead on the battlefield. The poet dwells on the pain of this loss, and that

---

[43] *AU*, 937. 6, 384–7. Dumville, *Wessex*, 149. Smyth, *Scandinavian York and Dublin*, ii, 31–9 and 43–4; Woolf, *From Pictland*, 168–75. See plate 11.

of kindred and friends (lines 37a–52b); he gloats over the totality of the defeat of men once renowned for their military prowess. Next, he shows in parallel the contrast between the dejected departure of the humiliated remnant of the Norsemen, from *Dingesmere* over the sea to Dublin, and the triumphant return of the English king and prince to Wessex (lines 53–9).

In the aftermath of the fighting (60–65a), the dead are portrayed as carrion for scavenging by birds and animals: black raven, white-tailed eagle, hungry hawk and grey wolf all shared in the 'heap of carnage' left on the field. Finally (65b–end), the poet shows the significance of this battle not just for the generation of Englishmen whose security under West Saxon rule the brothers' victory ensured, but in comparison with the whole of Anglo-Saxon history to date. Stressing the magnitude of this triumph, the poet sets the battle in the longest possible temporal context in a formal climax that describes this as a greater victory than that won by any English force since the first Germanic migration to British shores: never before had an army 'been put to greater slaughter at the edge of the sword'. Here the poet moves beyond the dynastic focus of his opening, a feature that had characterized the entries in the Chronicle and Mercian Register in the reign of Edward the Elder, to shape the success within a 'nationalizing narrative': 'Wessex is still the Chronicle's homeland, but the victory at *Brunanburh* is portrayed as a victory not just for Wessex but for all the Anglo-Saxon peoples'.[44] Æthelstan appears as heir to the *bretwaldas*, those earlier English kings who had also achieved military success against the British, among whom was his ancestor Ecgberht. Even so, little detailed attention is paid to the king's personal military prowess and his tactical skill in deploying his troops on the battlefield, achievements which are praised by implication only: this is a victory of a nation, not just of its royal leaders. That nation has here proved itself triumphant over the greatest of its rivals of recent decades, the rulers of the kingdom of York.[45] It is hard not to imagine that both Æthelstan and his brother would have enjoyed hearing themselves presented as the leaders of successful and all-conquering armies, the true heirs of the earliest warrior Anglo-Saxon kings and rightful rulers of the Northumbrian realm.[46]

Exaggerating the importance of this victory is difficult, for had Æthelstan's opponents won, the West Saxon hegemony over the whole mainland of Britain would have disintegrated. A Scots–Norse victory would have recreated the Norse kingdom of York (from which Olaf's

---

[44] Thomas Bredehoft, *Textual Histories: Readings in the Anglo-Saxon Chronicle* (Toronto, 2001), 102. Also Simon Walker, 'A Context for *Brunanburh*?', in *Warriors and Churchmen*, ed. Timothy Reuter (London, 1992), 22.

[45] As Alfred P. Smyth has argued, 'West Saxon writers of the period . . . were well aware that the outcome of the struggle between Wessex and Scandinavian York would, in the end, decide who was to be ruler of England', *Scandinavian York and Dublin*, ii, 98.

[46] Matthew Townend, 'Pre-Cnut Praise-Poetry in Viking Age England', *Review of English Studies*, n.s. li, 203 (2000), 366–7.

father had been expelled in 927) and reinforced the importance of the
York–Dublin axis. With York once more in Scandinavian hands, the
security of northern Mercia would have been imperilled and the future of
the recently conquered eastern Danelaw perhaps also placed in doubt.
Since the Dublin Norse did in fact overrun Mercia immediately after
Æthelstan's death and at the same time re-established the Norse kingdom
of York, these were not in 937 unreasonable anxieties.[47] On which side
Northumbrian loyalties lay it is hard to determine. A verse passage from a
twelfth-century panegyric about Æthelstan which William of Malmesbury
quoted at length asserted that the Northumbrians sided with the attacking
force: 'To this raging fury, with the consent of the king of the Scots, the
northern land lends its support with no misgivings; . . . the whole region
yields to their presumption.'[48] Further, the Annals of Clonmacnoise stated
that the invading allies fought with the support of Danes in England,
presumably either men of Danish extraction from Northumbria, or
from the eastern Danelaw, but this does not entirely corroborate the statement in William's poem.[49] The Chronicle poet makes much of the fact
that the English army consisted of West Saxon and Mercian contingents
fighting together, stressing the unity of Æthelstan's people. The enemies'
alliance would particularly have threatened Mercian interests and indeed
it seems likely that the Norse forces began their campaign by ravaging
Mercia, on whose northern borders the battle itself may have been
fought.[50]

The site of the battle

No one has ever satisfactorily determined the location of the site of the
battle of *Brunanburh*. One of the difficulties arises from the variety of
names given to the battlefield in the separate medieval sources that
mention the campaign; on the basis of those versions at different times
writers have advanced more than forty alternative identifications of the
battle site. These range geographically from Devon in the south-west, to
Burnswark in Dumfriesshire, and on the eastern side of the country from

---

[47] Smyth, *Scandinavian York and Dublin*, ii, 31–6, 43–5, 89–100. See also Smyth, *Warlords and Holy Men*, 203–5.

[48] *GR*, ii, 135, pp. 220–1; Michael Wood, 'Brunanburh Revisited', *Saga Book of the Viking Society*, xx.3 (1980), 201.

[49] Annals of Clonmacnoise, *s.a.* 931 = 937, ed. Murphy, p. 151. Stenton thought it signif-icant that no evidence records that the Danes in Northumbria sided with the invaders in 937: *Preparatory to Anglo-Saxon England*, ed. Doris M. Stenton (Oxford, 1970), 162.

[50] *Battle of Brunanburh*, lines 20b–28; John Dodgson, 'The Background of Brunanburh', *Saga Book of the Viking Society*, xiv (1956–7), 313–14; Wood, 'Brunanburh Revisited', 201–3; Nick Higham: 'The Context of Brunanburh', in *Names, Places and People: an Onomastic Miscellany in Memory of John McNeal Dodgson*, ed. Alexander Rumble and A.D. Mills (Stamford, 1997), 152.

one of the Bournes (in Cambridgeshire or Lincolnshire) to sites in Northumberland. Among antiquarian suggestions, cases were made for Axminster in Devon,[51] for sites in both Northumberland and Cheshire,[52] and even for Malmesbury in Wiltshire.[53] If none of these notions other than the Cheshire suggestion inspire much confidence, neither do many of the additional proposals advanced in more recent times.[54]

Various routes into unravelling this problem present themselves. One can explore place-name evidence looking for places that sound like, or were once spelt like *Brunanburh*. Alternatively, one may search for similarities between specific place-names and the variant versions of the name of the site of the battle offered by the tenth-century West Saxon chronicler Æthelweard (*Brunandun*), the twelfth-century writers Simeon of Durham ('... apud Weondune, quod alio nomine Aet Brunnanwerc uel Brunnanbyrig appelatur', i.e. at *Weondune*, which is called by another name *Æt Brunnanwerc* or *Brunnanbyrig*), and Geoffrey Gaimar (*Bruneswerce*).[55] Alternatively, accounts of the battle (in the *Brunanburh* poem in the

---

[51] Leland argued for Axminister in Devon on the grounds that the church there preserved the tombs of 'many noble Danes slain in King Æthelstanes time at a batel on Brunesdoun thereby; and the scepultres likewise of sum Saxon lordes slain on the same field': *The Itinerary of John Leland in or about the Years 1535–1543*, ed. L. Toulmin Smith, 5 vols (London, 1964), i, 243.

[52] William Camden held out for *Brumridg* or *Brumeford*, while Edmund Gibson preferred Bromborough in Cheshire: William Camden, *Britannia; sive florentissimorum regnorum Angliae Scotiae, Hiberniae, et insularum adjacentium ex intima antiquitate chorographica descriptio* (6th edn, London, 1607), 671. Compare *Britannia: or a Chorographical Description of Great Britain and Ireland, together with the Adjacent Islands*, ed. Edmund Gibson (London, 1753), 1097, where the identification with *Brumeford* is described as *dubitante*. See further, Alistair Campbell, *The Battle of Brunanburh* (London, 1938), 58–9.

[53] In his topographical notes on Wiltshire, the seventeenth-century antiquary John Aubrey reported that in return 'for the good service this towne did him against the Danes' Æthelstan gave to Malmesbury a vast and rich common and other privileges; that battle, he thought had taken place on Danys-hill nearby. A conviction that the battle of *Brunanburh* had been fought at Wynyard, on the south-east side of Malmesbury, near to a place called 'War-Ditch' was still maintained locally in the mid-nineteenth century, a confidence supported by the supposed burial of the king's fallen nephews in the abbey church there. See *Wiltshire: the Topographical Collections of John Aubrey FRS, AD 1659–70, corrected and enlarged by J.E. Jackson* (Devizes, 1862), 252; James T. Bird, *The History of the Town of Malmesbury and of its Ancient Abbey* (Malmesbury, 1876), 43–7.

[54] For a recent list see Paul Hill, *The Age of Athelstan: Britain's Forgotten History* (Stroud, 2004), 141–2; compare John Henry Cockburn, *The Battle of Brunanburh and its Period elucidated by Place-Names* (London and Sheffield, 1931), 40–8. As Page has remarked: 'it is hardly enough to look round for the nearest modern name beginning with Br and identify that as *Brunanburh*': R.I. Page, 'A Tale of Two Cities', *Peritia*, i (1982), 344.

[55] Æthelweard, iv. 5, p. 54; *Symeon of Durham, Libellus de Exordio atque Procursu istius, hoc est Dunelmensis, Ecclesie*, ed. and trans. David Rollason (Oxford, 2000), 138–9. Gaimar, *L'Estoire des Engleis*, line 3517, ed. Alexander Bell, Anglo-Norman Texts, 14–16 (Oxford, 1960), 112. This is the reading of only one manuscript of Gaimar's history; others read *Burneweste* and *Brunewerche*.

Anglo-Saxon Chronicle and also – more dubiously – in the narrative of *Vínheiðr* in *Egils saga*, chs 50–5, see below) may shed light on the topography of the battlefield and so perhaps support one putative place-name over another. Relevant to that discussion is John of Worcester's assertion that Olaf and Constantín, king of the Scots, entered the mouth of the Humber with a strong fleet, causing Æthelstan and his brother Edmund to go and meet them at *Brunanburh*. Simeon of Durham claimed similarly that the attacking fleet sailed up the Humber.[56] Otherwise one might have assumed that the attack came from the west, Constantín meeting up with a Norse fleet from Dublin to attack at some point on England's western seaboard.

From the Old English poem we see that the battle took place neither in Wessex nor in the lands of Constantín of the Scots, for both kings travelled to the battlefield from some distance. Further, the site apparently lay either near the coast or not far from a river that flowed out to open sea, since the enemy forces were close enough to their landing point to be able to escape to their ships and sail away, albeit having to ride hard, with the English in pursuit, in order to get there. According to the poem, the West Saxon troops harried the fleeing enemy 'all day long', cutting down fugitives from behind with 'sharpened swords' (lines 20b–24a). Some have taken this to imply that the landing place (*Dingesmere*) to which the remnant of the Dublin Norse army withdrew lay at some distance from the battlefield, but that does not necessarily follow, particularly if we reconsider the meaning of the compound *eorodcistum* used of the West Saxons in these lines. Although this compound has often been assumed to include a reference to horses and so to imply that a mounted West Saxon force pursued the fugitives (and so their landing place lay far away), Paul Cavill has recently demonstrated the error of that presumption. He has shown that the word has no reference either to cavalry (or, as others have thought, to chosen bands) but relates rather to gatherings of men in specific formations, or simply to assemblages of men en masse.[57] In these lines, the poet offers a tribute to the tenacity of the West Saxons as a troop, following that commendation immediately with a similar statement about the Mercians, who 'did not refuse hard fighting to any of the warriors who in the ship's bosom had followed Anlaf over the tossing waters to our land to meet their doom in battle'(24b–28a). In fulfilling his intention of praising the common purpose of the combined English army, the poet cared more for the impact of his verse than for the accuracy of his representation of military detail. Literary licence, not factuality thus determined much of the content of the Chronicle poem, which will not support close textual readings to determine the details of either the fighting or its aftermath.

[56] JW, *s.a.* 937, pp. 392–3; *HR*, *s.a.* 937, ed. Arnold, p. 125. Hill, *Æthelstan*, 145.
[57] Paul Cavill, '*Eorodcistum* in *The Battle of Brunanburh*', *Leeds Studies in English*, n.s. xxxix (2008), 1–15.

Nothing in the text of the poem requires us to argue that the battlefield lay at any great distance from the shore where the Dublin Norse force had landed.

Analysis of variant versions of the place-name using linguistic and grammatical arguments has led Paul Cavill to demonstrate that elements of the place-name including a genitive ending -s (such as Bromswold or Burnswark) cannot derive from the same root as *Brunanburh*. That name means either 'the *burh* or fortified place of a male person called Bruna', or (if the form is not that of a strong masculine personal noun but a weak feminine one), it could mean 'the fortified place at a river-name meaning the dark, brown or shining one'. Simeon of Durham's alternative *Brunnanwerc* or *Brunnanbyrig* provides two versions of the place-name with the same meaning: -*werc*, from the Old English *(ge)weorc*, which can refer to earthworks but often denotes a fortification, so acting synonymously with a -*burh*/-*byrig* ending. Further, Cavill has dismissed suggestions that the poet of the Chronicle verses invented the name *Brunanburh* in order to fit better with his metre, which would have opened up the possibility of arguing that the place actually had a name ending in -*dun*, -*feld*, -*ford* or -*werc*. The poetical account of the battle occurs only in manuscripts A–D of the Anglo-Saxon Chronicle; the E and F versions report the event in prose, but they, too, located it at *Brunanbyrig*. There would, Cavill argued, 'be no reason for these chronicles to give the *burh* form unless the place was known with that element . . . There can be no doubt that the place of the battle, for all the alternatives which appear in the later tradition, was widely and prosaically known as *Brunanburh*.'[58] With Cavill's conclusions in mind, it is more profitable to consider this question from an historical and logistical point of view.

A location in northern Britain appears the most likely. John of Worcester maintained that the Norse landed at the mouth of the River Humber, but no other source reports this and it seems implausible that a fleet setting sail from Dublin would have taken the difficult route round the north of Britain in order to attack from the east. John of Worcester may have extrapolated from the fact that Harald Hardrada and Sven of Denmark both landed on the Humber when they attacked England in 1066 and 1069.[59] Among the numerous identifications proposed, three merit further exploration.

Brinsworth, South Yorkshire

A plausible case could be made for the battle having been fought at Brinsworth (*Brynesford* in Domesday Book) near the Roman fort of

---

[58] Paul Cavill, 'The Site of the Battle of Brunanburh: Manuscripts and Maps, Grammar and Geography', in *A Commodity of Good Names*, ed. O.J. Padel and David N. Parsons (Donington, 2008), 313–15.

[59] JW, *s.a.* 937, pp. 392–3.

Templeborough (in modern times a huge steelworks, now converted into a heritage site called the Magna Centre).[60] While locating the battle in the Don valley would fit well with both John of Worcester's statement that Olaf landed at the Humber and the generally accepted view that the Norse-Scots *Brunanburh* campaign began with raids in Mercia, the onomastic problem remains insuperable: Brinsworth (first attested as *Brinesford* in Domesday Book) cannot derive from *Brunanburh*; nor could anywhere in this vicinity equate to Simeon of Durham's *Weondune/Wendune*. Appealing as is the notion that Brinsworth and Tinsley are sites of historic significance, particularly to one who used to teach in Sheffield, the case is unsustainable.

Burnswark, Dumfries and Galloway

If we ignore John of Worcester's assertion about a Humber landing, we might reasonably surmise that a force coming from Ireland would have landed on England's western coast, either at a point on the same latitude as Dublin (to which the other forces in this alliance would also have travelled by water), or at a place rather further north, if the Irish Norse had sailed to meet the forces of the Scots and Owain of Strathclyde nearer to the latter's homeland. Among various western locations that have attracted attention, one of the most plausible lies in south-west Scotland on the Solway Firth, near Ecclefechan in Dumfriesshire, an Iron Age hill fort, with a Roman camp on its summit. At first sight, Burnswark appears logistically a likely site for the battle. Olaf Guthfrithsson fought military engagements in Ireland in the summer of 937, including a battle against his rivals in Limerick on Lough Ree in early August; so he cannot have arrived on the British mainland before the end of that month, or even early in September. Little time remained thereafter for campaigning so late in the year, nor would it have proved easy to support an Irish army over the winter in northern England to launch a campaign in the spring of 938. The northern part of Æthelstan's realm might have faced a two-pronged assault: Constantín and Owain attacking by land in August, and being joined by Olaf's fleet in September. When Æthelstan had mustered a joint Mercian and West Saxon army to confront this dual threat, the enemy then retreated to a fortified and defensible place; topographically that could have been the hill fort at Burnswark. From a Scottish perspective, this

---

[60] This case was first made by John Henry Cockburn, a lawyer for the coal industry, who lived and worked in the Don valley: Cockburn, *The Battle of Brunanburh*, 35–70. A.H. Byrne offered strong support for his theory on grounds of 'inherent military probability' in his *More Battlefields of England* (London, 1952), 44–60. In an evocative essay, Michael Wood discussed his schoolboy ventures into South Yorkshire from Manchester and got excited over Tinsley Wood and the view from White Hill (which reminded him of the topography of the battlefield as described in *Egils Saga*): Wood, 'Brunanburh Revisited', 200–17; also his *In Search of England: Journeys into the English Past* (London 1999; Harmondsworth, 2000), 203–21.

argument has much to commend it. The probability that neither Owain nor Constantín could readily have handled the logistics of campaigning a long way from home strengthens the case; that no public memory of its importance as the site of so convincing an English victory appears less implausible given that this area lay firmly within medieval Scotland, not England.[61]

Considering the matter from an English viewpoint, however, the logistics look more difficult. Plentiful evidence attests to the progress made by Æthelstan's army as it made its way north up the eastern side of England towards Scotland in 934; his court stopped certainly at Nottingham, York and Chester-le-Street, and perhaps also at Ripon and Beverley. That constituted a major expedition requiring substantial forward planning (for seaborne forces as well as a land army). No sources even hint at a similar westbound advance in August/September 937 and it is extremely hard to identify likely places in Lancashire and Cumberland where the king, his immediate retinue and larger army could have stayed. We know of no estates in the north-west that belonged to the West Saxon kings, nor do we know of any monastic houses active north of Cheshire in the first half of the tenth century. Only estates belonging to the church of York (such as Amounderness, which Æthelstan had granted them in 934), or perhaps lands held by the community of St Cuthbert could have had the infrastructure and material resources to provide such hospitality. Yet neither church has any surviving record of such a visit (for which one might expect the king to have 'paid' with lavish gifts). Furthermore, it seems that far from campaigning in the north-west while Æthelstan gathered his army together, the Scandinavian forces had been attacking Mercia before they engaged the English at *Brunanburh*.

The place-name evidence for identifying Burnswark with *Brunanburh* would depend on the support this place gives for the evidence of the twelfth-century historian Gaimar that the battle was fought at *Bruneswerc*, a name which Simeon of Durham's alternative for *Brunanburh*, *Etbrunnanwerc* might conceivably reinforce.[62] Burnswark in Annandale first occurs in a text of 1542 as *Burnyswarke* (seventeenth-century texts give variously *Burniswork*, *Burneswark*, and *Burnswark*). Those who have argued that this place-name refers to the *Brunanburh* of the Chronicle poem have all

<hr/>

[61] Kevin Halloran, 'The Brunanburh Campaign: A Reappraisal', *Scottish Historical Review*, lxxxiv (2005), 133–48.

[62] Thomas Hodgkin first made the case for Burnswark in the *Athenaeum*, 15 August 1885, 239. Support came from George Neilson, '*Brunanburh* and Burnswork', *Scottish Historical Review*, vii (1909), 37–9; Charles Oman, *A History of England before the Norman Conquest* (London 1924), 521; and W.S. Angus, 'The Battlefield of Brunanburh', *Antiquity*, xi (1937), 283–93. More recently the idea has been enthusiastically adopted by Kevin Halloran, '*Brunanburh* reconsidered', *History Today*, lvi.6 (June 2006), 2–3; Halloran, 'The *Brunanburh* Campaign'.

maintained that the name in all of its variant spellings denotes 'the work, or fortification of a man called Bruna', the work in question being the Roman camp on the hill at Burnswark. But serious doubt has now been cast on this interpretation: Burnswark means 'hill-fort/(earth)work of or by the burn(s)'.[63]

Thus, on grounds of military logistics, Burnswark may work well for the Scottish forces, but it sits uneasily with what we can determine about Æthelstan's movements and with the evidence that this campaign began in Mercia. Onomastically, the modern place-name Burnswark cannot derive from the Old English poet's name for the battlefield of *Brunanburh*; arguments that the poet invented a new name for a place otherwise known by a different name we have already rejected. The best evidence that *Brunanburh* was fought at Burnswark comes in post-Conquest texts, specifically the history by Geoffrey Gaimar; to prefer the authority of one writing in the 1130s over a near-contemporaneous poem seems, on the face of it, contrary.

Bromborough, Cheshire

An identification of *Brunanburh* with Bromborough in Cheshire has much to recommend it for both onomastic and strategic reasons. Bromborough lies on the Mersey, an estuary often used by Viking raiders moving between Ireland and the British mainland and where there is evidence of considerable Scandinavian settlement from the late ninth century onwards. Not only would this have made the area a likely landing point for a fleet from Dublin, it would also have made the provisioning and support of a Scandinavian army in the field substantially easier than would a location in south-western Scotland, where they would have had to depend on Scottish support. Thirteenth-century charters point to an original Old English form for Bromborough: *Brunanburh*.[64] Identification of the place-name is extremely helpful but it does not of course prove that this Bruna's stronghold was the same fortification near which the battle was fought. Simeon of Durham's alternative name for the battlefield, *Weondune*, presents a difficulty; however, there is nearby a place called Rice Wood, near a small fortification, which was in the fourteenth century called *Welondrys* or *Welandrys*. This just might represent a later echo of the first element of Simeon's *Weondune*.[65]

Bromborough's proximity to a place called Thingwall may also prove helpful in identifying the site and explaining another element of the

[63] Cavill, 'The Site of the Battle', 311.

[64] The case was first made by A.H. Smith, 'The Site of the Battle of Brunanburh', in *London Mediaeval Studies*, ed. R.W. Chambers, F. Norman and A.H. Smith (London, 1937), i, 56–9. It received more authoritative support from John Dodgson, 'The Background of Brunanburh', 303–16; and his *Place-Names of Cheshire*, 4 vols (Cambridge, 1972), iv, 237–40. Dodgson's solution has further been supported by Higham: 'The Context of Brunanburh', 144–56.

[65] Richard Coates, 'A Further Snippet of Evidence for Brunanburh=Bromborough', *Notes and Queries*, xl.3 (1998), 288–9.

narrative given in the Old English poem. The 'ding' of *Dingesmere* in the poem (line 54), where the defeated Norsemen retreated to their ships before sailing back to Dublin in humiliated defeat, could refer to the *þing* of Thingwall (meaning 'the place where an assembly meets'). *Dingesmere* may refer to the wetland or marshland by the assembly meeting point, not to the Irish Sea, as some have tried to suggest. It is important to remember the propaganda purpose of the Old English poem, which strove to exalt the exploits of the West Saxon and Mercian forces and so to diminish and shame their opponents. Stressing that the Norse fugitives had to depart from an unsuitable place in wetland, or coastal marshland, before they could get to the deeper water and sail full tilt for Dublin, the poet highlighted the fact that they had made their stronghold near their own *þing*, a centre of Scandinavian power in the locality and a symbol of Scandinavian independence and self-determination. In light of that irony, the English victory – greater than any known since first the Anglo-Saxons had come to British shores – looks the sweeter.[66] Identifying the battlefield with Bromborough serves to place the battle at the boundary between the Norse Wirral and Anglo-Saxon-controlled Mercia, strategically a highly significant location.[67] This battle was as crucial for the future of Mercia as it was for the maintenance of Æthelstan's hold over northern England and his hegemony over the rest of Britain. Bromborough thus seems the most likely identification for the place called *Brunanburh* by the Chronicle poet.[68]

Egils saga

As well as the Chronicle poem, a further detailed account of this battle appears in the thirteenth-century Icelandic saga known as *Egils saga*, which provides a long, apparently circumstantial narrative of a battle at a place called *Vínheiðr* at which Olaf, king of the Scots fought against Æthelstan. Despite the different place-name, it is generally accepted that this refers to the battle of *Brunanburh*, but the evidence of the saga sheds little light on the circumstances of the battle; it seems to offer an image of a conventional conflict, rather than a reliable narrative of the events on this specific battlefield. The saga's author attempted to set the fight in an historical context, placing the events at the start of the reign of Æthelstan 'the Victorious' whom he identified as the grandson of King Alfred and son of Edward. A rudimentary summary of the politics of mid-tenth-century Britain refers to a king Olaf the Red, who ruled in Scotland (a region

---

[66] Paul Cavill, Stephen Harding and Judith Jesch, 'Revisiting *Dingesmere*', *Journal of the English Place-Name Society*, xxxvi (2003–4), 25–38, at 36. Now see also Cavill, 'Coming back to *Dingesmere*', in *Language Contact in the Place-Names of Britain and Ireland*, ed. Paul Cavill and George Broderick (Nottingham, 2007), 27–41.

[67] See also Smith, 'The Site of the Battle, 56–9; and Coates, 'A Further Snippet', 288–9.

[68] I am particularly grateful to Paul Cavill for help with the onomastic details of this argument.

'considered a third of the kingdom of England') while Æthelstan held Northumbria (one fifth of England, 'the furthest north next to Scotland'), where formerly Danish kings had governed. Æthelstan had put earls in charge of the district around York to guard against the onslaughts of Scots, Danes and Norwegians who frequently raided in the land and thought they had a claim to authority there. Welsh kings were subordinate also to the English ruler; but when Æthelstan succeeded 'hostilities began among the chieftains who had lost their power to his ancestors; they thought now would be the easiest time to claim it, while a young king ruled the kingdom'. Unfavourable comparison between Æthelstan and both his father and grandfather leads the author to note laconically, 'many became disloyal who earlier had offered good service'.[69]

While some historical understanding may underlie elements of this introductory material, there is no known source on which its author might have depended. The saga's account of the fight itself is as a literary creation (of some significance to the saga as a whole) not an historically reliable narrative, even though some of what it reports agrees with what is known of the battle fought in 937.[70] One of the difficulties here, as elsewhere in Æthelstan's reign, is that there is so little contemporary material to set beside the later sources. The poem celebrating the battle in the Anglo-Saxon Chronicle offers no prelude to the conflict but launches straight into the fighting; here the saga's author may be a better witness in reporting that Olaf had been raiding in Northumbria and had succeeded in bringing much of it under his authority before the English king could mobilize an army against him.[71] Where the saga may preserve a further element of truth is in its contention that Æthelstan had some men of Norse extraction fighting as mercenaries on his side, among whom the saga identified by name Thorolf and his brother Egil.[72]

William of Malmesbury offered some rather surprising criticism of Æthelstan before the battle of *Brunanburh*, at odds with his generally

[69] *Egils Saga*, §§50–51, trans. Christine Fell (London, 1975), 74–5. For the possibility that some kernels of historical fact lay behind the saga see Magnús Fjalldal, 'A Farmer in the Court of King Athelstan: Historical and Literary Considerations in the Vínheiðr Episode of *Egils Saga*', *English Studies*, lxxvii (1996), 16–18.

[70] Ian McDougall, 'Discretion and Deceit: a Re-Examination of a Military Stratagem in *Egils Saga*', in *The Middle Ages in the North-West*, ed. Tom Scott and Pat Starkey (Oxford, 1995), 112; Fjalldal, 'A Farmer', 26.

[71] *Egils Saga*, §52, trans. Fell, 75.

[72] Ibid., §50, trans. Fell, 74. A post-Conquest chronicler John of Wallingford (who may have had access to Anglo-Saxon materials now lost), said that the number of Danes in England had increased ever since Æthelstan's time, for he had held them in high regard, and that West Saxon kings were accustomed to use Danish mercenaries in their attacks on the provinces of their neighbours: *The Chronicle attributed to John of Wallingford*, ed. R. Vaughan, Camden Miscellany, xxi Camden 3rd ser. xc (London, 1958), 60; discussed by Shashi Jayakumar, 'The "Foreign Policies" of Edgar the Peaceable', *Haskins Society Journal*, x (2001), 26; and see also Alistair Campbell, *Skaldic Verse and Anglo-Saxon History* (London, 1971), 5–7.

favourable account of the king. He quoted a verse panegyric which, although describing Æthelstan as 'youthful and self-confident', charges him with having 'long ago given up war and passed his time in indolent leisure' while his enemies 'ruined everything by continual raids', until the reports of such widespread waste and misery galvanized him into tardy military action. Perhaps these were the sentiments of the original poet (whose verse William recast to conform to his own notions of literary style); either that poet sought some explanation for how the peace settlement of 934 could so swiftly have gone wrong, or he wanted to account for Æthelstan's failure to prevent Scottish and Irish raids in Northumbria and Mercia before the battle.[73]

Less plausible than the notion that several raids and skirmishes preceded the decisive battle at *Brunanburh/ Vinheiðr*, or the saga's suggestion that it took Æthelstan some while to raise an army and march it north, are the saga author's accounts of the threefold stratagem adopted by the English to delay the onset of the battle and his detailed description of the topography of the battlefield. The latter appears not for reasons of historical authenticity but in order to set the stage for the saga's literary denouement. A site was chosen, agreed on by both sides and then marked out with hazel stakes; the moor where the fighting would take place lay on level ground, but on one side a river flowed down and on the other there was a big wood. Egil had Æthelstan's men pitch their tents in rows in the narrow gap between the wood and the river, deceiving the enemy (who could not see over them) into thinking they were opposed by a much larger force than was really the case.[74] Here the author demonstrates the brilliance of Egil's strategic planning and the effectiveness of his deceitful stratagems, while at the same time preparing the reader for the fall of his brother, Thorolf. Had the enemy fought within the designated area, as they had agreed to do, the outcome would have been different, but their failure to keep to the rules left the hero Thorolf victim of their treachery.[75] Egil laments his fall in verse as he buries his brother before going to King Æthelstan for his reward. The meeting between the king and Egil is the climax of this episode, not the battle of *Vinheiðr* itself which was merely the preparation for that scene.

If we reject the witness of *Egils saga*, we have only the near-contemporary poem in the Anglo-Saxon Chronicle as a source for the details of the fighting.

[73] *GR*, ii, 135, pp. 220–1. Thomson, *Commentary*, 116–18.

[74] *Egils Saga*, §52, trans. Fell, 77. Some scholars have tried to locate the battlefield on the basis of this topographical material, for example Cockburn, *The Battle of Brunanburh* and Angus, 'The Battlefield of Brunanburh'; but that this was unwise, bearing in mind that the literary, not historical, nature of the text was argued as long ago as 1933: L. Hollander, 'The Battle on the Vin– heath and the Battle of the Huns', *Journal of English and Germanic Philology*, xxxii (1933), 33–43; see also Campbell, *The Battle of Brunanburh*, 69–70 and McDougall, 'Discretion', 117–24.

[75] Fjalldal, 'A Farmer', 28

William of Malmesbury seems not to have known of the Chronicle poem for he offered a rather different reading of the battle the first time he described it, erroneously counting Constantín, king of the Scots, among the fallen.[76] His independent contributions to the events surrounding the battle take the form of an account of Anlaf (Olaf) disguising himself as a harpist and going to spy on the English king in his tent (a story in which one might have more faith had William not already recounted a similar narrative about King Alfred on the eve of the battle of Edington)[77] and a miracle attributed to St Aldhelm of Malmesbury. Discovering that they had been spied upon, Æthelstan's army supposedly moved their tents to another place to prevent the enemy from launching an immediate attack. Despite this, Anlaf did fall upon the English forces during the night, taking the sleeping Æthelstan by surprise, but when the king called on God and St Aldhelm for aid, he put his hand to his scabbard and found there a wonderful sword. With this in his hand the king was able to lead his army into the field and fight tirelessly all day long until his enemies were put to flight. As well as Constantín, there fell five other kings, twelve jarls 'and almost the whole horde of barbarians', the few who lived being taken prisoner to be converted to Christianity.[78] In William's slightly confusing narrative of Æthelstan's reign, this circumstantially detailed but fundamentally unconvincing account appears before he talks about the 'ancient volume' in which he had found a panegyric about the king written during Æthelstan's lifetime. There is no reason to imagine that William drew on anything other than his own imagination and a stock repertoire of anecdotes in military history in order to craft this, the first of his versions of events in 937. On the second occasion on which he described the battle of *Brunanburh*, William quoted at length from the verse account of the king already mentioned; again this provides no new information about the battle itself, but merely consists of various laudatory remarks about the number of the king's troops (an improbable 100,000 men), their valour and the inevitable slaughter of many thousands of the undeserving pirate enemy.[79] One additional and equally unlikely piece of information William had obtained from Eadmer of Canterbury and inserted into his account of the bishops of England. Reporting that the future archbishop of Canterbury, Oda, had stood at Æthelstan's side during this battle, William recounted how he prayed for the miraculous replacement of the king's sword in its scabbard when he had come near to falling into the hands of his enemies and lost his

---

[76] *GR*, ii, 131, pp. 206–9.

[77] *GR*, ii, 121, pp. 182–5. C.E. Wright was more inclined to take this story seriously, since he thought it had 'an unmistakable ring of truth about it' and that the incident it described was 'by no means impossible or incredible'. He suggested that William might have obtained it from a short vernacular saga current at the royal court: *The Cultivation of Saga in Anglo-Saxon England* (Edinburgh and London, 1939), 145–6.

[78] *GR* ii, 131, pp. 208–9.

[79] *GR*, ii, 135, pp. 220–3.

weapon.[80] William may have stood on rather firmer ground when he claimed that two of those who had fallen on the English side at *Brunanburh* were buried at his own abbey of Malmesbury: the king's cousins Ælfwine and Æthelwine. These were the sons of Æthelstan's uncle, Æthelweard, and were apparently laid to rest to the right and left of the altar at Malmesbury.[81]

Whatever the difficulties of the various reports of this engagement, we cannot doubt its significance: it was a resounding victory. The Old English poet gloated more over the ignominy of Olaf's flight, yet in many ways the defeat was more crushing for Constantín; his son was dead and his credibility among his own people seriously weakened, a point noted by the later tenth-century chronicler, Æthelweard, who observed that after this battle the Scots had been forced to bow their necks. It was probably not long after this that Constantín abdicated and retired to St Andrews.[82] Non-English sources also recorded the victory of the West Saxons. To the annalist of Ulster, this was a 'great victory' that Æthelstan enjoyed, following the cruelly fought battle between the Saxons and the Norsemen, in which several thousand Norsemen died as well as a large number of Saxons, but from which the Norse king, Amlaíb, escaped with a few followers. Scottish and Welsh texts also noted the battle and its outcome.[83]

ÆTHELSTAN: A KING VICTORIOUS BECAUSE OF GOD

After the decisive English victory at *Brunanburh*, the country faced no further outside attack or invasion for the remainder of Æthelstan's reign. The king did, however, engage in one more foreign expedition, sending a fleet in 939 to Flanders allegedly, according to Flodoard, to assist Louis IV

---

[80] *GP*, i, 14, pp. 26–7; Eadmer, *Vita sancti Odonis*, PL 133, cols 931–4; see Lapidge, 'The Hermeneutic Style', 138; Brooks, *The Early History*, 222. Compare also *GP*, ii, 73, pp. 228–31 where Theodred, bishop of London, was also said to have been present at the battle and involved in the prayer for a new sword for the king.

[81] *GR*, ii, 136, pp. 222–3; compare ii, 135, pp. 220–1; *GP*, v, 246, pp. 592–3.

[82] Æthelweard, iv, 5, p. 54. Hudson has argued that Constantín was no more than a client king for his last years and suggested that he retired c.943: *Kings of Celtic Scotland*, 81–2.

[83] *AU* 937, 384–5. The Chronicle of the Kings of Alba noted the death of the son of the Scots king at the battle of *Duin Brunde*: ed. and trans. Benjamin Hudson, 'The Scottish Chronicle', *Scottish Historical Review*, lxxvii (1998), 150 and 157. The Pictish Chronicle (a tenth-century compilation) reported the battle within an account of the reign of Constantín III: 'Et bellum Duinbrunde in xxxiiii. ejus anno ubi cecidit filius Constantini.': *Chronicles of the Picts, Chronicles of the Scots*, ed. William F. Skene (Edinburgh, 1867), 9. The Welsh *Annales Cambriae* mentioned a '*Bellum Brune*' c.938: *Annales Cambriae*, ed. John Williams ap Ithel, Rolls Series (London, 1860), 17. The Irish Annals of Clonmacnoise, *s.a.* 931 = 937 reported a battle between the Danes of Dublin and the Danes of England against the Saxons on the plains of *othlynn* where there was a great slaughter (numbered improbably in thousands), among whom was Constantín's son, Cellach: ed. Murphy, p. 151; see Campbell, *Battle of Brunanburh*, 159; Smyth, *Scandinavian York and Dublin*, ii, 38–40.

in his struggle with rebellious magnates in Frankia. Whatever this expedition should have achieved, it seemingly failed, for instead of going into western Frankia, the fleet turned aside and attacked the coast of Flanders, before returning to England, its intentions unfulfilled. Thereafter Arnulf, count of Flanders, apparently allied himself with King Louis's enemies.[84] While we have only scant details about this engagement, we have already seen that the English king had interests in the region west of Flanders at Montreuil which he had exploited when he intervened in Breton affairs in 936–7, and Arnulf had sent the family of the count of Ponthieu into exile at the English king's court earlier that year. English and Flemish priorities appear to have coincided here. MacLean has offered an imaginative suggestion about the king's preparations for this expedition, linking them to his grant to his sister Eadburh, a nun at the Nunnaminster, of land on a river at Droxford in Hampshire (south-east of Winchester, near the coast). Since Arnulf had probably inherited his mother Ælfthryth's interest in land at Wellow on the nearby Isle of Wight (bequeathed to her by her father, King Alfred), MacLean wondered if Arnulf might have played a direct role in the strategic organization of this cross-Channel venture.[85] If Æthelstan had thereby hoped to help his nephew Louis, he did not succeed and this would prove his last military or naval engagement, for he died the following year.

Writing early in the eleventh century the celebrated Old English homilist, monk of Cerne Abbey and later abbot of Eynsham, Ælfric, wrote a short tract on kingship to serve as an epilogue to a translation he had made of the Old Testament Book of Judges. There he commented on three West Saxon kings, Alfred, Æthelstan and Edgar (957/9–975), who were 'victorious because of God'. Alfred fought frequently against the Danes until he gained victory and so protected his people; Edgar 'mightiest of all the kings of the English people', spread the praise of God everywhere and brought peace to his people. Æthelstan's achievement was to have fought against Anlaf, slaughtered his army and put him to flight and afterwards to have dwelt in peace with his people.[86] It is interesting that it should be for the victory at *Brunanburh* that Æthelstan was best known sixty years after his death,[87] for it is that achievement for which he remains the most celebrated and which has dominated all the later historiography of his

---

[84] Flodoard, 939 (21D); MacLean, 'Making a Difference', 177. Philip Grierson, 'The Relations between England and Flanders before the Norman Conquest', *TRHS*, 4th ser., xxiii (1941), 89.

[85] Flodoard, 939 (21B); above, ch. 2; S 446 (grant of Droxford to Eadburh); S 1507 (will of Alfred); MacLean, 'Making a Difference', 176–8.

[86] *The Old English Version of the Heptateuch: Ælfric's Treatise on the Old and New Testament and his Preface to Genesis*, ed. S.J. Crawford (London, 1922), 416–17; Dumville, *Wessex*, 141.

[87] Dumville wondered whether the king was already as shadowy a figure as he is today: *Wessex*, 142.

reign. His military prowess attracted the attention of his contemporaries, too; we have already seen the military commander portrayed in the poem *Carta dirige gressus*, where the poet Petrus depicted the king arming the army of the English for battle throughout Britain,[88] and in the verses *Rex pius Æðelstan*, which stressed that God had set Æthelstan as king over the English 'plainly so that this king himself, mighty in war, might be able to conquer other fierce kings, treading down their proud necks'.[89] On the basis of his conquest of Northumbria in 927, his crushing of the Scottish rebellion in 934 and his overwhelming victory at *Brunanburh* in 937, that reputation seems not unfounded. Æthelstan was one of the most remarkable English military leaders of the pre-Conquest period. Yet his achievements spread far beyond the military sphere.

---

[88] *Carta dirige gressus*, stanza 4; Lapidge, 'Poems', 98.
[89] *Rex pius Æðelstan*, lines 5–6; Lapidge, 'Poems', 95–6.

Chapter 7

DEATH

King Æthelstan died on 27 October 939, almost exactly forty years after his grandfather, Alfred, having ruled for fourteen years and ten weeks. Thus reported the various manuscripts of the Anglo-Saxon Chronicle, their authors reckoning the length of Æthelstan's reign from the day of his coronation on 4 September 925, not from the point at which he first assumed royal power the previous year.[1] Just one manuscript supplied the further information that the king died at Gloucester, and John of Worcester, who reckoned this the sixteenth not the fifteenth year of his reign, added the fact that the body of this vigorous and glorious king (*strenuous et gloriosus rex*) was buried at Malmesbury.[2] We learn more about Æthelstan's funeral and burial from William of Malmesbury, whose particular interest in this king can at least in part be explained by the presence of Æthelstan's tomb at his own abbey. William could, for example, attest from his own observation that the king had had fair hair: 'as I have seen for myself in his remains, beautifully intertwined with gold threads'.[3]

For William, Æthelstan's choice of burial place reflected his devotion to Malmesbury Abbey and respect for the memory of its seventh-century abbot Aldhelm (later bishop of Sherborne, d. 709), who also lay there. Previously Æthelstan had indicated a preference for Malmesbury over other monastic churches in Wessex when he elected to inter at the head of St Aldhelm's tomb the bodies of his cousins who had fallen fighting on his behalf at the battle of *Brunanburh*. According to William the king had 'such a veneration for the place thereafter that he thought nowhere more desirable or more sacred', declaring from the time of his kinsmen's burial that he intended this to be where his own body also should lie, even though Malmesbury Abbey cared for the cults of no other members of the West Saxon royal family.[4]

---

[1] ASC, *s.a.* 940 ABCD; 27 October was a Sunday in 939. Since the chroniclers' year began in September, October 939 was, by their reckoning, the year 940. King Alfred had died on 26 October 899. The regnal list written in the reign of Edward the Martyr (d. 978) which originally followed the B manuscript of the Chronicle but now survives as a single leaf (BL, Cotton MS Tiberius A. iii, fo. 178; called β by Charles Plummer, *Two of the Saxon Chronicles Parallel*, 2 vols (Oxford, 1892–9), i, 2–3; ii, lxxxix–xc) provided a more accurate calculation for the length of Æthelstan's reign of fourteen years, seven weeks and three days; see Whitelock, *EHD* I, no. 1, pp. 146–8.

[2] ASC, *s.a.* 940D; JW *s.a.* 940, pp. 394–5. See plate 16.

[3] *GR*, ii, 134, pp. 214–15.

[4] *GR*, ii, 136, pp. 222–3; compare ii, 135, pp. 220–1. See above, 183.

Instead, the New Minster at Winchester had, by the early tenth century, become that family's main mausoleum, holding the tombs of Æthelstan's father, Edward the Elder, both his grandparents, Alfred and Ealhswith, his uncle Æthelweard (father of those cousins who died at *Brunanburh*), and his eldest half-brother, Ælfweard. One might wonder whether Æthelstan's preference for Malmesbury arose not so much from his veneration for Aldhelm as from his reluctance to patronize or consign his perpetual memory to an establishment in Winchester so closely associated with his rival for the throne in 924.[5] He could, however, have chosen one of the other local religious houses where different members of his extended family had been buried, notably one of those in Dorset. Sherborne and Wimborne both had care of kings' tombs, and the royal foundation at Shaftesbury, already the resting-place of a king's daughter, would in future acquire its own yet more prestigious royal saint.[6] Perhaps geographical considerations drove Æthelstan's decision: Malmesbury lay in northern Wiltshire, near the old Mercian border and the county of Gloucestershire. Our study of the king's movements in the middle years of his reign suggested that he had a particular liking for Wiltshire, a preference he might have wanted still to articulate in death, for which purpose Malmesbury was ideal. An historic abbey, with the tomb of a notable West Saxon saint, it lay firmly within the king's ancestral homeland yet near enough to that realm's northern border to reach out towards subjects in the old kingdom of Mercia and those farther afield who had never previously known subjection to a West Saxon monarch.

Not just custodians of his earthly remains and cultivators of his eternal memory, Malmesbury's monks had cause to remember Æthelstan with grateful affection as a significant benefactor of their abbey. This factor may in part account for the substantial attention William devoted to this king's life and deeds in his history of the English kings. William provided additional material in praise of Æthelstan in the final book of his *Gesta pontificum*, which concerned the history of his own abbey and the life of its most famous saint, Aldhelm. Æthelstan, he averred, showed particular devotion to St Aldhelm, to whom he believed himself to be related and who once came to his support in battle; the king donated generously to Malmesbury, giving the abbey estates, vestments, sacred objects made of gold and even a portion of the Lord's cross which he had received from Hugh, duke of the Franks.[7] Lamenting the impatience of fate in cutting short his great deeds, William declared the king's death at Gloucester in 939 had come too early; Æthelstan's body was carried to Malmesbury to be buried in the

<hr>

[5] Alan Thacker, 'Dynastic Monasteries and Family Cults: Edward the Elder's Kindred', H&H, 254.

[6] King Æthelbald (d. 860) and his brother Æthelberht (d. 865) were buried at Sherborne; Æthelred (d. 871) at Wimborne; Alfred's daughter Æthelgifu was presumably buried at her nunnery in Shaftesbury, whither the remains of Edward the Martyr were translated in 979.

[7] *GP*, v, 246, pp. 592–3; for St Aldhelm's intervention at the battle of *Brunanburh* see above, 182.

tower, under the altar of St Mary. Describing the funeral in his *Gesta regum*, William added that 'many gifts from him in silver and gold were carried before the body, and many relics of the saints, bought in Brittany, for such were the objects on which he expended – warned it is said in a dream – the treasure accumulated and left untouched by his father'.[8] The epitaph on his tomb in the abbey – probably composed by William himself – read:

> Here lies one honoured by the world and grieved by his land:
> Path of rectitude, thunderbolt of justice, model of purity.
> His spirit has gone to heaven, its covering of flesh dissolved:
> An urn receives those triumphant relics.
> The sun had lit up Scorpio with its twelfth dawn
> When he struck down the king with his tail.[9]

William believed Malmesbury Abbey owed Æthelstan a substantial debt of gratitude for his grant of the relics of numerous saints.[10]

Even by the standards of his age, Æthelstan proved a notably pious king, attentive to the state of his soul and his need to answer for his deeds to a higher throne after his death. As well as his generosity in alms-giving (and his promotion of the spiritual value of caring for the poor through recommendations made in his charters and law codes) and his liberal donations to churches across his realm, Æthelstan demonstrated a substantial, indeed a remarkable, interest in the cult of the saints throughout his life. Æthelstan was the most celebrated collector of the remains of saints (and of objects associated with them and their cults) among early English kings and his reputation for interest in such sacred objects spread to the continent. Indeed, his passion for this pursuit represents one of the aspects of the king's character and personality on which a biographer may comment authoritatively without any recourse to imaginative surmise.

THE KING'S OWN RELIC COLLECTION

Royal interest in the cult of saints and the collection of relics was far from unusual. Æthelstan's grandfather, King Alfred, had received a piece of the cross from Pope Marinus and always, according to Asser, took the 'holy relics of a number of God's chosen saints' with him everywhere. Æthelstan's youngest brother, Eadred, had in his household priests specifically charged with care of the royal relics.[11] Possession of the remains of the saints could witness tangibly to a king's piety and his devotion to the memory of the holy,

---

[8] *GR*, ii, 140, pp. 228–9.

[9] *GP*, v, 246, pp. 594–5; for William's authorship of the epitaph, see Michael Winterbottom, 'William of Malmesbury, *versificus*', in *Anglo-Latin and its Heritage*, ed. S. Echard and G.R. Wieland (Turnhout, 2001), 109–27, at 119 and 125.

[10] *GP*, v, 247, pp. 294–5.

[11] ASC, *s.a.* 885 ADEF; 886 BC; Asser, chs 71 and 104; *SEHD*, no. 35.

as well as to the wider Church; gifts of relics to churches and monasteries reflected the generosity, power and wealth of a king, conferring spiritual benefit on both donor and recipient.[12] Royal saints were of particular interest to kings because of the example they presented of holy living and righteous deeds. They could also usefully serve political purposes when local loyalties to a prominent saint proved malleable in the shaping of regional and supra-regional identities. In Æthelstan's efforts to unite his disparate subjects into one English people after his conquest of Northumbria, he found the promotion of the cult of native English saints especially valuable; even before his accession, he had participated in his aunt and uncle's promotion of the cult of Northumbrian saints in Mercia. If we may believe the account of Abbo of Fleury, stories about saints and martyrs were recounted at Æthelstan's court, including tales about the sainted King Edmund of East Anglia, martyred at the hands of the Danes in 869. Equally popular according to a German witness were, apparently, accounts of the passion of the martyrs of Cologne and their leader Ursula.[13] The king's enthusiasm for the saints and interest in the notion of sanctity extended beyond his listening to tales of the heroic deeds of earlier saintly kings, or his generous donations to churches and religious communities with care of the cults of particular saints. He accumulated a relic collection of his own of some size and spiritual significance witnessing to an almost preternatural interest in bones and other objects associated with the holy; his reputation for especial enthusiasm for such remains was such that it reached continental churches. Medieval lives of a Flemish saint, Bertulfus, reported that an official from eastern Brittany, Electus, attempted unsuccessfully to steal the saint's remains in order to sell them to King Æthelstan.[14] The king's famed interest in such sacred objects caused other Frankish clerics and nobles to make him more conventional gifts of the remains of Breton and other saints.[15]

Our earliest evidence for Æthelstan's personal possession of relics occurs in the text of a manumission entered on to a blank space on the reverse of one of the leaves of an eighth-century English gospel book which presumably belonged to the king. Written in Old English, in a contemporary hand, the text reads:

King Æthelstan freed Eadhelm very soon after he first became king. Ælfheah the mass priest and the household (*se hired*), Ælfric the reeve, Wulfnoth the White, Eanstan the provost, and Beornstan the

---

[12] David Rollason, 'Relic-Cults as an Instrument of Royal Policy *c.*900–*c.*1050', *ASE*, xv (1986), 91–3.

[13] Abbo, *Passio*, 67; W. Levison, 'Das Werden der Ursula-Legende', *Bonner Jahrbucher*, cxxxii (1928), 142–57, and 58–90; Karl Leyser, 'The Ottonians and Wessex', in *Communications and Power in Medieval Europe*, ed. Timothy Reuter (London, 1994), 79.

[14] Patrick Geary, *Furta Sacra: Thefts of Relics in the Central Middle Ages* (Princeton, NJ, 1978), 60 and 140.

[15] See further below, 190–3.

mass-priest were witnesses of this. He who averts this, may he have the
disfavour of God and of all the relics which, by God's mercy, I have obtained
in England. And I grant the children the same as I grant the father.[16]

The phrase 'very soon after he first became king' could imply that Æthelstan
freed his slave Eadhelm on the day of his coronation and recorded the
manumission in the gospel book on which he had just sworn his coronation
oath. Later in the Middle Ages this book belonged to St Augustine's
Canterbury, but it may not have done so as early as 925, nor would the archbishop plausibly have borrowed a suitable gospel book for the coronation
from his monastic neighbours in Canterbury rather than using one from
Christ Church's own collection. These gospels probably belonged to
Æthelstan's personal book collection, in which case the witnesses to this
grant of freedom – among them two mass-priests and some secular office-
holders – would have come from the royal household. We may date this
text to the earliest months of Æthelstan's reign in the period soon after the
death of his brother Ælfweard on 1 August 924 and hence locate it after
Æthelstan's acceptance as king not just in Mercia but in the whole of the
realm his father had ruled. It thus demonstrates that even at this early stage
in his reign, the young king owned a relic collection of some note and held
it in sufficient esteem to use it for oath-swearing. One of those named as
witnesses may have had responsibility for the care of these relics.[17]

An additional indication of Æthelstan's early interest in relic cults comes in
one of the only two pieces of correspondence to survive from his reign: a letter
from a Breton cleric, Radbod, prior of the cathedral church of St Samson's at
Dol accompanying a gift of the bones of some Breton saints to the English
king. The text of the letter shows not only that Æthelstan's reputation for
interest in the cult of saints had travelled beyond British shores, but that the
king was esteemed by foreign clerics as a possible patron. Radbod wrote from
exile in central France, his congregation having fled Brittany because of
Norman attacks on the region. William of Malmesbury claimed to have found
the text of his letter in a *scrinium* (perhaps meaning a box in which archives
were stored, rather than a shrine) at the abbey of Milton Abbas in Dorset, a
church founded by King Æthelstan.[18] Written after Æthelstan's accession – for
Radbod addressed him as king – the letter has conventionally been dated to
before 927. Æthelstan must, however, have been on the throne for long enough

[16] BL, MS Royal I. B. vii, fo. 15v; *SEHD*, no. 19; trans. Keynes, 'Books', see plate 6. 185,
n. 201.

[17] Keynes, 'Books', 185–9. Also discussed above, 65.

[18] For the translation of *scrinium* as archive see R.M. Thomson, *William of Malmesbury,
'Gesta Pontificum Anglorum' II: Introduction and Commentary* (Oxford, 2007), 407. William entered
the text of this letter in the margin of a manuscript of his *Gesta pontificum* as an addition
beside his account of Æthelstan's donation of relics to Malmesbury: *GP*, v, 249, pp. 597–9;
he added the text also to the later redaction of his *Gesta regum*, where it follows William's
account of the king's gifts to Malmesbury and his description of the two churches there
(dedicated to St Peter and St Mary): *GR*, 138B, pp. 820–3. It is edited also in *C&S*, I, no. 9;
and translated in *EHD*, no. 228.

for his reputation to have travelled abroad if Radbod meant to offer more than generic compliments when describing him as 'a glorious king, holy exalter of the Church and subduer of the wicked heathen (*gentilitatis humiliator prauae*)'. Had that last remark alluded to the king's conquest of Northumbria we might date the letter to after that event in 927. Given the Dol brothers' situation and the wider political problems in Brittany after 919, one can see why they might have imagined Æthelstan as a possible patron and sought his prayers, especially if they knew that some of their compatriots, including the count of Poher and his son, had taken refuge in his kingdom.[19] One further factor may have led them to hope for a favourable response: by Radbod's account Æthelstan's father, King Edward, had also contacted St Samson's at Dol, commending himself by letter to the confraternity of St Samson; in other words entering into an agreement for mutual prayer with the congregation. Radbod now promised that the clergy from Dol (he and twelve canons) would recite psalms, offer masses and pray for both Edward and his son in the hope that King Æthelstan would not forget their plight.[20]

More remarkably, Radbod continued his letter by saying that he was sending with it, as a gift to the king, relics which he knew were 'dearer to Æthelstan than any earthly property', namely the bones of St Senator, St Paternus and St Scubilio. Formerly these three had lain in the sepulchre of his church: Paternus (St Pair, a sixth-century bishop of Avranches) in the centre, with Senator (also bishop of Avranches, died before 578) and Scubilio (Paternus's teacher, who died on the same day as he in 564) to Paternus's right and left.[21] That the Breton clergy were willing to send the relics of these saints abroad says much for the desperation of their situation; obviously they anticipated that Æthelstan could ensure the relics' safe-keeping, but they hoped further that the gift would advance their own cause with the king.[22] Despite his presumed pleasure in the gift, Æthelstan did not apparently retain these relics in his own collection; according to William, he gave the relics of St Paternus to Malmesbury, where they were kept in a shrine at the abbey, bearing the legend: 'This work King Æthelstan, ruler of Britain and of many peoples round about, ordered to be made in honour of St Paternus.'[23]

---

[19] See J.M.H. Smith, *Province and Empire* (Cambridge, 1992), 196–201; Dumville, *Wessex*, 156–8, 163; and above, 93. Compare also the other extant letter to Æthelstan, also written by a Breton pilgrim seeking the king's support, discussed above, 103–4.

[20] Earlier, I compared this confraternity agreement with the others made via Bishop Cenwald of Worcester's visit to monasteries in Germany in 929, including St Gall and Reichenau: above, 102.

[21] D.H. Farmer, *Oxford Dictionary of Saints* (Oxford, 1978), 312; Thomson, *Commentary*, 298. Whitelock wrongly identified these relics with those of the St Senator who was a fifth-century bishop of Milan: *EHD*, 892; *C&S*, I, 40, n. 2.

[22] Rollason, 'Relic-Cults', 94. Ferdinand Lot, 'Date de l'exode des corps saints hors de Bretagne', *Annals de Bretagne*, xv (1899–1900), 60–76; L. Gougaud, 'Mentions anglaises des saints Bretons et de leurs reliques', *Annales de Bretagne*, xxxiv (1919–21), 273–7.

[23] *GP*, v, 248, pp. 596–7.

King Æthelstan had access to Breton relics beyond those given him by the displaced congregation from Dol, some of them perhaps donated by the Breton exiles found in Wessex during his reign to whom liturgical and other evidence points.[24] He gave relics of St Samson of Dol to the church he had founded at Milton (for the soul of his dead brother, Edwin); Samson's remains were not among those given to the king by the brothers of Dol but rather, apparently, relics that he had bought for himself in Brittany.[25] The now lost register of Milton Abbey claimed that the king had given them an arm and some bones of St Samson and the arm of St Branwalader (a companion of Samson in his missionary work in Cornwall, the Channel Islands and Brittany) together with other relics, all being remains of saints that the king had brought from the holy Roman Church and Britain across the sea (i.e. Brittany).[26] An eleventh-century list of saints' resting-places also located relics of Branwalader at Milton; the church at Exeter claimed the remains of a number of Breton saints as part of its substantial collection, much of which it acquired through Æthelstan's generosity.[27] Æthelstan's ownership of these relics and his donations to favoured religious houses sent signals about his reputation and authority in Brittany that resonated not only with Breton exiles in Wessex but also with his English subjects, and their Welsh and British neighbours.[28]

Knowledge of Æthelstan's enthusiasm for the cult of the saints extended beyond Brittany and found expression in a vastly more elaborate gift of relics of great holiness (and substantial political significance) from Hugh, duke of the Franks, made when he sued for Æthelstan's sister's hand in 926. William of Malmesbury provided the fullest details of this embassy to the court of the West Saxon king, then meeting in council at Abingdon, although contemporary Frankish sources report the marriage itself and the thirteenth-century Chronicle of Abingdon also gave a briefer account.[29] According to William, Hugh sent 'Adulf' (i.e. Adelolf) son of Baldwin, count of Flanders and his wife 'Æthelswith', daughter of Edward (i.e. Ælfthryth, Edward's sister), the king's cousin, to make his case before King Æthelstan and his council. Adelolf 'produced gifts on a truly

---

[24] *TSD*, 73–5; C. Brett, 'A Breton Pilgrim in England in the Reign of King Æthelstan' in *France and the British Isles in the Middle Ages and Renaissance*, ed. Gillian Jondorf and D.N. Dumville (Woodbridge, 1991), 47.

[25] *GP*, v, 249, pp. 598–9; cf. *GP*, ii, 85, pp. 292–3. Another sixth-century figure, St Samson came originally from Dyfed and remained in Wales until his episcopal ordination, when he journeyed through Cornwall and Brittany, dying at Dol, his second monastic foundation, some time in the late sixth century. Nora Chadwick, *Early Brittany* (Cardiff, 1969), 250–5; some give a date of AD 565 for Samson's death, but this cannot be verified.

[26] *TSD*, 74; Brett, 'A Breton Pilgrim', 46.

[27] F. Liebermann, *Die Heiligen Englands* (Hanover, 1889), §47, p. 19; for the Exeter relics, see further below.

[28] Rollason, 'Relic-Cults', 95.

[29] *Historia ecclesie Abbendonensis*, MS B, §62, ed. and trans. John Hudson, *History of the Church of Abingdon*, 2 vols (Oxford, 2002–7), i, 282–3.

magnificent scale, such as might instantly satisfy the desires of a recipient however greedy', including spices, jewels, many swift horses with their trappings, an elaborate Byzantine onyx vase, carved so skilfully with pastoral scenes as to look almost lifelike, a precious crown 'of solid gold, and yet more precious from its gems'; and a number of objects closely associated with the Carolingian royal family, including relics of enormous significance in Christian history associated with the Crucifixion:

> the sword of Constantine the Great, with the ancient owner's name in gold letters, while on the scabbard over stout plates of gold you could see fixed an iron nail, one of four which the Jewish rabble had got ready for the tormenting of our Lord's body; Charlemagne's lance which, if the invincible emperor brandished it as he led the army against the Saracens, 'brought him the victory and it never failed' (it was said to be that same lance which, when driven by the centurion's hand into our Lord's side, opened Paradise to hapless mortals by the precious wound it made); the banner (*vexillum*) of Maurice, blessed martyr and general of the Theban legion, with which that same king [i.e. Charlemagne] in his Spanish war was wont to break and put to flight the enemy squadrons however fierce and closely packed; . . . a small piece of the holy and wonderful Cross enclosed in crystal, which the eye can penetrate, solid rock though it is, and discern the wood, its colour and its size; a small portion too, mounted in the same fashion, of the crown of thorns, which the raving soldiers set upon that sacred head in mockery of His kingship.[30]

If William had genuinely seen a now lost life of King Æthelstan and extracted from it the information about these spectacular presents, then he would witness here to gifts of quite extraordinary significance. Possession of objects and relics with Carolingian associations would substantially have enhanced Æthelstan's standing among his own people and – perhaps more importantly – among the other peoples of Britain, allowing him to benefit from both Charlemagne's imperial charisma and the *virtus* of the holy relics. As the greatest Germanic ruler of post-Roman Europe, the king who had extended the bounds of the Frankish realm across much of western Europe and been crowned as emperor in St Peter's Church in Rome by the Pope in 800, Charlemagne was unquestionably the most significant of the barbarian heirs of the Roman empire. Comparison with him raised Æthelstan to a level no earlier Anglo-Saxon monarch had ever attained. Such gifts testified both to Æthelstan's imperial pretensions, even at this early stage of his reign (earlier than the

---

[30] *GR*, ii, 135, pp. 218–21; the marriage itself was discussed fully, 47–8, above. For these relics, see Karl Leyser, 'The Tenth Century in Byzantine–Western Relationships', in his *Medieval Germany and its Neighbours, 900–1250* (London, 1982), 116–17; Karl Leyser, *Rule and Conflict in an Early Medieval Society: Ottonian Saxony* (London, 1979), 88 and nn.

Ottonians began to advance similar claims and share an interest in the cult of the warrior saint, Maurice), and to Frankish recognition of those aspirations.[31]

Even had William drawn on an earlier source for information about the Frankish embassy to Æthelstan's court, he might well have embellished that tenth-century narrative in the light of his own knowledge about the development of the cult of Charlemagne since the tenth century.[32] In particular, one might question whether Hugh's gifts really included the holy lance. Leaving aside this passage in William of Malmesbury's history and the problems associated with dating any source on which it drew, the earliest text to associate Charlemagne with the lance with which the centurion had pierced Christ's side as he hung on the cross is the *Chanson de Roland*, *c.*1100 (and thus after the discovery of the holy lance-head at Antioch by soldiers of the First Crusade in 1098), the *Chanson* placed the tip of the lance in the Frankish king's hands as he fought the Saracens.[33] A chronicle from St Riquier completed in 1088 (which supposedly drew on an earlier ninth-century account), reported that Charlemagne's son, Louis the Pious had given the tip of the Passion lance to the monastery of St Riquier, whence it was taken for safe-keeping from Viking attack to the cathedral church of Sens, *c.*888.[34] Since the Robertian family from which Hugh came had links with the archbishops of Sens, they might plausibly have assisted the duke in locating Carolingian treasures to give away to a foreign power (something at which churches with more obvious pro-Carolingian sentiments would probably have baulked). Yet, although we may have a record here conveying in essence the same legend connecting the holy lance with the Carolingian house as that found in the *Chanson de Roland*, its preservation in an eleventh-century text does not enable us to argue with any more confidence that the story had emerged substantially earlier than this. Nor does William's presumed use of a tenth-century account of Æthelstan.

Intriguingly, in 926 just as Hugh's embassy conveyed these precious gifts to Æthelstan's court, the Saxon king, Henry the Fowler supposedly bought the holy lance from Rudolf of Burgundy, and acquired at the same time a

---

[31] Leyser, *Rule and Conflict*, 88. Maurice, a third-century Christian soldier, led the Theban legion fighting on the empire's behalf in Gaul; having refused the emperor Maximian's instruction to sacrifice to pagan gods before a battle, the Christian soldiers of the Theban legion were martyred.

[32] Full discussion of the problems associated with William's account lies in Appendix I.

[33] *Chanson de Roland*, Laisse 183, lines 2503–6; *The Song of Roland: An Analytical Edition*, ed. and trans. Gerard J. Brault, 2 vols (University Park, PA and London, 1978), ii, 152–3; Thomas S. Asbridge, 'The Holy Lance of Antioch: Power, Devotion and Memory on the First Crusade', *Reading Medieval Studies*, xxxiii (2007), 3–36, at 31, n. 2.

[34] *Hariulf, Chronique de l'abbaye de Saint-Riquier (Ve siècle–1104)*, ed. Ferdinand Lot (Paris, 1894), iii, 5 and iii, 20, pp. 100, 141–2; cf. p. xxviii and n. 1. Michael Wood, 'The Making of King Æthelstan's Empire: an English Charlemagne?', in *Ideal and Reality in Frankish and Anglo-Saxon Society*, ed. Patrick Wormald *et al.* (Oxford, 1983), 266, n. 80.

spear that had belonged to the Emperor Constantine, decorated with crosses made from holy nails from the Crucifixion (whereas, by William's account, Æthelstan had the emperor's sword, with a nail from the Passion embedded in its scabbard). Although only Liudprand of Cremona (writing before 972) told of Henry's purchase, plentiful other tenth-century evidence witnesses to the Ottonians' energetic promotion of the cult of the holy lance and that of St Maurice in Saxony.[35] The two stories only seem independent from one another if we can confidently assert that William had all this information from his tenth-century source; once that is in question, the foundations for his claim start to disintegrate. We might choose to decide that William used his own imagination and a degree of rhetorical licence when he included the holy lance in the list of wonderful gifts made by the non-Carolingian Duke Hugh to Æthelstan. Ottonian claims certainly appear the stronger, and the notion of a connection between the lance and Charlemagne seems not to have emerged in literary form until the second half of the eleventh century.[36] On the other hand, we should note the visual evidence for interest in relics of the Crucifixion, including the lance that pierced Christ's side, in Æthelstan's circle conveyed by two miniatures added in his lifetime to the manuscript known as the Æthelstan Psalter. Of continental origin (from the Liège area) this was in England in Æthelstan's reign when some Greek texts were added (above, Chapter 4), as well as four miniatures which together form a pictorial litany probably deriving from a Last Judgment. Two depict Christ in Majesty; in the first he sits enthroned with angels, patriarchs, prophets and apostles, the lance, cross and sponge prominently displayed beside him; in the second, where martyrs, confessors and virgins surround Christ, he uncovers his breast to reveal the wound made by Longinus's spear.[37] Since Dodwell has argued that this was the first time in Western art that Christ was associated with these two particular instruments of the Passion, their depiction by an artist working in Æthelstan's intellectual sphere seems, in the light of the gift of Hugh of the Franks, highly significant, even if we hesitate over William of Malmesbury's association of both these objects with Charlemagne.[38]

[35] Liudprand of Cremona, *Antapodosis*, iv. 25, trans. *Liudprand of Cremona, The Embassy to Constantinople and Other Writings*, ed. John Julius Norwich (London, 1993), 114–15, represents the sole source for Henry I's purchase of the holy lance from Rudolf; Leyser, *Rule and Conflict*, 88. Widukind of Corvey first mentioned the use of the holy lance in a military context: *Rerum gestarum Saxonicarum*, i, 25 and iii, 46, ed. H.-E. Lohmann, MGH, SRG 60 (Hanover, 1935), 38, 127–8.

[36] Such legends might have circulated orally, of course, but that cannot now be verified.

[37] BL, Cotton Galba A. xviii, fos 2v and 21r; see plates 12 and 13. C.R. Dodwell, *The Pictorial Arts of the West 800–1200* (New Haven and London, 1993), plate 77; J.J.G. Alexander, 'The Benedictional of St Æthelwold and Anglo-Saxon Illumination of the Reform Period', in *Tenth-Century Studies*, ed. David Parsons (London, 1975), 171–2; Wood, 'The Making', 267–8 and his plates IV and V. For a more cautious reading, noting that the miniatures could have predated Hugh's embassy, see Keynes, 'Books', 194–5.

[38] Dodwell, *Pictorial Arts*, 95–6.

More promising is William's mention of a *vexillum* of St Maurice that he alleged had formerly belonged to Charlemagne. St Maurice d'Agaune (the site of the saint's martyrdom with his 6,000 companions of the Theban legion in *c*.03) represented an important staging post on the journey across the Alps via the St Bernard Pass. Charlemagne may have stayed there on his way to Rome, and he sent his son Charles to meet Pope Leo III at St Maurice in 804 and escort him to the court at Quierzy.[39] Records of Charlemagne's gifts to the church there and of the relics of the martyr he supposedly acquired when visiting the church are not authentic. We may, however, have more confidence in the claims of the abbey church at St Riquier and the cathedral church at Sens to possess relics of St Maurice.[40] The emperor Charlemagne gave a collection of relics to Sens in 809 including some of St Maurice (and those of many other early Christian, Roman and Gallo-Roman saints).[41] Given the demonstrable interest in St Maurice's cult in ninth-century Frankia, the connections between Charlemagne and churches claiming to possess his relics, and between the Robertian family and Sens, we can more confidently imagine that Duke Hugh might have found something there associated with the early Christian martyr (and with the emperor Charles) and have decided to give that to Æthelstan. Whether that object was a banner or in fact another lance is less clear. William of Malmesbury's statement that it was with this *vexillum* that Charlemagne was wont to 'break and put to flight the enemy squadrons however fierce and close packed', suggests that he, at least, imagined something more substantial than a banner or flag.[42] The precious crown of solid gold decorated with gems could also have come from the cathedral treasury at Sens, having belonged to some earlier Carolingian king.[43] Hugh's motives

[39] Rosamond McKitterick, *Charlemagne: the Formation of a European Identity* (Cambridge, 2008), 52 and 292.

[40] Angilbert of St Riquier had a famous relic collection, and his church also received generous presents from Charlemagne; one of the chapels in the abbey church was dedicated to St Maurice, whose relics were carried in solemn procession annually on his feast-day, 22 September. Angilbert of St Riquier's *Libellus* (preserved in Hariulf's Chronicle) lists his church's Maurician relics: *Hariulf: Chronique*, ed. Lot, chs 8–10, pp. 61–70; McKitterick, *Charlemagne*, 327.

[41] An inventory of the cathedral's relics from 1192 records the gift in the time of Archbishop Magnus with an elaborate statement about that donation and the silver reliquary in which it was preserved, and a surviving ninth-century label once attached to some of the relics also notes the gift and dates it to 809. Laura H. Loomis, 'The Holy Relics of Charlemagne and King Athelstan: the Lances of Longinus and St. Mauricius', *Speculum*, xxv (1950), 444; McKitterick, *Charlemagne*, 327.

[42] Loomis, 'Holy Relics', 446 refers also to the fourteenth-century *Chronicon* of Henry Knighton, which associates William's gift story to Æthelstan with the romance of Guy of Warwick, in which his warrior hero goes out to fight on behalf of King Æthelstan armed with the sword of Constantine and the lance of St Maurice in his hand. Another late tradition has Æthelstan wearing one of Hugh's relics around his neck as he fought against the pagans at *Brunanburh*: *Eulogium Historiarum III*, ed. F.S. Haydon (Rolls Series 1863), 10–11; see Wood, 'The Making', 267.

[43] Wood, 'The Making', 266.

for sending objects with such overt Carolingian associations may reflect as much his antipathy to his own royal family as his admiration for Æthelstan. Yet his desire to forge a marriage alliance with the West Saxon house suggests an awareness of the potential benefits to him (and to his future children) of such a connection, one that gifts of such holy and imperial significance could only enhance.

Yet more valuable still, and capable of conveying yet more sacred power, the relics relating to the Crucifixion included in Hugh's gift flattered the English king and played even more directly to Æthelstan's known penchant for holy memorabilia. Not only did Constantine's sword have one of the nails from the cross fixed on its scabbard, over plates of gold, but Hugh also gave a relic of the cross itself, enclosed in crystal and a piece of the crown of thorns, similarly set. In 872 the Byzantine emperor Basil I sent letters and gifts to Louis the German, including a crystal of marvellous size decorated with gold and precious stones and quite a large piece of the salvation-bringing cross.[44] Could it have been this relic – passed into West Frankish hands by some other exchange of royal gifts – that Hugh sent to Æthelstan? Other features of Hugh's gift to Æthelstan have marked Byzantine features; Karl Leyser suggested that Hugh might deliberately have tried to imitate Greek practice in assembling this collection of precious items. Association with the Greek emperors would have added yet further to Æthelstan's perceived status and he showed himself far from unconscious of the potential implications of such comparisons, electing to be described in some of his charters as *basileus*, the title used of the Greek emperors.[45] Charlemagne had certainly seen his own imperial power as equivalent to that of the Byzantine emperors, even though it took twelve years from his coronation as emperor before Byzantine envoys came to his court and acclaimed him, calling him emperor and *basileus*.[46] Onyx chalices formed part of tenth-century Byzantine embassies to the West, perhaps inspiring Hugh to select from the Carolingian royal treasury an older, classical onyx vase carved with pastoral scenes; certainly this range of gifts resembles those described by Widukind in his accounts of embassies to Otto's court in Saxony.[47] While the cross relic might, therefore, have been Eastern in origin, it could have been engraved in western Europe. A Carolingian rock crystal engraved with the Crucifixion now in the British Museum might conceivably be the one Hugh gave Æthelstan, although nothing is known of its provenance before 1867.[48] Whatever their origins all these artefacts fulfilled a similar purpose for Hugh as he collected them in preparation for his suit for Æthelstan's half-sister's hand in marriage: they transferred to the West Saxon king (soon, Hugh

---

[44] *Annals of Fulda*, s.a. 872, trans. T. Reuter (Manchester, 1992) 67.

[45] Below, 213.

[46] McKitterick, *Charlemagne*, 114–18.

[47] Leyser, 'The Tenth Century', 42–3.

[48] Thomson, *Commentary*, 125; see G.A. Kornbluth, *Engraved Gems of the Carolingian Empire* (Philadelphia, PA 1995), 89–94, no. 14; plate 14.

hoped, to become his brother-in-law) some of the *virtus* and divine favour that Charlemagne and other Carolingian kings had enjoyed.[49] Æthelstan and his court, we may imagine, saw them in a similar light. One of the panegyric poems written in Æthelstan's honour recast verse originally dedicated to Charlemagne, suggesting that contemporaries did indeed associate this king directly with the great Frankish emperor.[50] According to William, Æthelstan reciprocated by making Hugh gifts of equivalent status and by agreeing to the contracting of the marriage.[51]

ÆTHELSTAN'S RELIC DONATIONS

Several English monasteries claimed to own relics identifiable with items from Hugh's gift; indeed the sacred items in the collection had a profound impact on later medieval literature, which witnesses to considerable competition between different religious houses for possession of these marvellous objects.[52] We should not doubt that Æthelstan did distribute many of the sacred objects in his own possession to the churches and monasteries in his realm, nor that he expected to gain spiritual benefit from such largesse. Yet that he had a reputation for such generosity meant that later generations of monks frequently tried to enhance the virtue of their own relic collections by connecting them with the name of this exceptionally pious king.

According to William of Malmesbury, the secular objects acquired from the Franks Æthelstan preserved for his successors on the throne, but the pieces of the cross and the crown of thorns the king gave to Malmesbury, where their presence continued to bolster the abbey in his own day.[53] However, the church at Milton also claimed to have acquired a piece of the true cross from Æthelstan, together with the Breton relics discussed earlier.[54] Exeter Cathedral, which purported to own one third of all of the king's relic collection, argued in an eleventh-century Old English list of the cathedral's relics that they had possession of a piece of the true cross, as well as a piece of the lance with which our Lord's holy side was opened on the cross, and a relic of St Maurice, though not his banner.[55] Slightly

[49] Leyser, 'The Tenth Century', 42; D.R. Rollason, *Saints and Relics in Anglo-Saxon England* (Oxford, 1989), 160–2.

[50] The poem, *Carta dirige gressus* is discussed above, 112; cf. Loomis, 'Holy Relics', 440; Wood, 'The Making'.

[51] *GR*, ii, 135, pp. 220–1.

[52] Laura H. Loomis, 'The Athelstan Gift Story: its Influence on English Chronicles and Carolingian Romances', *Proceedings of the Modern Language Association*, lxvii (1952), 521–37.

[53] *GR*, ii, 135, pp. 220–1.

[54] *TSD*, 74; W. Dugdale, *Monasticon Anglicanum* (1655–73; new edn by J. Caley, *et al.*, 6 vols in 8, London, 1817–30), ii, 349–50.

[55] Old English relic-list in Oxford, Bodleian Library MS. Auct D. 2. 16; fos 8r–14r: §5 (Æthelstan's gift of one third of his relics); §7 (holy cross); §12 (lance); §73 (St Maurice), ed. Patrick Conner, *Anglo-Saxon Exeter: a Tenth-Century Cultural History* (Woodbridge, 1993), 177–83.

later Latin versions of this list refer to a sword as well as to the lance, which might conceivably corroborate William of Malmesbury's account (or, alternatively, have inspired him to embellish his source by including those items in his own narrative).[56]

Abingdon's monks did not miss out either on the possibilities presented by Æthelstan's posthumous reputation for generosity with his relics: William had said that Æthelstan received Hugh's embassy at Abingdon, so the monks retold the story in their abbey's history: this was a full meeting of the king's court, which took place at Easter and was attended by his earls and barons, in the time of Abbot Godescealc;[57] messengers of the 'king' of France, Hugh surnamed Capet, came, offering the king gifts made of precious metals and others more valuable than gold and silver; that is, precious relics to be treated with all reverence and afterwards to be venerated, specifically part of a thorn of the crown and part of a nail of the Lord, and the standard of St Maurice, the most glorious martyr and leader of the Theban legion, with a precious finger of St Denis the martyr. King Æthelstan gave Abingdon all these relics, 'concealed with all honour in a silvery reliquary', and they continue to protect the house, the abbey's thirteenth-century chronicler argued.[58] An early twelfth-century Abingdon relic-list laid claim to the holy nail and the finger of St Denis but not to the rest of these items, suggesting that although the house chronicler's account may partly reflect twelfth-century relic holdings, it was probably also influenced, and thus enhanced, by the much fuller narrative provided by William of Malmesbury.[59]

In Winchester, interest in the cult of St Maurice in the later pre-Conquest period is shown by the dedication of a church north of the New Minster and close to the royal palace to the martyred leader of the Theban legion.[60] This need not have any connection with Hugh's supposed gift to Æthelstan and indeed, given what I have already argued about Æthelstan's ambivalent relations with the church in Winchester, we might not expect Æthelstan to have donated much of his collection to any of the Winchester houses. Yet, the New Minster claimed to have acquired at least some of the king's treasures, for the *Liber vitae* includes one list of relics 'kept in the

[56] For William's possible dependence on the Exeter lists, see below; Latin list from the Leofric Missal: Bodleian Library Bodley 579, fo. 6rv: §8 'De mucrone et de lancea unde latus Domini fuit apertum', ed. Conner, *Anglo-Saxon Exeter*, 193. Rollason, *Saints*, 161.

[57] *TSD*, 36; S.E. Kelly, *Charters of Abingdon*, 2 vols (Oxford, 2000–1), i, 109.

[58] *Historia ecclesiae Abbendonensis*, MS B, §62, ed. Hudson, i, 282–3 and see discussion ibid., i, clxxiii–clxxiv. See also *TSD*, 80.

[59] See also I.G. Thomas, 'The Cult of Saints' Relics in Medieval England', PhD thesis, University of London, 1974, 153–4.

[60] Martin Biddle *et al.*, *Winchester in the Early Middle Ages: an Edition and Discussion of the Winton Domesday* (Oxford, 1976), 316, 329n and 330; in the early eleventh century, monks' funeral processions visited the church of St Maurice: Maurice Keene with Alexander R. Rumble, *Survey of Medieval Winchester* (Oxford, 1985), 540; also C.H. Turner, 'The Churches of Winchester in the Eleventh Century', *Journal of Theological Studies*, xvii (1916), 65–8.

shrine made by Ælfwold the *cyricweard* (sacristan)', which begins with an item: 'all the relics which were in King Æthelstan's treasury and the bones of St Sebastian'. In addition, a thirteenth-century collection of Winchester annals alleged under the year 924 that Æthelstan had given the head of St Justus the martyr to the Old Minster.[61] One portion of the wood of the cross supposedly made its way from Æthelstan to Westminster and another piece to Glastonbury.[62] Clearly, medieval English houses competed to advance on behalf of their own communities a title to these wondrous objects brought to England by the duke of the Franks. None of these state-ments other than portions of that in the Exeter relic-list pre-date William's narrative in his *Gesta regum*, however, which makes Exeter's claim to part of the holy lance (and, associated with that, a sword) particularly interesting.

Æthelstan's gift of relics to Exeter[63]

Although I cast doubt earlier on William of Malmesbury's account of Æthelstan's 'conquest' of Exeter and expulsion of the Cornish from the town in 927 (above, Chapter 6), Æthelstan certainly did visit Exeter on more than one occasion, issuing charters there in 928 and 932, and convening there – perhaps at Christmas in 931 – the council from whose discussions emerged the law code conventionally numbered *V Æthelstan*.[64] Eleventh-century relic-lists from the cathedral church at Exeter, as we saw, provide important additional – and independent – testimony about the king's concern for the minster church in the city. A church existed in Exeter before Æthelstan's time, for King Alfred gave it to Asser, with all its jurisdiction in the Saxon land and in Cornwall; even if Æthelstan did not (as the Old English relic-list claimed) found the minster, he may have arranged for it to be rebuilt, or possibly for the erection of another church on the site of the earliest foundation.[65] None of the surviving charters in Æthelstan's name in Exeter's favour are genuine but the late texts in his

[61] Keynes, *Liber Vitae*, 106 (§ xxii); Walter de Gray Birch, *Liber Vitae: Register and Martyrology of New Minster and Hyde Abbey, Winchester* (London and Winchester, 1892), lxv, 162–3; *TSD*, 78–9; Rollason, 'Relic-Cults', 93. 'Annales monasterii de Wintonia (AD 519–1277)', *s.a.* 924, ed. H.R. Luard, *Annales Monastici*, 5 vols (Rolls series, 1864–9), ii, 10; *TSD*, 78.

[62] William of Malmesbury, *De antiquitate*, ed. J. Scott *The Early History of Glastonbury* (Woodbridge, 1981), 114–15; John of Glastonbury, *Chronicon*, ed. J. Carley, *The Chronicle of Glastonbury Abbey* (Woodbridge, 1985), 138–9.

[63] C. Henderson and P. T. Bidwell, 'The Saxon Minster at Exeter', in *The Early Church in Western Britain and Ireland*, ed. S.M. Pearce (Oxford, 1982), 145–75; J.P. Allan, C.G. Henderson and R.A. Higham, 'Saxon Exeter', in *Anglo-Saxon Towns in Southern England*, ed. J. Haslam (Chichester, 1984), 385–414. F.M. Rose-Troup, 'The Ancient Monastery of St Mary and St Peter at Exeter, 680–1050', *Report & Transactions of the Devonshire Association for the Advancement of Science, Literature and Art*, lxiii (1931), 179–220, at 189–93.

[64] Compare Appendix II, 'When King Æthelstan was where'; S 399–400 and S 418a.

[65] Asser, ch. 81; Nicholas Orme, *Exeter Cathedral: the First Thousand Years, 400–1400* (Exeter, 2009), 8.

name may preserve elements of original donations from him to the minster;[66] Exeter lost its early documents in a fire in the minster's archive after a Viking attack on the town in 1003 and Bishop Leofric may rightly have claimed that Æthelstan had donated a number of the church's Devon estates, even if he had to fabricate the evidence to prove it.[67] Exeter's claim to have benefited substantially – more indeed than any other church – from generous donation of relics from Æthelstan's collection does not, in this context, seem wholly implausible.

Exeter had constructed four lists of its relics before the end of the twelfth century, the earliest of which – written in Old English and copied on a gathering inserted near the front of a tenth-century gospel book from Landévennec in Brittany – probably dates either from the first half or from the middle of the eleventh century.[68] Among the relics it lists are some of saints whose lives post-dated King Æthelstan: Ælfgifu, wife of King Edmund, who died in 944; Oda, archbishop of Canterbury, who died in 958; and Edward the Martyr, who died in 978, but his cult was instituted only in 1008, so the list presumably post-dates that time.[69] Not all of the relics recorded in this list can, therefore, have come from Æthelstan's donation, but that need not cause us to doubt its central contention that the core of Exeter's relic collection came directly to the minster in Exeter from King Æthelstan.

More than an inventory of sacred objects to which the church laid claim, the Old English list takes the form of a sermon, with a hortatory style indicating that it was crafted to be read aloud, perhaps during a mass or procession for the feast of the relics at Exeter. Much more effectively than a mere list of the saints whose remains the church could show to visiting pilgrims, this text publicized the nature, extent and spiritual importance of Exeter's relic collection, with brief but emotionally intense summaries of individual saints' passions interspersed between the catalogues of names.[70] A prologue set the scene, attributing lofty motives to the king in making such a donation:

> At this place is set out in this document what concerns the holy relics which Æthelstan the honourable king gave to the minster of St Mary & St Peter at Exeter for God's praise, for the deliverance of his own soul

[66] Pierre Chaplais, 'The Authenticity of the Royal Anglo-Saxon Diplomas of Exeter', *BIHR*, xxxix (1966), 1–8.

[67] Orme, *Exeter Cathedral*, 9–10.

[68] Oxford, Bodleian MS Auct D. 2. 16; fos 8r–14r, copied in a hand datable to the second half of the eleventh century; N.R. Ker, *Catalogue of Manuscripts containing Anglo-Saxon* (Oxford, 1990), 351, no. 291; for the date see Conner, *Anglo-Saxon Exeter*, 171–5. The first gathering of the manuscript (fos 1–7) contains an inventory of the lands and books which Bishop Leofric (1050–72) gave to Exeter copied in a different hand of similar date; its opening deliberately echoes the wording of the Old English relic-list.

[69] Conner, *Anglo-Saxon Exeter*, 173.

[70] Ibid., 175–6.

and for the eternal salvation of all those who seek out and worship the holy place. Certainly it was the same King Æthelstan, when he had succeeded to kingship after his father Edward and through God's grace ruled all of England alone which before him many kings held among themselves, who then came on one occasion here to Exeter . . . and he began to meditate and to consider how best to use his royal treasury to further praise to God and to himself, and to the everlasting profit of his people.[71]

Inspired with the thought that perishable, earthly treasures might bring him imperishable, heavenly rewards, the king 'sent honest, discerning men over the sea', using his treasures as they travelled to buy 'the greatest of all relic collections, gathered far and wide from every place' and bringing it to the king. Then 'he commanded that here in Exeter – here where God had sent him the enlightening idea – a minster ought to be erected' to the honour of God, the Virgin Mary and St Peter; and he gave twenty-six manors for the support of the minster; 'and he had one third of the aforementioned collection of relics bestowed for the eternal deliverance of his soul, and as a help to all who seek out and faithfully worship the holy place where the relic-collection is kept'. William of Malmesbury also mentioned Æthelstan's dream-given inspiration to collect continental relics, connecting that *somnium* with his decision to use the treasure accumulated but left untouched by his father for the purchase of relics of the saints.[72] Since William had by his own account visited Exeter when looking for material about Æthelstan, he could of course have taken this idea directly from the Old English relic-list. The prologue concludes (§6) with a summary of what is to follow, showing the text's oral character once more:

Now we shall tell you without any deceit what the relics are which are here in this holy minster, and tell you this document straight away, which reveals without any deception what each one of the relics is.[73]

Thereafter, the text moves into catalogue mode, listing the relics the church claimed.[74] The oldest list of the church's collection, preserved in the Leofric Missal, also has something to say about the king as donor of the collection: 'These are the names of the holy relics which are kept at Exeter in the minster of St Mary and St Peter the Apostle, the largest part of which the most glorious and victorious King Æthelstan, that is to say the patron of the place, gave to it.' Thus, whereas the Old English text explicitly stated

[71] Ibid., 176–7.

[72] *GR*, ii, 140, pp. 228–9.

[73] Conner, *Anglo-Saxon Exeter*, 176–7.

[74] The relics ranged from those associated with the life and Passion of Christ, with other New Testament figures, to early church martyrs and confessors and then saints and holy men and a few women from the early medieval period.

that the entire collection had come from Æthelstan, the author of this version made a more modest, and perhaps more accurate claim.[75] Some relics listed in the Old English list do not appear in the Leofric Missal, possibly because the community had lost them in the time that elapsed between the creation of the two lists. The claim that together with a portion of the lance that had pierced Christ's side there was a sword, however, is new to the Leofric Missal. We might want to be cautious before making too much of this; the lance with which Christ's side was pierced (an object, after all, to which the Gospel of John testified)[76] represented as valuable a relic to devout collectors as did pieces of the infant Jesus's manger, stone from the mountain where he fasted, or bits of the table where the apostles ate the Last Supper with him, all of which Exeter also said it owned. No version of the list associates the spear with Charlemagne, or the sword with Constantine. That William of Malmesbury knew at least one version of these relic-lists seems likely; that recollection of Exeter's claim to these sacred objects inspired him to improve with additional detail a tenth-century account of Hugh of the Franks's gifts in order to take account of more recent legends connecting these with the cult of the great emperor, Charlemagne is not impossible. Exeter's relic-lists should not cause us to modify the conclusion reached earlier that William probably invented the idea that Hugh gave Æthelstan the holy lance with which Charles the Great had fought the Saracens. Together, lists of the Exeter relic collection witness to the generosity of King Æthelstan and to his great wealth, power and piety and to the extent of his continental connections, sufficient that he could assemble spiritual treasures of substantial worth from all over Christendom, not just from Britain and Britain across the sea.[77]

ÆTHELSTAN AND THE CULT OF ENGLISH SAINTS

Æthelstan's collection and acquisition of relics from the continent cast important light on his interest in sacred objects associated with Christ himself and the first witnesses to the faith in the Early Church, but we should not forget the importance he placed on native saints, something that we can trace back to his youth in Mercia. Roger of Wendover, writing in St Albans in the thirteenth century, recorded in his history under the year 929, 'in this year King Æthelstan decided to search out the relics of the saints of his kingdom in order to pray for God's grace'.[78] One might

[75] Conner, *Anglo-Saxon Exeter*, 190; Nicholas Orchard, ed., *The Leofric Missal*, 2 vols (London, 2002), ii, 8 and see i, 210.

[76] John, 19: 34.

[77] Rollason, 'Relic-Cults', 93.

[78] Roger of Wendover, *Flores historiarum*, s.a. 929, ed. H.O. Coxe, 5 vols (London, 1841–4), i, 387; Michael Wood, ' "Stand Strong against the Monsters": Kingship and Learning in the Empire of Æthelstan', in *Lay Intellectuals in the Carolingian World*, ed. Patrick Wormald and Janet L. Nelson (Cambridge, 2007), 202.

associate this statement with the telling of stories about King Edmund of
East Anglia at Æthelstan's court. In his *Passion of St Edmund*, written for the
monks of Ramsey in the early 980s, Abbo claimed that Dunstan, later
archbishop of Canterbury but then a young monk in Æthelstan's
entourage, had heard an eyewitness account of Edmund's death in 869, as
recounted to Æthelstan and his companions by King Edmund's armour-
bearer.[79] An historian at the abbey of Bury St Edmunds writing *c*.1100
argued that signs of the martyr king's sanctity had been manifest in King
Æthelstan's reign, when a group of *clerici* had tended his tomb (and
witnessed his miracles) at Bury.[80] We might imagine that Æthelstan took
some interest in this cult, but no concrete evidence of such concern
survives beyond the sources just mentioned. He did not translate the
saint's body from its original resting-place to Bury; no charter to the abbey
in Æthelstan's name survives, nor did later generations of monks there
apparently think it worth either constructing one in his name or including
him in one of their lists of benefactors. His brother Edmund can more
reliably be connected with his namesake's cult.[81] The king did apparently
imagine he had a direct blood link with another significant early English
saint, Aldhelm of Malmesbury. If, however, we extend our gaze firmly
outside Wessex, not just east but also northwards, then we can, as Michael
Wood has argued, discern a policy of co-opting important regional saints
into national saints, a search for new holy patrons to protect a newly
imagined realm.[82]

Oswald

Even before his accession, Æthelstan had participated in his aunt and
uncle's promotion of the cult of the seventh-century Northumbrian saint-
king Oswald at Gloucester. He continued to support that cult in maturity,
motivated perhaps less by immediate family loyalty to a saint whom his aunt
had revered than by the fact that he believed himself related to Oswald.

Gloucester had from the 670s onwards housed a well endowed double
minster, dedicated to St Peter and closely connected with the Mercian
royal family. The town's association with the local ruling power persisted
into the later ninth century, when the shire had come under the direct rule

[79] Abbo, *Passio*, 67; despite the substantial problems inherent in this account, it may
testify to an interest in this cult at Æthelstan's court.

[80] Hermann, *De miraculis sancti Eadmundi*, ed. Thomas Arnold, *Memorials of St Edmund's
Abbey*, 3 vols, Rolls Series 96 (London, 1890–6) i, 29–30; see Susan Ridyard, *The Royal Saints
of Anglo-Saxon England* (Cambridge, 1988), 213 and 222, n. 45. For Edmund's charter to Bury,
see S 507; Kathryn A. Lowe and Sarah Foot, *The Anglo-Saxon Charters of Bury St Edmunds
Abbey in Suffolk* (forthcoming), no. 2.

[81] *Contra* V.H. Galbraith, 'The East Anglian See and the Abbey of Bury St Edmunds',
EHR, xl (1925), 223, n. 2.

[82] Wood, ' "Stand Strong" ', 202.

of Ealdorman Æthelred and his wife, Æthelflæd, King Alfred's daughter. By 896 there was a royal palace at Gloucester, for a council met there in that year; the city was refortified and the street plan within the walls reordered around the year 900. Æthelred and Æthelflæd also founded a second minster in the town, which they dedicated at first, like the old minster, to St Peter. There they constructed a large crypt at the east end to house the shrine of a saint and their own tombs, indicating clearly that this should be seen as one of the premier ecclesiastical establishments at the heart of their Mercian realm.[83] Following a military expedition into Danish territory in 909 (possibly, as the West Saxon version of the Chronicle suggested, one masterminded by Edward the Elder, Æthelflæd's brother, but more plausibly an entirely Mercian enterprise), the bones of the martyred Northumbrian seventh-century king Oswald were translated from Bardney in Lincolnshire to the new minster at Gloucester.[84] That church was then rededicated to the northern saint.

Oswald's sanctity and his posthumous reputation as *christianissimus rex*, one of the great heroes of Bede's *Ecclesiastical History*, rested largely on the manner of his death in battle against the pagan Mercian king, Penda, at *Maserfelth* in 642.[85] Dismembered in order that the head, arms and hands might be displayed on stakes, Oswald's body had originally been buried in different places. Oswiu (Oswald's brother and successor) took the head, hands and arms back to Northumbria and interred his head at the monastery at Lindisfarne which Oswald had founded and where the remains of St Cuthbert also rested. When that community left their island home through pressure of Danish raiding in the 870s, they put Oswald's head into Cuthbert's coffin, and carried it with them in their wanderings. Between 675 and 679, Oswald's niece Osthryth, wife of the then Mercian king Æthelred, took the main portion of the body from its original resting-place to the royal monastery at Bardney in Lincolnshire.[86] Despite his Northumbrian origins (and the original antipathy of the Bardney monks to a foreign oppressor), subsequent Mercian kings actively promoted Oswald's cult, among them Offa, who adorned his shrine with 'silver, gold, gems and much finery'.[87] According to William of Malmesbury, Æthelred and Æthelflæd moved the relics because the whole

[83] Alan Thacker, 'Membra disjecta: the Division of the Body and the Diffusion of the Cult', in *Oswald: Northumbrian King to European Saint*, ed. Clare Stancliffe and Eric Cambridge (Stamford, 1995), 120. Also Alan T. Thacker, 'Chester and Gloucester: Early Ecclesiastical Organization in Two Mercian Burhs', *Northern History*, xviii (1982), 207. William of Malmesbury reported that Æthelred and Æthelflæd were buried at this new minster in Gloucester (*GP*, iv, 155, pp. 446–9); but the Mercian Register suggested their bodies rested at the old St Peter's: MR *s.a.* 918.

[84] ASC 909; MR 909; *GR*, i, 49, pp. 72–5.

[85] *HE*, iii, 9, pp. 240–3.

[86] *HE*, iii, 11, pp. 246–7.

[87] Alcuin, *The Bishops, Kings, and Saints of York*, ed. and trans. P. Godman (Oxford 1982), lines 388–91, pp. 34–5.

of Mercia was then under their control; their promotion of a saint so inti-
mately associated with previous rulers of Mercia made a clear statement
about their own ambitions within the remnant of that now divided
realm.[88]

The young Æthelstan probably attended the ceremonial reburial of the
Northumbrian king's remains in 909, and he demonstrated a continuing
interest in Oswald's cult into adulthood, perhaps moved in part by the
wonders that God often showed at Gloucester through the young Oswald's
virtue, as Ælfric recorded later in his Old English life of the saint.[89] A
charter supposedly produced in the year of Æthelstan's consecration as
king (925), but now surviving only in a transcript from York's archives
dating from 1304 and the reign of Edward I, asserts that Æthelstan gave
privileges to the church of St Oswald's, Gloucester, according to an agreement he had reached with his uncle and in order to fulfil his father's wishes:

> . . . the same king Æthelstan in the first year of his consecration,
> according to a pact of paternal piety which formerly he pledged with
> Æthelred, ealdorman (*primicerius*) of the people of the Mercians, simi-
> larly sedulously promoting the paternal wishes of king Edward, with
> the full agreement and permission of his nobles gave with eternal
> liberty and removed from all secular servitude and delivered to the serv-
> ices of Almighty God with clergy dedicated to God the minster called
> New, where the mortal remains of the holy body of the blessed martyr
> Oswald rest in felicity and that that aforesaid minster was founded and
> built by Æthelred outside the old wall of the town of Gloucester and
> circumscribed with very definite boundaries . . .[90]

So soon after his father's death, Æthelstan may well have acted as much
out of piety and devotion to his memory (and to that of his uncle, longer
dead) as from his commitment to promote the cult of Oswald. Yet in fact
we have other grounds for thinking that this particular saint mattered
considerably to Æthelstan personally, and that more than filial obligation
led him to act.

---

[88] *GP*, iv, 155, pp. 446–7; Thacker, 'Membra disjecta', 120; Thacker, 'Chester and
Gloucester', 209. David R. Rollason, *Saints and Relics in Anglo-Saxon England* (Oxford, 1989),
154.

[89] *Ælfric's Lives of the Saints*, ed. W. Skeat, EETS, o.s. 114 (London, 1900), no. 26, p. 142;
Thacker, 'Membra disjecta', 121.

[90] The text is printed in G.O. Sayles, *England Court of King's Bench, Select Cases in the Court
of King's Bench under Edward 1, III*, Seldon Society Publications, 58 (London, 1939), 141, and
trans. Michael Hare, 'The Documentary Evidence for the History of St. Oswald's,
Gloucester to 1086 AD', in *The Golden Minster: The Anglo-Saxon Minster and Later Medieval Priory
of St. Oswald at Gloucester*, ed. Carolyn Heighway and Richard Bryant, CBA Research
Report 117 (York, 1999), 43, n. 21. Hare has argued (36–7) that the text's circumstantial
detail and elaborate invocation of both Æthelstan's father and his uncle support a
presumption in favour of the text's essential authenticity. Also discussed above, 34.

We see further evidence for Æthelstan's promotion of the cult of Oswald in the context of his half-sister Eadgyth's marriage to Otto of Saxony in 929 or 930. Describing the making of the match and attesting to the nobility of Eadgyth's birth, Hrotsvitha of Gandersheim declared in her *Gesta Ottonis* that Eadgyth was 'born of the blessed lineage of King Oswald, whose praise the world sings because he yielded himself to death for the sake of Christ's name'. For a people only recently Christianized (the Saxons had received the faith no more than 130 years earlier) association with an historic Anglo-Saxon Christian king conferred obvious prestige.[91] Æthelstan himself may well have promulgated this dynastically convenient fiction, given his existing interest in the saint. But fiction it was, for no direct evidence attests to a blood tie between Oswald of Northumbria and the West Saxon royal line. Oswald did make an alliance with a king of Wessex *c.*635 when he acted as godfather to the first Christian West Saxon king, Cynegils, on his baptism and then took Cynegils's daughter (named in a twelfth-century source as Cyneburg) as his wife.[92] Yet, since Edward the Elder and his children claimed descent via Ecgberht from a different branch of the West Saxon royal family from Cynegils's, and given that Oswald's line died out after the death without issue of his son Oethelwald, any claim for association between the West Saxon royal family and the Northumbrian house of Bernicia rested only on the fact of Oswald's and Cynegils's marriage alliance. Even so, that alone apparently sufficed for Æthelstan's branch of the West Saxon house to claim kinship with the Northumbrian royal saint and thus to underpin Æthelstan's and his half-sister's promotion of St Oswald's cult.[93] The placing of Cynegils's name at the head of a tenth-century list of the kings of the West Saxons testifies to the significance of Cynegils's memory to the rulers of Wessex. This list was compiled at the New Minster in Winchester and preserved in its *Liber vitae*; it gave Edward the Elder a prominent place.[94] All Edward's children, not just those who ruled after him, could have benefited from the supposed association between their father's kingly predecessor Cynegils and the illustrious royal saint Oswald, accruing some of his *virtus* to themselves and to their wider kin. Certainly it did Eadgyth

---

[91] Hrotsvitha, *Gesta Ottonis*, lines 95–8, ed. W. Berschin, *Hrotsvit Opera Omnia* (Munich and Leipzig, 2001), 279. Dagmar Ó Riain-Raedel, 'Edith, Judith, Matilda: the Role of Royal Ladies in the Propagation of the Continental Cult', in *Oswald: Northumbrian King to European Saint*, ed. Clare Stancliffe and Eric Cambridge (Stamford, 1995), 212–15; Patrick Corbet, *Les Saints ottoniens : sainteté dynastique, sainteté royale et sainteté féminine autour de l'an Mil* (Sigmaringen, 1986), 46–7 and 111–14. This marriage was discussed in greater detail above, 48–52.

[92] *HE*, iii, 7, pp. 232–3.

[93] A useful genealogy of West Saxon rulers which shows the different branches of the line very clearly appears in Barbara Yorke, *Kings and Kingdoms of Early Anglo-Saxon England* (London, 1990), 134, table 16. See also Elisabeth van Houts, 'Women and the Writing of History in the Early Middle Ages', *EME*, i (1992), 57.

[94] Jan Gerchow, *Die Gedenküberlieferung der Angelsachsen: mit einem Katalog der libri vitae und Necrologien* (Berlin, 1988), 320–1. Keynes, *Liber Vitae*, 83.

no harm with her Saxon in-laws to promote a link with Oswald, whose cult also thrived on the continent.[95]

Cuthbert

St Cuthbert stands apart as the saint above all others with whose cult King Æthelstan had the closest association. Mention of the two names together instantly conjures an image of the one surviving manuscript portrait of the king, the frontispiece to the manuscript of Bede's Lives of St Cuthbert which we examined closely in Chapter 4 and which Æthelstan gave to the saint's community, then at Chester-le-Street.[96] The image of the crowned king bowing before the saint connects the past life and deeds of the seventh-century saint (recorded in the pages of the open book in the king's hands) with the present time of the picture's composition, when a West Saxon king has extended his direct authority over the lands where St Cuthbert once lived, preached and prayed. Æthelstan's cultivation of Cuthbert's memory cannot have lacked political overtones, given the advantages to the promotion of his claims to *imperium* over all Britain that would accrue from the support of the great patron of the north, yet we should avoid any temptation to advance too cynical or instrumental an interpretation of the king's behaviour. As well as Bede's prose and verse lives of St Cuthbert, this volume included a rhyming office for St Cuthbert, a hymn in his praise and a mass setting, all presumably intended for use in the royal chapel, which demonstrate that Cuthbert's cult already flourished in the south of England as well as in the saint's native Northumbria.[97] That Æthelstan believed that the saint could bring him material as well as spiritual benefits need not diminish our presumption that he uttered prayer and attended masses and offices in the saint's honour with genuine, heartfelt conviction.

West Saxon awareness of the possible benefits of the cult of St Cuthbert went back to Æthelstan's grandfather King Alfred, according to the mid-eleventh-century *Historia de sancto Cuthberto*, produced by the saint's community, then exiled from their island home on Lindisfarne because of the danger of Viking attack. Cuthbert had appeared to Alfred in a dream before the battle of Edington (erroneously identified as at *Assandune*) and

---

[95] The feast of his martyrdom, 5 August, was recorded in numerous calendars including a sacramentary from Essen, where later in the tenth century Edith's granddaughter Matilda was abbess; see Leyser, 'The Ottonians', 78–9; Peter Clemoes, *The Cult of St Oswald on the Continent*, Jarrow Lecture 1983 (Jarrow, 1984); Ó Riain-Raedel, 'Edith', 214–15.

[96] Cambridge, Corpus Christi College MS 183, fo. IV; Catherine E. Karkov, *The Ruler Portraits of Anglo-Saxon England* (Woodbridge, 2004), 55–60. See plate 1.

[97] Christopher Hohler, 'The Icononography', in *The Relics of St Cuthbert*, ed. C.F. Battiscombe (Oxford, 1956), 396–408; David Rollason, 'St Cuthbert and Wessex: the Evidence of Cambridge, Corpus Christi College MS 183', in *St Cuthbert his Cult and his Community to AD 1200*, ed. Gerald Bonner *et al.* (Woodbridge, 1989), 414; Thacker, 'Dynastic Monasteries', 255.

foretold not just his own imminent victory over the Danes, but also Edward's and Æthelstan's future military successes and the latter's hegemony over the island of Britain: 'Afterwards be joyful and strong without fear, since God has delivered your enemies into your hands, and likewise all this land, and established hereditary rule for you and your sons and the sons of your sons. Be faithful to me and to my people, for all Albion has been given to you and your sons. Be just, for you are chosen King of all Britain.'[98] Alfred repaid his debt to the saint at the end of his life by ordering his son Edward to give two armlets and a gold thurible to the saint and always to devote himself to his cult.[99] In his own last days, the aged King Edward did likewise, according to the *Historia*, which offers an account that fits ill with what we know otherwise about Edward's plans for the succession, perhaps reflecting both the geographical and chronological distance of its author from the West Saxon court in the early 920s:

> At that time King Edward, full of days and worn down by ripe old age, summoned his son Æthelstan, handed his kingdom over to him, and diligently instructed him to love St Cuthbert and honour him above all saints, revealing to him how he had mercifully succoured his father King Alfred in poverty and exile and how he had boldly aided him against all enemies, and in what way he had always very clearly come most promptly as his continual helper whenever there was need.[100]

For the monks of St Cuthbert, family loyalty thus played as important a role in inspiring Æthelstan to visit the shrine of the saint at Chester-le-Street in 934 as did his own pious motives: 'Therefore [i.e. in direct response to Edward's deathbed admonition], while King Æthelstan was leading a great army from the south to the northern region of Britain, taking it to Scotland, he made a diversion to the church of St Cuthbert and gave royal gifts to him, and then composed [a] signed testament and placed it at St Cuthbert's head.'[101] Since this passage implies that the saint's coffin was opened in Æthelstan's presence (for him to deposit the *testamentum*), his decision to stop at Chester-le-Street on his way north may have arisen in part from his knowledge that the head of King Oswald lay in St Cuthbert's coffin. Perhaps, given his former loyalties, Æthelstan wanted to see that relic more than to admire Cuthbert's incorrupt body.

Æthelstan's devotion to the cult of this all-powerful northern saint found expression in his visit to his shrine, where he had sight of the opened coffin, and in his substantial donation of books, liturgical and secular objects (including some money), and land, all of which were itemized in

[98] *HSC*, ch. 16, pp. 54–7. Thacker, 'Dynastic Monasteries', 255.

[99] *HSC*, ch. 19, pp. 58–9.

[100] *HSC*, ch. 25, pp. 64–5.

[101] *HSC*, ch. 26, pp. 64–5. For discussion of the background to the Scottish expedition see above, 164–7.

the testament of St Cuthbert preserved in the *Historia de sancto Cuthberto*.[102] In the event of his death on the Scottish expedition, the *Historia* alleged, he instructed his brother Edmund, who seems to have accompanied him on this northbound trip, to bring his body to St Cuthbert's shrine for burial.[103]

Interestingly, the king apparently made no attempt to acquire any of Cuthbert's relics to add to his own collection; nothing associated with Cuthbert appears in any version of the Exeter relic-list, for example. Perhaps he considered the saint's power would prove most efficacious if his body remained intact in its wooden coffin and any sacred objects associated with him stayed near his shrine. There Cuthbert's devoted congregation offered fitting praise, night and day, for the souls of all people, but especially – the king must have hoped – for the success of Æthelstan in life and the benefit of his soul in death. If Æthelstan had felt at all tempted to reunite Oswald's head with the rest of his remains now once again gloriously interred at Gloucester, he contrived to resist such a move. In fact, we might go so far as to argue that the king generally treated native saints differently from the remains of holy men and women who had lived and died outside England; he does not seem to have tried to augment his own collection, or those of churches within Wessex or Mercia, with the remains of earlier Anglo-Saxon saints. Maybe he believed that their *virtus* would work most effectively on behalf of the nation as a whole if their cults continued at the places where they had prayed and witnessed to the Gospel in their own lifetimes. Deracinating the remains of biblical or continental saints and adding them to his private collection manifestly caused the king fewer scruples.

No other early English king showed so consistent and devoted an interest in the cult of the sacred as Æthelstan; his name could add a veneer of verisimilitude to even the most far-fetched descriptions of a church's relic collection. A passion for the cults of the dead manifested by Æthelstan in his youth (something perhaps fostered by his uncle and aunt in Mercia) remained central to his articulation of his faith throughout his life and, if we may believe William of Malmesbury here, was remembered at his death in the organization and choreography of his funeral in the autumn of 939.

Tenth-century comments after King Æthelstan's demise illustrate how greatly his contemporaries honoured his achievements. Noting that Æthelstan died 'an untroubled death', one Irish annalist described the English king as the 'pillar of the dignity of the western world'.[104] From the perspective of the early eleventh century in England, Æthelstan's achievements and reputation seemed equally noteworthy. Ælfric, monk of Cerne

---

[102] Full details of his gift are provided above, 119–24.

[103] *HSC*, ch. 27, pp. 64–7.

[104] *AU*, 939.6, 386–7.

and later abbot of Eynsham, drew attention to English kings 'victorious because of God' in a discussion of the nature of kingship which forms the epilogue to his translation of the Old Testament Book of Judges. There he singled out Alfred, Edgar and Æthelstan 'who fought against Anlaf and slaughtered his army and put him to flight, and afterwards with his people dwelt in peace'.[105] The West Saxon Latin chronicler Æthelweard, writing early in the reign of Æthelred the Unready, also offered a retrospective assessment. To him, Æthelstan had been a very mighty king (*rex robustissimus*) and worthy of honour (*rex venerandus*); above all, Æthelweard drew attention to the consequences of Æthelstan's victory at *Brunanburh*, still popularly remembered in his day as the 'great battle'. His greatest achievement had been to enforce the submission of the Scots and the Picts, which brought significant and lasting consequences: 'The fields of Britain were consolidated into one, there was peace everywhere and abundance of all things, and [since then] no fleet has remained here having advanced against these shores, except under treaty with the English.'[106]

---

[105] *The Old English Version of the Heptateuch*, ed. S.J. Crawford (London, 1922), 416–17; quoted by Dumville, *Wessex*, 141, who dates this text to 1002×1005.

[106] Æthelweard, iv. 5, p. 54: 'uno solidantur Brittannidis arua, undique pax, omniumque foecundia rerum . . .'

Chapter 8

BRITISH MONARCH

Æthelweard's assessment of Æthelstan's peaceful unification of the fields of Britain usefully opens up a different perspective on Æthelstan's kingship from the one with which this study began. There, attention focused on Æthelstan's claim to be the first English monarch, he who first 'ruled all of England alone which before him many kings held among themselves'.[1] But the tenth-century chronicler Æthelweard dwelt not on Æthelstan's kingship of the English, but on his hegemony over the whole island of Britain.

KING OF THE ENGLISH AND RULER OF THE WHOLE OF BRITAIN

Giving a gospel book to Christ Church, Canterbury Æthelstan had the volume inscribed by a clerk from his household: 'Æthelstan, king of the English and ruler of the whole of Britain with a devout mind gave this gospel book to the primatial see of Canterbury, to the church dedicated to Christ.'[2] The scribe's apparent familiarity with the charter conventions of Æthelstan's day emerges from the striking relationship between the terms used to describe King Æthelstan in this dedicatory inscription (copied, presumably, towards the end of his reign) and the language of the king's later charters.[3] This manuscript inscription reinforces a presumption that the king, even if not directly responsible for choosing the language used to denote the nature and extent of his power, did approve the linguistic decisions made on his behalf. He thus found these terms as suitable for use in

---

[1] Eleventh-century list of relics belonging to the church at Exeter preserved in Oxford, Bodleian MS Auct D. 2. 16; fo. 8r, ed. and trans. Patrick Conner, *Anglo-Saxon Exeter* (Woodbridge, 1993), 176.

[2] BL, MS Cotton Tiberius A. ii, fo. 15v: *ÆDELSTAN Anglorum basyleos et curagulus totius Brytannie*; printed and trans. Keynes, 'Books', 149–50. The book dates from the late ninth or early tenth century and was originally from Lobbes in Belgium.

[3] Pierre Chaplais, 'The Anglo-Saxon Chancery: From the Diploma to the Writ', reprinted in *Prisca Munimenta*, ed. F. Ranger (London, 1973), 46–7; Keynes, *Diplomas*, 26. The same hand is found also in charters issued in the names of King Edmund and his successor, Eadred; he might have belonged to the community of the Old Minster, Winchester, but was probably a member of the royal household.

the religious context of a gift to the metropolitan church at Canterbury as for a grant of land to one of his thegns.[4]

Draftsmen in the royal circle responded swiftly to the changed political circumstances that followed from Æthelstan's acquisition of the previously independent kingdom of Northumbria in 927. The newly coined royal style *rex Anglorum*, 'king of the English', suggests contemporaries were aware of the magnitude of the king's achievement in uniting all the Anglo-Saxon kingdoms into one. Yet this title represented neither the sum total of the rhetorical capability of the king's scribes, nor the extent of his own desire to express the nature of his new powers. While the first charters issued after the submission at Eamont in 928 said merely that Æthelstan ruled as king of the English by gift of God, early in 931 charters produced on the king's behalf by 'Æthelstan A' began to style him 'king of the English, elevated by the right hand of the Almighty to the throne of the whole kingdom of Britain';[5] or, on one occasion: 'king of the English, elevated by the right hand of the Almighty to the summit of Albion'.[6] After 'Æthelstan A' apparently stopped working in the royal writing office, his successors continued to use the same exalted language, referring to the king as guardian (*curagulus*) or governor (*gubernator*) of the whole island of Britain or of Albion,[7] and calling Æthelstan not just king (*rex*) of the English but *basileus*, the Greek title for the ruler of the Eastern empire. Lest the implications of these elevated royal styles should pass unnoticed, one text glossed the meaning yet further, describing Æthelstan as *basileus* of the English and of all the peoples settled round about.[8]

In one of his Sandars lectures in bibliography delivered at Cambridge in 1898, W.H. Stevenson offered a vivid assessment of the language of Æthelstan's charters which merits repeating. Observing that these documents marked an important stage in the history of the Old English

---

[4] Compare S 430: 'Æðelstanus. nodante Dei gratia basileus Anglorum et equæ totius Bryttanniæ orbis curagulus'.

[5] S 412–13, 416–17, 418a, 418–19, 422.

[6] S 434: 'Æthelstanus rex Anglorum – per omnipatrantis dexteram. apice totius Albionis sullimatus.' For discussion of Albion, the archaic term for Britain recorded by Pliny in his *Natural History* and used by Bede (*HE*, i, 1), see A.L.F. Rivet and Colin Smith, *The Place-Names of Roman Britain* (London, 1979), 247–8; and Andrew Merrills, *History and Geography in Late Antiquity* (Cambridge, 2005), 250 and 255. For its adoption in the tenth century as a term of geographical and political significance, see Julia Crick, 'Edgar, Albion and Insular Domination', in *Edgar, King of the English*, ed. Donald Scragg (Woodbridge, 2008), 166–9.

[7] For example, S 430 (and S 431, 438, 440, 446–7): *totius Bryttanniae orbis curagulus*; cf. S 448: *tocius Brittannie orbis gubernator*; S 411 and 437: *totius Albionis gubernator*. Eric John, *Orbis Britanniae, and Other Studies* (Leicester, 1966), 48–51, 53–4.

[8] S 441 and 442: *basileus industrius Anglorum cunctarumque gencium in circuitu persistencium*; John, *Orbis Britanniae*, 52; Harald Kleinschmidt, 'Die Titulaturen englischer Könige im 10. und 11. Jahrhundert', in *Intitulatio III: Lateinische Herrschertitel und Herrschertitulaturen vom 7. bis zum 13. Jahrhundert*, ed. H. Kleinschmidt *et al.* (Vienna, Cologne, Graz, 1988), 93–4. Timothy Reuter, 'The Making of England and Germany, 850–1050: Points of Comparison and Difference', reprinted in his *Medieval Polities and Modern Mentalities*, ed. J.L. Nelson (Cambridge, 2006), 284–99, at 296–8, sets the royal styles in a useful wider context.

diploma, Stevenson commented on the pomposity of their language and inflated use of rhetoric:

> The tendency that we have noticed [previously] towards circumlocution is developed in Æthelstan's chancery to the highest perfection. The object of the compilers of these charters was to express their meaning by the use of the greatest possible number of words and by the choice of the most grandiloquent, bombastic words that they could find. Every sentence is so overloaded by the heaping up of unnecessary words that the meaning is almost buried out of sight. The invocation with its appended clauses, opening with pompous and partly alliterative words, will proceed amongst a blaze of verbal fireworks throughout twenty lines of smallish type, and the pyrotechnic display will be maintained with equal magnificence throughout the whole charter, leaving the reader, dazzled by the glaze and blinded by the smoke, in a state of uncertainty as to the meaning of these frequently untranslatable and usually interminable sentences.[9]

Certainly these documents make substantial demands of their readers or auditors; we reflected earlier on the difficulty that must have faced members of the king's council with limited Latin when the documents were read aloud at meetings. Their flamboyant and, indeed, pompous language was designed, as Lapidge has observed, to enhance the majesty of the donor and the importance of his gift. One has to wonder, however, how much beyond that general idea his ealdormen and thegns could have hoped to grasp, even if some kind (and highly educated) bishops standing nearby tried to translate the text for them, or at least paraphrase it sotto voce during its recitation.[10] Hermeneutic language of this sort – characterized by the 'ostentatious parade of unusual, often very arcane and apparently learned vocabulary' – is associated in England particularly with the writings of Aldhelm, the late-seventh-century abbot of Malmesbury, and again after Æthelstan's reign with writings linked to the tenth-century monastic revolution.[11] In some places, Lapidge shows, the authors of these texts borrowed their high-flown vocabulary from Aldhelm, but at others they may have drawn on glossaries. Lapidge noted further a predilection for the hermeneutic style in northern France in the early tenth century and especially in centres associated with reformed monasticism, which

---

[9] Stevenson never published the text of these lectures, but they have been transcribed from the manuscript versions surviving in St John's College, Oxford by Simon Keynes, who has made them available online: *http://www.trin.cam.ac.uk/chartwww/STEVEN~1/STEVINT.HTM* [accessed 1 Sept. 2009].

[10] Michael Lapidge, 'The Hermeneutic Style in Tenth-Century Anglo-Latin Literature', reprinted in his *Anglo-Latin Literature 900–1066* (London and Rio Grande, 1993), 137–8; James Campbell, *The Anglo-Saxon State* (London 2000), 40. Above, 133–4.

[11] Lapidge, 'Hermeneutic Style', 105.

may suggest another possible mode of its transmission to Æthelstan's court.[12] Oda, the future archbishop of Canterbury, could have played a role in that process, given his reputation for competence in both Latin and Greek, his continental contacts (especially with Fleury, a centre for Latin of this style) and his known closeness to the king.[13] Although Æthelstan's charter scribes first used Greek in this innovative fashion to ornament their diplomatic language, draftsmen of charters for Eadwig and Edgar subsequently adopted the same habit, so that these words came in time to form part of conventional charter language.[14]

Even those unfamiliar with the writings of Aldhelm, who had never consulted, far less tried to make use of a Latin–Greek glossary, could have absorbed important messages from the language and rhetoric of Æthelstan's charters. Their bombastic proems made grandiose statements about the king's concerns of the fickleness of mortal existence in comparison with eternal blessedness, about the need for all to defend the poor and regularly give alms, the importance of concentrating the mind on the things above. They confirmed to those able to grasp their gist (if not their finer points of detail) an impression they might have obtained from elsewhere – and, if they knew the king, acquired from their own observation – that religion and proper religious observance mattered to Æthelstan. Yet the inflated royal styles arguably served a more important function. For the king's titles revealed to courtly intimates, ealdormen of distant shires, subordinate Welsh kings and visiting dignitaries something they had *not* previously known. Æthelstan no longer claimed to rule as king of the Anglo-Saxons, or even as king of the English. As ruler of the whole of Britain, he laid stake to hegemony over the entire island and all the lesser kings and princes therein. His was an imperial domain. That was precisely the message conveyed in the inscription recording the king's donation of the gospel book to Canterbury; a poem added in the king's lifetime to the same manuscript (*Rex pius Æðelstan*) celebrated the munificence shown by this donation, and stressed Æthelstan's military ability to conquer and subdue other kings.[15]

Visually, Æthelstan's court bore further witness to the quasi-imperial nature of his rule as shown in the splendid objects given to him by foreign leaders, especially the wonderful gifts sent by Hugh, duke of the Franks, when he petitioned for one of Æthelstan's sisters in marriage. Close connection between some of the relics in that collection and the Carolingian royal family, especially between the royal regalia and the first

[12] The career of the future archbishop Oda and that of others who had spent time at Fleury represent one obvious contact here: Lapidge, 'Hermeneutic Style', 107–11; on contacts between the French and English churches in this period see above, 100–10.

[13] Lapidge, 'Hermeneutic Style', 115–17, 138. For Oda's connection with the royal court see above, 97–100.

[14] Lapidge, 'Hermeneutic Style', 138.

[15] 'Rex pius Æðelstan', lines 5–6, ed. and trans. Lapidge, 'Poems', 96. Above, 94.

Carolingian emperor, Charles the Great, enhanced Æthelstan's standing enormously. Neither party to that transaction can have entered into it unaware of the underlying implications of the gift exchange for their respective standings.[16] Manuscripts associated with the royal circle also pointed towards a self-conscious awareness of the king's standing on a national stage, and indeed to some recognition of that enhanced status in other parts of Europe. At the same time, the king started to use another medium to convey the nature of his power to an audience far beyond the restricted circle of the royal court: his coins.

In new issues minted soon after 927 the king articulated his authority over all the English kingdoms (and the British rulers who had sworn him obedience) via a fresh written legend, the simple, yet highly effective phrase 'king of all Britain': *rex totius Britanniae*. Beyond this, from the early 930s – in a move that parallels the contemporaneous shift in the diplomatic language of his charters – the design of the king's coins changed to employ an entirely different kind of visual imagery. Instead of a design with a cross in the centre and an inscription running around the circumference of the face, the obverse of Æthelstan's coins now bore a portrait of the king's crowned bust. Previous Anglo-Saxon kings had normally been depicted on their coins wearing diadems, so Æthelstan's choice of a crown apparently of contemporary design seems significant and merits more detailed consideration than we gave this matter when we looked at this coinage in our discussion of Æthelstan's rule over his kingdom. Let us now pause for a while and consider the iconographic and ideological implications of Æthelstan's decision to have himself portrayed wearing a crown, starting with the image found on his coins.

Crowns as symbols of royal and imperial authority

Late-Roman models seem the most obvious sources for the iconographical symbolism of Æthelstan's crowned bust on his coins, but more recent Carolingian (and conceivably Byzantine) images could also have played a role. The idea of a portrait coinage was not new: the depiction of busts on coins represented one of the most enduring legacies of Roman coinage in the early medieval West, those portraits being used, like their Roman exemplars, to convey political messages. Most early Germanic coinage adopted the style of a bust in profile in the style of the Roman *tremissis* (a coin valued at one third of a solidus), although some early Anglo-Saxon coins did show facing heads. From the end of the sixth century, Byzantine coins had depicted busts face-on; some continued a tradition of showing the emperor wearing armour, including a helmet, and holding a shield, but crowns and diadems became increasingly common as the chief insignia of the imperial office. The style of Byzantine crowns, however, differs fundamentally from that worn by Æthelstan. Byzantine models probably do not lie behind

---

[16] Above, 192–8.

Æthelstan's design, which appears rather to imitate older Roman models, reinforced perhaps by Carolingian profile busts.[17]

On Roman imperial coins, crowns to symbolize victory were normally made of leaves, attached to a band and tied at the back of the head. Laurels symbolized peace, so a crown or wreath of laurels was given to victorious generals who had brought peace to the Romans. Other Roman imperial issues depicted a style of radiate crown (i.e. one with rays coming out of a circular band) derived ultimately, as Gannon has explained, from Greek representations of the sun god Helios. Examples of coins bearing draped busts wearing radiate crowns appear in Anglo-Saxon England from the mid-seventh century, modelled on such late Roman examples. On those Roman coins, the spikes of the crown that rise vertically from the band around the emperor's head tend to be discrete, standing proud above the hair, whereas in the earlier Anglo-Saxon examples the verticals often merge with the hair and form triangular patterns in fields of dots.[18] Iconographically Æthelstan's crowned-bust type was not obviously derived from early examples of Anglo-Saxon coins depicting crowned busts, but it could have been modelled directly on the above mentioned late Roman examples of imperial coins. If so, Æthelstan's moneyers stuck more closely than had earlier English craftsmen to that potential Roman model in separating the spikes clearly from one another, and from the king's hair. However, where Roman radiate crowns had vertical spikes with sharp points, the three prongs on Æthelstan's crown each end with a circular ball, in an apparently unique numismatic style.

In choosing a Roman imperial image to convey ideas about the changed nature of his power to his English (and British) subjects, Æthelstan's portrait coinage followed an ideological precedent set by the Carolingians, even though his coins were not stylistically close to Carolingian ninth-century examples, which depicted their subjects wearing not crowns but laurel wreaths. During the first half-century of Carolingian rule Frankish royal coins bore a variety of images, none of which depicted the kings themselves; that changed after Charlemagne's imperial coronation, and specifically after 812 and Charles's recognition as emperor in Constantinople. Then Charles issued coinage depicting his bust in profile, facing right, with a laurel wreath about his head and a *paludamentum* round

---

[17] Anna Gannon, *The Iconography of Early Anglo-Saxon Coinage: Sixth to Eighth Centuries* (Oxford, 2003), 23 and 25–30 (for facing heads); Ildar H. Garipzanov, 'The Image of Authority in Carolingian Coinage: the *Image* of a Ruler and Roman Imperial Tradition', *EME*, viii (1999), 197–218. Philip Grierson, *Byzantine Coins* (London, 1982), 30–2, 51. G.P. Galavaris, 'The Symbolism on the Imperial Costume as Displayed on Byzantine Coins', *American Numismatic Society Museum Notes*, viii (1958), 99–117, at 101, 104.

[18] Gannon, *Iconography*, 42–3. See Pierre Bastien, *Le Buste monétaire des empereurs romains*, 3 vols (Wetteren, 1992–4), i, 103–16; plates 34.3 (Titus); 37.2 (Domitian); compare H. Mattingly and E.A. Sydenham, *The Roman Imperial Coinage II: Vespasian to Hadrian* (London, 1926), plate VI, 101 (Domitian); XV, 307 (Trajan); or for later examples, R.A.G. Carson, *Coins of the Roman Empire* (London, 1990), plate 36, 529–31 (Diocletian).

his shoulders. This style of clothing resembles that worn by emperors on Roman coins issued between the early fourth century (the time of Constantine the Great) and the death of Justin II in 578; Byzantine imperial costume changed in the ninth century, so Carolingian coins of this period clearly imitate Roman not Eastern examples. Louis the Pious adopted most of the features of this coinage after his accession in 814, and struck a similar issue in gold after his imperial coronation in 817, yet after about 818 portrait coins disappeared in Frankia and were minted only on special occasions (as, for example, in 822–3 when Lothar became king in Italy, or in 848 when Pippin II conquered Aquitaine).[19] Might we not see Æthelstan's acquisition of sole authority over Britain as a similar special occasion, meriting an equivalent ideological statement, articulated visually through an image that deliberately evoked the dress of a Roman emperor as well as via the imperial language of the charters?[20] Whatever the reality of the power he might hope to wield over the whole British Isles, Æthelstan was unquestionably the first sole ruler to lay claim to so broad a hegemony since the departure of the Romans in the early fourth century. That he looked to Roman models for visual imagery and probably also to the heirs of Rome – the Carolingian emperors in the West – should not surprise us.

Iconographically, the crown Æthelstan wore on this coinage appears to owe little to numismatic exemplars and to resemble more closely a simplified version of the crowns worn in manuscript portraits by ninth-century Carolingian rulers such as Charles the Bald. These share the same essential design of a circlet with vertical stalks, although the Carolingian examples generally appear more elaborate than Æthelstan's, having jewels or other decoration on the band and stalks adorned with more complicated foliate endings standing upright around the king's head.[21] If Carolingian images were to hand when this new coinage was designed, no one followed

---

[19] Garipzanov, 'Image', 207–10; Simon Coupland, 'Charlemagne's Coinage: Ideology and Economy', in *Charlemagne: Empire and Society*, ed. Joanna Story (Manchester, 2005), 223–7; and S. Coupland, 'Money and Coinage under Louis the Pious', *Francia*, xvii (1990), 45–8.

[20] For the ideological symbolism of this Roman coinage, see Garipzanov, 'Image', 210; Bastien, *Le Buste monétaire* i, 61–80, 235–57.

[21] W.J. Andrew, 'Evolution of Portraiture on the Silver Penny', *British Numismatic Journal*, v (1908), 366–7, argued that Charles the Bald was depicted wearing a similar crown to Æthelstan's, but he was so depicted only in manuscript portraits, never on his coins. Most such Carolingian ruler-portraits depict their subjects wearing crowns far more elaborate than Æthelstan's, for example that worn by Charles the Bald, who is seated enthroned and surrounded by members of his court (including the manuscript's donor) in the so-called Vivian Bible: Paris: Bibliothèque Nationale de France, Ms. Lat. 1, fo. 423r. Closer to Æthelstan's crown in its basic design is the crown worn by the same king in an image of him seated on his throne holding an orb and sceptre, painted late in his life and found in his Psalter: Paris, BN Bibliothèque nationale, MS Lat., 1152, fo. 3v. That crown has a decorated band around the king's head, unlike Æthelstan's simpler circlet, from which protrude stalks with foliate ends, rather than the simple balls worn by Æthelstan.

them slavishly. In the context of the manuscript images, however, it is striking that the king's portrait in the copy of Bede's Lives of St Cuthbert that he gave to Chester-le-Street illustrates him wearing precisely the same sort of crown as that depicted on his coins.[22] In fact, the closest stylistic parallels for Æthelstan's crown as shown both on his coins and in the frontispiece to the manuscript of the Bede Lives seem not to be Carolingian, but Ottonian and may reflect the exchange of political and artistic ideas between England and Saxony during the tenth century.

Ottonian ruler portraits of the later tenth and early eleventh centuries convey contemporary political ideas about the derivation of Ottonian kings' royal (and quasi-sacerdotal) authority from Christ, the celestial king of kings, reflecting a shift away from Carolingian conceptions of the royal office which had depended more on Old Testament exemplars like David and Solomon. New representations of Christ crowned and of images of the Magi as kings, wearing crowns (rather than the Phrygian hats conventionally drawn in earlier representations of wise men with the infant Christ) first appear in contemporary manuscripts from Germany and England in the third quarter of the tenth century. Anglo-Saxon and Ottonian coronation *ordines* of the same period also demonstrate this evolution in the theology of rulership, stressing the parallelism between their earthly kings and the heavenly Christ. At the same time, English and German monarchs articulated imperial claims to hegemonic power: Otto to an empire based in Rome, heir to Charlemagne's; Edgar, like Æthelstan, to imperial rule over all of Britain. While not expressed in its fully developed form until after Æthelstan's day, some of the roots of this new ruler-theology may first have found expression at his court and been fostered by the close relationship between his circle and that of Otto I. Since the earliest extant examples both of a crowned *Christus rex* and of Magi wearing crowns occur in the Benedictional of Æthelwold (963×984, perhaps 970×975), it seems, as Deshman argued, that the iconography of crowned Magi and the crowned Christ was invented first in England and spread from there to Germany. Further, however – and more significantly for this argument – it appears that tenth-century English courts discussed crowns and experimented with ways to depict them visually.[23] We might thus pause for a moment to look at some representations of crowns that post-date Æthelstan's day.

In the Benedictional of Æthelwold, the Magi are depicted wearing crowns more elaborate than Æthelstan's but similar in essential design:

[22] Plate 1. We can only speculate as to the design of the second contemporary portrait of the crowned king that once illustrated BL, MS Cotton Otho B. ix; see above; 107, 121–2.

[23] BL, Add. MS 49598, fo. 24v; illustrated in Andrew Prescott, *The Benedictional of St. Æthelwold: A Masterpiece of Anglo-Saxon Art: A Facsimile* (London, 2002); see Robert Deshman, '*Christus rex et magi reges*: Kingship and Christology in Ottonian and Anglo-Saxon Art', *Frühmittelalterliche Studien*, x (1976), 367–405. Simon Keynes, 'Edgar, *rex admirabilis*', in *Edgar, King of the English, 959–975*, ed. Donald Scragg (Woodbridge, 2008), 25.

gold circlets surround each head, each with three vertical stalks with foliate ends; the first king presents a golden diadem to the infant Christ seated on the Virgin's lap. The crown worn by King Edgar in the full-page frontispiece attached to his grant of privileges for the New Minster, Winchester foundation is similar, with slightly more slender verticals.[24] Much closer to Æthelstan's crown are those given to the Magi in an image dating from the third quarter of the tenth century, depicting the Magi presenting their gifts to the infant Christ in the Fulda Sacramentary. These are grander than Æthelstan's in that the gold circlet round the heads of the Magi has jewelled decoration and the balls stand higher and prouder of their heads than on Athelstan's, but in essence they have the same design.[25] One might compare also a slightly later Ottonian image in the Warmund Sacramentary of c.1000 which shows the Virgin Mary investing Otto with a crown in the form of a circlet with a decorated band from which protrude five stalks, each ending in a ball.[26] Even closer in style to Æthelstan's, if perhaps slightly more elaborate, is the crown worn by Henry III in an image from an Echternach manuscript datable to 1039×1034.[27] The close contacts first established between the Ottonian and West Saxon courts by the marriage of Otto I to Eadgyth, Æthelstan's half-sister, which we know involved the exchange of gifts and manuscripts, may well have led to some sharing of ideas about crowns and crown-wearing between the two courts, as well as discussions of theories of Christian rulership. We know that those connections continued beyond

---

[24] Prescott, *The Benedictional*, 13. BL, Cotton Vespasian A. viii, fo. 2: *The Golden Age of Anglo-Saxon Art 966–1066*, ed. J. Backhouse, D.H. Turner and L. Webster (London, 1984), 47 (no. 26); Catherine E. Karkov, *The Ruler Portraits of Anglo-Saxon England* (Woodbridge, 2004), 84–118.

[25] Göttingen, Universitätsbibliothek, Hs. Theol. 231, fo. 19r. *Sacramentarium Fuldense*, ed. Gregor Richter and Albert Schönfelder (Fulda, 1912; reprinted Henry Bradshaw Society, ci, Farnborough, 1982), plate 16. For the date of the image, see H. Hoffmann, *Buchkunst und Königtum im ottonischen und frühsalischen Reich*, 2 vols (Stuttgart, 1986), i, 150.

[26] Ivrea, Biblioteca Capitolare MS. LXXXVI, fo. 16v; Robert Deshman, 'Otto III and the Warmund Sacramentary: a Study in Political Theology', *Zeitschrift für Kunstgeschichte*, xxxiv (1971), 1–20, fig. 1. Other Ottonian crowns are often more elaborate, for example those worn by the figures offering gifts to a crowned, enthroned Otto in the Gospel Book of Otto III, made at Reichenau, c.1000: Munich, Bayerisch Staatsbibliothek, Clm 4453, fos 23v and 24r; Henry Mayr-Harting, *Ottonian Book Illumination: an Historical Study*, 2 vols (2nd edn, London, 1999), i, plates XX and XXI. One might look also at the various crowns depicted in the Bamberg Apocalypse (another Reichenau manuscript of the same date): Bamberg, Staatsbibliothek, MS Bibl. 140. Although none resembles Æthelstan's closely in style, one type (worn by the lions who appear as the angel blows the fifth trumpet, fo. 23), has spherical decorations, but these balls sit on the angled headband round each lion's brow, not raised up on stalks: Mayr-Harting, ii, figs 2, 3 and 140.

[27] Bremen, Staats- und Universitätsbibliothek MS B 21, fo. 3v; illustrated in colour in *Das Reich der Salier, 1024–1125: Katalog zur Ausstellung des Landes Rheinland-Pfalz* (Sigmaringen, 1992), 298; and in black and white in Michael Hare, 'Kings, Crowns and Festivals: the Origins of Gloucester as a Royal Ceremonial Centre', *Transactions of the Bristol and Gloucestershire Archaeological Society*, cxv (1997), 42.

Æthelstan's reign, and indeed into the eleventh century. While Cenwald or another English ecclesiastic travelling in Ottonian Saxony might have seen some Ottonian scribes' early efforts at designing crowns, given that the earliest examples of Æthelstan's crowned coinage date from the early 930s and the ruler portraits were drawn in his lifetime, the predominant influence may have been from Wessex to Saxony rather than the other way round.[28]

Can we determine in which medium the image of Æthelstan wearing his crown first appeared? Did the king's moneyers have his crowned manuscript portraits in mind when they designed the crown for his new portrait coinage? If so, that might have led them to reject not just the Carolingian example of the laurel-wreath crown, but also the potential presented by the diadem, derived originally from the Greek fillet given to victorious athletes, which had become another potent symbol of conquest and power. Adorned with gems and pearls, even with *pendilia* (trailing cordonets on either side), such diadems had appeared on earlier English coins, in Carolingian manuscript ruler-portraits, and were often worn by Byzantine emperors.[29] Alternatively, did the court painters have examples of crowned-bust coins before them when they designed the portraits of their monarch to go in the manuscripts destined for the shrine of St Cuthbert?

A third possibility seems more promising (and does not require us to show how manuscript art influenced coin design or vice versa): supposing both moneyers and court painters depicted the king as they had seen him on ceremonial occasions, wearing a crown that consisted of a simple, unadorned circlet, with vertical prongs surmounted by spherical balls. Festal crown-wearing was a Carolingian habit, associated particularly with the major liturgical festivals of Christmas and Easter. The first concrete evidence for the same kind of festival court-holding in England comes from Æthelstan's court and from the early 930s.[30] We should not forget that the crown had been one of the symbols of royal power given to Æthelstan at his coronation, replacing the helmet that had previously denoted royal status. If his predecessors had not often worn crowns, or at least not in the same formal contexts as Æthelstan would choose to wear them, can we guess what sort of crown the archbishop placed on the

[28] I am extremely grateful to Henry Mayr-Harting for advice on this point, and am mindful of his warning that one can attach too much significance to different types of crown: *Ottonian Book Illumination*, ii, 42–3. See also J.R. Maddicott, *The Origins of the English Parliament 924–1327* (Oxford, 2010), 20–1.

[29] For example, the portrait of Lothar, emperor and ruler of the Middle Kingdom that prefaces the gospel book, Paris, BN Lat. MS 266, for iv (illustrated in Bullough, *Carolingian Renewal*, 37, fig. 4). See Gannon, *Iconography*, 45–51, for the use of diadems on coins. Byzantine crowns in this period were generally considerably more elaborate than the plain, unadorned crown worn by Æthelstan; headbands were highly ornate, often set with jewels, which might also hang down around the emperor's (or empress's) ears.

[30] Rosamond McKitterick, *Charlemagne* (Cambridge, 2008), 170, 173. Hare, 'Kings, Crowns'; Wormald, *MEL*, 434–5.

newly anointed king's head in September 925? He might have used a simple gold band, or something more elaborate, such as the bejewelled circlet used for crowning a prince depicted in the Sacramentary of Charles the Bald produced in Metz, *c*.870.[31] Of course, it is possible that in the interval between Æthelstan's acceptance as ruler in both Wessex and Mercia and his coronation in September the following year, while Archbishop Æthelhelm drafted a new liturgical *ordo*, craftsmen in the royal workshop designed and made a crown for use in that ceremony at Kingston. If so, the king could have continued to wear that crown on ceremonial occasions; this would have made it the obvious choice for depiction in the visual media we have been discussing. The coincidence of the inception of festal crown-wearing, the minting of the crowned-bust coins, the innovative commissioning of portraits of the crowned king, and the articulation of grandiose statements about the almost imperial nature of Æthelstan's hegemony over the whole orb of Britain all suggest otherwise, however.

To my mind, the period after 927 appears the most likely moment for designing a crown fit for a king 'elevated by the hand of the Almighty to the summit of Albion', its visual iconography mirroring the new charter language (echoed also in manuscript dedications). In style, this new crown owed something to the available iconographic models associated with earlier Roman and Carolingian imperial rulers. Yet the finished product as revealed to us on the coins and in the manuscript portrait resembled closely none of those pre-existing symbols of imperial power, or any of the known examples of royal headgear worn by previous Anglo-Saxon kings. Nor (if we place any reliance on William of Malmesbury's account of this embassy) did the king's new regalia apparently owe much to the example of the crown included with the gifts sent by Hugh, duke of the Franks when he sought Æthelstan's half-sister in marriage: 'a precious crown of solid gold and yet more precious from its gems, of which the brilliance shot such flashing darts of light at the beholders that the more anyone strove to strain his eyes, the more he was dazzled and obliged to give up.'[32] Even allowing for William of Malmesbury's hyperbole, this sounds much more like the crowns seen in Carolingian (and later in Ottonian) manuscripts, than the one Æthelstan wore. Æthelstan's crown appears to have been unique, arguably deliberately so. In having himself depicted with this style of headgear, the king conveyed a subtle but significantly novel message. Sharing neither a Roman nor a Carolingian imperial agenda, and heir to no previous historical tradition, Æthelstan's hegemonic power required fresh

---

[31] Paris, BN Lat. MS 1141, fo. 2v; illustrated in C.R. Dodwell, *The Pictorial Arts of the West, 800–1200* (New Haven and London, 1993), 62, fig. 49. Janet L. Nelson, 'The Earliest Surviving Royal *Ordo*: Some Liturgical and Historical Aspects' (1980) reprinted in her *Politics and Ritual in Early Medieval Europe* (London and Ronceverte, 1986), 356–8; Hare, 'Kings, Crowns', 48.

[32] *GR*, ii, 135, pp. 218–19.

modes of expression, appropriate to these unprecedented British circumstances. Earlier West Saxon kings had proved enormously successful in
their appointed role; Æthelstan's grandfather Alfred had achieved rulership
over Angles *and* Saxons, not just the men of an expanded Wessex. But
Æthelstan ruled over all Britain; we need to think further about what a
claim to such authority might mean. What might *Britannia* have conveyed
to a tenth-century audience, Anglo-Saxon or British?

THE IDEA OF BRITAIN

As a geographical notion, the idea of Britain resonated readily in tenth-
century minds. Bede had begun his *Ecclesiastical History* with a description of
the ocean island of Britannia, once called Albion (as reported by Pliny in his
Natural History). The Old English Bede retained his opening, making the
geographical description accessible to those who lacked the Latin to read the
original.[33] After the preface, the first substantive entry of the (vernacular)
Anglo-Saxon Chronicle located the story of the island of Britain (*Bretenlond*)
within the history of the Roman empire by starting with Julius Caesar's
conquest in 60 BC. Beyond that spatial entity – ancestral home to Britons
and adopted country of settled Anglo-Saxons, and latterly Danes – it is,
however, hard to determine what *Britannia* might have signified to its tenth-
century inhabitants and their neighbours. Even the most cursory reading of
Bede or the Chronicle would reveal that the island as a whole had never
constituted a unitary state, nor did its partial unification under Roman
imperial rule survive the withdrawal of Roman troops early in the fourth
century. *Britannia* the island thereafter encompassed a number of different
polities, reduced by the early tenth century from the profusion that had
characterized earlier centuries, but a plurality none the less.

Bede differentiated between the peoples of Britain (English, Britons,
Irish and Picts) on linguistic grounds, seeing Latin – the fifth language of
the island and in general use among all those peoples – as a potential
source of unity.[34] One of Bede's purposes in writing his history was to
promote a sense of such unity and common cause among the Germanic
Christians of the island. Despite their separate ethnic and political origins,
he sought to demonstrate that the Anglo-Saxons had been brought
together into one *gens* by the unifying power of the Christian faith, trans-
mitted to them by Rome.[35] His argument concerned spiritual authority

---

[33] *HE*, i. 1, pp. 14–15; *The Old English Version of Bede's Ecclesiastical History of the English
People*, I. 1, ed. Thomas Miller, EETS, o.s. 95–6 (Oxford, 1890; reprinted 1959), 24–5:
'Breoton ist garsecges ealond, ðæt wæs iu geara Albion haten.'

[34] *HE*, I. 1, pp. 16–17.

[35] Sarah Foot, 'The Making of *Angelcynn*: English Identity before the Norman Conquest',
TRHS, 6th ser. vi (1996), 39; Patrick Wormald, 'Bede, the *Bretwaldas* and the Origins of the
gens Anglorum', in *Ideal and Reality in Frankish and Anglo-Saxon Society*, ed. Patrick Wormald
et al. (Oxford, 1983), 99–129.

and the potential of religion to bind disparate groups into one; a putative political dimension lay only in his discussion of kings who held wide power (*imperium*) over more than one English kingdom.[36] There he did not intend to demonstrate that early Anglo-Saxon kings (Ælle, a fifth-century king of the South Saxons, Ceawlin of Wessex, Æthelberht of Kent, Rædwald of East Anglia, and three Northumbrian kings of the seventh century: Edwin, Oswald and Oswiu) had held any sort of imperial office extending across the whole island of Britain. Rather he may have been trying to hint, as I have argued previously, that 'just as one faith and one language *can* unify disparate groups, so, bearing in mind the demonstrable unity provided by the centralizing authority of the Church, *could* a single political authority serve as one means of binding otherwise distinct political groups into a common cause: the promotion of the true faith and the making of a people with a single, Christian identity'.[37] For just one king, Edwin of Northumbria, did Bede explicitly claim authority over 'all the inhabitants of Britain, English and Britons alike', although he implied that all three Northumbrians held similar sway. By his account the last named in this list, Oswiu, even overwhelmed and made tributary the tribes of Picts and Irish who inhabited the northern parts of Britain. A northern hegemony extending over *Britannia* could seemingly be imagined in Bede's day, even if its reality might have proved short-lived at best.[38] Æthelstan, who also ruled over English and Britons alike, could claim to be heir to that *imperium*, and could find West Saxon precedent for so doing.

The ninth-century compilers of the Anglo-Saxon Chronicle used the same list of Bede of seven kings who had once held *imperium* to a rather different end. Noting the point at which a West Saxon king – Ecgberht, grandfather of Alfred – first claimed authority over all of England south of the Humber, the chronicler gave him a new and otherwise unknown title: *bretwalda* (or in some manuscripts, *brytenwalda*), namely, 'ruler of Britain'. By adding Ecgberht's name to this list of glorious rulers, the chronicler argued by implication that Ecgberht's power after his conquest of Mercia in 829, although short-lived, was equivalent to that of the Southumbrian kings named by Bede who exercised *imperium* over the lands south of the Humber. To their number we should add one further king, not in Bede's original list but described by him in similar terms: Æthelbald of Mercia (716–56). In his survey of the state of Britain in his day made at the end of his *History*, Bede named the bishops of all the southern English diocesan sees, observing that 'all these kingdoms and the other southern kingdoms which reach right up to the Humber, together with their various kings, are subject to Æthelbald, king of Mercia'. Grandiose claims had

---

[36] *HE*, II. 5, pp. 148–51.

[37] Foot, 'Making of *Angelcynn*', 41.

[38] *HE*, II. 5, pp. 148–51; John, *Orbis Britanniae*, 6–7: 'that Adomnan in his Life of St Columba described Oswald as *totius Britanniae imperator* would provide independent support for the presumption that such a hegemony was imaginable'.

been advanced for the nature of Æthelbald's rule in some quarters in his realm. One contemporary charter (surviving as an apparent original) described King Æthelbald in the body of the text as 'king not only of the Mercians but also of all provinces which are called by the general name "South English" (*sutangli*)'; in the witness-list he attested with the title king of Britain: *rex Britanniae*. Boniface, the Anglo-Saxon missionary to the Germans, wrote to Æthelbald in terms that seem to echo that charter, saying in his letter's salutation that Æthelbald was 'preferred in the love of Christ to all other kings and wielded the glorious sceptre of imperial rule over the English (*Angli*)'.[39]

From these disparate pieces of evidence we establish a sense that even while the Anglo-Saxon kingdoms of England remained fundamentally independent, before England (and an English 'state') had yet been imagined, from time to time individual kings wielded hegemonic power beyond their own realms and thereby created a polity of a different sort. Æthelbald held sway over all the kingdoms south of the Humber; to at least one of his scribes that made him *rex Britanniae*, king of Britain. *Britannia* had become a political expression in English usage by the eighth century and one that could denote either a Northumbrian or a Southumbrian hegemony. When the chronicler called Ecgberht the eighth *bretwalda*, he made a similar statement about the authority of the ninth-century king of Wessex: Ecgberht, too, ruled over Britain. It was to these political traditions that Æthelstan claimed to be heir; his hegemony over both English and Britons (and his supremacy over subject British rulers) made him the ninth *bretwalda*. His court's use of visual iconography and verbal rhetoric reinforced that message. The poem *The Battle of Brunanburh* resonates with that claim to lordship over Britain, especially in its closing lines. By comparing Æthelstan's triumph in this battle to earlier Anglo-Saxon victories over the British the poet, in Simon Walker's words, sought to 'rank him among the small band of kings accorded the title *bretwalda* who held the rule over all the kingdoms of the southern English. The implicit comparison is, indeed with Northumbrian kings such as Edwin, Oswald and Oswiu who "had still greater power and ruled over all the inhabitants of Britain, English and Britons alike".'[40] Although the poet appears never to have ventured near a battlefield, he could still express national and patriotic sentiments well. As Edward Irving argued, 'a nation

---

[39] ASC 829; *HE*, V, 23, pp. 558–9; S 89. Boniface and seven other missionary bishops to Æthelbald, AD 746–7, ed. M. Tangl, *Die Briefe des Heiligen Bonifatius und Lullus*, MGH, Epistolae selectae I (Berlin, 1916), no. 73; trans. *EHD*, no. 177. John, *Orbis Britanniae*, 10.

[40] Simon Walker, 'A Context for *Brunanburh*', in *Warriors and Churchmen*, ed. Timothy Reuter (London, 1992), 23. See also John, *Orbis Britanniae*, 7–11; Dumville, *Wessex*, 153–4, 169–71; M. Wood, 'The Making of King Æthelstan's Empire: an English Charlemagne', in *Ideal and Reality in Frankish and Anglo-Saxon Society*, eds P. Wormald *et al.* (Oxford, 1983), 250–2, 271–2; and Sarah Foot, 'Where English Becomes British: Rethinking Contexts for *Brunanburh*', in *Myth, Rulership, Church and Charters*, ed. Julia Barrow and Andrew Wareham (Aldershot, 2008), 139–40.

is being born here, in a swelling surge of triumphant recognition of the fact . . . The literate *Brunanburh* poet understands enough history to recognize that his own English ancestors once swarmed just as hungrily over Britain as the recent invaders swarmed over the field at Brunanburh', the essential difference being that the army he celebrated won its crucial, nation-building engagement.[41]

Æthelstan's court announced and finessed an ideology about Britain as a single political unit and about this king as ruler over the whole of that polity, equivalent to the geographical island of Britain. Some in his circle also played with the ancient geographical term for the island, Albion, in seeking new ways to convey the magnitude of Æthelstan's achievement.[42] Æthelweard's recognition that Æthelstan had consolidated Britain territorially into a single unit fits into this context. Non-English texts promoted the same notion of Æthelstan's British authority. The Welsh prophecy poem *Armes Prydein*, written *c.*930, called Æthelstan the 'Great King', his conquests completing the theft of land from the British begun by Hengest and Horsa.[43] A later Welsh history of kings also stressed Æthelstan's significance; speaking of the Saxons it reported, 'and thus after casting off the lordship of the Britons from them they thereupon ruled all England with Edelstan as their prince who first of the English wore the Crown of the Island of Britain'. Geoffrey of Monmouth ended his *Historia regum* with reference to Adelstan, the king under whom the Saxons had thrown off the dominion of the British. For Geoffrey, the battle of *Brunanburh* represented a turning point for English and British alike.[44] Æthelstan was, indeed, a British monarch. His court conveyed the magnitude of that status through visual imagery and powerful use of language, making his contemporaries fully aware of the novelty and also potentially of the enduring significance of what this king had achieved (even though, in the event, that would prove distinctly short-lived).[45] We should thus remember his public glories and his private, more personal triumphs.

---

[41] Edward B. Irving, 'The Charge of the Saxon Brigade: Tennyson's *Battle of Brunanburh*', in *Literary Appropriations of the Anglo-Saxons*, ed. Donald Scragg and Carole Weinberg (Cambridge, 2000), 174–93, at 183–4.

[42] Crick, 'Edgar, Albion and Insular Domination', 161 and for the ecclesiastical elements of these ideological claims to insular domination, 163–4.

[43] *Armes Prydein: the Prophecy of Britain from the Book of Taliesin*, ed. Ifor Williams and Rachel Bromwich (Dublin, 1982), lines 17–22: 'Myrddin foretells that they will meet in Aber Peryddon, the stewards of the Great King. (And though it be not in the same way, they will (all) lament death) with a single will they will offer battle. The stewards will collect their taxes – in the armies of the Cymry, there was nobody who would not pay.'

[44] J. Rhys and J.G. Evans, *The Text of the Bruts from the Red Book of Hergest* (Oxford, 1890), 255; quoted in *Armes Prydein*, ed. Williams and Bromwich, xviii. *The Historia Regum Britannie of Geoffrey of Monmouth. 1, Bern, Burgerbibliothek, MS. 568*, §207, ed. Neil Wright (Cambridge, 1984), 147; trans. Lewis Thorpe, *Geoffrey of Monmouth* (Harmondsworth, 1966), 284; see Michael Wood, *In Search of England* (London, 1999; paperback, 2000), 151.

[45] Campbell, *The Anglo-Saxon State*, 51.

Epilogue

MEMORY, OBLIVION, COMMEMORATION

King Æthelstan's unquestionable attainments in military, political, legal, diplomatic, religious and cultural spheres found recognition in the widespread regard expressed for him by his contemporaries, from which we might anticipate that the king's fame would long have outlived him. Effusive notices marked his death, as we saw in Chapter 7, and Æthelstan retained a prominent position in the West Saxon consciousness at the end of the tenth century. His expanded realm and overlordship over the other rulers of Britain did not survive his death – his successor Edmund had to refashion that for himself – but West Saxon control over Northumbria was secured after 954 and the kingdom of the English re-established permanently after King Edgar (Edmund's younger son) acquired the whole united realm on the death of his brother Eadwig in 959. Edgar went on in time to lay claim to imperial titles no less exalted than his uncle's. Æthelstan's claim to undying glory, won with the sword's edge on the field at *Brunanburh*, but sustained thereafter by the grateful prayers of his own kin and by members of those religious houses whom he had so generously endowed, should have proved secure, even against the inevitable temporal decay of transitory affairs much lamented in his charter proems. Yet if one asked a group of educated Britons to name three Anglo-Saxon kings, few would now number Æthelstan among those they could recall. Alfred who burnt the cakes would top any list, followed swiftly by Harold (he who died with an arrow in the eye at the battle of Hastings) and then perhaps Æthelred the Unready, or Edward the Confessor.[1] In his homeland, outside the few places with monuments to his memory, Æthelstan has become England's forgotten king, an almost entirely unknown figure of a remote past no longer seen as relevant to modern culture, or included in a national school curriculum. Farther afield in my experience, even in anglophone societies, his name arouses little more than polite bemusement. Despite the magnitude of his achievements and the validity of his claim to be reckoned England's first monarch and ruler of the whole of Britain, at the start of the third Christian millennium, Æthelstan's name

---

[1] T.A. Shippey, 'The Undeveloped Image: Anglo-Saxon in Popular Consciousness from Turner to Tolkien', in *Literary Appropriations of the Anglo-Saxons*, ed. Donald Scragg and Carole Weinberg (Cambridge, 2000), 216.

hardly resonates outside the restricted circles of academe. How could so great a king have been thus forgotten?

MEMORY

From the perspective of the late tenth century it had seemed clear that Æthelstan should take the credit for having laid the foundations of the unitary realm that the West Saxon monarch now enjoyed as ruler (*rex* or *basileus*) of the English and of the peoples round about. Yet in one important – perhaps critical – sense, Æthelstan may have contributed to his own forgetting by having failed to beget heirs of his own who would ensure the perpetuation of his memory. His nephew Edgar, under whom the English found themselves once more securely united after the uncertainties of the intervening years, adopted the same two identities as had Æthelstan. He called himself king of the English and claimed also to rule with an authority extending over all the peoples in Britain. As Keynes has argued, 'the consistent usages of Edgar's reign represent nothing less than a determined reaffirmation of the polity created by Æthelstan in the 930s'. Edgar and his direct heirs had no particular reason to commemorate an increasingly remote uncle rather than fathers and grandfathers. Even so, one indication of Æthelstan's posthumous standing within the royal family in that period comes in the choices King Æthelred (978–1016) made when naming his sons. He looked to his predecessors on the West Saxon throne, calling his eldest Æthelstan and the next Ecgberht (after the eighth *bretwalda*), before working through Æthelstan's successors in sequence. Only after having reached his immediate predecessor (Edward) did Æthelred turn for his eighth son to the name Alfred.[2] Æthelred himself has a poor reputation, and one that lingers in the popular memory through his unfortunate epithet 'unready', widely believed to refer to his inability to resist the concerted efforts at conquest by co-ordinated armies led by Cnut, the Danish king. After Æthelred's death, his defeat of his son, Edmund Ironside in 1016, and subsequent assumption of the English throne, Cnut did much to try and reconcile his new subjects by constructing an image of himself as an archetypically 'English' king. He wrote to his new subjects stressing that he would rule as a gracious lord and a faithful observer of God's rights and just secular law, and urged that the nation should observe Edgar's law. His lengthy two-part law code again sought to stress continuity with a peaceful past. Æthelstan's example may have persuaded Cnut additionally to become a significant benefactor to the Church, making gifts of valuable manuscripts to different churches; one such book given to the New Minster at Winchester he had prefaced with a

---

[2] Simon Keynes, 'Edgar, *rex admirabilis*', in *Edgar, King of the English, 959–975*, ed. Donald Scragg (Woodbridge, 2008), 3–58, at 25. For a late-tenth-century royal style, see S 876, a charter of Æthelred of 993, attested by his four eldest sons. For the sequence of Æthelred's sons, see Keynes, *Diplomas*, 187, n. 116.

portrait of himself and his wife Emma as donors.[3] The new Norman regime after 1066 sought similarly to legitimize itself by claiming continuity with the English past and trying to make William direct heir of Edward the Confessor, and promoter of the laws of Edward.[4]

William the Conqueror did not look back as far as Æthelstan's time for precedents for his rule, but Æthelstan's reputation did not wane after the Norman Conquest; indeed, if anything it grew as a consequence of the historical revival in England in the early years of the twelfth century. Monastic writers looked back nostalgically to an English past before the evils they experienced in their time, which they traced back to the fateful day of the Conquest. As Richard Southern has argued, 'circumstances forced scholarly monks all over England to become historians, to examine the historical content of material which had never been used in this way before, and to extract from unpromising documents a new picture of antiquity'.[5] In that process, Æthelstan often played a significant role, especially, but not exclusively, in the historical materials written at monastic houses that he had patronized. Historians tracing the history of the English kings afforded him due prominence; his status as the first of the Anglo-Saxon kings to rule over all the English attracted attention, and he acquired generally positive and flattering epithets from those who wrote about his life and deeds. To the Anglo-Normans, Æthelstan deserved remembrance since he stood out as the founder of a united English realm, but also – and perhaps more significantly – for having asserted lordship over his Celtic neighbours in Britain. Those achievements resonated particularly as the Normans sought to impose their authority over the whole island.[6]

Above all, William of Malmesbury, who in Southern's words, 'extended to the whole kingdom the corporate aims of each monastic researcher of his day', provided a substantial account of King Æthelstan, dwelling not just on his military and diplomatic achievements, or merely his generosity to William's own house at Malmesbury, but also on his personality and character. William set the tone for much subsequent discussion of Æthelstan by the way he introduced his lengthy narrative, referring to traditions current in his own day about the extent of Æthelstan's education and his interest in law, and claiming to have found additional

---

[3] M.K. Lawson, *Cnut: the Danes in England in the Early Eleventh Century* (London and New York, 1993), 150–60; Catherine E. Karkov, *The Ruler Portraits of Anglo-Saxon England* (Woodbridge, 2004), 119–56, and fig. 17 (BL, MS Stowe 944, fo. 6r).

[4] Simon Keynes, 'The Cult of King Alfred the Great', *ASE*, xxviii (1999), 229.

[5] R.W. Southern, 'Aspects of the European Tradition of Historical Writing, 4: The Sense of the Past', *TRHS*, 5th ser., xxiii (1973), 248.

[6] Dumville, *Wessex*, 168. The thirteenth-century St Albans chronicler John of Wallingford remembered Æthelstan as the only king of the southern English to whom the Northumbrians had been subject since the first coming of the English to the island of Britain: *The Chronicle Attributed to John of Wallingford*, ed. R. Vaughan, Camden Miscellany, xii (London, 1958), 45.

material about this king in 'an ancient volume in which the writer was at odds with the difficulty of his material, finding it hard to express his opinions as he would have wished'. Because William claimed to have paraphrased this fresh evidence, 'subjoining a few points in ordinary language which may perhaps make some contribution to the evidence for his good qualities', his testimony provided the basis for most later discussions of Æthelstan's reign, until the authenticity of that 'ancient book' came under closer scrutiny in the 1980s.[7] Southern saw William's attempt to construct a life of Aldhelm in his *Gesta pontificum* as William's masterpiece of historical method. One could equally apply Southern's remarks about that biographical portrait to William's almost monographic treatment of Æthelstan in the *Gesta regum*: 'the attempt to evoke a figure of so distant a past from such fragmentary materials – for he had no contemporary biography to guide him – was a daunting task'.[8] Whatever that 'ancient book' had provided for William, it can scarcely have offered a biographical treatment equivalent to Asser's Life of Alfred. Yet William's heroic efforts to flesh out a character for Æthelstan did something to blur the significance of that disparity between the quantity and nature of the materials to have survived from Alfred's and Æthelstan's courts, by supplying popular and legendary material about our subject that would feed into later romance. In William's hands, Æthelstan became not just a king worthy of remembrance, but one about whom there were stories and vignettes worth recalling, and indeed repeating.

Æthelstan's chances of retaining a significant place in a popular appreciation of 'great' kings of the pre-Conquest past depended much on the prominence accorded his deeds by such historians as William and John of Worcester, on whom I have drawn at several points in this study, and Henry of Huntingdon. To Henry, Æthelstan 'clearly was splendidly famous in his deeds, attacked as he was by the strongest but never defeated in war'. Beyond translating the 'strange words and figures of speech' of *The Battle of Brunanburh* poem into Latin for his audience, however, Henry had little to say about those deeds.[9] Any bid to have that 'undying glory won at the sword's edge' translated into genuine immortality would depend on the capacity of Æthelstan's reputation to overcome the competition presented by conflicting claims to greatness advanced not just for Alfred but also for the British King Arthur (given a huge boost by Geoffrey of Monmouth) and the sainted Edward the Confessor.

---

[7] *GR*, ii, 132, 210–11; Lapidge, 'Poems'. See further, Appendix I.

[8] Southern, 'Aspects', 255.

[9] HH, V. 18–19, pp. 310–15. We might note that Henry attributed no blame to Æthelstan for the death of his brother Edwin in 933, seeing this as merely an act of adverse fortune (V. 18, 310–11); compare E.A. Freeman, 'The Mythical and Romantic Elements in Early English History' (1866), reprinted in his *Historical Essays*, series 1 (Oxford, 1886), 10–15.

Most problematically for Æthelstan's cause, Alfred was frequently hailed as the first king to hold sway over the whole of England. Orderic Vitalis made that claim first, but its energetic promotion by monks of St Albans probably had more impact on English popular perception. Roger of Wendover, writing at St Albans early in the thirteenth century, asserted confidently that the general submission to Alfred and restoration of London in 886 made him, from that time forward, the monarch of all England. His successors conveyed the same argument yet more forcefully, Matthew Paris even reporting that 'in view of his merits Alfred was called the Great'. So high did Alfred stand in the ranks of former monarchs that Henry VI tried in 1441 to get Alfred, 'the first monarch of the famous kingdom of England', canonized, but without success.[10] Attempts to make a saint of Edward the Confessor had begun soon after his death; eulogized in a poetic obituary notice in the Anglo-Saxon Chronicle, Edward was the subject of a *Vita* written by a monk of St Omer on behalf of his widow in 1065–67. His cult developed in the twelfth and thirteenth centuries when Osbert of Clare produced a new, much fuller life, which with other testimonials proved sufficient for Pope Alexander III to canonize him in 1161.[11] No one seems to have mounted a similar effort on Æthelstan's behalf, which might seem surprising. In Æthelstan we have, like Edward, a monarch who devoted much time and energy to the promotion of religious matters and the patronage of the Church. One might have thought a claim to chastity, preserved on spiritual grounds, notably easy to advance for Æthelstan, given that he had never married, nor produced any illegitimate offspring. Where he differed from Edward, of course, was in his martial prowess, which would fit ill with conventional hagiographical stereotypes advancing the claims of saints as promoters of a gospel of peace.

While neither great nor saint, Æthelstan nonetheless continued to have a high profile in Latin and vernacular literature written in England in the later middle ages, proving a far from forgotten monarch. His martial success attracted a good deal of attention, as for example in the account of the battle of *Brunanburh* given by Gaimar in his *L'Estoire des Engleis*, written *c.*1135–40.[12] In his poetic chronicle of Britain, *Roman de Brut*, Wace included an account of King Æthelstan which Layamon developed further in his *Brut* (*c.*1190), making Æthelstan into a strong Christian king who issued law and restored the payment of Peter's pence to Rome after a period of desuetude. Here Æthelstan's illegitimate birth occupied a

---

[10] Keynes, 'Cult of Alfred', 231–7.

[11] Frank Barlow, 'Edward [St Edward; *known as* Edward the Confessor] (1003×5–1066)', *Oxford Dictionary of National Biography*, Oxford University Press, September 2004; online edn, May 2006 [http://ezproxy.ouls.ox.ac.uk:2117/view/article/8516, accessed 23 September 2009]

[12] *L'estoire des Engleis by Geffrei Gaimar*, lines 3509–24, ed. Alexander Bell (Oxford, 1960), 112.

prominent place and Æthelstan did not succeed his father naturally but had to come to London to be appointed king before he could be duly anointed and crowned. Even so, he had the distinction of being 'the first Englishman to gain possession of the whole of England' (line 15944). Æthelstan supposedly made a number of administrative reforms to England: establishing courts of law and setting up assemblies, establishing shire courts and making enclosures for game, setting up manorial and hundred courts and founding many important guilds as well as refashioning churches (lines 15972–9). The historicity of much of this is problematical, as Elaine Treharne has shown, but the anachronisms that place his rule soon after Ine of Wessex, or claim him as parliament's founder have less significance for us than do the allusions to the illegitimacy of his birth – derived ultimately from William of Malmesbury, via Wace – and the remark, almost tossed away, that Æthelstan ruled unjustly (line 15987).[13]

In Layamon we see a far from unequivocal portrait of the king and the same negativities can be paralleled in other Anglo-Norman and Middle English texts. Æthelstan played a role in the Anglo-Norman *Gui de Warewic* (*c*.1230) and variant English versions of the poem dating from the fourteenth and fifteenth centuries. There he appeared as a royal figure often in the background of the action although some elements of one battle scene, where the king's enemy is Sir Anlaf of Denmark, may owe something to the *Brunanburh* poem. Æthelstan apparently had the status of a representative Anglo-Saxon king with a known name available to authors from this period looking to locate their narrative in a pre-Conquest past; his fictionalized reputation had steadily deteriorated, however, since the early post-Conquest period. Now he often appeared weak, unable to take sound advice and even neglecting the spiritual.[14] Quite why this should have happened we can only speculate but it seems likely that familiarity with William of Malmesbury's stories about both the unsuitability of his mother and his part in organizing his brother's death played key roles in dimming his reputation.

Æthelstan fared rather better in the Life of St Oswald of Worcester in the *South English Legendary* (the earliest manuscripts of which date from the late thirteenth century), where he made a cameo appearance because of his connection with Oswald's uncle, Archbishop Oda. At a battle against heathen men (obviously based loosely on *Brunanburh*) Oda, the king's highest counsellor, urged the king to take his scabbard and seize his sword in order to overcome his foe. Æthelstan here demonstrated how true

---

[13] Elaine M. Treharne, 'Romanticizing the Past in the Middle English *Athelston*', *Review of English Studies*, n.s. l (1999), 6–7.

[14] John Frankis, 'Views of Anglo-Saxon England in Post-Conquest Vernacular Writing', in *Orality and Literacy in Early Middle English*, ed. Herbert Pilch (Tübingen, 1996), 242–3; Treharne, 'Romanticizing', 7–8.

Englishmen behave: his function in this part of Oswald's life was primarily to underscore Oswald's Englishness and high political connections.[15]
Æthelstan's military victories and his piety played central roles in
fourteenth-century English chronicles such as the anonymous *Short Metrical
Chronicle*, the *Boke of Brut* (*c*.1327), or John of Trevisa's translation of the
Polychronicon of Ranulph Higden (1387): in all those texts Æthelstan was
depicted as pious, victorious and, above all, English. As a memorable
figure, Æthelstan proved valuable in focusing the minds of later medieval
audiences on the pre-Conquest past and so helped these authors in their
aim of creating a sense of unbroken English history from Anglo-Saxon
times to the fourteenth century.[16] In these different accounts, Æthelstan's
patronage of the Church and interest in book-learning were not forgotten;
indeed in some quarters they were amplified beyond his known achievements. When Tyndale sought to justify his own translation of the Bible, he
reported having read as a child a statement in the English Chronicle that
'King Athelstan caused the Holy Scripture to be translated into the tongue
that then was in England', and that the bishops supported him in this.[17]
Æthelstan had a further not inconsiderable afterlife in Norse saga.
We have already had cause to consider the depiction of the battle of
Brunanburh (relocated to a field called *Vinheiðr*) in *Egils saga* and should
recall that Egil Skallagrímsson reputedly addressed Æthelstan in verse.
Æthelstan appeared also in prose sagas of the later medieval period, not
least because of his role in assisting Hákon, known as *Aðalesteins fóstri*.[18]

Returning to English literature, little of the heroic comes across in the
fourteenth-century poem named *Æthelston*. There the eponymous hero, in
Treharne's words 'a troubled, insecure king', was not portrayed 'through
chivalric gestes, but as a fallible human monarch'. Only with the aid of the
archbishop and his absolution after Æthelstan's repentance could he
become a pious king, overcome crisis and gain moral strength.[19] *Æthelston*
did not pretend to offer an historical account of tenth-century English
affairs, or to convey a genuine pre-Conquest ruler. The poem's concerns,
Helen Young has argued, clearly occupy a fourteenth-century space,
preoccupied as it is with issues of government and English identity. The
usefulness of the Anglo-Saxon past to the poet lies centrally in its capacity
to give a continuity to English history that the Conquest had not severed:

[15] Jill Frederick, '*The South English Legendary*: Anglo-Saxon Saints and National Identity',
in *Literary Appropriations of the Anglo-Saxons*, ed. D. Scragg and C. Weinberg (Cambridge,
2000), 57–73, at 61.
[16] Helen Young, '*Athelston* and English Law: Plantagenet Practice and Anglo-Saxon
Precedent', *Parergon*, n.s. xxii (2005), 98.
[17] William Tyndale, *The Obedience of a Christian Man* (1528), ed. David Daniell (London,
2000), 19. See plate 19.
[18] Judith Jesch, 'Skaldic Verse in Scandinavian England', in *The Vikings and the Danelaw*,
ed. James Graham-Campbell *et al.* (Oxford, 2001), 313–17; M. Fjalldal, *Anglo-Saxon England
in Icelandic Medieval Texts* (Toronto, 2005), 87–90 and 94–100.
[19] Treharne, 'Romanticizing', 20.

Anglo-Saxon monarchs disagreed with their archbishops of Canterbury just as had various post-Conquest kings, but, the poem suggested, 'Plantagenet problems of government could be solved with recourse to Anglo-Saxon remedies'.[20] The poem might have been called Edgar, Edmund, or even Alfred; the precise choice of king was less relevant than that his name should convey instantly the pre-Conquest past which the poet sought to evoke. Æthelstan's name echoed peculiarly in thirteenth- and fourteenth-century ears, suggesting that despite his supposed char- acter flaws, enough of his successful deeds lived on to ensure him a place in popular memory.

OBLIVION

From the early modern period onwards, we see a shift in King Æthelstan's place in popular memory as the reputation of his grandfather Alfred increasingly eclipsed that of all Anglo-Saxon kings. With other notable pre-Conquest monarchs, Æthelstan came at best to play a bit-part in the story of England's past. Even though Æthelstan's name had maintained some currency in the later middle ages he appeared less often from the sixteenth century onwards either as a figure worth remembering in his own right, or when an author sought a generic pre-Conquest king. Æthelstan gradually disappeared from popular consciousness. While we cannot trace a simple inexorable narrative of Æthelstan's forgetting, the comparison between his albeit slightly mixed fourteenth-century reputa- tion and his relative insignificance in nineteenth-century narratives of England's history is stark and mirrors the rise during the same period of King Alfred as 'the archetypal symbol of the nation's perception of itself'.[21]

Queen Elizabeth's reign saw an increasing interest in the history of England before the Norman Conquest. Antiquarian scholars collected manuscript texts from that period and arranged for their publication, opening up to a wider audience knowledge of what Archbishop Parker termed 'the antient Monuments of the learned men of our Nation'. Matthew Parker arranged for the publication of numerous texts to encourage the study of the early English language and enhance under- standing of early English history in the hope of providing a more secure historical underpinning for the newly created 'Ecclesia Anglicana'. Among the texts Parker edited and printed was Asser's Life of King Alfred (1574), which did much to increase popular understanding of Alfred's qualities as a ruler and to build his reputation as a scholar and statesman at the expense of all other pre-Conquest kings for whom no such

---

[20] Young, '*Athelston*', 116–17.
[21] Keynes, 'Cult of Alfred', 225.

biographical material survives.[22] John Foxe drew on printed accounts of England's past in crafting an extended account of English history in the edition of his *Actes and Monuments* published in 1570. In his survey of kings from Egbert to William the Conqueror he gave Æthelstan due attention, describing him as a 'prince of worthy memory, valiant in all his acts' and – in a telling phrase that suggests Æthelstan needed some extra support – 'nothing inferior to his father Edward'. Foxe gave him credit for 'reducing this realm under the subjection of one monarchy, for he both expelled the Danes, subdued the Scots, and quieted the Welshmen, as well in North Wales as also in Cornwall' but struggled over his role in the death of his brother Edwin.[23] Yet Alfred far outshone his grandson in Foxe's account in virtues and in achievement. In the theatre, Æthelstan's name fared little better. Only one Elizabethan play dealt directly with an Anglo-Saxon topic and it celebrated Edmund Ironside; after the Restoration, plays on Anglo-Saxons remained rare, although not wholly unknown. Edgar's youthful exploits provided valuable material for playwrights, as did the liaison between the young king Eadwig and his cousin Ælfgifu. The novelist and poet Jane West wrote a play called *Edmund Surnamed Ironside* (1791). Yet authors could still continue to expect their audiences to rise to the name and reputation of Æthelstan. A play of 1756 called *Æthelstan* by Dr John Brown, in which Garrick took the leading part in performance in Drury Lane, did not concern the king at all, however, but dealt with a rebel Saxon earl of the same name, who fought valiantly against the Danes.[24]

One historic British (now worldwide) social institution, an important but often disregarded medium for preserving and disseminating the Anglo-Saxon past, continues to trace its mythological origins back to King Æthelstan and so contrives among its number to keep his name alive. Freemasons, whose origins lie in the medieval guilds of stonemasons who used to meet in lodges built for their purposes on building sites, emerged as wider social groups that admitted gentlemen as well as working stone-masons in Scotland in the sixteenth century and, in a slightly less organized fashion, in England in the seventeenth century. The establishment of the Grand Lodge in London in 1717 marked the beginning of modern Freemasonry in Britain, whence it spread rapidly across Europe and America; by the late eighteenth century there were over a thousand Masonic lodges in Britain with perhaps 30,000 members. Masons invoke the name of Æthelstan (and his 'son', Edwin) in a foundation legend, first recorded in Middle English verse in manuscripts of the fifteenth century

[22] Ibid., 240–1, and references cited there.

[23] John Foxe, *Acts and Monuments*, 1570 edn, book iii, 195–8 [http://www.hrionline.ac.uk/johnfoxe/main/3_1570_0195.jsp, accessed 26 January 2010]

[24] Donald Scragg, 'Introduction', in *Literary Appropriations*, ed. Scragg and Weinberg, 17–18.

and still promoted by the order today. According to this narrative, the art of building had fallen into neglect in early tenth-century England but Æthelstan reintroduced it: his 'son' loved the stonemasons and was initiated into their secrets. Thanks to Edwin's good offices, Æthelstan gave the stonemasons a charter allowing them to hold an annual assembly, the first of which Edwin convened at York, giving the society rules of organization and ordinances governing their craft. Later versions of the story expand Æthelstan's involvement and the details of the ordinances agreed at Edwin's York assembly substantially, reflecting specific conditions in the building industry in England in the sixteenth century.[25]

Our interest in this material lies not in the legend itself (which has no intrinsic historical merit) but in the fact of its association with Æthelstan's name. It acquired some modifications when further historical research by early Masons revealed the impossibility of Æthelstan's having a son called Edwin and questioned the likelihood of identifying this character with the king's brother Edwin, whose death at sea the Anglo-Saxon Chronicle recorded in 933. Yet the claim that Æthelstan played a role in the society's formation has proved surprisingly tenacious. Eighteenth-century texts such as James Anderson, *The Constitution of the Free-Masons* (1723) and William Preston's *Illustrations of Masonry* (1775) which both dealt with these legends and the historical evidence for the king's reign had an enormous effect in popularizing the story of Edwin's drowning. As Andrew Prescott has argued, 'for many members of Masonic lodges in provincial towns and cities in eighteenth-century England, [these two books] were probably one of the chief means by which they were made aware of Anglo-Saxon history and the life of Æthelstan'.[26] Today, the English order continues to call itself 'The Masonic Order of Æthelstan'. A Masonic lodge established in London in 1769 in 1816 the Royal Æthelstan Lodge, took the name of still thrives, as do the Athelstan lodges at Atherstone, Warwickshire and Philadelphia, Pennsylvania, both consecrated in 1870. The Athelstan Lodge established at Mobile, Alabama in the same year had, however, by 1873, reinvented itself as a independent men's social club, perhaps because of the order's prohibition on alcoholic drinks or because Catholics (prominent in the city and among its business and professional elite) could not join;[27] the Athelstan Club in Battle Creek, Michigan, now only a social club, probably also once had Masonic connections. Just how little some of Mobile's twentieth-century residents knew about King Æthelstan (or indeed Anglo-Saxon

[25] Andrew Prescott, ' "Kinge Athelston That Was a Worthy Kinge of England": Anglo-Saxon Myths of the Freemasons', in *The Power of Words*, ed. Hugh Magennis and Jonathan Wilcox (Morgantown, WV, 2006), 397–434. The first version of the Masonic foundation legend is found in British Library, MS Royal 17 A. i: discussed by Prescott, ' "Kinge Athelston" ', 404–8. A more elaborate version was preserved in BL Add. MS 23198: 408–15.

[26] Prescott, ' "Kinge Athelston" ', 431.

[27] Don Harrison Doyle, *New Men, New Cities, New South: Atlanta, Nashville, Charleston, Mobile, 1860* (Chapel Hill, NC, 1990), 247, and 351, n. 63.

history generally) is revealed in a report in *The Times* of London about plans made in October 1983 for a British Faire in Mobile to include an exhibit on the Kings and Queens of England. The promoter reported the involvement of the Athelstan Club in this event, since 'Athelstan was king of Wessex and grandson of Albert the Great who reigned in the tenth century'.[28]

Beyond the Masonic Order, a wider educated British public in the eighteenth and nineteenth centuries would most plausibly have encountered the historical Æthelstan and his deeds in history books, either those written specifically for children, or general histories of England. Simon Keynes's exploration of the eighteenth-century pictures and engravings made to accompany contemporary English histories reveals which events and persons were thought worthy of commemoration. In this medium, too, Alfred had greater prominence than any other pre-Conquest king. Neither of the images Keynes located in which Æthelstan appeared relates to incidents reported in any medieval historical texts. 'Æthelstan saves his father's life by taking Leofrid the Dane prisoner' depicts an episode reported in Montague's *New and Universal History of England* of 1771 which cannot be connected with any event in the king's life to which any medieval text bears witness. A legend that a Leofrid the Dane, who had settled in Ireland, assisted by Griffith ap Madoc, brother to the prince of West Wales, landed on the north-western English coast and penetrated as far as Chester in 920, where they were defeated by Edward with Æthelstan's assistance, had some currency in eighteenth-century popular histories and is still remembered in modern-day Chester.[29] The engraving showing 'Æthelstan ordering the Bible to be translated into the Saxon language', which illustrates Russel's *New and Authentic History of England* (1777), derives ultimately from Tyndale's assertion quoted above.

Much the most important and influential single work to promote Anglo-Saxon studies was Sharon Turner's *History of the Anglo-Saxons*, first published in four volumes between 1799 and 1805 and reprinted in at least six further editions before Turner's death in 1847. Turner did much to revise contemporary views of a people once thought barbarous. In his third edition, as part of a wider analysis of social and cultural aspects of Anglo-Saxon life, he expanded an original section on 'Their Poetry, Literature, Arts and Sciences', to include his own translation of the Chronicle's poem on *Brunanburh*, omitted from the first edition on the grounds that previous translations existed in print. Even in the later edition Turner had little complimentary to say about the verses: he observed their 'artless order' and described this as 'poetry in its rudest form, before the art of narration was

---

[28] Reported in *The Times* Diary, 24 August 1983, p. 8.

[29] Temple Sydney, *A New and Complete History of England* (London, 1773), *s.a.* 920. I owe this reference to Simon Keynes. For the memory that the heads of Gruffydd and Leofrid had been set on the gates of the city of Chester after their defeat see http://www.chesterwalls.info/ northgate3.html (accessed 20 February 2010).

understood'.[30] Yet he helped to establish *Brunanburh* as a key battle in English history, an engagement which he described as 'of such consequence that it raised Æthelstan to a most venerated dignity in the eyes of all Europe'.[31] Alfred received more attention in Turner's history than any other single figure: five substantial chapters on the military events of his reign concluded the first volume of the third edition, and six more opened Volume II, tackling Alfred's intellectual and moral character and his public conduct, his translations and poetical compositions. In comparison, the treatment of Æthelstan seems slight; nonetheless this does not constitute an insubstantial survey of the king's deeds and personality. Turner's account drew heavily on William of Malmesbury but also on a range of other sources, including *Egil's saga*, in order to craft a vivid and dramatic narrative, especially when recounting the battle of *Brunanburh*. This 'dangerous and important conflict . . . effectively secured to [Æthelstan] the throne of his ancestors; the subjugation of the Anglo-Danes was so decisive that he has received the fame of being the founder of the English monarchy'. Considering the claims of others to that epithet, Turner concluded: 'The truth seems to be that Alfred was the first monarch of the Anglo-Saxons, but Æthelstan was the first monarch of England . . . After the battle of *Brunanburh* Æthelstan had no competitor: he was the immediate sovereign of all England. He was even nominal lord of Wales and Scotland.'[32] Interestingly, Turner did not pursue the question of Æthelstan's overlordship of Britain, even though (in support of his argument that Æthelstan should have the title 'first English monarch') he quoted a charter of King Edgar that referred to Æthelstan's subjection of all the peoples of Britain. Generally he gave a favourable account of Æthelstan's personality and deeds, covering his marriage alliances and fostering of foreign princes ('thus it became the glory of Æthelstan that he nurtured and enthroned three kings in Europe'); his generosity to the poor and to the Church; and his laws (quoting William of Malmesbury in asserting 'It was a common saying of the Anglo-Saxons of Æthelstan that no one more legally or more learnedly conducted a government'). The lengthy eulogy ends, however, with the king's murder of his brother Edwin, a deed that 'stained his memory': 'for seven years, Æthelstan mourned his death with a penitence which proved that he gained nothing by the crime, but self-reproach and infelicity – the most usual consequence of guilt'.[33]

[30] Sharon Turner, *The History of the Anglo-Saxons*, 3rd edn, 3 vols (Paris, 1840), iii, 166–7. Edward B. Irving, 'The Charge of the Saxon Brigade: Tennyson's *Battle of Brunanburh*', in *Literary Appropriations of the Anglo-Saxons*, ed. Donald Scragg and Carole Weinberg (Cambridge, 2000), 179.

[31] Turner, *The History*, ii, 120.

[32] Ibid., 120–1.

[33] Ibid., 131–2.

By devoting more space to Æthelstan than to any other pre-Conquest king apart from Alfred and offering generally a highly positive reading of Æthelstan's character and achievements (in stark contrast to his account of Edgar, which dwelt primarily on that king's moral weaknesses), Turner did much to increase awareness of Æthelstan in the wider population. *Little Arthur's History of England*, first published in 1835 but reprinted throughout the nineteenth century, shows some debts to Turner in devoting much attention to the pre-Conquest period. The (childless) Lady Maria Callcott wrote it for a real 'Little Arthur' in the hope that it might instil in him the foundations of patriotism; she found numerous moral messages in the country's Anglo-Saxon past with which to edify him. Alfred attracted her particular attention, but she had a good deal to say about Æthelstan also, commending him for his intelligence and bravery, and lauding his recognition that England needed to have a great many ships, for both defensive and mercantile purposes. She credited him – wrongly – with the introduction of a law that every man who built a ship and went to sea twice would acquire thane (thegn) status, which means, she explained to her childish readers, 'that he should be called lord instead of mister when he was spoken to'.[34] Lady Maria then told a highly colourful account of the aftermath of Æthelstan's victory at *Brunanburh*, drawing ostensibly on an old book written by a man who had talked to one who survived the battle, called 'Egill'. That text praised Æthelstan for his clemency to the defeated and offered some domestic details about the furnishings of the king's hall and the sorts of entertainment and diet enjoyed by the royal court and its foreign visitors: 'they all drank a great deal of ale, and while they drank there were several men, called minstrels, singing to them about the great battles they had fought, and the great men who were dead'.[35]

Little Arthur's History stands somewhat apart from other general histories of England written during the nineteenth century with children in mind. The majority tended to conform to a pattern we might now find predictable: those that dealt at all with pre-Conquest kings paid the most attention to Alfred; their treatment of kings other than Harold (because of his defeat at Hastings) proved highly variable. So a *History of England in Easy Dialogues for Young Children by a Lady* (1816) names only three English kings before William the Conqueror (Alfred, who was 'one of the best of our early kings', Cnut and Harold). Similarly, *Aunt Anne's History of England on Christian Principles for the Use of Young Persons* (1841) declared that 'there were many Saxon kings after Alfred but as I think there is not much to interest you in their reigns, I think my best plan will be to give you a list of their names and afterwards relate anything interesting'. Announcing that

[34] This provision was in fact made in a text about wergelds and social status closely associated with Archbishop Wulfstan of York, called by Liebermann, *Geþynco*, §6, trans. *EHD*, no. 51.

[35] Lady Maria Callcott, *Little Arthur's History of England* (London, 1835, twentieth thousand edn, 1846), ch. 10, pp. 30–3.

the first four reigns after Alfred were full of contests with the Danes, she moved rapidly to Eadred, never mentioning Æthelstan at all. Those texts that devoted more attention to England's earlier history and to the period of the Heptarchy, gave considerable prominence to Alfred's grandfather, Ecgberht, often claimed as the first king of England, and supposedly crowned with that title at Winchester in 828. A *Catechism of the History of England* supplied Ecgberht's name in answer to the question, 'Who was the first king of England?' and went on to devote substantial attention to Alfred's reign, requiring not just knowledge of his military exploits but that pupils 'relate the remarkable events of Alfred's reign besides his defeating the Danes'. Æthelstan required no such feats of memory: 'Q. Did Æthelstan perform anything worthy of notice? A. Yes, he obtained a great victory over the Danes in Northumberland, after which he reigned in tranquillity being regarded as one of the ablest kings of those ancient times.'[36]

Not all such writers dismissed Æthelstan so readily, especially not those whose knowledge of the Anglo-Saxon past clearly came in part from Sharon Turner. Henry Tyrrell's *History of England for the Young*, published in the 1850s, had Ecgberht crowned at Winchester as the first to rule over one united kingdom of England. However, he followed Turner in asserting that Æthelstan ('who was worthy to be a grandson of the great king Alfred; he governed wisely and defended the land in a skilful and powerful manner') was 'the first who called himself "king of the English", for even Alfred, though ruler of the whole land, only bore the modest title of King of the West Saxons'. Æthelstan's achievements also encompassed the reform of the law, regard for the poor, and a great admiration for the Bible, which he was anxious to have translated.[37] The Venerable Charles Smith (Archdeacon of Jamaica) extrapolated yet further beyond the facts in claiming that Æthelstan had placed copies of the Saxon scriptures in the churches of England.[38] After a lengthy consideration of Alfred, presenting him not as a political but as a moral exemplar for the nation's youth, Charles Dickens devoted just one paragraph to Æthelstan in his *Child's History of England*. According to Dickens, Æthelstan governed England well, reduced the turbulent people of Wales, forcing them to pay tribute, restored old law fallen into disuse, cared for the poor, and defeated an alliance forged against him (i.e. at *Brunanburh*). 'After that he had a quiet reign; the lords and ladies about him had leisure to become polite and

---

[36] *The Catechism of the History of England from its Earliest Period to the Present Time: Written in Easy Language, for the Use of Young People*, by a friend to youth (Newbury, [not before 1820]), 16–20.

[37] Henry Tyrrell, *A History of England for the Young* (London, 1853?–1856?), 18, 27.

[38] Charles John Smith, *History of England for Young Students from the Earliest Times to the Present* (London, 1867).

agreeable; and foreign princes were glad (as they have sometimes been since) to come to England on visits to the English court.'[39]

Among general histories aimed at a wider adult readership we might pause over just one: *A History of England under the Anglo-Saxon Kings*, translated by Benjamin Thorpe from the original German of the first volume of J.M. Lappenberg's *Geschichte von England*, first published in 1834, which appeared in English in 1845. Lappenberg gave some attention to Æthelstan's military exploits during his father's reign, including that somewhat unlikely story of the young prince's defeat of 'Leofred, a Dane', and then devoted a whole chapter to Æthelstan's deeds during 'a reign which though not long yet pre-eminent in glory each year of which appeared destined to witness a new exaltation of the Anglo-Saxon name'. Drawing heavily on William of Malmesbury, Lappenberg had much, unsurprisingly, to say about Æthelstan's foreign relations, supplementing English narratives with German and Frankish sources. Not all his comments were favourable: 'no merits, no exertions were sufficient to obliterate the injurious stain which in the eyes of his prejudiced countrymen was attached to the birth of Æthelstan, and which, through his efforts to remove it, only appeared the greater'. His role in the murder of his brother Edwin, and the latter's cup-bearer, thus received full, and critical, treatment.[40]

Nineteenth-century interest in the Anglo-Saxons found further expression beyond the works of history in literary texts, again inspired in part by Sharon Turner's demonstration of the vitality of pre-Conquest culture. Here we see how processes involved in the creation of a national identity suitable for an age of intense nationalism which had also a marked romantic ethos served to mould popular historical consciousness of pre-Conquest kings and their deeds. In that process, Alfred's role became yet more prominent at the inevitable expense of his grandson. Ignored entirely by Wordsworth in his chronological sequences of sonnets on Anglo-Saxon themes, *Ecclesiastical Sketches* (1822), Æthelstan's wider reputation received a substantial boost from Tennyson's translation of the Chronicle poem *The Battle of Brunanburh* and the slightly earlier 'dramatic chronicle' by George Darley: *Ethelston or The Battle of Brunanburh* (1841). Darley saw his play as putting down a marker for one of the many heroes of our race who as yet sleeps without a memorial, among whom he obviously numbered Æthelstan.[41] Alfred, Lord Tennyson (then Poet Laureate) wrote his verse translation of *The Battle of Brunanburh* in 1876 and published it in 1880. Generally Anglo-Saxon poetry received little critical acclaim in this period, but the American poet Longfellow, in a lengthy review article covering several recent texts in Anglo-Saxon studies including

---

[39] Charles Dickens, *A Child's History of England* (London, 1852–4), 43; Clare A. Simmons, *Reversing the Conquest: History and Myth in Nineteenth-Century British Literature* (New Brunswick, NJ and London, 1990), 25.

[40] J.M. Lappenberg, *A History of England under the Anglo-Saxon Kings*, trans. Benjamin Thorpe (London, 1845; rev. edn, 2 vols, 1881), ii, 136–7.

[41] Scragg, 'Introduction', 17.

Bosworth's *Dictionary of the Anglo-Saxon Language* (1837) and Kemble's *Beowulf* (1833), responded positively as a poet to Old English verse forms. He offered his own translation of the *Brunanburh* poem, remarking: 'we consider this ode, as one of the most characteristic specimens of Anglo-Saxon poetry. What a striking picture is that of the lad with flaxen hair, mangled with wounds; and of the seven earls of Anlaf, and the five young kings, lying on the battle field, lulled asleep by the sword! Indeed the whole ode is striking, bold and graphic.'[42] Tennyson had not always had positive things to say about *Brunanburh*, which he had a thane mock and parody in his play *Harold*: 'Mark'd how the war-axe swang, / Heard how the war-horn sang, / Mark'd how the spear-head sprang, / heard how the shield-wall rang, / Iron on iron clang, / Anvil on hammer bang –' Longfellow, too, had noted how the short emphatic lines of this verse ring like blows of hammers on anvils. In making this translation, however, Tennyson showed a greater appreciation not just of its basic rhythms (which he conveys relentlessly in a sequence of short lines) but also of its heroic qualities. He wrote, of course, as Irving has noted, for a Victorian audience: 'his version of *Brunanburh* must have told thousands of readers that there was some quite exciting and rather different-sounding verse to be discovered back in the dim English past (though it also sounded comfortably modern)'.[43] Yet, despite the popularity of Anglo-Saxon subjects among Victorian painters, neither Æthelstan nor his great battle at *Brunanburh* found visual commemoration in any picture exhibited at the Royal Academy between 1769 and 1904. King Alfred once more dominated these canvasses, the only other kings depicted being Cnut, Harold, Eadwig and Edward the Martyr.[44] Alfred, not Æthelstan, took the central role in the creation of a national myth of English and British origins. The beginnings of political stability in Britain – to be celebrated in the mid-nineteenth century in contrast to the upheavals elsewhere in Europe – went back to Alfred's day. He was, in the words of Edward Augustus Freeman, 'the most perfect character in history'; having compared Alfred favourably with a range of historical figures including Charlemagne, Edward I and George Washington, Freeman concluded, 'there is no other name in history to compare with his'.[45] In comparison with fame on this scale, Æthelstan faded into oblivion.

[42] H.W. Longfellow, 'Review of Anglo-Saxon Literature', *North American Review*, xlvii (1838), 115–18. Irving, 'The Charge', 179–80.

[43] Longfellow, 'Review,' 100. Irving, 'The Charge', 186–7. That there is still an audience for this verse is indicated by its inclusion in the *Oxford Book of War Poetry*, chosen and edited by Jon Stallworthy (Oxford, 1984; paperback 1988), 19–23. I owe this reference to my father, M.R.D. Foot.

[44] Roy Strong, *And When Did You Last See Your Father? The Victorian Painter and British History* (London, 1978), 114–18 and see his Appendix, 'Subjects from British history from the Ancient Britons to the outbreak of the Napoleonic Wars exhibited at the Royal Academy', 155–6. I am grateful to Richard Gameson for drawing this list of paintings to my attention.

[45] E.A. Freeman, *The History of the Norman Conquest of England*, 6 vols (Oxford 1867–79; 2nd edn, 1870), i, 48–52; quoted Keynes, 'Cult of Alfred', 344–5.

COMMEMORATION

Yet Æthelstan has not proved entirely forgotten, for his name continued to resonate securely in the popular English imagination in those places that had, or claimed to have, a direct association with the king in life, or in death. Writing in 1856, Charles Knight expressed some surprise in his *Popular History of England* at the extent to which the king's memory persisted among the populace of Malmesbury, where his tomb lay. The townsfolk apparently believed that the ruined arches of the Norman abbey dated from Æthelstan's day and attributed some of their common-rights (to pasture, for example) to Æthelstan's generosity, earned suppos-edly by the assistance their forebears had offered the king in a great battle against the Danes. In the restored abbey church at Malmesbury Æthelstan is commemorated by a late medieval tomb chest in perpendicular style, now in the north aisle. The king's recumbent, full-length effigy lies beneath a heavy traced canopy; the original head has been removed and replaced with another of unknown date.[46] A charming tale relating to the circumstances of Æthelstan's grant to Malmesbury given by John Aubrey links that gift with an annual ceremony on Trinity Sunday when prayers were said praising God 'that moved the hearts of King Athelstan and Dame Maud his good queen, to give this ground to our forefathers and to us'.[47] We know nothing of this supposed queen, whom we must assume to have been a figment of local imaginations that saw marriage as essential to all good kings. Other towns also recalled the king's name; as Palgrave had observed in his *History of the Anglo-Saxons*, 'throughout the west of England there is scarcely a town in which a statue of Æthelstan has not been erected'.[48] A medieval sequence of statues once found on the west front of Lichfield cathedral (but removed, because much decayed, in 1749), might have included a figure representing Æthelstan. However, the statues replacing those earlier images, which were commissioned by the dean and chapter in 1821, apparently included Alfred – with a harp – but not his grandson.[49]

At Beverley in the East Riding of Yorkshire, the population recalled this king fondly. Æthelstan had supposedly visited Beverley on his way to fight

---

[46] James T. Bird, *The History of the Town of Malmesbury and of its Ancient Abbey* (Malmesbury, 1876), 43–7. Nikolaus Pevsner, *Wiltshire*, 2nd edn, revised Bridget Cherry (Harmondsworth, 1975), 326. See plate 16.

[47] *Wiltshire: the Topographical Collections of John Aubrey FRS, AD* 1659–70, corrected and enlarged by J.E. Jackson (Devizes, 1862) 252, 272. See also S 454, Susan Kelly, *Charters of Malmesbury Abbey* (Oxford, 2005), no. 48 and pp. 292–3.

[48] Charles Knight, *The Popular History of England: An Illustrated History of Society and Government from the Earliest Period to our Own Times* (London, 1856), 128–9; Francis Palgrave, *History of the Anglo-Saxons* (London, 1837; 1867 edn), 182.

[49] J.C. Woodhouse, *A Short Account of Lichfield Cathedral* (8th edn, London, 1885), 38–42; I am grateful to Simon Keynes for this reference. C. Harradine, *Hand Guide to Lichfield Cathedral containing a Detailed Account of the Sculpture on the West Front* (Lichfield, 1891).

a major battle in the north (either the Scottish expedition of 934, or the *Brunanburh* campaign in 937) and paused to pray for victory in his forthcoming expedition at the shrine of St John of Beverley (a prominent figure in Bede's *History*, and an early bishop of Hexham). Returning after a successful campaign, Æthelstan allegedly went on to refound the church as a collegiate community of canons and granted it land and a number of privileges including the right of sanctuary (a right claimed energetically until the Reformation, and still remembered in the minster today because of the frithstool, or peace stool, now located in the sanctuary), plus the right of the minster to receive thraves (a levy of corn) from all of the East Riding. The survival of a silver finger-ring of indeterminate medieval date, inscribed with the names of King Æthelstan and John 'archbishop' of Beverley and now preserved in a museum in Bury St Edmunds in Suffolk, offers further possible evidence at least of the memory of an association between the church of Beverley and the first king of all England.[50] Recollection of the privileges this king gave to the town is marked on the geography of medieval Beverley by a series of stone crosses one mile distant from the frithstool, the point where sanctuary could be claimed. Additionally the townspeople believed that the king had given them a charter, exempting them from certain tolls and conferring upon them important privileges. In fact no known source datable to before the reign of Stephen securely connects Æthelstan with the town, but this has not impeded the cultivation of his memory there.[51] Three monuments in the minster commemorate the king: a fourteenth-century corbel in the north choir aisle shows the heads of Æthelstan and St John, with the king in the act of handing his charter of liberties to the saint. Over the door of the south transept an early modern painting on wood (perhaps early sixteenth century in date, first mentioned in an eighteenth-century account of the church) depicts two figures, representing Æthelstan once more in the act of giving his charter to the saint, to which is added the words:

Als free, make I the[e]
As hert may thynke, or eyh can see.

On the north side of the archway leading into the choir is a canopied niche holding an eighteenth-century statue of a life-size warrior cast in lead, set on a pedestal: Æthelstan, holding a drawn sword in his right hand

---

[50] E. Okasha, 'A Rediscovered Medieval Inscribed Ring', *ASE*, ii (1973), 167–71; see also Susan E. Wilson, 'King Athelstan and St John of Beverley', *Northern History*, xl (2003), 5–23. See plate 17.

[51] Richard Kieckhefer, *Theology in Stone: Church Architecture from Byzantium to Berkeley* (Oxford and New York, 2004), 109–73. George Oliver, *The History and Antiquities of the Town and Minster of Beverley in the East Riding of Yorkshire* (Beverley, 1829), 57–60, 326. D.M. Palliser, 'The Early Medieval Minster', in *Beverley Minster: An Illustrated History*, ed. Rosemary Horrox (Beverley, 2000), 24. Susan E. Wilson, *The Life and After-Life of John of Beverley* (Aldershot, 2006), 119 and cf. 109–10.

and a charter in his left. A similar figure of John stands on the south side of the arch. Both were cast in 1781 by William Collins and added to an elaborate choir screen in mixed classical and Gothic style set up in 1731 (possibly to a design by Hawksmoor), which was dismembered in 1875.[52]

The cathedral church of Ripon in North Yorkshire claimed a link with Æthelstan on terms similar to those advanced by the church at Beverley. A spurious writ in Æthelstan's name (perhaps modelled on one of Henry I) alleged that Æthelstan had confirmed the privileges of the church and chapter of Ripon. Like Beverley and York, the church of Ripon sought in the later Middle Ages to claim that Æthelstan had promised it privileges when he came to Yorkshire on his way to fight the Scots; he supposedly vowed then that, should he prove successful, he would endow northern churches as a mark of his gratitude. A rhyming Middle English version of the charter (perhaps dating from the late thirteenth century) gives the privilege of sanctuary to the church: On ilke side the kyrke a mile/For all ill deedes and ylke agyle / And within yair kyrke yate, / At ye stan ya grithstole hate . . .'[53] The boundary of this place of refuge was, by the late thirteenth century, marked by eight crosses around the church called mile crosses, three of which survived into modern times: Athelstan's cross on the road between Ripon and Nunwick, close to a field called Athelstanesclose; a stump of an Archangel cross on a lane in Ripon leading from the Navigation bridge to Bondgate; and Sharrow cross, which stands on the road from Sharrow to Ripon.[54] Tamworth in Staffordshire also recalls its pre-Conquest past via a life-size statue of a bellicose Æthelflæd, Æthelstan's aunt, erected in 1913 to mark the millenary anniversary of the fortification of the town. Æthelflæd brandishes a sword in her right hand, while her left arm comforts the child Æthelstan, who clings to her skirts.[55]

Kingston upon Thames in Surrey can claim significant links with the Anglo-Saxon past, as the site of the coronation of pre-Conquest kings from Æthelstan onwards. The town's inhabitants have ensured the preservation of what they believe to be the historic coronation stone in the marketplace. A piece of Greywether sandstone, or sarsen (a glacial boulder) with a flat top, this may once have formed part of a prehistoric stone circle and stands nearly 31 inches high. Formerly the stone stood inside the chapel of St Mary, a medieval church (believed to date from

---

[52] Nikolaus Pevsner and David Neave, *Yorkshire: York and the East Riding*, 2nd edn (Harmondsworth, 1995), 293. Horrox, *Beverley Minster*, plates 7 (corbel) and 9 (painting on boards). See plate 18.

[53] 'For a mile on each side of the church, for all evil works and each guilty act, and within the enclosure* of the churchyard gate, at the stone called the grithstole.' *yair = enclosure, precincts of the church, etc.: *MED*, s.v. 'yerd'. I am grateful to Laura Ashe for advice on this point.

[54] S 456 (and rhyming Middle English version, S 457); John Richard Walbran, *A Guide to Ripon, Fountains Abbey, Harrogate, Bolton Priory and Several Places of Interest in their Vicinity* (Ripon, 1874), 7, 30–1.

[55] See plate 3.

before the Conquest, and perhaps originally dedicated to All Saints) which lay on the south side of the chancel of the current church until its destruction in 1730. Part of the roof and walls had fallen, burying a sexton trying to dig a grave too close to the foundations, and the rest was thereafter demolished. Statues of Eadred, Edward the Martyr and Æthelred the Unready had once been preserved inside it, but not apparently an effigy of Æthelstan. However, in his *Antiquities of Surrey* Aubrey reported that six crowned Anglo-Saxon kings had their portraits hung in St Mary's church, including Æthelstan, who he said had been crowned in the marketplace in the town. A letter published in *The Times* in 1956 sought to refute the long-standing misconception that coronation services had taken place outside in the marketplace of Kingston and not in the church, where surviving coronation *ordines* state clearly such ceremonies were performed.[56]

Some of that confusion arose from the modern location of the coronation stone. At first after the destruction of St Mary's chapel, the stone had stood by the entrance to the guildhall in the marketplace where it served as a mounting block. Mindful of their historic connections with Æthelstan and thus considering the stone's treatment unsuitable, the Masonic Order of Surrey played a prominent role in a campaign in the 1850s to resituate the relic in a more formal setting. In 1854 the Provincial Grand Master of Surrey inaugurated its new position at what was believed to be that of the Saxon palace, where it was mounted on a heptagonal base and surrounded by railings. The names of the seven kings believed to have been crowned on the stone were inscribed on the base, with the dates of their coronations, and a coin issued in each king's name. Æthelstan's name appears here, with the date 925. The other kings named are: Edward the Elder, Edmund, Eadred, Eadwig, Edward the Martyr and Æthelred. Re-laying the stone involved appropriate Masonic ceremonies, including checking its position with a square and level, and the sprinkling of the monument with corn, oil and wine. Kingston celebrated with a public holiday, marked by a Masonic procession, bands playing and a peal of bells.[57] In June 1924, the town of Kingston organized another historical procession and pageant to celebrate the millenary of Æthelstan's accession, an event which focused on the king's unification of the Anglo-Saxon kingdoms as first king of all England, but also on his efforts as an humanitarian, working for peace through unity, and his supposed convening of a court at Kingston in 937, attended by kings and queens of France, the Alps, Provence and Aquitaine and the emperor and empress of Germany.[58]

---

[56] John Aubrey, *The Natural History and Antiquities of the County of Surrey* (1718–19), facsimile reprint with introduction by J.L. Nevinson (Dorking, 1975), i, 20. Letter to the Editor from Patrick W. Montague-Smith, of Kingston upon Thames, *The Times*, 11 September, 1956, p. 9.

[57] W.E. St. L. Finny, *The Royal Borough of Kingston-upon-Thames, Surbiton and its Surroundings* (London, 1902), 33–5, 49–55; Prescott, ' "Kinge Athelston" ' 433–4. See plate 5.

[58] 'Millenary of Crowning of Æthelstan', report by our special correspondent, *The Times*, 10 June 1924, p. 9.

Twentieth-century royal coronations inspired historical reflection on the distant, pre-Conquest past. W.E. Finny wrote his little booklet on the history of the borough of Kingston - upon - Thames in coronation year, 1902. He dwelt on the resonance of the new king, Edward VII's name with that of his distant forebear, Edward the Elder, whom he believed to have been crowned in Kingston one thousand years previously. As the coronation of George VI approached in May 1937 (held on the date that had originally been planned for his elder brother, who would have been crowned Edward VIII had he not abdicated in December 1936), Anglo-Saxon historical precedents also came to mind. The Windsor Herald, A.T. Butler (an officer in the College of Arms in London) produced a lengthy essay for *The Times* on the new king's regnal style. Butler traced the style 'king of the English' to Ecgberht (Alfred's grandfather) and argued that King Æthelstan, exactly 1,000 years earlier, had been the first of the house of Cerdic to introduce the name of Britain into his royal style.[59] That the millennial anniversary of the battle of *Brunanburh* fell in the same year did not escape notice, either. W.E. Finny wrote to *The Times* to point out that as a consequence of Æthelstan's victory at *Brunanburh* in 937, 'His Majesty King George VI will be crowned at Westminster the king of the only kingdom in Europe which by the Grace of God has lasted 1000 years'.[60]

Without the spur provided by anniversary dates, Æthelstan's name has slipped again from public view since 1940 (when, as noted in the prologue, the millennium of his death attracted a brief newspaper notice). Frank Stenton's *Anglo-Saxon England,* published as the second volume of the *Oxford History of England* in 1943, gave a boost to the understanding of Æthelstan's significance beyond purely academic circles by devoting considerable attention to his achievements, but sixty years on, Stenton's general reader-ship is now more limited. Æthelstan has experienced something of a renaissance in the past thirty years, when scholars have paid increasing attention to the range of less conventional sources for the king's reign, especially the poetry written in his praise and manuscript books associated with his name. Historians now often set his reign in a wider cultural context and compare the king directly with his continental contempo-raries.[61] In Old English literary studies (as opposed to historical), Æthelstan has always had some part to play. Edward Irving wrote wryly about the experience of using *The Battle of Brunanburh* when teaching Old

[59] A.T. Butler, ' "By the Grace of God": The King's Style', *The Times,* 11 May 1937, p. 48.

[60] Letter to the Editor, *The Times,* 19 April 1937, p. 10.

[61] Lapidge, 'Poems'; Keynes, 'Books'; Michael Wood, 'The Making of King Æthelstan's Empire: an English Charlemagne?', in *Ideal and Reality in Frankish and Anglo-Saxon Society,* ed. Patrick Wormald *et al.* (Oxford, 1983), and his ' "Stand Strong against the Monsters": Kingship and Learning in the Empire of Æthelstan', in *Lay Intellectuals in the Carolingian World,* ed. Patrick Wormald and Janet L. Nelson (Cambridge, 2007); Karl Leyser, 'The Ottonians and Wessex', in *Communications and Power in Medieval Europe,* ed. Timothy Reuter (London, 1994).

English: 'a poem that is tidy but not especially exciting in any poetic sense, nonetheless a very useful one to have your students read early, mainly because it is completely conventional, a rich mass of clichés that students will need to learn in order to read . . . highly formulaic poetry'. Before students can move on to the excitements of *The Battle of Maldon*, *Beowulf* and the *Fight at Finnsburh*, they will have encountered Æthelstan and Edmund, the sons of Edward, confronting the seven strong earls of the army of Anlaf.[62] Similarly, modern university students of Anglo-Saxon history tracing the evolution of a unified kingdom of the English (and, especially if pupils of James Campbell, of the formation of an Anglo-Saxon state) have always encountered not just Chronicle accounts of this king's battles, but his coinage and his law codes. These different materials – literary, cultural and artistic as well as governmental and numismatic – have permitted us to create in these pages a rounded picture of this tenth-century king, whose claim to enduring fame rests on far more than military prowess. The validity of William of Malmesbury's assertion about the extent of Æthelstan's education may now appear to have more substance than once thought and not be mere empty rhetoric; equally, the poet John's prophecy that Æthelstan would 'be abundantly endowed with the eminence of learning' appears fulfilled in the mature king. The magnificence of the gifts apparently showered on the West Saxon king by foreign leaders seeking to make marriage alliances with Æthelstan also look in this context less excessive, and more commensurate with contemporaries' sense of his significance. That he might have been thought in some senses Charlemagne's equal, and certainly a worthy recipient of objects once treasured by the great Carolingian emperor, we might find explicable.

Sharon Turner thought it 'not at all surprising that Æthelstan was a favourite both among his own people and in Europe'. No modern historian would now write about Æthelstan in quite the language that Turner chose: '[Æthelstan] was certainly a great and illustrious character. He appears to have been as amiable as great. To the clergy he was attentive and mild; to his people affable and pleasant. With the great he was dignified; with others he laid aside his state, and was condescending and decently familiar . . . His people loved him for his bravery and humility; but his enemies felt his wrath.'[63] Yet my intention in this volume shares something with Turner's aims, for I, too, have sought the man behind the public figure who won battles, entertained dignitaries from overseas and convened royal councils on a seemingly unprecedented scale. Study of the person of the king rather than the institutions of his government has revealed much about Æthelstan's interests, tastes and preoccupations; above all, we now understand a great deal about his anxieties.

---

[62] Irving, 'The Charge', 183.
[63] Turner, *The History*, ii, 131.

Two images of Æthelstan have dominated his posthumous reputation: that of the successful warrior king, who defended the shores of a united England against combined forces from Scotland, Ireland and Scandinavia; and the pious king of the poem, the book- and relic-collector who proved a generous patron to the English Church and promoter of the cults of national saints. Both need revising. Exploration of Æthelstan's religious views and relationship with the Church beyond the evidence provided by the inscriptions in manuscripts associated with him and the relics he appears to have collected and donated, produces a more convincing picture of a man with a genuine inner spiritual life, and a serious concern for both the care of the poor and for his immortal soul. His statements about gifts made for his soul's good we should take as evidence for that preoccupation, just as his injunctions to the beneficiaries of some of his charters and in his laws that psalms be sung for his soul and alms given to the poor reflected more than empty rhetoric. From this perspective Æthelstan's decision to remain unmarried seems more readily explicable as a religiously motivated determination on chastity as a way of life. In the light of this more rounded picture of Æthelstan the man, we now also view his military exploits rather differently. The expeditions to Northumbria in 927, to Scotland in 934 and to *Brunanburh* (whether that field lay on the Wirral, in Dumfriesshire, or in the East Riding) all required substantial forward planning, a reliable supply chain and, above all, enormous wealth. These campaigns show us a military commander of skill and foresight, a more than competent soldier, supported by a staff of proven ability and unquestioned loyalty. His army's capacity on at least two (possibly three) major campaigns to supply itself so far from Wessex reveals much about Æthelstan's ability to harness the wealth of his expanded territory to his own ends. Mercian supply bases established during his father's wars must have played their part, but cannot have continued to feed, and organize quarters for, an army and a fleet active as far north as Caithness in 934. The quiet and bookish young man with his little bags of saintly bones has little in common with that king.

Kenneth Sisam, his mind fresh with Stenton's image of the national assemblies convened by Æthelstan and his vivid depiction of the king ('he possessed the physical energy without which no early king could govern well')[64] remembered Æthelstan as lying at the beginning of many developments. One can indeed dwell on that which Æthelstan did first: uniting the English people under a single authority; accepting the submission of all the other rulers of Britain and claiming hegemony over the whole island; wearing a crown and promoting his crowned portrait to the widest possible audience through his coinage; allying himself through marriage to the major powers of western Europe; legislating against Sunday trading and for the relaxation of the death penalty for juveniles. Yet, to do so

---

[64] Stenton, *ASE*, 356.

returns Æthelstan to the caricature of archetypical early medieval monarch from which I have sought so hard to release him. A biographical portrait of Æthelstan creates a series of interconnected images of a complex man, one who grew out of a rather difficult (and quite possibly, rather unhappy) childhood to become one of the most powerful rulers in the Europe of his day. It cannot begin to reveal what the tenth-century man was 'really' like. But it does show that one may not readily reduce Æthelstan to any single, stereotypical epithet. 'Very mighty', 'worthy of honour', 'his years filled with glory', 'pillar of the dignity of the Western world', 'pious King Æthelstan': each of these near-contemporary comments reflects aspects of our hero's achievement, yet none by itself encapsulates him as a person. Brought out of the shadows that have too long obscured his memory, Æthelstan now stands revealed in more than one dimension. His is a life not merely to commemorate but also to celebrate.

Appendix I

WILLIAM OF MALMESBURY AND A LOST LIFE OF KING ÆTHELSTAN[1]

William of Malmesbury wrote his 'Deeds of the English Kings' (*Gesta regum Anglorum*) in the second quarter of the twelfth century with the encouragement of Queen Matilda (1080–1118, daughter of Malcolm, king of the Scots and Margaret, granddaughter of Edmund Ironside, d. 1016) who had an interest in the history of her ancestors, the English kings.[2] As a member of the monastery at Malmesbury in Wiltshire since childhood, William showed a particular interest in King Æthelstan, his abbey's most significant pre-Conquest royal benefactor, who was buried in the abbey church. William's lengthy and detailed account of Æthelstan's reign, and especially the information he offers about his childhood in his *Gesta regum*, look particularly valuable to the biographer given the absence of any surviving narrative sources written either during Æthelstan's time, or during the reigns of his immediate successors. Many areas of Æthelstan's life would remain entirely unknown without William's narrative. However, precisely because William is a unique witness to so much of what he has to say, we need to treat his account cautiously.

William's narrative of the reign of Æthelstan falls into three discrete sections that were apparently written at two different times. The first part (Book II, §131) and also the third (II, §§136–40) rely on the Anglo-Saxon Chronicle and on various legendary sources and William probably wrote both sections at the same time. In between these two lies a later composition (§§132–5) constructed after William had discovered an ancient volume, written in a bombastic and rhetorical style; this middle portion apparently depends upon the testimony of the old book. Following immediately after his obituary notice for Edward the Elder, William first provides (§131) a concise narrative of the key events of Æthelstan's reign. Despite its lack of reference to specific dates other than that of Æthelstan's

---

[1] The account given here makes substantial use of an unpublished essay generously given to me by Michael Wood, 'The Lost Life of King Æthelstan: William of Malmesbury's Account of Æthelstan's Reign'. This new paper expands arguments Wood first advanced in 'The Making of King Æthelstan's Empire' and *In Search of England* (Harmondsworth, 2000), ch. 8: 'The Lost Life of King Athelstan'.

[2] *GR*, Ep. ii, pp. 6–9. An early version was completed around 1126, but William subsequently made a number of corrections and additions to the text on the basis of material not available to him when he was first writing.

accession, this seems to draw in part on a manuscript of the Anglo-Saxon Chronicle. William's text of the Chronicle did not, however, contain the verse account of the battle of *Brunanburh*, for he was unaware that Constantín of the Scots had survived the battle in which his son died.[3] Other than the Chronicle, William seems here to draw exclusively on legendary material, including the account of Anlaf spying in the English king's camp before the battle of *Brunanburh* and the miracle attributed to St Aldhelm, material which he embellished to fill out what would otherwise have been a distinctly scanty report.[4] The final part of William's tripartite narrative is similar in nature in that it adds little to what we can discover of his reign from other sources. Beginning with a description of the death of a certain Alfred to whose opposition to Æthelstan he had alluded earlier (§136), William used a (spurious) charter from Malmesbury to demonstrate the king's generosity to the abbey (§137) and then went on to recount further legends about the king that he claimed to have learned 'more from popular songs (*cantilena*) which have suffered in transmission than from scholarly books written for the information of prosperity'.[5] Thus, even he had little confidence in what he was about to recount: a story of King Edward (the Elder's) liaison with a shepherd girl, from which union Æthelstan himself was born; accounts of the rebellions of Alfred and Æthelstan's brother Edwin; and the king's role in the latter's death (§139). The whole concludes with a brief relation of Æthelstan's own death and burial at Malmesbury (§140).

According to William it seems that the passages just described originally constituted the whole of his account of Æthelstan's life and reign. He had cause to wish to add some fresh material only once he had discovered a new source:

> Concerning this king [Æthelstan] there is a vigorous tradition in England that he was the most law-abiding and best-educated ruler they have ever had; though it is only a very short time since I learned the extent of his education, from an ancient volume in which the writer was at odds with the difficulty of his material, finding it hard to express his opinions as he would have wished. I would add his words here in an abbreviated form, except that in the praise of his prince he rambles beyond reason, in the style which Cicero, king of Roman eloquence,

---

[3] *GR*, ii, 131, pp. 206–9.

[4] Discussed above, 182. For William's dependence on legend and specifically his use of ballads, see C.E. Wright, *The Cultivation of Saga in Anglo-Saxon England* (Edinburgh and London, 1939), 30–3. Wright argued (156) that the fullness of William's account suggested that Æthelstan 'must have been the subject of a very rich collection of vernacular sagas, which in William's own time had become popular ballads'.

[5] *GR*, ii, 137, pp. 224–5. The charter in question is S 436, of which William provided the only known text in *GP*, v, 250, pp. 598–601; he probably created this himself by conflating other charters for the abbey in the king's name: see Susan Kelly, *Charters of Malmesbury Abbey* (Oxford, 2005), no. 28, and above, 40–3.

calls in his *Rhetoric* 'bombastic'. His manner is excused by the practice of his time, and the excess of panegyric is countenanced by his enthusiasm for Æthelstan, who was then still living. I will therefore subjoin a few points in ordinary language which may perhaps make some contribution to the evidence for his good qualities.[6]

Clearly, William had recently read the account of the young king's education '*in quodam . . . uolumine uestusto*' (in a certain ancient volume) in which the writer 'was at odds with the difficulty of his material'. Only at a late stage in the construction of his History did William elect to include the additional material, taken from the old book but recast in more straightforward language. That extra information now constitutes the middle portion of his narrative; it is rather clumsily inserted into the pre-existing schema and, without thought for any consequent chronological confusion, traces again the whole span of the king's life from his father's death up to the battle of *Brunanburh*.[7] William stated explicitly that the reader should understand all this material to have come from his old volume, for he ended with a lengthy verse account of the battle of *Brunanburh* introduced with the statement: 'On the subject of the battle, this is the moment to set down the opinions of the versifier from whom all this has been extracted'.[8] From the historian's and still more the biographer's perspective, this central portion of William's account proves much the most useful. Here he told of a meeting between the child Æthelstan and his grandfather Alfred at which the king gave his grandson princely gifts; the young man's education at the court of his aunt Æthelflæd and her husband, Ealdorman Æthelred, and his coronation at Kingston;[9] his marriage alliance with Sihtric and subsequent conquest of Northumbria (into which account is inserted a lengthy and otherwise unattested report of the deeds of Sihtric's 'brother' Guthfrith and Æthelstan's siege of York);[10] and his subduing of first the Welsh and then the Cornish and imposition of substantial tributes on both.[11] On account of these achievements, William averred, 'the whole of Europe sang his praises and extolled his merits to the sky'.[12] There follows a lengthy account of Æthelstan's dealings with other European powers, including the marriages he arranged for his sisters and a detailed statement of the embassy sent by Hugh, duke of the Franks and the magnificent, imperial gifts the latter gave to his new brother-in-law.[13]

[6] *GR*, ii, 132, pp. 210–11.

[7] *GR*, ii, 133–5, pp. 210–23.

[8] *GR*, ii, 135, pp. 220–1: 'De quo bello tempus est ut illius uersifici, de quo omnia haec excerpsimus, sententiam ponamus.'

[9] Following the prose account of these events, William inserted thirty lines of verse, recapitulating the same themes: *GR*, ii, 133, pp. 210–12.

[10] See above, 19 and 162.

[11] *GR*, ii, 134, pp. 212–17.

[12] *GR*, ii, 135, pp. 216–17.

[13] *GR*, ii, 135, pp. 218–21.

Finally, William turned to the battle of *Brunanburh* and reverted to the verse already mentioned.

Historians used to take William's lengthy, if slightly confusing, treatment of Æthelstan's life as a key witness to Æthelstan's personality and behaviour, a useful supplement to the scanty narrative sources from the mid-tenth century. Crucially, William appeared to have based his account on material that had the 'authority of a contemporary'.[14] Michael Lapidge challenged that confidence in an article published in 1981, in which he demonstrated that the two verse passages which William included in the central portion of his narrative could not have derived from that 'certain ancient book' (as scholars have assumed, following Stubbs's edition of the *Gesta regum*); rather, on the stylistic evidence of their diction and rhyme-scheme, they must have originated in the late eleventh or early twelfth century.[15] Lapidge distinguished between the ancient (prose) book from which William said he would have quoted were it not for its barbarous style, and the separate, later poem from which William did provide excerpts. He assumed the poem had originated at Malmesbury (Æthelstan's burial place and an abbey to which he had made generous benefactions). Doubting that William himself wrote them, Lapidge attributed the verses to another Malmesbury monk, Peter Moraunt, a native of Bourges, a monk at Cluny before he came to England and later became abbot of Malmesbury (1141–*c*.58/9).[16] Lapidge rejected the poem's historical value in unequivocal terms:

> The confidence of historians in the antiquity of William's poem has thus been misplaced. Its statements can no longer be accepted as the evidence of a contemporary. In fact, under examination, the poem may be seen not to contain a single scrap of information which is not known from other sources or is not manifestly a flight of poetic fancy (I think of the account of Athelstan's early education in particular). It remains true that William of Malmesbury is an important source for Athelstan's reign in preserving information not found elsewhere. But we can affirm that the poem in rhyming hexameters from which he quotes two long extracts was *not* the source of this information.[17]

Without the poem from which he quoted at length in his description of Æthelstan's life and deeds William would have, as Dorothy Whitelock observed, 'added only legendary matter to our knowledge'.[18] As we have seen, the first and third sections of his account are historically almost

[14] Stenton, *ASE*, 339, n. 2.
[15] Lapidge, 'Poems', 62.
[16] Ibid., 70–1.
[17] Ibid., 71.
[18] Whitelock in *EHD*, 303.

entirely worthless. Yet if we reject the middle section and William's unconfirmed testimony about the king's youth and upbringing as without foundation, we could have little further to say about Æthelstan's early life before he started to appear directly in contemporary sources at the time of his accession in 924 and coronation the following year.[19] Some historians, reluctant entirely to condemn William's narrative, have tried to find ways of reinstating its authority, despite the evident dangers of such an approach.[20] Michael Wood has perhaps defended the essential usefulness of the *Gesta regum* most energetically; his cause has received some support from the most recent editors of William's text. Commenting in detail on these sections, R.M. Thomson concluded that both the verse and prose passages found in the *Gesta regum* represent not verbatim quotations from the 'old volume' which William had found, but rather William's adaptation of the original to conform to his own ideas about style.[21]

One way to approach this question is to try and identify the very old volume from which William was working. Lapidge suggested that this might have been an acrostic poem prophesying a glorious future for a young prince; which he attributed to John the Old Saxon (a scholar at the court of King Alfred).[22] If correct, this persuasive argument would require us to set aside everything William has to say about Æthelstan in the middle portion of his account beyond, perhaps, his description of the young prince's investiture by King Alfred.[23] However, as Michael Wood and latterly R.M. Thomson have argued, William stated explicitly that *all* the material included in the central portion of his narrative came from the old book, not just the verse extracts.[24] While the verses quoted are certainly not tenth century in origin, their inclusion does not conflict with William's statement that he would not quote the barbaric language of his text verbatim but intended rather to retell the story in a familiar style. As we have already seen, the middle section falls into two halves, in each of

[19] Dumville, *Wessex*, 146.

[20] Dumville has articulated the dangers of placing any reliance on William's testimony: *Wessex*, 142–3, n. 9, 150; see also R.I. Page, 'A Tale of Two Cities', *Peritia*, i (1982), 341–3. Simon Keynes offers a balanced view of the conflicting arguments: 'Books', 144, n. 15.

[21] Michael Wood, 'The Making of King Æthelstan's Empire: an English Charlemagne?', in *Ideal and Reality in Frankish and Anglo-Saxon Society*, ed. Patrick Wormald *et al.* (Oxford, 1983), 265–7; Thomson, *Commentary*, 116–28. See also Michael Winterbottom, 'William of Malmesbury, *versificus*', in *Anglo-Latin and its Heritage*, ed. S. Echard and G.R. Wieland (Turnhout, 2001), 120–5, for a detailed analysis of the metre of the verses William rewrote from the earlier, obscure and pompous material.

[22] Lapidge, 'Poems', 72–83; the poem opens ' "Archalis" clamare, triumuir, nomine saxI' (You, prince, are called by the name of 'sovereign stone'). A full translation and alternative suggestion as to the date of the poem's composition are provided above, 32–3.

[23] For which occasion he thought it possible that John had written his acrostic: Lapidge, 'Poems', 79–81.

[24] Wood, 'The Making', 265–7; Thomson, *Commentary*, 116–18.

which essentially the same information is provided first in prose and then in verse. Thomson has suggested that the original work on which William depended was written in both prose and verse, like the eleventh-century *Life of King Edward* (the Confessor) and that he modernized both the prose and the verse to make them more palatable to a twelfth-century audience. To imagine that the quantity of otherwise unattested information which William supplies for Æthelstan derived not from this certain ancient book but from yet another equally ancient, but also lost text is to take scepticism too far.[25] We should look elsewhere for William's source.

A library catalogue datable to 1247/8 from the abbey of Glastonbury in Somerset now in the library of Trinity College, Cambridge lists a book under the title: 'Epistole Alquini, Albini et Karoli et bella Etheltani regis et exposiciones diuersorum uerborum gramaticales. Vita sancti Wilfridi. leg[ibilis]'.[26] This composite manuscript, containing letters of Alcuin (who wrote under the pseudonym 'Albinus') and Charlemagne, an account of the wars of King Æthelstan, a glossary and one of the lives of Wilfrid no longer survives. It has attracted considerable attention from scholars as a possible source for William. If Glastonbury's account of the wars of Æthelstan had been written in the hermeneutic Latin cultivated in tenth-century England (a style that might reasonably be described as bombastic),[27] readers would indeed have been grateful to find a glossary in the same manuscript.[28] Other than this, the different elements of the manuscript have little in common. Such a bald catalogue entry tells us nothing about whether this was originally designed as a single codex or (if, as seems more likely, these were once separate texts) when the disparate parts were bound together inside one set of covers. While a number of the letters of Alcuin and Charlemagne do discuss ideas about kingship, that is

---

[25] Thomson, *Commentary*, 118: ' "Ockham's razor" must surely apply'. James Campbell has also accepted that William must have had one or more tenth-century sources for much of what he relates about Æthelstan and that it is not improbable that some of that material was written in verse: *The Anglo-Saxon State* (London and New York, 2000), 138.

[26] Cambridge, Trinity College, MS R. 5. 33, fo. 103v; this catalogue has been edited by James Carley in *English Benedictine Libraries: the Shorter Catalogues*, ed. R. Sharpe, J.P. Carley, R.M. Thomson and A.G. Watson, Corpus of British Medieval Library Catalogues 4 (London, 1996), p. 199 (B39.261).

[27] Michael Lapidge, 'The Hermeneutic Style in Tenth-Century Anglo-Latin Literature', *ASE*, iv (1975), 67–111; reprinted in his *Anglo-Latin Literature 900–1066* (London and Rio Grande, 1993), 105–49.

[28] It was not uncommon for difficult texts to be preserved with copies of glossaries; a mid-tenth-century copy of Frithegod's *Breviloquium sancti Wilfridi* survives in a manuscript now in St Petersburg with an early tenth-century copy of Priscian's *Ars de nomine* (St Petersburg Public Library, MS O. v. XV. 1); and the difficult third book of Abbo of St Germain-des-Prés, *Bella Parisiacae urbis* was frequently copied with grammatical materials and supplied with glosses: Lapidge, 'Hermeneutic Style', 113–14. Michael Wood has suggested that the title of the lost work *Bella Ethel(s)tani regis* echoes the title of Abbo's work and wondered whether this was a model for the Æthelstan work, but this seems rather far-fetched.

not a theme either of Stephanus's eighth-century prose life of Wilfrid, nor of the tenth-century hexameter *Breuiloquium uitae Wilfridi* by the Frankish author Frithegod of Canterbury.[29] Readers of that poem – described by Lapidge as 'probably the most difficult Latin poem ever composed in pre-Conquest England'[30] – would also have needed the assistance of a glossary, but it is rash to leap to the conclusion that Frithegod's verse lay in this Glastonbury manuscript, since a separate copy of the same text appears later in the thirteenth-century catalogue.[31] To describe the lost Glastonbury manuscript as a tenth-century manual on kingship or a mirror for princes, as Michael Wood has done, is unwarranted. Nevertheless, the evidence that there had in the thirteenth century been at Glastonbury a text, whether in verse or prose we cannot tell, that offered an account of King Æthelstan's wars is promising, especially since we know that William of Malmesbury was a frequent visitor to the abbey while he was writing the *Gesta regum*.[32]

Michael Wood has made a detailed analysis of information to be derived from William's version of the king's life and particularly of the language of the poetic extracts he chose to include. On this basis Wood has argued that the central section of the narrative about Æthelstan in the *Gesta regum* is a Carolingian-styled royal biography of the tenth century, an encomium written in hermeneutic Latin verse. He has proposed that William relied for all of this portion of his text on a single source, an account of the king's reign that certainly extended from his coronation to the battle of *Brunanburh*, and possibly also covered his death and burial; that source further provided information about Æthelstan's education and upbringing, included specifically to testify to his fitness to hold royal office and to counter the rumours of his illegitimate birth. Wood has associated this supposed verse work with the circle of Æthelwold, abbot of Glastonbury and later bishop of Winchester, a man who in adolescence had been a protégé of the king, as we saw above (Chapter 4). We do not need to follow all of Wood's arguments in detail in order to make a case for reinstating the testimony of William of Malmesbury as an independent witness to the events of Æthelstan's reign. Lapidge's counter-case rests exclusively on his analysis of the poetics of the verse quoted, which cannot have been written before the latter years of the eleventh century.[33] But that the verse failed tests of Latinity and style does not clinch this argument and indeed Lapidge himself used elements of William's account to support his interpretation of John the Old Saxon's acrostic.

[29] Michael Lapidge, 'A Frankish Scholar in Tenth-Century England: Frithegod of Canterbury/Fredegaud of Brioude', *ASE*, xvii (1988), 45–65; reprinted in his *Anglo-Latin Literature 900–1066* (London and Rio Grande, 1993), 157–81.

[30] Lapidge, 'Frithegod', 181.

[31] *English Benedictine Libraries*, 99.

[32] William Stubbs, *Willelmi Malmesbiriensis monachi De gestis regum Anglorum libri quinque*, 2 vols (Rolls Series, London, 1887–9), i, xxvii–xxx; Thomson *Commentary*, xxxii, n. 25.

[33] Lapidge, 'Poems', 69.

William of Malmesbury provides evidence for many aspects of
Æthelstan's reign to which no other authority bears witness. By his own
account, some elements of his narrative derive from popular and
legendary sources, but these he clearly demarcated within the structure of
this part of Book II of the *Gesta regum* from the material he had derived
from 'a certain old book'. That was written in a pompous fashion at odds
with twelfth-century notions of style and accessibility of language; so
William preferred to reshape its information in a more straightforward
form, and retell the narrative in both prose and verse. As was often his
wont, William adapted the source in front of him to suit his own sense of
his readers' needs and desires, here interpolating dialogue into his
legendary material, there replacing barbaric, hermeneutic verse with a
poetic rendition of the same essential information in verses he probably
crafted himself.[34] In the central, fullest, account of the king's life William
certainly drew on some source now lost; I incline to agree with Thomson
and Wood that this was a single text and that it dated from the tenth
century. Either it was written during the king's lifetime (if William stated
correctly that the king still lived when the panegyric were crafted), or
someone composed it within living memory of the king's life and deeds.
Since whatever work William relied on reached its climax with the battle
of *Brunanburh*, it might have been written to celebrate that victory.[35]
William's account of Æthelstan's life remains a treacherous one, not least
because – in the absence of that lost text – we have no means of establishing just how far his 'improvement' of the original extended beyond
stylistic embellishment to outright fabrication. Wherever the *Gesta regum*'s
testimony cannot be elsewhere corroborated, we must continue to question its strict accuracy. But that William had succeeded in finding a unique
source of information about the king's reign seems certain; for that the
biographer must express cautious gratitude.

---

[34] That William could be quite cavalier in his use of pre-existing texts is well known and
even when he claimed to be quoting verbatim, he often made substantial alterations; see
M. Winterbottom and R. Thomson, *William of Malmesbury Saints' Lives* (Oxford, 2002), xvi;
Winterbottom, 'William of Malmesbury', 127.

[35] Wood's suggestion that its authorship be sought in the Æthelwoldian circle would put
its composition a little later, although its author could still have known the king personally.

WHEN KING ÆTHELSTAN WAS WHERE

It is impossible to provide a meaningful itinerary for King Æthelstan. There are certain days on which he can be shown to have been at specific places, often because he issued charters that were copied by a scribe who chose to indicate the precise date and location of their confirmation. From these isolated references we cannot, however, draw any conclusions about his movements in between the points at which his whereabouts can be determined. That he stayed in Wiltshire over Christmas and during January 933 might seem plausible, bearing in mind not only that this was a religious feast but that travel at the turn of the year would have been difficult. But to infer that he made a gradual westward progress from Colchester in Essex, through Hampshire and on to Devon during the spring and summer of 931 would be unwarranted. Again, that we do not know him to have issued charters or law-codes at many places in the former Mercian kingdom does not necessarily mean that he did not spend much time in the midland counties, or that he failed to summon his leading men to join him there.

Within those limits, this table seeks to list what we can determine about when the king spent time at a specific place. Some of this, despite the caveats just noted, remains necessarily speculative; *italics* indicate particular uncertainty; items inside square brackets denote events involving people other than the king. Information about the period before his accession in 924 and coronation to a united realm in 925 is even scantier, most of the information here deriving only from William of Malmesbury.

Date	Place	Source	Comments
*c.*894	Unknown; probably in Wessex	WM, *GR*, ii, 133, pp. 210–11	Birth. Date depends on William of Malmesbury's statement that Æthelstan was 30 in 924
Before 899	Unknown, in Wessex	*GR*, ii, 133, pp. 210–11	Investiture by King Alfred

c.899–909	*Mercia*	*GR*, ii, 133, pp. 210–11	*Brought up at Mercian court after King Edward's second marriage c.899*
909	Gloucester	MR 909	Translation of St Oswald's relics from Bardney
912–918	*Mercia?*		*Possible participation in Æthelflæd's fortification of burhs in north-west Mercia*
918–924	*Mercia?*		*Possible participation in King Edward's wars in Mercia*
924	*Mercia*		Election as king in Mercia
925	[*Tamworth?*]	S 395 (Burton, no. 2)	Acting apparently as Mercian king: *rex Anglorum*
4 Sept. 925	Kingston - upon - Thames	ASC 924; S 394 St Augustine's	Coronation
30 Jan. 926	Tamworth, Staffordshire	ASC D	Marriage of Sihtric and Æthelstan's sister
926	Abingdon	WM, *GR*, ii, 135, pp. 218–21. Date, but not location, from Flodoard, 9268E	Embassy to Æthelstan led by Adelof, son of Baldwin of Flanders on behalf of Hugh, duke of the Franks to arrange latter's marriage to Eadhild
12 July 927	York	WM, *GR*, ii, 134, pp. 214–15	Capture of city of York after death of Sihtric

After 12 July 927	Eamont, nr Penrith	ASC D	Submission of northern princes to Æthelstan's rule
Summer 927	Hereford Cornwall	WM, *GR*, ii, 135, pp. 214–16	Submission of Welsh; submission of Cornish
16 April 928 3 days after Easter (13 April)	Exeter, Devon (<u>in arce regia</u>)	S 400 (Old Minster archive)	*rex Anglorum* land in Wiltshire
16 April 928 3 days after Easter (13 April)	Exeter, Devon (<u>in arce regia</u>)	S 399 (Glastonbury archive)	Land in Wiltshire
929			Embassy to Æthelstan's court from Henry the Fowler seeking a bride for his son Otto
[929	Germany		Visit of Cenwald, bishop of Worcester, to monasteries in Germany]
3 April 930 [Easter 18 April]	Lyminster, Sussex <u>in uilla omnibus notissima</u>	S 403 (Selsey archive)	Land in Sussex to Bp Selsey
29 April 930	Chippenham <u>in uilla omnibus notissima</u>	S 405 (Exeter archive)	Land in Devon to Crediton
7 June 930 for 934 (Trinity Sunday 1 June 934)	*London <u>in ciuitate omnibus nota</u>*	*S 428 (Worcester archive)*	*Dubious. Forged charter, similar dating problems to S 407 on which probably modelled*
c.930	*Abingdon*	*S 1208 (Abingdon, no. 28)*	*Dubious; a spurious charter clearly drawn up after the event, possibly relating to a transaction effected before 931*

11 Jan. 921 for 931	*Wilton*	*S 379* (*Wilton archive*)	*Dubious*
23 March 931 [Easter 10 April]	Colchester in uilla omnibus notissima	S 412 (Old Minster archive)	Land in Hampshire
20 June 931	King's Worthy, Hants	S 413 (Abingdon, no. 23)	Land in Hampshire
15 July 931	East Wellow, Hants in uilla regali	S 1604 (Abingdon, no. 24)	
6 Oct. 931	*Kingston, Surrey*	*S 450* (*Exeter archive*)	*Doubtful charter, granting land in Cornwall.*
12 Nov. 931	Lifton, Devon in uilla omnibus notissima	S 416 (Single sheet, Old Minster)	Land in Wiltshire
30 Aug. 932	Middeltun (in uilla noblissima): either Milton Regis in Kent or Milton Abbas in Dorset	S 417 (Old Minster archive)	Land in Hampshire
9 Nov. 932	Exeter in ciuitate famosissima	S 418a (Barking archive)	Land in Essex (?)
24 Dec. 932	Amesbury in uilla omnibus notissima	S 418 (New Minster, no. 10)	Land in Hampshire; beneficiary required to provide for 120 destitute daily
24 Dec. 932	Amesbury, Wilts	S 419 (Shaftesbury, no. 8)	Land at Fontmell, Dorset
11 Jan. 933	Wilton in civitate notissima	S 379 (New Minster, no. 8)	Land in Wiltshire; beneficiary required to provide food for destitute once a year

26 Jan. 933	Chippenham, <u>in uilla omnibus notissima in uilla celeberrima</u>	S 422 (Sherborne no. 7)	Land in Dorset Monks required to sing all psalter on 1
		S 423 (Sherborne, no. 8)	Nov. annually Land in Dorset Same obligation
[933		ASC 933 E	Death of Æthelstan's half-brother Edwin, 'drowned at sea']
16 Dec. 933	*Kingston <u>in regali uilla</u>*	S 420 *(Chertsey archive)*	*Dubious*
2nd day of Easter 834 (for 934) [Easter Day 6 April]	*Dorchester*	*S 391 (Milton archive)*	*Dubious*
28 May 934 [Pentecost 25 May]	Winchester <u>in ciuitate opinatissima</u>	S 425 (original Christ Church, Canterbury)	Land in Sussex (or Kent)
7 June 934	Nottingham <u>in civitate omnibus notissima</u>	S 407 (York Minster archive)	Amounderness charter
Early summer 934	Chester-le-Street	*HSC* ch. 25	Visit to shrine of St Cuthbert
Summer 934	Scotland	ASC	Ravaged Scotland with naval and land force
13 Sept. 934	Buckingham <u>in uilla</u>	S 426 (Glastonbury archive)	Land in Wiltshire
16 Dec. 934	*Frome, Somerset in regali uilla*	*S 427 (Old Minster archive)*	*Land in Hampshire; uncertain*
21 Dec. 935	Dorchester <u>in ciuitate celeberrima</u>	S 434, 435: (Malmesbury nos 26–7)	Land in Wilts to Malmesbury; dated 937 for 935
935	Cirencester	S 1792: (St Pauls, no. 11)	

936	York	Flodoard, 936 (18A). Richer, *Historiae*, i. 2, Æthelstan received Frankish embassy at York, seeking return of Louis IV to France at York	Compare William of Malmesbury, *GR* ii, 135, pp. 216–17, for a Norwegian embassy to York (undated)
937	<u>Brunanburh</u>	ASC	Battle of *Brunanburh*
27 Oct. 939	Gloucester	ASC D	Death

Movements not precisely datable

924x933 (possibly 924x926)	Winchester	S 1417 (New Minster, Winchester)	Lease alienating land from the New Minster to one of the king's thegns. Royal style – 'Angelsaxonum Denorumque rex' might suggest this issued before the conquest of Northumbria.
924x939	?	I *Æthelstan*	'Tithe ordinance'
924x939 [926xc.930, chs 13.1–18 probably earlier than the main code, ?928x930]	Grately, Hampshire	II *Æthelstan*	No direct evidence of king's presence
Christmas 924x938; ?931 [post-dates Grately; earlier than *As III* and *IV*]	Exeter	V *Æthelstan*	King was present, Wulfhelm was not. Not 932 when at Amesbury for Christmas; could have been issued 930, 931 or 934

924x939	Faversham, Kent	No text survives	King apparently present. Provisions mentioned *III As* 2–3; *IV As* 1; *VI As* 10
924x939	Kent	*III Æthelstan*	King not present (local report by bishops, thegns, nobles and commoners of Kent, addressed to the king in second person)
924x939	Thunderfield, nr Horley, Surrey	*IV Æthelstan*	Archbishop Wulfhelm presided, no evidence king was present
924x939 [after Grately, Exeter and Thunderfield]	London	*VI Æthelstan*	Ordinance of bishops and reeves of London
924x939	Whittlebury, Northants	*VI Æthelstan*, 12.1	King present

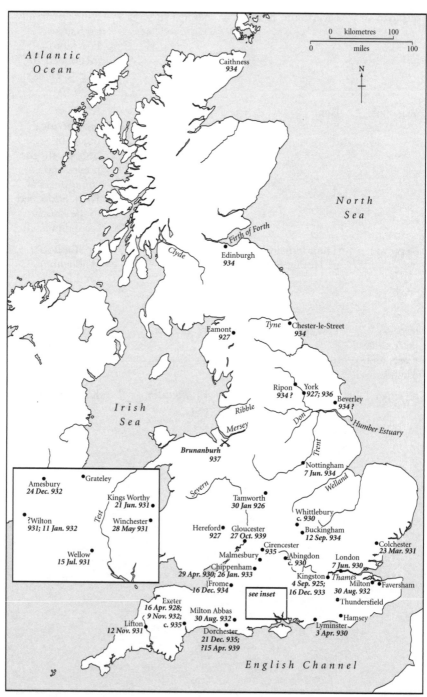

Map 4. When Æthelstan was where.

BIBLIOGRAPHY

MANUSCRIPTS

Cambridge, Corpus Christi College, MS 183
Coburg, Landesbibliothek, MS 1 (the Gandersheim Gospels)
London, British Library, MS Cotton Claudius B. v
London, British Library, MS Cotton Domitian A. viii
London, British Library, MS Cotton Galba A. xviii
London, British Library, MS Cotton Tiberius A. ii
London, British Library, MS Royal 1. A. x
London, British Library, MS Royal 1. B. vii
London, Lambeth Palace, MS 1370
Oxford, Bodleian Library, MS Auct. D. 2. 16

PRIMARY SOURCES

Abbo of Fleury, *Passio S. Eadmundi*, ed. M. Winterbottom, *Three Lives of English Saints* (Toronto, 1972)

The Anglo-Saxon Chronicle: A Collaborative Edition, 5 MS C, ed. K. O'Brien O'Keeffe (Cambridge, 2001)

The Annals of Clonmacnoise, ed. D. Murphy (Dublin, 1896 and Felinfach, 1993)

The Annals of Ulster (to AD 1131), Part I, Text and Translation, ed. S. Mac Airt and G. Mac Niocaill (Dublin, 1983)

Armes Prydein: the Prophecy of Britain from the Book of Taliesin, ed. I. Williams and R. Bromwich (Dublin Institute for Advanced Studies, 1982)

Asser's Life of King Alfred: together with the Annals of Saint Neots erroneously ascribed to Asser, ed. W.H. Stevenson (Oxford, 1904; 1959 edn)

'B', *Vita S Dunstani*, ed. W. Stubbs, *Memorials of St Dunstan*, Rolls Series 63 (London, 1874), 3–52

Byrhtferth, *Vita S Oswaldi*, ed. and trans. Michael Lapidge, *Byrhtferth of Ramsey, the Lives of St Oswald and St Ecgwine* (Oxford, 2009)

Charters of Abingdon Abbey, ed. S.E. Kelly, Anglo-Saxon Charters VII–VIII (Oxford, 2000–1)

Charters of Bath and Wells, ed. S.E. Kelly, Anglo-Saxon Charters XIII (Oxford, 2007)

Charters of Burton Abbey, ed. P.H. Sawyer, Anglo-Saxon Charters II (Oxford 1979)

Charters of Malmesbury Abbey, ed. S.E. Kelly, Anglo-Saxon Charters XI (Oxford, 2005)

Charters of the New Minster, Winchester, ed. S. Miller, Anglo-Saxon Charters IX (Oxford, 2000)

Charters of St Augustine's Abbey, Canterbury and Minster-in-Thanet, ed. S.E. Kelly, Anglo-Saxon Charters IV (Oxford, 1995)

Charters of St Paul's London, ed. S.E. Kelly, Anglo-Saxon Charters X (Oxford, 2004)

Charters of Selsey, ed. S.E. Kelly, Anglo-Saxon Charters VI (Oxford, 1998)

Charters of Shaftesbury Abbey, ed. S.E. Kelly, Anglo-Saxon Charters V (Oxford, 1996)

Chronicle attributed to John of Wallingford, ed. R. Vaughan, Camden Miscellany, xxi Camden 3rd ser. xc (London, 1958)

Chronicle of Æthelweard, ed. A. Campbell (London, 1962)

La Chronique de Nantes, ed. R. Merlet (Paris, 1896)

Councils and Ecclesiastical Documents relating to Great Britain and Ireland, ed. A. Haddan and W. Stubbs, 3 vols (Oxford, 1869–79)

Egils Saga, trans. C. Fell (London, 1975)

Flodoard, *Annals*: ed. P. Lauer, *Les annales de Flodoard, publiées d'après les manuscrits, avec une introduction et des notes* (Paris, 1905); trans. S. Fanning and Bernard S. Bachrach, *The Annals of Flodoard of Reims, 919–966* (Peterborough, Ont., 2004)

Folcuin, *Gesta Abbatum Sithiensium*, ed. O. Holder-Egger, [*Supplementa tomorum I–XII, pars I*], ed. G. Waitz, *MGH Scriptores* [folio], 13 (Hanover, 1881), 607–35

Gaimar, *L'Estoire des Engleis*, ed. Alexander Bell, Anglo-Norman Texts, 14–16 (Oxford, 1960)

Hariulf, Chronique de l'abbaye de Saint-Riquier (Ve siècle – 1104), ed. Ferdinand Lot (Paris, 1894)

Henry of Huntingdon, *Historia Anglorum*, ed. and trans. D.E. Greenway (Oxford, 1996)

Historia de Sancto Cuthberto, ed. and trans. T. Johnson South (Cambridge, 2002)

Historia ecclesie Abbendonensis = the History of the Church of Abingdon, ed. and trans. J. Hudson, 2 vols (Oxford, 2002–7)

Hrotsvitha of Gandersheim, *Gesta Ottonis*, ed. W. Bershin, *Hrotsvit Opera Omnia* (Munich and Leipzig, 2001), 271–305

Liber Eliensis, ed. E.O. Blake, Camden Society, 3rd ser. xcii (London, 1962)

The Old English Version of the Heptateuch: Ælfric's Treatise on the Old and New Testament and his Preface to Genesis, ed. S. J. Crawford (London, 1922)

Richer von Saint-Remi, Historiae, ed. Hartmut Hoffmann, MGH *Scriptores* 38 (Hanover, 2000)

Roger of Wendover, *Flores historiarum*, ed. H.O. Coxe, 5 vols (London, 1841–4)

The Sacramentary of Ratoldus (Paris, Bibliothèque Nationale de France, lat. 12052), ed. Nicholas Orchard (Cranbrook, 2005)

Two of the Saxon Chronicles Parallel, ed. C. Plummer, 2 vols (Oxford, 1892–9)

Widukind of Corvey, *Res gestae Saxonicae*, ed. P. Hirsch and H.E. Lohmann, *Die Sachsengeschichte des Widukind von Korvei*, 5th edn, MGH SRG (Hanover, 1935)

William of Malmesbury, *De antiquitate Glastonie ecclesie*, ed. J. Scott, *The Early History of Glastonbury, An Edition, Translation and Study of William of Malmesbury's De antiquitate Glastonie ecclesie* (Woodbridge, 1981)

William of Malmesbury, *Gesta pontificum Anglorum = The History of the English bishops*, ed. and trans. M. Winterbottom with the assistance of R.M. Thomson (Oxford, 2007)

William of Malmesbury, *Gesta regum Anglorum = The History of the English Kings*, ed. and trans R.A.B. Mynors, completed by R.M. Thomson and M. Winterbottom, 2 vols (Oxford, 1998–9)

Wulfstan of Winchester, *Vita S Æthelwoldi: The Life of St. Æthelwold*, ed. M. Lapidge and M. Winterbottom (Oxford, 1991)

SECONDARY SOURCES
(CITED MORE THAN ONCE)

Abels, R., *Alfred the Great: War, Kingship and Culture in Anglo-Saxon England* (London, 1998)

—— 'Royal Succession and the Growth of Political Stability in Ninth-Century Wessex', *Haskins Society Journal*, xii (2002), 83–97

—— 'Alfred and his Biographers: Image and Imagination', in *Writing Early Medieval Biography*, ed. D. Bates *et al.* (Woodbridge, 2006), 61–75

Abrams, L., 'Edward the Elder's Danelaw', in *Edward the Elder, 899–924*, ed. N.J. Higham and D.H. Hill (London and New York, 2001), 128–43

Alexander, J.J.G., 'The Benedictional of St Æthelwold and Anglo-Saxon Illumination of the Reform Period', in *Tenth-Century Studies*, ed. D. Parsons (London, 1975), 169–83

Althoff, G., *Otto III*, trans. P.G. Jestice (University Park, PA, 2003)

Angus, W.S., 'The Battlefield of Brunanburh', *Antiquity*, xi (1937), 283–93

Archibald, M.M. and C.E. Blunt, *Sylloge of Coins of the British Isles 34, British Museum Anglo-Saxon Coins V, Athelstan to the Reform of Edgar 924–c.973* (London, 1986)

Bailey, M., 'Ælfwynn, Second Lady of the Mercians', in *Edward the Elder, 899–924*, ed. N.J. Higham and D.H. Hill (London and New York, 2001), 112–27

Barker, E.E., 'Two Lost Documents of King Æthelstan', *ASE*, vi (1977), 137–43

Barrow, J., 'Chester's Earliest Regatta? Edgar's Dee-Rowing Re-visited', *EME*, x (2001), 81–93

Bates, D., J. Crick and S. Hamilton, eds, *Writing Medieval Biography: Essays in Honour of Frank Barlow* (Woodbridge, 2006)

Battiscombe, C.F., *The Relics of Saint Cuthbert: Studies by Various Authors Collected and Edited with an Historical Introduction* (Oxford, 1956)

Birch, W. de Gray, *Liber Vitae: Register and Martyrology of New Minster and Hyde Abbey, Winchester* (London and Winchester, 1892)

Blackburn, M., 'Mints, Burhs, and the Grately Code, Cap. 14.2', in *The Defence of Wessex: the Burghal Hidage and Anglo-Saxon Fortifications*, ed. D. Hill and A. Rumble (Manchester, 1996), 160–75

Blunt, C.E., 'The Coinage of Athelstan, 924–939: a Survey', *British Numismatic Journal*, xliv (1974), 36–160

Bonner, G., D. Rollason and C. Stancliffe, eds, *St Cuthbert, His Cult and His Community to AD 1200* (Woodbridge, 1989)

Bredehoft, T.A., *Textual Histories: Readings in the Anglo-Saxon Chronicle* (Toronto, 2001)

Brett, C., 'A Breton Pilgrim in England in the Reign of King Æthelstan', in *France and the British Isles in the Middle Ages and Renaissance*, ed. G. Jondorf and D.N. Dumville (Woodbridge, 1991), 43–70

Brooks, N., *The Early History of the Church of Canterbury: Christ Church 597–1066*, Studies in the Early History of Britain (Leicester, 1984)

—— 'The Career of St Dunstan', in *St Dunstan: His Life, Times and Cult*, ed. N. Ramsay *et al.* (Woodbridge, 1992), 1–23

—— 'The Anglo-Saxon Cathedral Community, 597–1070', in *A History of Canterbury Cathedral*, ed. P. Collinson, N. Ramsay and M. Sparks (Oxford, 1995), 1–37

Bullough, D., 'The Continental Background', in *Tenth-Century Studies*, ed. David Parsons (London, 1975), 20–36

Byrne, A.H., *More Battlefields of England* (London, 1952)

Campbell, A., *The Battle of Brunanburh* (London, 1938)

—— *Skaldic Verse and Anglo-Saxon History* (London, 1971)

Campbell, J., 'Anglo-Saxon Courts', in *Court Culture in the Early Middle Ages: the Proceedings of the First Alcuin Conference*, ed. C. Cubitt (Turnhout, 2003), 155–69

—— 'What is not Known about the Reign of Edward the Elder', in *Edward the Elder, 899–924*, ed. N.J. Higham and D.H. Hill (London and New York, 2001), 12–24

—— *The Anglo-Saxon State* (London, 2000)

—— 'Anglo-Saxon Courts', in *Court Culture in the Early Middle Ages*, ed. C. Cubitt (Turnhout, 2003),

Cavill, P., 'The Armour-Bearer in Abbo's *Passio sancti Eadmundi* and Anglo-Saxon England', *Leeds Studies in English*, n.s. xxxvi (2005), 47–61

—— 'The Site of the Battle of Brunanburh: Manuscripts and Maps, Grammar and Geography', in *A Commodity of Good Names: Essays in Honour of Margaret Gelling*, ed. O.J. Padel and D.N. Parsons (Donington, 2008), 303–19

Cavill P., S. Harding and J. Jesch, 'Revisiting Dingesmere', *Journal of the English Place-Name Society*, xxxvi (2003–4), 25–38

Chaplais, P., 'The Anglo-Saxon Chancery: From the Diploma to the Writ', *Journal of the Society of Archivists*, iii (1966), 160–76; reprinted in *Prisca Munimenta*, ed. F. Ranger (London, 1973), 43–62

—— 'The Authenticity of the Royal Anglo-Saxon Diplomas of Exeter', *Bulletin of the Institute of Historical Research*, xxxix (1966), 1–34; reprinted with an addendum in his *Essays in Medieval Diplomacy and Administration* (London, 1981), no. XV

—— 'The Royal Anglo-Saxon "Chancery" of the Tenth Century Revisited', in *Studies in Medieval History presented to R.H.C. Davis*, ed. H. Mayr-Harting and R.I. Moore (London and Ronceverte, 1985), 41–51

Charles-Edwards, T., 'Alliances, Godfathers, Treaties and Boundaries', in *Kings, Currency and Alliances*, ed. M.A.S. Blackburn and D.N. Dumville (Woodbridge, 1998), 47–62

Clemoes, P., *The Cult of St Oswald on the Continent*, Jarrow Lecture 1983 (Jarrow, 1984)

Coates, R., 'A Further Snippet of Evidence for Brunanburh = Bromborough', *Notes and Queries*, xl.3 (1998), 288–9

Conner, P.W., *Anglo-Saxon Exeter: a Tenth-Century Cultural History* (Woodbridge, 1993).

Crick, J., 'Edgar, Albion and Insular Domination', in *Edgar, King of the English*, ed. D. Scragg (Woodbridge, 2008), 158–70

Davidson, M.R., 'The (Non)submission of the Northern Kings in 920', in *Edward the Elder, 899–924*, ed. N.J. Higham and D.H. Hill (London and New York, 2001), 200–11

Davies, W., *Wales in the Early Middle Ages* (Leicester, 1982)

Dodgson, J., 'The Background of Brunanburh', *Saga Book of the Viking Society*, xiv (1956–7), 303–16; reprinted in *Wirral and its Viking Heritage*, ed. P. Cavill, S.E. Harding and J. Jesch (Nottingham, 2000), 60–9

—— *Place-Names of Cheshire*, iv (Cambridge 1972).

Dodwell, C.R., *The Pictorial Arts of the West 800–1200* (New Haven and London, 1993)

Downham, C., 'The Chronology of the Last Scandinavian Kings of York', *Northern History*, xl (2003), 25–51

Dumville, D.N., 'The Ætheling: a Study in Anglo-Saxon Constitutional History', *ASE*, viii (1979), 1–33

—— 'Brittany and "Armes Prydein Vawr" ', *Etudes Celtiques*, xx (1983), 147–59

—— 'The West Saxon Genealogical Regnal List: Manuscripts and Texts', *Anglia*, civ (1986), 1–32

—— *Wessex and England from Alfred to Edgar: Six Essays on Political, Cultural and Ecclesiastical Revival* (Woodbridge, 1992)

—— 'Mael Brigte mac Tornáin, Pluralist coarb (†927)', *Journal of Celtic Studies*, iv (2004), 97–116

Fjalldal, M., 'A Farmer in the Court of King Athelstan: Historical and Literary Considerations in the Vínheiðr Episode of *Egils Saga*', *English Studies*, lxxvii (1996), 15–31

—— *Anglo-Saxon England in Icelandic Medieval Texts* (Toronto, Buffalo and London, 2005)

Foot, S., 'The Making of *Angelcynn*: English Identity before the Norman Conquest', *TRHS*, 6th ser. vi (1996), 25–49

—— *Veiled Women: the Disappearance of Nuns from Anglo-Saxon England*, 2 vols (Aldershot, 2000)

—— 'Finding the Meaning of Form: Narrative in Annals and Chronicles', in *Writing Medieval History*, ed. N. Partner (London, 2005), 88–108

—— *Monastic Life in Anglo-Saxon England, c.600–900* (Cambridge, 2006)

—— 'Where English becomes British: Rethinking Contexts for Brunanburh', in *Myth, Rulership, Church and Charters: Essays in Honour of Nicholas Brooks*, ed. J. Barrow and A. Wareham (Aldershot, 2008), 127–44

—— 'Dynastic Strategies: the West Saxon Royal Family in Europe', in *England and the Continent in the Tenth Century*, ed. D. Rollason, C. Leyser and H. Williams (Brepols, 2011), 241–57

Frank, R., 'Skaldic Verse and the Date of *Beowulf*', in *The Dating of Beowulf*, ed. C. Chase (Toronto, 1981), 123–39

Gameson, R., *The Role of Art in the Late Anglo-Saxon Church* (Oxford, 1995)

Gannon, A., *The Iconography of Early Anglo-Saxon Coinage: Sixth to Eighth Centuries* (Oxford, 2003)

Garipzanov, Ildar H., 'The Image of Authority in Carolingian Coinage: the *Image* of a Ruler and Roman Imperial Tradition', *EME*, viii (1999), 197–218

Geary, P., *Furta Sacra: Thefts of Relics in the Central Middle Ages* (Princeton, NJ, 1978)

Gerchow, J., *Die Gedenküberlieferung der Angelsachsen: mit einem Katalog der libri vitae und Necrologien* (Berlin, 1988)

Goffart, W., '*Hetware* and *Hugas*: Datable Anachronisms in *Beowulf*', in *The Dating of Beowulf*, ed. C. Chase (Toronto, 1981), 83–100

Graham-Campbell, J., R. Hall, J. Jesch and D.N. Parsons, eds, *Vikings and the Danelaw: Select Papers from the Proceedings of the Thirteenth Viking Congress* (Oxford, 2001)

Grierson, P., 'The Relations between England and Flanders before the Norman Conquest', *TRHS*, 4th ser., xxiii (1941), 71–112

Griffiths, D., 'The North West Frontier', in *Edward the Elder, 899–924*, ed. N.J. Higham and D.H. Hill (London and New York, 2001), 167–87

Halloran, K., 'The Brunanburh Campaign: A Reappraisal', *Scottish Historical Review*, lxxxiv (2005), 133–48

—— 'Brunanburh Reconsidered', *History Today*, lvi.6 (June 2006), 2–3

Hare, M., 'Kings, Crowns and Festivals: the Origins of Gloucester as a Royal Ceremonial Centre', *Transactions of the Bristol and Gloucestershire Archaeological Society*, cxv (1997), 41–78

—— 'The Documentary Evidence for the History of St. Oswald's, Gloucester to 1086 AD', in *The Golden Minster: The Anglo-Saxon Minster and Later Medieval Priory of St. Oswald at Gloucester*, ed. C. Heighway and R. Bryant, CBA Research Report 117 (York, 1999), 33–45

Hart, C., *The Danelaw* (London and Rio Grande, 1992)

Heighway, C., 'Gloucester and the New Minster of St Oswald', in *Edward the Elder, 899–924*, ed. N.J. Higham and D.H. Hill (London and New York, 2001), 102–11

Higham, N.J. 'The Context of Brunanburh', in *Names, Places and People: an Onomastic Miscellany in Memory of John McNeal Dodgson*, eds A. Rumble and A.D. Mills (Stamford, 1997), 144–56

—— and D.H. Hill, eds, *Edward the Elder, 899–924* (London and New York, 2001)

Hill, D., *An Atlas of Anglo-Saxon England* (Oxford, 1981)

——, 'The Shiring of Mercia – Again', in *Edward the Elder, 899–924*, eds N.J. Higham and D.H. Hill (London and New York, 2001), 144–59

Hill, P., *The Age of Æthelstan: Britain's Forgotten History* (Stroud, 2004)

Hudson, B., *Kings of Celtic Scotland* (Westport, CT and London, 1994)

Insley, C., 'Assemblies and Charters in Late Anglo-Saxon England', in *Political Assemblies in the Earlier Middle Ages*, ed. P.S. Barnwell and M. Mostert (Turnhout, 2003), 47–59

—— 'Where Did All the Charters Go?', *ANS*, xxiv (2001), 109–27

Irving, E.B., 'The Charge of the Saxon Brigade: Tennyson's *Battle of Brunanburh*', in *Literary Appropriations of the Anglo-Saxons*, ed. D. Scragg and C. Weinberg (Cambridge, 2000), 174–93

Jackson, R.A., *Ordines Coronationis Franciae: Texts and Ordines for the Coronation of Frankish and French Kings and Queens in the Middle Ages*, 2 vols (Philadelphia, PA, 1995)

Jesch, J., 'Skaldic Verse in Scandinavian England', in *The Vikings and the Danelaw*, ed. J. Graham-Campbell *et al.* (Oxford, 2001), 313–25

John, E., *Orbis Britanniae, and Other Studies* (Leicester, 1966)

Karkov, C.E., *The Ruler Portraits of Anglo-Saxon England* (Woodbridge, 2004)

Kelly, S., 'Anglo-Saxon Lay Society and the Written Word', in *The Uses of Literacy in Early Mediaeval Europe*, ed. R. McKitterick (Cambridge, 1990), 36–62

Keynes, S., *The Diplomas of King Æthelred 'the Unready': a Study in their Use as Historical Evidence* Cambridge Studies in Medieval Life and Thought, 3rd ser., xiii (Cambridge, 1980)

—— 'King Æthelstan's Books', in *Learning and Literature in Anglo-Saxon England*, ed. M. Lapidge and H. Gneuss (Cambridge, 1985), 143–201

—— 'Regenbald the Chancellor (sic)', *ANS*, x (1988), 185–222

—— 'Royal Government and the Written Word', in *The Uses of Literacy in Early Mediaeval Europe*, ed. R. McKitterick (Cambridge, 1990), 226–57

—— 'The Control of Kent in the Ninth Century', *EME*, ii (1993), 111–31

—— 'The West Saxon Charters of King Æthelwulf and his Sons', *EHR*, cix (1994), 1109–49

—— 'Anglo-Saxon Entries in the *Liber Vitae* of Brescia', in *Alfred the Wise*, ed. J. Roberts, J.L. Nelson and M. Godden (Cambridge, 1997), 99–119

—— 'King Alfred and the Mercians', in *Kings, Currency and Alliances*, ed. M.A.S. Blackburn and D.N. Dumville (Woodbridge, 1998), 1–45, at 34–9

—— 'The Cult of King Alfred the Great', *ASE*, xxviii (1999), 225–356

—— 'England c.900–1016', in *NCMH* III, ed. T. Reuter (Cambridge, 1999), 456–84

—— 'Edward, King of the Anglo-Saxons', in *Edward the Elder, 899–924*, ed. N.J. Higham and D.H. Hill (London and New York, 2001), 40–66.

—— 'Edgar, *rex admirabilis*', in *Edgar, King of the English, 959–975*, ed. D. Scragg (Woodbridge, 2008), 3–58

—— and M. Lapidge, *Alfred the Great: Asser's Life of Alfred and other contemporary sources* (Harmondsworth, 1983)

Kieckhefer, R., *Theology in Stone: Church Architecture from Byzantium to Berkeley* (Oxford and New York, 2004)

Kleinschmidt, H., 'Die Titulaturen englischer Könige im 10. und 11. Jahrhundert', in *Intitulatio III: Lateinische Herrschertitel und Herrschertitulaturen vom 7. bis zum 13. Jahrhundert*, ed. H. Kleinschmidt *et al.* (Vienna, Col, Graz, 1988), 75–129

Kornbluth, G.A., *Engraved Gems of the Carolingian Empire* (Philadelphia, PA, 1995)

Lapidge, M., 'The Hermeneutic Style in Tenth-Century Anglo-Latin Literature', *ASE*, iv (1975), 67–111; reprinted in his *Anglo-Latin Literature 900–1066* (London and Rio Grande, 1993), 105–49

—— 'Some Latin Poems as Evidence for the Reign of Athelstan', *ASE* ix (1981), 61–98; reprinted in his *Anglo-Latin Literature 900–1066* (London and Rio Grande, 1993), 49–86 [citations in the text are given to the pagination of the original]

—— 'Israel the Grammarian in Anglo-Saxon England', in *From Athens to Chartres: Neoplatonism and Medieval Thought. Studies in Honour of Edouard Jeauneau*, ed. H.J. Westra (Studien und Texte zur Geistesgeschichte des Mittelalters, 35) (Leiden, 1992), 97–114, reprinted in his *Anglo-Latin Literature 900–1066* (London and Rio Grande, 1993), 87–104 [to which all citations are made]

—— 'Byrhtferth and Oswald', in *St Oswald of Worcester: Life and Influence*, ed. N. Brooks and C. Cubitt (London and New York, 1996), 64–83

Lappenberg, J.M., *A History of England under the Anglo-Saxon Kings*, trans. Benjamin Thorpe (London, 1845; rev. edn, 2 vols, 1881)

Larson, L.M., *The King's Household in England before the Norman Conquest*, Bulletin of the University of Wisconsin, 100, History series i. 2 (Madison, WI, 1904)

Lauer, P., *La Règne de Louis IV d'Outremer* (Paris, 1900)

Lavelle, R., 'The Use and Abuse of Hostages in Later Anglo-Saxon England', *EME*, xiv (2006), 269–96

Levison, W., 'Das Werden der Ursula-Legende', *Bonner Jahrbucher*, cxxxii (1928), 1–164

Leyser, K., *Rule and Conflict in an Early Medieval Society: Ottonian Saxony* (London, 1979)

—— 'The Tenth Century in Byzantine–Western Relationships', in *Relations between East and West in the Middle Ages*, ed. D. Baker (Edinburgh, 1973), 29–63, reprinted in his *Medieval Germany and its Neighbours, 900–1250* (London, 1982), 103–37

—— 'The Ottonians and Wessex', in *Communications and Power in Medieval Europe: the Carolingian and Ottonian Centuries*, ed. T. Reuter (London, 1994), 73–104

Loomis, L.H., 'The Holy Relics of Charlemagne and King Athelstan: the Lances of Longinus and St. Mauricius', *Speculum*, xxv (1950), 437–56

—— 'The Athelstan Gift Story: its Influence on English Chronicles and Carolingian Romances', *Proceedings of the Modern Language Association*, lxvii (1952), 521–37

Loyn, H.R., 'Wales and England in the Tenth Century: the Context of the Æthelstan Charters', *Welsh History Review*, x (1980–1), 283–301; reprinted in his *Society and Peoples: Studies in the History of England and Wales c.600–1200* (London, 1992), 173–99

—— *The Governance of Anglo-Saxon England 500–1087* (London, 1984)

Lyon, S., 'The Coinage of Edward the Elder', in *Edward the Elder, 899–924*, ed. N.J. Higham and D.H. Hill (London and New York, 2001), 67–78

McDougall, I., 'Discretion and Deceit: a Re-Examination of a Military Stratagem in *Egils Saga*', in *The Middle Ages in the North-West*, ed. T. Scott and P. Starkey (Oxford, 1995), pp. 109–42

McKitterick, R., *Charlemagne: the Formation of a European Identity* (Cambridge, 2008)

MacLean, S., 'Making a Difference in Tenth-Century Politics: King Athelstan's Sisters and Frankish Queenship', in *Frankland: the Franks and the World of the Early Middle Ages: Essays in Honour of Dame Jinty Nelson*, ed. P. Fouracre and D. Ganz (Manchester, 2008), 167–90

Maddicott, J.R., *The Origins of the English Parliament 924–1327* (Oxford, 2010)

Mayr-Harting, H., *Ottonian Book Illumination: an Historical Study*, 2 vols (2nd edn, London, 1999)

Nelson, J.L., 'The Problem of King Alfred's Royal Anointing', *Journal of Ecclesiastical History*, xviii (1967), 145–63; reprinted in her *Politics and Ritual in Early Medieval Europe* (London and Ronceverte, 1986), 309–27

—— 'The Second English *Ordo*', in her *Politics and Ritual in Early Medieval Europe* (London and Ronceverte, 1986), 361–74

—— 'The Franks and the English in the Ninth Century Reconsidered', in *The Preservation and Transmission of Anglo-Saxon Culture*, ed. P.E. Szarmach and J.T. Rosenthal (Kalamazoo, MI, 1997); reprinted in her *Rulers and Ruling Familes in Early Medieval Europe* (Aldershot, 1999), no. VI

—— 'Reconstructing a Royal Family: Reflections on Alfred, from Asser Chapter 2', in *People and Places in Northern Europe, 500–1000*, ed. I.N. Wood and N. Lund (Woodbridge, 1991), 47–66, reprinted in her *Rulers and Ruling Familes in Early Medieval Europe* (Aldershot, 1999), no. III

—— 'Rulers and Government', in *NCMH* III, ed. T. Reuter (Cambridge, 1999), 95–129

—— 'Alfred's Carolingian Contemporaries', in *Alfred the Great*, ed. T. Reuter (Aldershot, 2003), 293–310

—— 'Eadgifu (d. in or after 951)', *Oxford Dictionary of National Biography*, Oxford University Press, Sept. 2004 [http://www.oxforddnb.com/view/article/39220]

—— 'Did Charlemagne have a Private Life?', in *Writing Medieval Biography, 750–1250: Essays in Honour of Professor Frank Barlow*, ed. D. Bates, J. Crick and S. Hamilton (Woodbridge, 2006), 15–28

—— 'The First Use of the Second Anglo-Saxon *Ordo*', in *Myth, Rulership, Church and Charters*, ed. J. Barrow and A. Wareham (Aldershot, 2008), 117–26

Okasha, E., 'A Rediscovered Medieval Inscribed Ring', *ASE*, ii (1973), 167–71

Ó Riain-Raedel, D., 'Edith, Judith, Matilda: the Role of Royal Ladies in the Propagation of the Continental Cult', in *Oswald: Northumbrian King to European Saint*, ed. C. Stancliffe and E. Cambridge (Stamford, 1995), 210–29

Orme, N., *Exeter Cathedral: the First Thousand Years, 400–1400* (Exeter, 2009)

Ortenberg, V., 'Aux périphéries du monde carolingien: Liens dynastiques et nouvelles fidélités dans le royaume anglo-saxon', in *La Royauté et les élites dans l'Europe carolingienne (début IXe siècle aux environs de 920)*, ed. R. le Jan (Lille, 1998), 505–17

Page, R.I., 'The Audience of *Beowulf* and the Vikings', in *The Dating of Beowulf*, ed. C. Chase (Toronto, 1981), 113–22

—— 'A Tale of Two Cities', *Peritia*, i (1982), 335–51

Poole, R.L., 'The Alpine Son-in-law of Edward the Elder', *EHR*, xxvi (1911), 310–17

Pratt, D., *The Political Thought of King Alfred the Great* (Cambridge, 2007)

Prescott, A., *The Benedictional of St. Æthelwold: A Masterpiece of Anglo-Saxon Art: A Facsimile* (London, 2002)

—— ' "Kinge Athelston That Was a Worthy Kinge of England": Anglo-Saxon Myths of the Freemasons', in *The Power of Words: Anglo-Saxon Studies presented to Donald G. Scragg on his Seventieth Birthday*, ed. H. Magennis and J. Wilcox (Morgantown, WV, 2006), 397–434

Reuter, T., *Germany in the Early Middle Ages c.800–1056* (London, 1991)

—— 'Assembly Politics in Western Europe', in *The Medieval World*, ed. P. Linehan and J.L. Nelson (Routledge, 2001), 432–50

Ridyard, S.J., *The Royal Saints of Anglo-Saxon England: a Study of West Saxon and East Anglian Cults* (Cambridge, 1988)

Robinson, J.A., *The Saxon Bishops of Wells. A Historical Study in the Tenth Century*, British Academy supplemental papers (London, 1918)

Rollason, D.W., 'Relic-Cults as an Instrument of Royal Policy c.900–c.1050', *ASE*, xv (1986), 91–103

—— *Saints and Relics in Anglo-Saxon England* (Oxford, 1989)

—— 'St Cuthbert and Wessex: the Evidence of Cambridge, Corpus Christi College MS 183', in *St Cuthbert, his Cult and his Community to AD 1200*, ed. G. Bonner et al. (Woodbridge, 1989), 413–24

Sawyer, P.H. ed., *Anglo-Saxon Charters: an Annotated List and Bibliography*, Royal Historical Society guides and handbooks, 8 (London, 1968), no. 520; also available electronically at: *http://www.trin.cam.ac.uk/sdk13/chartwww/eSawyer.99/eSawyer2.html*

—— 'The Royal *tun* in Pre-Conquest England', in *Ideal and Reality*, ed. P. Wormald *et al.* (Oxford, 1983), 273–99

Scragg, D., 'A Reading of *Brunanburh*', in *Unlocking the Wordhord*, ed. M. C. Amodio and K. O'Brien O'Keefe (Toronto, 1998), 109–22.

—— 'Introduction', in *Literary Appropriations of the Anglo-Saxons from the Thirteenth to the Twentieth Century*, ed. D. Scragg and C. Weinberg (Cambridge, 2000), 1–21

Sharp, S., 'England, Europe and the Celtic World: King Æthelstan's Foreign Policy', *Bulletin of the John Rylands University Library of Manchester*, lxxix (1997), 197–220

—— 'The West Saxon Tradition of Dynastic Marriage: with Special Reference to Edward the Elder', in *Edward the Elder, 899–924*, ed. N.J. Higham and D.H. Hill (London and New York, 2001), 79–88

Shippey, T.A., 'The Undeveloped Image: Anglo-Saxon in Popular Consciousness from Turner to Tolkien', in *Literary Appropriations of the Anglo-Saxons from the Thirteenth to the Twentieth Century*, ed. D. Scragg and C. Weinberg (Cambridge, 2000), 215–36

Smith, J.M.H., *Province and Empire: Brittany and the Carolingians* (Cambridge, 1992)

Smyth, A.P. *Scandinavian York and Dublin: the History and Archaeology of Two related Viking Kingdoms*, 2 vols (Dublin, 1975–9)

—— *Warlords and Holy Men: Scotland AD 80–1000* (Edinburgh, 1984)

Southern, R.W., 'Aspects of the European Tradition of Historical Writing, 4: The Sense of the Past', *TRHS*, 5th ser., xxiii (1973), 242–63

Stafford, Pauline, *Unification and Conquest: a Political and Social History of England in the Tenth and Eleventh Centuries* (London, 1979)

—— 'The King's Wife in Wessex, 800–1066', *Past and Present*, xci (1981), 3–27

—— *Queens, Concubines and Dowagers: the King's Wife in the Early Middle Ages* (London, 1983)

—— 'Charles the Bald, Judith and England', in *Charles the Bald: Court and Kingdom*, ed. M. Gibson and J.L. Nelson (2nd edn, Aldershot, 1990), 139–53

—— 'Succession and Inheritance: a Gendered Perspective on Alfred's Family History', in *Alfred the Great: Papers from the Eleventh-Centenary Conferences*, ed. T. Reuter (Aldershot, 2003), 251–64

—— 'Writing the Biography of Eleventh-Century Queens', in *Writing Early Medieval Biography: Essays in Honour of Frank Barlow*, ed. D. Bates *et al.* (Woodbridge, 2006), 99–109

Stenton, F.M., 'The Supremacy of the Mercian Kings', *EHR*, xxxiii (1918), 433–52; reprinted in *Preparatory to Anglo-Saxon England: Being the Collected Papers of Frank Merry Stenton*, ed. D.M. Stenton (Oxford, 1970), 48–66

—— *Anglo-Saxon England* (Oxford, 1943; 3rd edn, 1971)

Stevenson, W.H., 'A Latin Poem Addressed to King Athelstan', *EHR*, xxvi (1911), 482–7

Tanner, H.J., *Families, Friends and Allies: Boulogne and Politics in Northern France and England c.879–1160* (Leiden and Boston, 2004)

Thacker, A.T., 'Chester and Gloucester: Early Ecclesiastical Organization in Two Mercian Burhs', *Northern History*, xviii (1982), 199–211

—— 'Membra disjecta: the Division of the Body and the Diffusion of the Cult', in *Oswald: Northumbrian King to European Saint*, ed. C. Stancliffe and E. Cambridge (Stamford, 1995), 97–127

—— '*Peculiaris patronus noster*: the Saint as Patron of the State in the Early Middle Ages', in *The Medieval State: Essays presented to James Campbell*, ed. J.R. Maddicott and D.M. Palliser (2000), 1–24

—— 'Dynastic Monasteries and Family Cults: Edward the Elder's Kindred', in *Edward the Elder, 899–924*, ed. N.J. Higham and D.H. Hill (London and New York, 2001), 248–63

Thundy, Z.P., '*Beowulf*: Date and Authorship', *Neuphilologische Mitteilungen*, lxxxvii (1986), 102–16

Townend, M., 'Pre-Cnut Praise-Poetry in Viking Age England', *Review of English Studies*, n.s. li, 203 (2000), 349–70

Treharne, E.M., 'Romanticizing the Past in the Middle English *Athelston*', *Review of English Studies*, n.s. l (1999), 1–21

Turner, S., *The History of the Anglo-Saxons*, 3rd edn, 3 vols (Paris, 1840)

Van Houts, E., 'Women and the Writing of History in the Early Middle Ages: the Case of Abbess Matilda of Essen and Aethelweard', *EME*, i (1992), 53–68

Wainwright, F.T., 'The Submission to Edward the Elder', *History*, xxxvii (1952), 114–30, reprinted in his *Scandinavian England*, 325–44

—— *Scandinavian England: Collected Papers*, ed. H.P.R. Finberg (Chichester, 1975)

—— 'North-West Mercia AD 871–924', *Transactions of the Historic Society of Lancashire and Cheshire*, xciv (1942), 3–55; reprinted in *Wirral and its Viking Heritage*, ed. P. Cavill, S.E. Harding and J. Jesch (Nottingham, 2000), 19–42

Walker, S., 'A Context for *Brunanburh*?', in *Warriors and Churchmen*, ed. T. Reuter (London, 1992), 21–39

Wasserstein D.J., 'The First Jew in England: "The Game of the Evangel" and a Hiberno-Latin Contribution to Anglo-Jewish History', in *Ogma: Essays in Celtic Studies in Honour of Próinséas ní Chatháin*, ed. M. Richter and J.-M. Picard (Dublin, 2002), 283–8.

Werner, K.F., *Histoire de la France, I: Les origins (avant l'an mil)* (Paris, 1984)

Whitelock, D., *Some Anglo-Saxon Bishops of London*, The Chambers Memorial Lecture, 1974 (London, 1975), reprinted in her *History, Law and Literature in 10th–11th Century England* (London, 1981), no. II

—— 'Some Anglo-Saxon Charters in the Name of Alfred', in *Saints, Scholars, and Heroes: Studies in Medieval Culture in Honour of Charles W. Jones*, ed. M.H. King and W.M. Stevens, 2 vols (Collegeville, MN, 1979), I, 77–98

Wieland, G.R., 'A New Look at the Poem "Archalis clamare triumuir" ', in *Insignis Sophiae Arcator: Essays in Honour of Michael W. Herren on his 65th Birthday*, ed. G. R. Wieland, C. Ruff and R.G. Arthur (Turnhout, 2006), 178–92

Williams, G., 'Hákon Aðalsteins fóstri: Aspects of Anglo-Saxon Kingship in Tenth-Century Norway', in *The North Sea World in the Middle Ages: Studies in the Cultural History of North-Western Europe*, ed. T.R. Liszka and L.E.M. Walker (Dublin, 2001), 108–26

Wilson, S.E., 'King Athelstan and St John of Beverley', *Northern History*, xl (2003), 5–23

—— *The Life and After-Life of John of Beverley* (Aldershot, 2006)

Winterbottom, M., 'William of Malmesbury, *versificus*', in *Anglo-Latin and its Heritage: Essays in Honour of A.G. Rigg on his 64th Birthday*, Publications of the Journal of Medieval Latin iv, ed. S. Echard and G.R. Wieland (Turnhout, 2001), 109–27

Wollasch, J., 'Monasticism: the First Wave of Reform', *NCMH III*, ed. T. Reuter (Cambridge, 1999), 162–85

Wood, M., 'Brunanburh Revisited', *Saga Book of the Viking Society*, xx.3 (1980), 200–17

—— *In Search of the Dark Ages* (London, 1981; 1991 edn)

—— 'The Making of King Æthelstan's Empire: an English Charlemagne?', in *Ideal and Reality in Frankish and Anglo-Saxon Society*, ed. P. Wormald *et al.* (Oxford, 1983), 250–72

—— *In Search of England: Journeys into the English Past* (London, 1999; Harmondsworth, 2000)

—— ' "Stand Strong against the Monsters": Kingship and Learning in the Empire of Æthelstan', in *Lay Intellectuals in the Carolingian World*, ed. P. Wormald and J.L. Nelson (Cambridge, 2007), 192–217

Woolf, A. 'View from the West: an Irish Perspective', in *Edward the Elder*, ed. N.J. Higham and D.H. Hill (London and New York, 2001), 98–101

—— *From Pictland to Alba 789–1070* (Edinburgh, 2007)

Wormald, P., 'Bede, the *Bretwaldas* and the Origins of the *gens Anglorum*' in *Ideal and Reality in Frankish and Anglo-Saxon Society*, ed. P. Wormald, D. Bullough and R. Collins (Oxford, 1983), 99–129

—— '*Engla lond*: The Making of an Allegiance', *Journal of Historical Sociology*, vii (1994), 1–24

—— *The Making of English Law* (Oxford, 1999)

—— 'On þa wæpnedhealfe: Kingship and Royal Property from Æthelwulf to Edward the Elder', in *Edward the Elder 899–924*, ed. N.J. Higham and D.H. Hill (London and New York, 2001), 264–79

—— 'Living with King Alfred', *Haskins Society Journal*, xv for 2004 (2006), 1–39

Wright, C.E., *The Cultivation of Saga in Anglo-Saxon England* (Edinburgh and London, 1939)

Yorke, B., 'Æthelwold and the Politics of the Tenth Century', in *Bishop Æthelwold*, ed. B. Yorke (Woodbridge, 1988), 65–88

Yorke, Barbara, 'Edward as Ætheling', in *Edward the Elder 899–924*, ed. N.J. Higham and D.H. Hill (London and New York, 2001), 25–39

Young, H., '*Athelston* and English Law: Plantagenet Practice and Anglo-Saxon Precedent', *Parergon*, n.s. xxii (2005), 95–118

UNPUBLISHED MATERIAL

Little, G.R., 'Dynastic Strategies and Regional Loyalties: Wessex, Mercia and Kent, *c.*802–939', PhD thesis, University of Sheffield, 2007

Thomas, I.G., 'The Cult of Saints' Relics in Medieval England', PhD thesis, University of London, 1974

Wood, M., 'The Lost Life of King Æthelstan: William of Malmesbury's Account of Æthelstan's Reign', unpublished paper, kindly lent by the author

INDEX